A GUIDE TO
CATHOLIC READING

A GUIDE TO
CATHOLIC READING

•

JACK F. BERNARD

AND

JOHN J. DELANEY

Doubleday & Company, Inc.
Garden City, New York
1966

Nihil obstat: John A. Goodwine, J.C.D.
                 Censor Librorum
Imprimatur: ✠Terence J. Cooke, D.D., V.G.
             Archdiocese of New York
             July 20, 1966

CONTENTS

To Harold C. Gardiner, s.j.
who has done so much to advance
the cause of Catholic letters

INTRODUCTION

In a book of this kind, it is desirable at the outset that the authors define for the reader rather precisely their aim in compiling the work, the limits they assign to it, and any technical aspects which the reader should know of before he embarks on it. Though there is a lively difference of opinion among authors as to whether any introduction is ever read, the authors of this *Guide* felt a short statement of its purpose and what it is meant to accomplish should be made for those readers who do read an Introduction.

The first point we wish to make is that this *Guide* is meant for the general reader. Its genesis took place at the conclusion of numerous lectures I have delivered over the past decade when listeners told me they were convinced of the desirability of expanding their Catholic reading and asked me how to begin. A survey of available literature on Catholic reading revealed a complete lack of any over-all guide which could serve as a basis for a practical reading program for the general reader in the field of Catholic books. When this fact became apparent, I resolved to do something about it and this *Guide* is the result of that resolution.

It should be emphasized that it was not primarily written for the scholar or for the non-reader. The former will be unhappy that many books of a technical nature in his specialty are not included. Our answer is that we have deliberately omitted technical treatises. In some areas certain books are included which might be so described. But in any such cases, the works are of such importance that no bibliography on that particular subject could be compiled without including them. With all such books, the descriptions clearly point out any difficulties which are inherent in the work so that the general reader is aware of the content of the work in question. In so far as the non-reader is concerned, this *Guide* is definitely not a primer; it is a guide. Both the scholar and the non-reader, we feel sure, can benefit from the books included herein. But essentially this *Guide* is designed for the intelligent individual who wishes to learn more of the available books that are encompassed by that somewhat amorphous term "Catholic reading." Our hope is that he be enticed into a full awareness of such riches by a planned course of reading based on the subject headings and books described in this *Guide*.

Next to be stressed is the fact that this *Guide* is a *selection*. There was no intention on the part of the authors to present every book on a given subject. Rather the selection is a personal one based on my more than forty years in the book world. Though it is personal, it is meant to cover the whole spectrum of Catholic reading. Critics or readers may be disappointed at not finding a particular favorite listed, but I trust that over-all they will agree that each of the more than 750 books included is outstanding in its field. I dare say that anyone who reads all of these books will have a magnificent insight into things Catholic.

A word about the descriptions. They are meant to give in short compass the substance of the book described, something about the author's style, and where necessary a caution when the book is more than ordinarily difficult for the general reader. The descriptions are straightforward and reflect general critical opinion about each work. As a result of this approach, the reader can immediately discern whether this book is suitable for his reading tastes or purposes in seeking a book in a particular field.

We have covered a wide range of intellectual levels in the books selected, so there is reading material in this *Guide* for every reading taste. One exception to this generalization must be made. We have deliberately refrained from listing works that can only be defined as "junk." For inclusion, we have adopted literary norms which are generally recognized. This does not mean that any book not included is *ipso facto* an illiterate work. We have already pointed out this is a selection, not an all-embracing collection. But it does mean we have arbitrarily ruled out certain books which have been best-sellers because their literary standards or professional approach is such that we would not wish to include them in a recommended list of this nature. The standards for inclusion are high, we admit, but on the other hand we feel only the best should be included in a recommended list of Catholic reading.

We have deliberately, with rare exceptions, not listed out-of-print books. Obviously, there are books now out of print which belong in any list of outstanding Catholic books. But the criterion for inclusion is that the book be understandable to the general reader and also that it be fairly readily available. If the general reader does not have access to a particular book, then we felt it should be eliminated from consideration for inclusion. In some cases, this decision caused the authors not to list works we felt could be read by the general reader with great benefit. But if he has no access to the book, then a listing would be of no value for him. In some few instances we have listed a book no longer in print but only when we felt such a title was still rather widely available in local libraries readily accessible to the general reader. Obviously this rules out books still available in specialized libraries to which only the scholar or specialist has access.

We have not included textbooks, missals and prayer books, and juveniles. Textbooks by their nature are not for the general reader since they are not specifically designed for reading but rather for study in a class or group. Missals and prayer books were excluded as, strictly speaking, this type of book is not meant for reading in the accepted sense of the word. And finally, since this *Guide* is for adult readers, juveniles were ruled out. Further, juveniles present particular problems and are of such scope that a complete guide should be devoted exclusively to them.

In listing the titles we have tried to give information pertinent to the would-be reader, such as author, publisher, year of publication, number of pages, and special features such as introductions, translators, illustrations, maps, index, etc. In addition we have appended additional items of information we thought would be useful for the reader. We have indicated the price of the edition listed. We emphasize that these prices are based on the latest information available when this *Guide* went to press. In a period of inflation such as we are currently experiencing, prices can change very rapidly. But even in such an eventuality, at least the reader will have some idea of whether he is contemplating a $2 book or a $15 book.

Also, wherever a paperback edition exists we have so indicated this fact. Paperbacks have been and continue to be the greatest boon for reading and book ownership the book trade has evolved in this century. A veritable flood of literary treasures is available at prices anyone can afford—and we do mean anyone. For the interested reader, they provide the means for building a home library fitted to any individual's purse as can readily be seen from a perusal of the home library suggestions you will find in the appendix. At the same time it should be pointed out that frequently you will find a paper book of such merit and importance that you will want it in a more permanent, hard-cover form. Where only the paperback edition is listed, it means that only that edition is currently in print.

At the end of the *Guide*, we have listed all the publishers mentioned in the text with their addresses. Further information on any of the titles may be obtained from them. Before writing the publisher though, we suggest you first discuss your book problems or needs with your local Catholic or general bookseller. Even more strongly do we urge that you find a good bookseller in your area and patronize him. He can be most helpful and a good bookstore is a treasure trove that you should be constantly exploring for the wealth of back titles and the constant stream of new books which can bring so much knowledge, information, inspiration, entertainment, and pleasure into your life.

For your convenience, we have also prepared an alphabetical listing of all the books and authors mentioned in the *Guide* so that you may easily find the description of a particular title or the books of a particular author. Also, we have prepared a section on Catholic periodicals and newspapers, and Catholic book clubs as a guide for you in these fields.

We have tried throughout to make this *Guide* as usable as possible for the general reader. To this end the subjects are listed alphabetically as we felt this was the most practical listing for quick and easy reference. Under each subject, books are listed alphabetically by author—with two exceptions. In the Biography section the books are listed alphabetically under the name of the subject of the book rather than by author. Obviously if a person wants to read a biography of Teilhard de Chardin it would be much simpler to find it under that entry rather than under the author's name. In the History section we have listed the books under chronological eras and under each of these historical sections alphabetically by author. Again we felt it would be much simpler for the reader to find a book on the Renaissance, for example, under that heading rather than under an author's name. Further, in both of these exceptions, since there is an author-title index at the back of the book, it is a simple matter for the reader who knows an author's name to trace the book by looking him up in this index.

And as a final point, the opinions expressed in the section headings are those of this author. Unlike most introductions to the different sections of catalogues which merely describe the section, I have attempted to give some background to the subject under treatment. In the course of this treatment, usually there can be no disagreement with the facts presented. In some few cases, opinions are stated which may differ from those of some of the readers of this *Guide*. In such cases I plead only that they are based on this author's interpretation of certain facts and occurrences. In no case are they ever in conflict with the dogmatic teachings of the Church—nor, in view of this author's unqualified allegiance to the Church, could they ever be.

J.J.D.

1. THE ARTS

It is a lamentable fact that the arts, which for so many centuries found their chief source of subject and inspiration in Christian themes, have become so divorced from the Church that Christian art has reached its lowest ebb in our time. Even the most superficial survey of art in Western culture prior to the modern era reveals the dependence of the greatest artists, architects and sculptors on Christian tradition. Not only was the subject of all great art, in the thousand years from the fall of Rome until modern times, Christian in motif, but the very inspiration for the great artist was the Christian story.

The reason for that state of affairs was to be found in the complete Christianization of every facet of human culture in that millennium. By the thirteenth century, all of Western culture was Christian. As Christopher Dawson so brilliantly demonstrated in *Religion and the Rise of Western Culture*, the development of Western civilization and culture is inexplicable except in the context of its Christian roots.

A culture is best illuminated by its literature and the fine arts. So this Christian Era is reflected by its painting, its architecture, its sculpture. And if ever an era of human history was gloriously depicted, the centuries when the Church dominated Western thought is that period. Never in the history of mankind before or since has man wrought the wonders and beauties of the palette, the chisel, and architectural planning with such magnificence as during the period culminating in the Renaissance, when men such as Michelangelo, Raphael, Rembrandt, Leonardo da Vinci, Fra Angelico, Donatello, Giotto, El Greco, Tintoretto, Cellini, Titian, Botticelli—to mention just a few—were creating those breath-taking and indescribable works of art which are the glory and pride of Western civilization.

In this cascade of unequaled creativity, two facts stand out. First and foremost is the source of inspiration for these artists. All in their own talented way are offering their genius to God through their own particular medium. Their concept of life was that of Christian belief; they were thoroughly imbued with the spirit of Christianity and their work reflects their Christian heritage and belief. Scenes from the life of Christ, our Lady, the great Biblical figures and the saints, are the subjects of most of the great art of this period. The Bible was the artists' source book, their vision and imagination the creative ferment, and their talent the practical application—an amalgam which produced the unrivaled masterpieces which centuries later we still enjoy. But the key to it all is Christianity. Without the beliefs taught by the Church and accepted by all men this art simply could never have come into existence.

As with painting, so too with architecture. Man has never since approached the sublimity and ethereal beauty of the medieval cathedral. Never has architecture produced so perfect a form for a particular purpose as the medieval Gothic cathedral built as a paeon of praise to God as well as for the more mundane purpose of providing a place of worship for God's people. Who can ever view the rose windows of Chartres, with the afternoon sun streaming through and bathing the whole interior of the cathedral with heavenly color, without feeling close to almighty God? It causes one to stand in awe and admiration for the men who created this joyful tribute to God. For centuries the fruit of their labors has silently offered its beauty and its majesty to the Lord of all.

All over Europe, other monuments stand giving their mute but almost celestial testimony to the faith and beliefs of dedicated artisans and architects—a Christian faith inspiring a worthy response from its followers. Chartres, Mont St. Michel, Cologne, Notre Dame, San Marco, and hundreds of churches and cathedrals all over Europe stand as shrines to the Christian heritage.

Other fine arts too reached their height in this period. Sculpture—Michelangelo's *Pietà* and *Moses*, Ghiberti and Donatello's bronze reliefs, the baptistry door and the Medici Chapel in Florence; tapestry—the Bayeux tapestry; stained glass—the windows of Chartres; illuminated manuscripts—the Duke of Berry's illuminated *Book of Hours*. Turn to any of the fine arts, and the list is endless, and the story is the same.

Art in its every form was magnificent and the inspiration was always the same—the desire to offer praise and thanks to God through man's artistry and craftsmanship. In the arts Christianity generated masterpieces that have remained unsurpassed in beauty, technique, and vision.

But the Church, besides being the inspiration for this treasure, was also the means by which it was brought into being. For the leading patrons of artists and artisans in this period were the churchmen. Time and again a bishop or a cardinal or a pope would commission a work which, when executed, became one of the masterpieces which thrill all who see it. For centuries the main source for the practical aspect of financing these works was the ecclesiastic who wanted a particular work for his church or cathedral, library or monastery, palace or dwelling. Granted the genius of the artist, also of prime importance was the wherewithal to turn his dream into reality. And so often this was provided through the largess of the prelate or churchly patron.

In the fullest sense of the concept, then, the great art of the Middle Ages and the Renaissance was directly attributable to the Church. The Church provided the inspiration, the means; and through her children, the artists, she produced a beauty, a magnificence, and a glory which have endured for conturios and will continuo for conturios to como.

But toward the end of the Renaissance, and set into full motion by the Reformation, a new trend set in. With the Reformation, a new spirit was abroad and the forces which have molded the modern world came into play. The unity of Europe was disrupted; nationalism began to exert its hold; unknown lands were discovered and cried for exploration and exploitation; men's thoughts began to turn from mainly religious considerations to more worldly interests. No longer were religious themes the sole subjects for the artist. The increasing role of commerce and trade created a new class of mercantile princes who increasingly became patrons for the artist.

The rending of Europe by the Reformation also was an important factor in the changing art scene. No longer the undisputed all-powerful court of last resort in Europe, the Church was fighting for her very existence. Art no longer was a leading preoccupation with churchmen; they were now more concerned with defending the truths of their faith. A consequence of this whole development was the fortress type of reaction to attacks on the Church; in a situation of danger such as that facing the Church, there was the inevitable closing of ranks, a rejection of innovation, and a closed-mind dogmatic approach to all aspects of human action. An art which is boxed in, limited in technique and subject, and not free to experiment, is doomed. The lifeblood of any human activity is development and growth, which are stimulated by experimentation and innovation. But art in the Christian camp of the period after the Reformation was caught up in the over-all posture of defense which the Church felt obliged to assume. And the result was inevitable: Christian art was stultified.

Not only was art in general in the Church caught up in this defensive mechanism of the Church, but so was the individual artist. Bound by the dictates of his Church, he was no longer free to explore new forms and experiment with new techniques. He must conform to the siege mentality and produce only what was imitative of art in the Church at the height of its glory. For instance, the Gothic church was the epitome of Church architecture. Consequently for centuries after the Gothic period, churches all over the world were designed in the Gothic style. No attempt was made to adapt new architectural forms to church architecture. So it was with other art forms. Art was bound hard and fast in the thralldom of tradition. Small wonder that the individual Catholic artist has made little, if any, contribution to art during the past four centuries. Only when he broke the stifling shackles of a narrow, closed-in, ghetto type of art was he able to make a contribution to the mainstream of art.

By the twentieth century, generally speaking and with rare exceptions, the fine arts in the Christian sense were in an arrested state. Mainly they had degenerated into an unimaginative, pietistic, unreal form which was so banal that it is a cause of wonder that it has taken so long for revulsion to set in. It reflected what had taken place in the Church generally. Because of the desperate need to defend the Church against the very real perils of modern civilization, the

Church retreated from the world and defended her members from the world by denouncing the world and all it offered. In doing so, it so overemphasized traditional positions that it lost all contact with the very real advances made in so many areas by modern man. Not until Pope Leo XIII were the first tentative advances made which were to bear such heady fruits in the pontificate of Pope John XXIII.

As in so many other fields, then, Catholic art reflected the defensive, tradition-bound posture of the Church. Sporadic efforts were made in the intervening centuries, but not until our own times have the artists and architects and all the other practitioners of various art forms been able to break out of the suffocating mediocrity which had imprisoned them for so long. But once the Church decided to bring her message to the world, then the fetters were snapped and Catholic art began to come alive. The final thrust was provided by the liturgical movement with its emphasis on a return to the basic meanings of public worship. With this new emphasis, liturgical art was brought to life again and a revival set in motion which in time will revolutionize Church art. This coupled with the very real growth of cultural appreciation by our Catholic people as the result of increased educational backgrounds, higher social and economic levels of living, and increased leisure should provide an artistic revival which may yet bring back in a modern manner the artistic glories of another age in the Church.

ADAMS, HENRY. *Mont-Saint-Michel and Chartres.* Anchor, 1959. xiv, 422 p., index. pa. $1.45.

Henry Adams was renowned during his lifetime as an authority on American history. It is ironic, perhaps, that since his death he is best remembered for this great contribution to an understanding of the mind and faith of the Middle Ages. Essentially, the book is an examination of the faith that brought into being the great Gothic cathedrals, and one of its primary concerns is architecture as a manifestation of religious faith; but it is also concerned with such matters as the literature of the period, the earthly queens and the Heavenly Queen, and with such churchmen as Abelard,

Francis of Assisi, and Aquinas. This work is a modern classic, and a brilliant interpretation of the Middle Ages for the twentieth-century reader.

GETLEIN, FRANK and HAROLD C. GARDINER (S.J.). *Movies, Morals, and Art.* Sheed, 1961. vii, 179 p. $3.50.

Part I of this work, by Mr. Getlein, views the art of the movie in its historic and aesthetic context, comparing movie-making with the other arts; the thesis of this section is that the cult of film "personalities" is destroying the value of the cinema as narrative art. In Part II, Father Gardiner discusses the moral evaluation of films, concluding that all human acts are legitimate themes for art, and that the moral value of a film must be judged more on the basis of a theme's treatment than on the theme itself. This is one of the most stimulating, and certainly the best written, of the books available on art and morality in the movies.

GILSON, ETIENNE. *The Arts of the Beautiful.* Scribner, 1965. 182 p. $4.50.

Professor Gilson has one purpose in this book: "From beginning to end, art is bent upon *making;* this book says nothing else." In other words, he regards art as a practical thing, as a means of expressing to the senses the beauty of that Truth which is God, and within that context he defines artistic beauty as the splendor, or shining forth, of Truth. He shows the historical derivation of his thesis by giving an historical summary of the earlier philosophers' position on art and beauty, especially that of Aquinas, and then examines whether or not, and if so to what extent, that classical position is taken into account in modern art. This is not, properly speaking, a technical work; yet, because of the abstract way in which the author discusses principles, it requires careful reading.

GILSON, ETIENNE. *Painting and Reality.* Pantheon, 1957. xxiv, 367 p., bibliography, index. $7.50. Meridian, 1959. pa. $1.55.

In this series of essays, Gilson concentrates specifically on a single problem of aesthetics: is there a real difference between "painting" and "pictures" and, if so, what is that difference. The problem, stated in other words, is whether painting is really a creative art or merely a process for duplicating what the eyes see in the external world. This is probably as authoritative and definitive a discussion of the subject as has ever appeared and, although it presumes a certain basic familiarity with the terminology of scholasticism and with the history of art, a careful reading will be of much value to those interested in creative art.

LEONARDO DA VINCI. *The Notebooks of Leonardo da Vinci.* Translated and edited by Pamela Taylor. Mentor, 1960. 253 p., plates. pa. 75¢.

Leonardo's notes covered his investigations on almost every field of art and science. This collection consists of excerpts from those notes, and reveals Leonardo as one of the most universal geniuses of history. In addition to his insights into the nature of the fine arts, he foresaw and completed designs for many inventions that lay centuries in the future: the airplane, the submarine, tanks, poison gas, and he anticipated such milestones as the theory of gravitation, of the circulation of the blood, and the heliocentric theory. This collection makes fascinating, and sometimes amusing, reading.

MÂLE, EMILE. *Religious Art.* Pantheon, 1948. 256 p., illustrations, index. $4.50.

This work, by one of the great historians of art, discusses religious art from the twelfth to the eighteenth century, covering clearly and carefully the development of a truly Christian artistic beauty in such diverse fields as the illustration of manuscripts, the painting of frescoes, the erection of the great medieval cathedrals, the masterpieces of the artists of the Renaissance, and the relative decadence of seventeenth-century French and Italian religious painting. The book may be recommended as the non-technical treatment of a technical subject, and it will be of interest to the general reader as well as to those interested in art and its history. (This is an abridged version of a larger work by the same author.)

MARITAIN, JACQUES. *Art and Poetry.* Translated by E. duP. Matthews. Philosophical Library, 1943. 104 p. $1.75.

This small work comprises three essays. The first treats of the work of three modern painters: Marc Chagall, Georges Rouault, and Gino Severini. The second essays, entitled "Dialogues," is concerned mostly with the relationship of art and morality in the novel, and within that context examines some of the work of Mauriac, Dostoevsky, and Gide. The third, "Freedom of Song," discusses music as an art in modern times, and deals with Stravinsky, Lourie, and Satie. The thesis throughout the book is that artistic greatness cannot exist unless the artist knows God and possesses humility, intelligence, and love. This work, despite its excellent translation, is not always easy reading, but it may be recommended as a brief but incisive statement of principles on the relation between artistic and spiritual beauty.

MARITAIN, JACQUES. *Art and Scholasticism and Other Essays.* Translated by Joseph W. Evans. Scribner, 1962. vi, 234 p., notes, appendices. $5.00. Scribner, 1964. pa. $1.45.

This is a collection of essays concerning the nature of art, of aesthetics, and of beauty, by the most respected Catholic philosopher of modern times. Maritain's thesis is that, for an object to be called "beautiful," it must conform to the end for which it was created. Art, as an interpretation of nature, must also be judged by that standard; thus, what the artist produces must relate the subject to its end. And since the final end of all creation is God, then the artist must show creation in relationship to God. If he succeeds, his work partakes of the subsistent Beauty which is God, and is beautiful. Maritain's explanation of his thesis, in these essays, requires in the reader an adequate background in Scholastic metaphysics as well as the patience to read carefully and thoughtfully.

MARITAIN, JACQUES. *Creative Intuition in Art and Poetry.* Pantheon, 1953. viii, 423 p., notes, plates. $7.50. Meridian, 1955. pa. $1.55.

The most esteemed Catholic philosopher of modern times explains his concept of creative intuition as the mark of genius in art. He also applies that criterion to poetic values and to the evaluation of painting, illustrating his points by extensive quotations from famous poets and by the use of excellent reproductions of works of art. This book is, in effect, the synthesis of Maritain's thought on aesthetics. It is not easy reading, but it is highly recommended to those involved or interested in the literary or plastic arts.

ROBERTSON, ALEC. *Christian Music.* Hawthorn, 1961. 157 p., bibliography. $3.50.

This is a volume (number 125) of *The Twentieth Century Encyclopedia of Catholicism,* treating of the history and development of Christian musical art through the ages. An introductory chapter discusses the existence and nature of pre-Christian religious music, while subsequent sections trace the development of a specifically Christian mode of musical expression, from a pre-Gregorian period through the establishment of Gregorian chant as the liturgical music par excellence. There are treatments of the introduction and development of polyphonic music in the Middle Ages, English church music up to the Reformation, the reformations of the Council of Trent in the sixteenth century, the introduction of the use of solo, chorus and orchestra in the great baroque monuments of the seventeenth and eighteenth centuries, and the romanticism of the nineteenth century. The book concludes with a discussion of the liturgical use of the organ. This is a book that will appeal to the cultivated Christian in general, and presupposes no background knowledge of music.

SYNDICUS, EDUARD (s.J.). *Early Christian Art*. Translated by J. R. Foster. Hawthorn, 1962. 188 p., illustrations, bibliography. $3.50.

This is an outline of the history of Christian art from the first century after Christ to the age of Charlemagne. Father Syndicus discusses and explains the primitive art and symbolism of the early Christians as found in the Roman catacombs, the dovolopment of the basilica form of churches, the early Church's images of Christ, the influence of Byzantine art on the West, the great masterpieces of Byzantium in Constantinople and in Ravenna, and the renewal of Christian art in the West during the reign of Charlemagne. (Volume 121 of the *Twentieth Century Encyclopedia of Catholicism*.)

WINEFRIDE, WILSON. *Modern Christian Art*. Hawthorn, 1965. 175 p., illustrations, bibliography. $3.50.

This survey of Christian art in modern times begins with the Romantic Movement of the eighteenth and nineteenth centuries and shows how the expressive artists of today owe a debt to the traditional Christian artists of earlier centuries. Then, in short analyses, the author discusses modern painting and sculpture, with emphasis on such well known twentieth-century figures as Eric Gill, Sir Jacob Epstein, David Jones, and many others. There are separate sections on architectural trends, ceramics, textiles, and stained glass.

This book (Volume 123 in *Twentieth Century Encyclopedia of Catholicism*) is a book on art for the reader who knows nothing about art. It is non-technical, clearly written, and highly informative.

VAN ZELLER, HUBERT (O.S.B.). *Approach to Christian Sculpture*. Sheed, 1959. 191 p., index. $3.75.

This short essay studies, in language that the non-artist can understand, the expression in stone of religious faith. Although Father Van Zeller is concerned primarily with that belief's sculptured representation, he lays down the general principles which must govern all religious art—and, indeed, art in general—in whatever form it takes.

2. THE BIBLE

Of the many factors which have led to the present widespread and unprecedented renewal and reform of the Catholic Church, it is safe to say the single most important factor has been the tremendous resurgence of interest in the Bible and the consequent effect of that revival on every sphere of the Church's activity. For centuries now the average Catholic has believed the Bible to be a divinely inspired book and, with tradition, the source of all Catholic teaching. But he has also been admonished to exercise the utmost care in his approach to Bible reading and encouraged to read it preferably under close clerical or religious supervision. Most Church authorities argue, and rightly so, that the Church never officially forbade the individual Catholic to read approved Catholic versions of the Bible; but, by the same token, most lay Catholics of the older generation will agree that reading the Bible without proper supervision was frowned on by most Catholic priests and nuns.

Happily the situation has changed radically and today Catholics are urged, exhorted, and entreated on every side to read the Book of Books. The reading of the repository of divine revelation, the Bible, is wholeheartedly recommended by popes and cardinals, theologians and teachers, priests and nuns, as the inspired word of God telling of God's intervention in human history and God's plan for our salvation. More than ever before, Catholics are reading and studying the Bible to learn from it what God has wrought with his Chosen People and what he offers through his divine Son. It is indeed worthy of every man's effort that he learn of these all important events and promises from their source.

Though men have always recognized the great merit of the Bible as the written record of God's relations with man, in the past all too frequently it was regarded as the province of the scholar and the exegete. Now, due to the inspired leadership of a series of enlightened popes—notably Leo XIII and Pius XII—the gates have been thrown open and the richest treasure of the Judeo-Christian world has been revealed to us through fruits of Biblical research unequalled and unparalleled in the Christian era.

And what is this book so extravagantly extolled by the great of all ages? First and foremost, it is the inspired, written word of God, spoken through the instrumentality of human authorship. It is a sacred book because of its divine origins and because of its contents. As St. Paul put it: "All Scripture is inspired by God" (2 Tim. 3:16) and as such should be accorded the reverence of a most sacred heritage.

All Christians accept the belief that the Bible is of divine origin but are often puzzled by the seeming errors and inconsistencies to be found in various sections. This confusion arises because they overlook the fact that the actual writing was done by human beings subject to the state of knowledge extant in the culture and civilization of their times and by their own state of life. God himself did not write the Bible; he inspired men to do the writing. The significance of this fact is simply that men, in writing of certain events and occurrences, recounted them as well as they were able from their own backgrounds. Consequently, the *telling* often contains errors. But the *content*, the salvation message, is never in error. If these two points are understood, then it will be realized that the full meaning of the Bible unfolds more clearly and more meaningfully as men advance in knowledge and are able to apply that knowledge to understanding the meanings in the Bible. There are many examples of how men's increased knowledge revealed the true meaning of certain passages and even now, despite twenty centuries of study, there are portions of the Bible just revealing their true meaning in the light of new scientific discoveries or greater knowledge of the period or new methods brought to bear on old dilemmas. Fantastic as has been the increase in our Bible knowledge in the past century as the result of dedicated and persistent study, it only drives home forcefully the fact that there is still and incredible distance to go in understanding fully what God is telling us in the Bible.

If, then, one keeps in mind that men actually wrote the Bible and that it was written by many different men in different ages of human development, it will be a great step forward in understanding the Bible. Couple with this the fact that we do not have the text of a complete Old Testament dating back to the days when the ancient writers were at work, or even of a New Testament from the time when the Evangelists were writing (the last book written of the New Testament was by John who died between A.D. 90 and 100), and you can begin to understand some of the problems of the Bible scholar. For instance, the earliest substantial texts of the New Testament are the more than one hundred pages of the Chester Beatty papyri dating from the early third century and the manuscript of the Gospel of John known as Papyrus Bodmer II dated about A.D. 200. After these, the manuscripts available date to the fourth century A.D. and later. Imagine what could have happened to a manuscript which was the product of countless scribes copying from a previous manuscript over a period of centuries. It is small wonder that agreeing on a text is not the least problem facing Biblical scholars. In the same way, the original copies of the Hebrew Old Testament have all perished and the oldest known complete manuscript of the Old Testament dates back to about A.D. 950, more than two thousand years after the generally agreed upon date for the completion of the last book of the Old Testament—though a fragment containing the Ten Commandments and Deuteronomy 6:4 (the first verse of the Jewish prayer, the *Shema*), known as the Nash fragment and dating from the first or second century B.C., and fragments discovered in Old Cairo and dating from the seventh century A.D., do exist. This fact will explain the tremendous excitement generated among scholars at the news of the discovery of the Dead Sea Scrolls in 1947. These fragments of the Old Testament are generally agreed to date from the first or second century B.C. and they offer an unparalleled opportunity to check the texts of existing versions of a later date. More recent discoveries are believed to date from the second and third century B.C. It is no small tribute to the scholars and scribes who copied and passed on to the next generation their precious manuscripts that close comparisons have thus far revealed little significant variation.

Another interesting problem facing the scholar is the language used originally in writing the books of the Bible and the historical background of each period. The Old Testament was written in Hebrew and Aramaic—the latter having replaced Hebrew as the language of the Jews after the Exile (586 B.C.)—over a period of a thousand years. The New Testament was written in Greek, except for Matthew's Gospel which was written in Aramaic. Just imagine the changes that must have taken place in a language over the centuries as in the case of Old Testament Hebrew. The task of unraveling the different meanings of the same word at different periods in itself is monumental. Complicating this problem are other interesting factors. For example, many of the books of the Old Testament were written long after the events described. The events recorded in Deuteronomy are generally agreed to have taken place in the thirteenth century B.C.; the book itself as we know it dates from the seventh century B.C. The authorship of the various books is mainly anonymous, and frequently it is obvious that several authors were involved in writing a particular book.

The science of language is only one of the methods used by scholars to give us more precise information about the Bible. The discoveries in archaeology in the past century have been of inestimable worth in unearthing knowledge of the civilizations and cultures affecting the destinies of the Jews. Such scientific discoveries as the application of the carbon method of dating objects, the new knowledge made available by the broadening of astronomical research, the application of modern medical discoveries to some Biblical figures to explain some of their actions—all these and a thousand other discoveries of modern science have been eagerly and conscientiously used by Biblical scholars to advance our knowledge of the Word of God. The magnitude of their interest and their application of the knowledge of the sciences is staggering.

But science is not the only tool used to broaden our knowledge of the Bible. The whole concept and application of literary forms have enormously increased our understanding of whole sections of the Bible. The expression "literary form" designates simply the literary devices used by the ancient writers. Scholars are just beginning to understand some of the literary forms employed in the Bible and with that understanding emerge whole new concepts. For instance, today we all understand a work of fiction. But, four thousand years from now, the novel may have been a discarded and forgotten literary form for thousands of years. Scholars of that far-off day would then be unable to have any understanding of a great fictional classic of our times and, because of this ignorance, could misinterpret whole sections of a novel. So, too, the ancient Bible writers used literary forms that have been discarded and forgotten. As scholars try to learn of these forms and apply interpretations to them, whole new vistas are being revealed.

From all the scholars' study and research and meticulous care there is emerging a body of knowledge never before available. Fortunately, these dedicated men have been aware of their responsibility to make this knowledge available to their less knowledgeable fellow men. The result has been a welcome and unprecedented flood of books on every aspect of the Bible, written for every intellectual level.

From all we have said above it is obvious that the Bible presents many problems which require the aid of the specialist for their unraveling. As modern scholarship reveals hidden meanings and new interpretations, the wisdom of the Church in insisting that any interpretation of the Bible must not be made by whim or one's personal fooling or desires is clearly evident. It is far too complex a volume to be left to casual or uninformed explanation. After all, what is at stake is the whole history and plan of salvation for all mankind. Small wonder that the Church has always been concerned that any version of the Bible be under her aegis, so that approved versions may be the result of expert study and explanations by specialists in the field of Biblical study.

The Bible is truly the most important book in the world. With the books now available on and about the Bible, there is no excuse for anyone's not knowing the Bible to the best of his ability. It is the most important book in any man's life, for as St. Paul says the Scriptures "are able to instruct us unto salvation by the faith which is in Christ Jesus. All Scripture is inspired by God and useful for teaching, for reproving, for correcting, for instructing in justice; that the man of God may be perfect, equipped for every good work." (II Tim.

3:15–17), and St. Jerome says "A man who is well grounded in the testimonies of the Scripture is the bulwark of the Church." For our personal salvation and for the good of the Church, we should study the Bible. We think you will find in the list below books which will help in your study of the Bible and help you on the way to these laudable goals.

ENGLISH VERSIONS OF THE BIBLE

There are various versions of the Bible in English which are authorized for reading and study by Catholics. Only these versions are listed in this *Guide*, but there are of course Jewish and Protestant versions as well. It is an interesting fact that Biblical scholars of all denominations are now working together exchanging views, information, and discoveries. With this closer cooperation, for the first time, there is a possibility that at some future date a joint effort of Catholic, Jewish, and Protestant scholars will produce a common Bible acceptable to all Christian faiths. A step in this direction is the Anchor Bible which, though not a Catholic Bible, has been highly praised by Catholic scholars. It is not a co-operative-effort Bible, but scholars of all three faiths are involved in its translation. Because of the great interest in the Anchor Bible we have included a description of it below. It should be pointed out, though, that it is still a law of the Church that Catholics should do their Bible reading from approved Catholic versions.

Before considering the actual versions of the Bible, it should be noted that *all* Bibles in English are translations. If the reader will keep this fact in mind he will understand why various versions differ. Obviously even with a modern foreign language, two translators may use different expressions for translating the same foreign word. It should be evident then, particularly in view of some of the difficulties we have discussed above, that two equally dedicated and learned men can very easily use different expressions and styles to translate certain words and phrases. Also literary styles vary. One man may translate literally and concern himself only with accuracy; another, equally qualified, may translate in a figurative sense, determined to provide a translation in felicitous English. Both are perfectly acceptable in the eyes of the Church which wisely realizes that men's literary tastes vary and that there is room for a variety of styles.

All Catholic translations of the Bible in the past have been made from the Vulgate. The Vulgate is the Latin version of the Bible made by St. Jerome in the late fourth and early fifth centuries. It soon became the accepted version of the Bible and was used through the centuries as the authentic version by all scholars. It was officially declared authentic and authoritative by the Council of Trent. It must be realized though that St. Jerome's Bible was a translation from the original Hebrew, Aramaic, and Greek, into Latin which, in Jerome's day (342-420), was the vernacular language.

The Vulgate served the Church well for centuries when Latin was the language of all Europe. But with the rise of national states, national vernacular languages began to develop. At first this presented no real problem since all learned men understood and used Latin. Books and correspondence were written in Latin long after vernacular languages were widely used. By the beginning of modern times, though, the need for translations of the Bible into the various national languages had become increasingly apparent. In 1560 the Catholic Church was outlawed in England and the Catholics there were faced with English versions of the Bible which contained notes offensive to Catholics and which had been distorted in translation for sectarian purposes. An authorized Catholic version in England became essential for English-speaking Catholics.

A group of exiled English Catholic scholars produced such a version with the publication of the New Testament at Rheims, France, in 1582 and the Old Testament in Douay, Flanders, in 1609, both translated from the Vulgate. This translation soon became widely known as the Douay-Rheims version and, with occasional revisions, it was to remain the standard Catholic Bible in English for more than three centuries. The most comprehensive revision was made by Bishop Richard Challoner, vicar apostolic of London, in 1749-50 and again in 1752, so that this version came to be referred to as the Douay-Challoner-Rheims version.

It was not until the 1940s that new English translations appeared. By that time, it was evident that a new version, in modern English, was needed for the twentieth-century Catholic. Changes in the language over three centuries had rendered many of the Biblical passages obsolete, and to the modern ear many of the expressions used were strange and meaningless. In the United States, the Confraternity of Christian Doctrine, under the sponsorship of the American hierarchy, began a new English translation and published the New Testament in 1941. This New Testament translation was a thorough revision of the Douay-Challoner-Rheims version with close attention to the Vulgate. However, for the Old Testament, the scholars involved decided to base their translation on the original Hebrew, Aramaic, and Greek. With the completion of the Old Testament, a new translation of the New Testament based on the original Greek and Aramaic is planned. Commonly known as the Confraternity Version, this is the first Catholic version in English of the Bible based on original sources.

In England, in the 1940s, the well known English scholar-priest, Ronald Knox, was requested by the English hierarchy to produce a new translation; this Bible, known familiarly as the Knox Bible, was published in 1944–50. Monsignor Knox used the Vulgate as the basis for his translation, though he consulted the original languages where the Latin of the Vulgate was obscure.

In 1966 the fourth celebrated English translation of the Bible was published, the Jerusalem Bible. Based on the famed *Bible de Jérusalem*, the product of fifty years' labor by French Dominicans and published under the direction of Father Roland de Vaux of L'Ecole Biblique de Jerusalem, it was hailed on its publication in France in 1956 as *the* great Bible of modern times. It was translated into English by a group of English Biblical scholars under the direction of Father Alexander Jones, who checked each translated book against the original Hebrew, Aramaic and Greek.

These four translations are the accepted Catholic versions of the Bible in English. A fifth version should be noted. It is the Catholic edition of the Protestant Revised Standard Version of the Bible which was adapted for Catholic use in

1965–66 at the invitation of the Scottish Catholic bishops. Its various national editions carry the *imprimatur* of Scottish, American and Australian bishops.

Also to be noted are two English versions of the New Testament which many scholars consider to be excellent translations: the Spencer translation of the New Testament, made by Aloysius Spencer o.p. from the Greek and published in 1940; and the Kleist-Lilly New Testament, also translated from the Greek by James A. Kleist, s.j. and Joseph L. Lilly, c.m. and published in 1954.

There are all kinds of editions of these Bibles and New Testaments ranging from inexpensive paper editions to expensive, magnificently illustrated, morocco-bound volumes. We describe below the distinctive qualities of each version though we make no attempt to list the numerous editions; these you should examine at your book store. But one fact must be emphasized before we conclude this section. If there is a single book that every Catholic should possess, it is the Bible. One of the versions available will suit your needs, but we urge you as strongly as we can to own one and above all to read it regularly.

THE BIBLE

The Holy Bible, Douay-Challoner-Rheims Version.

This edition of the Scriptures, popularly known as the "Douay Bible," is a translation of the Latin version (the *Vulgate*) made by St. Jerome at the end of the fourth century. The Douay Bible was the work of Dr. Gregory Martin and a group of exiled English scholars, and it was intended to furnish the outlawed Catholic Church in England with a faithfully translated vernacular Bible. It is called "Douay" and "Rheims" because the New Testament was printed at Rheims in 1582, and the Old Testament at Douay in 1609–10. The Douay-Rheims was the standard version for Catholics until the late eighteenth century, when Bishop Challoner of London revised the entire work in order to modernize its language. From that time until very recently, the Douay-Challoner-Rheims Version was that commonly in use among

English-speaking Catholics, both for private reading and for
use in public reading during liturgical services. Despite the
majestic prose of this edition, however, and despite the
familiarity of Catholics with its wording, the Douay Bible
is being increasingly abandoned in favor of translations that
use more modern, colloquial English. For the twentieth-
century reader, the Douay contains too many obsolete words
and archaic expressions, and too many inaccuracies in the
light of modern Biblical scholarship, for it to be able to compare favorably with newer versions. (There is a wide range
of prices for this version, depending upon quality of binding,
of paper, etc. All Catholic book stores carry a wide selection of Bibles, and we suggest that you examine those in your
book store for the edition most suited to your needs.)

The Holy Bible, Confraternity Version.

Since 1952, scholars of the Catholic Biblical Association
under the patronage of the Episcopal Committee of the Confraternity of Christian Doctrine have been publishing, piece-
meal, a new translation of the Bible, done from the original
languages and making use of the latest advances made in
Scriptural studies by both Catholic and Protestant scholars.
There are three volumes currently available of this translation,
all containing Old Testament books: Volume I: Genesis,
Exodus, Leviticus, Numbers, Deuteronomy, Joshua, Judges,
and Ruth; Vol. III: Job, Psalms, Proverbs, Ecclesiastes,
Canticle of Canticles, Wisdom, and Sirach; Vol. IV: the
Prophetic Books. Still not available in the new translation,
therefore, are the Old Testament books of Kings, Paralipo-
menon, Esdras, Tobias, Judith, Esther, and Machabees; for
them, the old Douay Version is used. The New Testament
known as the "Confraternity Version" is not a part of this
new translation, but of an older one made from the Latin
Vulgate and first published in 1941. Eventually, it is planned
that the entire Bible, both the Old Testament and the New,
will be available in the new translation.

The purpose of the new translation is to make available
the whole Bible in modern English, eliminating the inaccuracies and ambiguities of the older versions and incor-
porating the advances made by modern Biblical scholarship.
To a large extent that purpose has been realized in the books
that have already appeared, although the reader may find
that the explanatory notes accompanying the text are comparatively inadequate. The New Testament currently avail-

able in this Version, however, has sacrificed much of the
majesty of the Douay wording, and yet retained many of
that older version's scholarly deficiencies.

Along with the Douay Version, the Confraternity Version
is widely used in this country. It is available at any book
store at a variety of prices.

The Holy Bible, Knox Version. Prefaced by Bernard Cardinal
Griffin. Sheed, 1956. Old Testament: 913 p., maps, notes;
New Testament; 285 p., maps, notes.

Monsignor Ronald A. Knox's translation of the Bible was
one of the first, and certainly one of the most successful, attempts to present the Word of God in twentieth-century
colloquial English. Knox was one of the great literary stylists
of his time, and although his translation may not be strictly
considered authoritative—since it was made from the Latin
Vulgate, in the light of the Hebrew and Greek originals,
rather than from the original languages themselves—it remains a monumental achievement in its clarity of expression
and beauty of style.

The Jerusalem Bible. Doubleday, 1966. xvi, 2016 p., notes,
tables, maps. $14.95.

The Jerusalem Bible is the latest version to appear in English of the entire Bible. It is a translation of the famous
Bible de Jérusalem, the French version published under the
direction of the Biblical Institute of Jerusalem (hence its
name) and acclaimed as the most authoritative of all vernacular renditions of the Bible. Under the direction of Father
Alexander Jones, the eminent Scripture scholar, a team of
experts, both Biblical and literary, worked for a decade
translating the French version into English and comparing
it with the original-language manuscripts for accuracy of
rendition. The result has been an English Bible that is, in
many respects, superior even to the French version, for it
takes into account events in Biblical scholarship which have
taken place since the French translation was published.

There is a general introduction to the Old Testament,
and one to the New Testament, as well as introductions to
each of the individual books of both Testaments. These introductions are in fact complete and comprehensive essays
explaining clearly such interesting factors of Bible study as
authorship, date and place of composition, structure of the
books, historical character of the books and literary *genre,*

and the individual book's connection with preceding and succeeding books. In addition, explanatory notes accompany the text of each book, clarifying the meaning of the more difficult passages and providing pertinent historical, literary, geographical, and linguistic information and referring the reader to other Biblical passages and books of parallel or complementary interest.

Given, then, this version's attention to literary quality as well as to accuracy and clarity and the quality of the introductory and explanatory apparatus, the *Jerusalem Bible* may be said to be the most up-to-date, easy to read, and certainly the most instructive, version to appear in modern times. The language is thoroughly modern, yet it has managed to retain that majesty of expression that is usually associated with the King James and Douay versions, while the introductions and notes surpass in coverage, quality, and relevance, anything to which the non-scholar hitherto has had access.

The Holy Bible, Revised Standard Version, Catholic edition. Nelson, Liturgical Press, 1965.

The "Catholic edition" of the Revised Standard Version is that edition of the Revised Standard Version which has received the *imprimatur* of Catholic bishops. It differs from the Protestant Revised Standard Version only in the wording of a few sentences, and it is the closest that Catholics and Protestants have come to having a "common" Bible. The Revised Standard Version was prepared from the American Standard Version, which itself was an edition of the King James Version published in 1611 during the English Reformation. The Revised Standard Version incorporates all of the most recent results of Biblical study and modern critical methods, and it has been acclaimed as a translation that combines accuracy, clarity of meaning, and beauty of language. As with most other versions, there is a wide range of prices. In mid-1966 the *Oxford Annotated Edition* of the R.S.V. was published by Oxford University Press. This edition bears the *imprimatur* of Richard Cardinal Cushing.

The Anchor Bible. Foxwell Albright and David Noel Freedman, Editors-in-Chief. Doubleday, 1965. (38 vols.) $5.00 to $7.00 per volume.

The Anchor Bible is, in effect, a collection of individually translated books of the Bible. The translations are done from the original languages by highly respected Biblical authorities, Jewish, Protestant and Catholic. Some of the individual volumes, therefore—those done by Catholic scholars—bear the *imprimatur*. *The Anchor Bible* offers a most readable scholarly translation, fully documented and supported by the most up-to-date Biblical, historical, and archaeological scholarship. Each book is accompanied by a very detailed commentary; in several cases, more than half the volume is devoted to commentary. The series, by reason of such extensive commentary and of its size and scope, is intended for Biblical scholars, for libraries, and for trained specialists in ecclesiastical disciplines.

THE NEW TESTAMENT

The New Testament, Kleist-Lilly Version. Translated by James A. Kleist and Joseph L. Lilly. Preface by Joseph Husslein, s.j. Bruce, 1954. xii, 690 p., notes. $6.00.

This modern translation of the New Testament is a lively rendition into contemporary American English. Although the use of idiomatic American is occasionally jarring, the translators manage to convey the meaning of difficult passages with often remarkable clarity and originality.

The Holy Bible, Westminster Version.

This version of the Bible was undertaken in 1913, with the purpose of presenting to the English-speaking world a vernacular Bible which would be on a par, both from the standpoint of literary beauty and of scholarly acumen, with the celebrated King James, or Authorized, Version of the Protestant churches. By 1934, the New Testament had appeared, and work is continuing on the translation of the Old Testament. The translators are working from the original languages, as they did for the New Testament translation. The beauty of style and accuracy aimed at by the translators was achieved in the New Testament, but modern Biblical scholarship has long since bypassed it, and the style of the translation seems rather old-fashioned to modern ears. The translators, a group of English scholars, are presently at work on the translation of the Old Testament.

BOOKS ON THE BIBLE

DANIEL-ROPS, HENRI. *Israel and the Ancient World.* Translated by K. Madge. Image, 1964. 435 p., notes, index. pa. $1.35.

This is a history of the Jewish people from the time of Abraham to the birth of Christ. The author places the events of the Old Testament narrative in their proper relation to the histories of the other civilizations and peoples of the ancient world. An especially interesting treatment is accorded to the borrowing of traditions by the Israelites from the Babylonians, Egyptians, Hittites, Assyrians, Persians, and Greeks—a borrowing which allowed elements of those civilizations to pass, by way of the Bible, into the consciousness of Western civilization. The book is not "light" reading, but it is indispensable for a proper understanding of the Old Testament, and very helpful in understanding the New. (Originally published under the title of *Sacred History.*)

DANIEL-ROPS, HENRI. *What Is the Bible?* Translated by J. R. Foster. Hawthorn, 1958. 128 p., bibliography. $3.50. Guild, 1962. pa. 85¢.

The present work is volume 60 of the *Twentieth Century Encyclopedia of Catholicism,* of which this author is the general editor. It discusses with clarity and insight the importance of the Bible, how it came to be written and by whom, and how the definitive list of the authentic books of the Bible was ascertained. This is a short work, excellent for use as an introduction to deeper studies in the Bible, and it will be especially valuable for the general reader.

DOUGHERTY, JOHN J. (MSGR.). *Searching the Scriptures,* revised edition. Doubleday, 1959. 160 p., appendices. $3.95. Image, 1963. pa. 75¢.

This is a popularly written introduction to the reading and study of the Bible, explaining what the Scriptures are, how and where they were written, who the authors were, and showing what we should look for in them. This small book is an excellent guide to Bible study for the lay reader.

FLANAGAN, NEAL M. (O.S.M.). *Salvation History.* Sheed, 1964. 245 p. $5.00.

Father Flanagan has written an introduction to the study of Biblical theology. His approach is historical rather than topical, covering the range of Biblical experience from its beginnings in the Old Testament through the New Testament. Of particular value are the author's efforts to make clear the unity and harmony existing between the two Testaments.

FREMANTLE, ANNE, Editor. *The Greatest Bible Stories.* Stephen Daye, 1951. 239 p. $3.50. Image, 1957. pa. 85¢.

This is a world anthology of Catholic fiction, all the selections having the Bible as the basis of their stories. The stories themselves—by such writers as François Mauriac, Ronald Knox, and Paul Claudel—are so arranged that the life of Christ unfolds chronologically.

HUNT, IGNATIUS (O.S.B.). *Understanding the Bible.* Sheed, 1962. xiv, 207 p., index. $3.95. Sheed, 1965. pa. $1.95.

Father Hunt, a well known Biblical scholar, presents a systematic and popularly written introduction to modern Biblical studies. He discusses, among other subjects, how present-day Biblical scholars use the findings of archaeology to confirm or interpret the recitals of the Old and New Testaments, how it is possible to decide with probability which of two ancient manuscripts of the Bible is the more reliable, how the science of linguistics can be put to work in deciding the meaning of a Biblical passage, and what is the significance of "higher criticism" and "lower criticism" in Catholic Biblical studies today. The general reader will find that this work will give him a surprising insight into the work that is currently being done in Scriptural studies.

JONES, ALEXANDER. *Unless Some Man Show Me.* Sheed, 1960. 162 p. $2.50. Paulist, 1964. pa. 95¢.

Father Jones is one of the leading Biblical scholars of our time. In this book, he deals with various problems of "Biblical interpretation"—i.e., he determines what some of the more puzzling texts of Genesis and Jonah were meant to signify, by establishing the historical and literary circumstances of the passages in question. This is an excellent introduction to a fascinating science: how to understand what the Bible *really* says, as opposed to the human tendency to make it say whatever we want it to say. The book does not require any special background in the reader, but it does demand careful reading.

KELLER, WERNER. *The Bible As History.* Translated by William Neil. Morrow, 1956. 452 p., illustrations, maps, diagrams, index. $4.95.

Only in recent years have scientific discoveries been used to document the events described in the Bible as history. Dr. Keller in this work has gathered together a mass of archaeological evidence supporting the historical authenticity of some of those events, relying chiefly upon modern discoveries in the Near East and in the Mediterranean countries, and step by step the book reveals the factual foundations of the Old and New Testaments. For example, he skillfully interweaves quotations from ancient Babylonian documents with the Bible's account of the Flood, showing that the Babylonian record of that event is substantially the same as the Hebrew account. The book makes fascinating reading and, if occasionally some of Dr. Keller's conclusions seem more definite than is warranted by the evidence he brings forward, that failing is amply compensated for by the over-all worth of the work.

McKENZIE, JOHN L. (s.j.). *Dictionary of the Bible.* Bruce, 1965. 976 p., tables, maps, illustrations. $17.95.

Father McKenzie has written almost two thousand separate articles, analyzing every book of both the Old and New Testaments. The reader will find practically every Biblical name identified, with essays on such major concepts as grace, faith, salvation, truth, etc., and with articles on the various civilizations of importance to Biblical study (Egyptian, Sumerian, Canaanite, Elamite, and Persian). Of particular value is the author's analysis of each book of the Bible according to content, literary character, date and time of composition, and themes. This is an excellent, easily understandable, reference work; it will be of great value for use in the home as well as in libraries.

McKENZIE, JOHN L. (s.j.). *Myths and Realities.* Bruce, 1963. 285 p., bibliography. $4.75.

Father McKenzie, a well-known Biblical scholar and writer, considers in these essays several sensitive areas in modern Catholic thought, such as the question of intellectual freedom in the Church, the relationship of inspiration to revelation, the distinction between myth and fact in the Old Testament, and the messianic mission of Christ. The author combines solid scholarship with a talent for clear exposition, and his work is recommended to the informed reader.

McKENZIE, JOHN L. (s.j.). *The Power and the Wisdom.* Bruce, 1965. 293 p., indices. $4.95.

This collection of essays constitutes a study of the New Testament. The author's primary purpose is to express, in intelligible terms, the mystery of Christ, and such is the unifying theme of the book. To this end, he furnishes information on the cultural, political, intellectual, and social milieu of Christ's time; then he treats of Jesus, his relationship to the Father, his nature, and the Redemption. There is a closing chapter on the "demythologization" of the Bible. The work is highly recommended as an introductory study of the New Testament.

McKENZIE, JOHN L. (s.j.). *The Two-Edged Sword.* Bruce, 1956. 317 p., index. $4.95. Image, 1966. pa. $1.25.

This introduction to the study of the Old Testament begins with Genesis and continues on through the books of the prophets, considering the topical ideas of each book in relationship to each other and to their counterparts in the modern world. There is ample information on such matters as the divine and human authorship of the books, the psychological processes of inspiration and prophecy, the Hebrew concept of history, and the literary forms in which they expressed that concept. Father McKenzie's book is highly recommended.

MONRO, MARGARET T. *Enjoying the New Testament.* Foreword by Cuthbert Lattery (s.j.). McKay, 1961. 197 p., appendices. $2.95. Image, 1962. pa. 75¢.

An introduction to the New Testament, this book provides a basic and systematic reading plan and points out to the reader the various problems which occur in interpreting the New Testament: the public for whom the various books were written, the intellectual and social conditions of the early Christians, the personalities of the authors of the New Testament books. This is a popularly written, well-organized, and easily understandable guide for beginners in Biblical studies, and it includes an excellent program for further reading.

MURPHY, ROLAND E. (O. CARM.). *The Dead Sea Scrolls and the Bible.* Newman, 1956. xi, 116 p., pa. $1.50.

One of the most fascinating discoveries of modern times was the unearthing in 1947 of the famous "Dead Sea Scrolls" in the Zumran cave along the shores of the Dead Sea. Among the important Biblical manuscripts and fragments contained in those documents are the oldest extant copy of the Book of Isaiah, commentaries on several books of the Old Testament, an Essene work called the Manual of Discipline (which has led to speculation that Christ belonged to the Essene sect of Judaism), and copies of the Damascus Document. Father Murphy explains briefly and clearly the importance of those documents to an understanding of the Bible, and the relationship between them and the Bible.

NEWLAND, MARY REED. *The Family and the Bible.* Random, 1963. 272 p., bibliography. $5.95.

A well known writer and mother of seven children tells how, with the aid of a Biblical scholar, she and her family read through the Old Testament. Mrs. Newland's book is a well written and often witty combination of Bible commentary for young people and guide to what to read in the Old Testament. It contains much practical advice and information for parents concerned with the religious education of their families.

ORCHARD, BERNARD (O.S.B.); EDMUND F. SUTCLIFFE (S.J.); R. C. FULLER, and RALPH RUSSELL (O.S.B.), Editors. *A Catholic Commentary on Holy Scripture.* xvi, 1289 p., maps, index. Nelson, 1953. $15.00.

This work is intended to be, and is in fact, a library of Scripture in a single volume. The editors provide a general introduction on the Bible as a whole, and individual introductions for the Old Testament and the New, situating the two in their historical and literary context and discussing authorship, literary characteristics, date of composition, etc. For the individual books, each verse has its own short commentary which explains what is meant by obscure or ambiguous words or phrases in that verse and which ties in the meaning of the verse either with the significance of the entire chapter or book or interprets it in the light of other books of the Bible. This is an excellent and comprehensive book which will be a great help to an intelligent understanding of the Sacred Scriptures for all Catholics, and, from the standpoint of clarity of treatment and completeness of coverage, it is to be highly recommended. Its only drawback is that it draws its Bible texts from the Douay version, a translation that is rapidly being displaced in this country by more modern and more scholarly translations.

RICCIOTTI, GIUSEPPE. *The Acts of the Apostles.* Translated by L. E. Byrne. Bruce, 1958. 420 p., maps. $8.00.

The *Acts of the Apostles* is, from a human standpoint, one of the most interesting of the books of the Bible, treating as it does of the early history of the Church. Ricciotti has taken the entire book and given a verse-by-verse commentary on it, clearing up many puzzling points of an historical nature as well as elucidating points of interest for an understanding of the initial missionary activities of the infant Church. The translation is sometimes awkward, but not so much so as to make for difficult reading.

VAN DEN BORN, ALFRED. *Encyclopedic Dictionary of the Bible.* Translated and adapted by Louis F. Hartman. Mc-Graw, 1962. 2634 p., illustrations, plates, maps, bibliographies. $27.50.

This is one of the most complete and useful one-volume Biblical encyclopedias available in English. It identifies and discusses practically every word, concept, and name to be found in either the Old Testament or the New, in entries ranging in length from a few lines to several thousand words. The entries take into account non-Catholic, as well as Catholic, Biblical studies. Despite the relative absence of English-language works in the bibliographies, and an occasional lapse into jargon, this book is an excellent reference work for libraries and for the general reader.

VAUX, ROLAND DE (O.P.). *Ancient Israel.* Translated by J. A. McHugh (O.P.). McGraw, 1961. xxiii, 592 p., indices, bibliography. $10.95.

The author of this work is one of the most eminent biblical scholars of the Catholic Church. His work is not, properly speaking, a history of Israel so much as a study of the life and institutions of that nation as recorded in the Old Testament. Among the subjects which receive extensive treatment are nomadism among the Israelites, the place of the family in society, and the nature and scope of the civil, military, and religious institutions of the Hebrews.

VAWTER, BRUCE (C.M.). *A Path Through Genesis*. Sheed, 1956. ix, 300 p. $4.00.

Probably no book of the Bible offers so many difficulties to the thinking Christian as does Genesis, with its account of the origins of the universe and of man, of original sin and of the early history of the human race. Father Vawter, one of America's outstanding Biblical scholars, examines those problems in this book, considering the general nature of Genesis (its composition, historical character, origin, and authorship) as well as the peculiar scientific and historical problems that it presents. This is probably the best such work available in English.

WOODS, RALPH L., Editor. *The Catholic Companion to the Bible*. Foreword by Bishop John J. Wright. Lippincott, 1956. 313 p., index. $3.95.

The present work is a collection of Catholic writings on the Bible, from the time of early Christianity to the present. The selections are both critical and inspirational in nature, ranging from Ronald Knox's "Some Problems of Bible Translation" to St. Augustine's essay on "Faith in the Authority of Scripture," and including such contributors as Bede Griffith, Thomas Aquinas, St. Jerome, Cardinal Gibbons, and many of the popes. The selections are divided into three groups, by subject: "The Nature, Value and Authority of the Bible"; "The Old Testament"; "The New Testament."

3. BIOGRAPHY

The lives of famous men and women have always evoked the greatest interest among their fellow men. With men and women in positions of great power, the reason for this interest is obvious, for the decrees promulgated and events set in motion by such personages have affected the lives of millions and have had repercussions which endured for centuries. Where the exercise of such authority affected one's destiny and decided matters of life and death, freedom and serfdom, economic well-being or peonage, it is obvious that the person wielding such power is bound to be the object of intense interest. How did these people attain their positions of influence, what motivated their decisions, what traits of character merged to make such individuals, what were the outside factors involved in their actions, what kind of persons were they—these are just a few of the questions that we want answered when we consider people in power. The wielder of power is always under close scrutiny, either by the people of his own time directly affected by his actions and directly involved or by those of another era interested in what he had accomplished.

But such interest in individuals does not limit itself to those in positions of authority. Artists, composers, musicians, authors, sculptors, architects, religious figures, physicians, scientists, philosophers—the whole spectrum of human activity is of interest to the reader. Always we are interested in these qualities which make a man stand out in his chosen profession. Often the interest is merely one of curiosity. What was there in Moses' makeup that persuaded the Jews to follow him for years in their seemingly aimless wanderings in the desert? What was there about an Innocent III that caused emperors and kings to bow before his will? Why, of all the great painters and sculptors of the Renaissance, was Michelangelo such a towering genius? What were the qualities that caused men to rally to Napoleon's banners time and again and follow him to death and destruction? What

were the magnetic qualities with which Churchill was so
richly endowed that he was able to lead his people from
certain defeat to ultimate victory? Such considerations as
these have interested men through the ages and do so today
just as strongly.

Often there is more than mere curiosity involved. For
though it has so often been said—and how truly—that each
generation must learn through its own errors, it is nonetheless true that individuals are constantly learning from those
who have preceded them on the stage of history or, on a
more mundane level, those who have shown the way in one's
profession or calling. Certainly Plato must have learned much
from Socrates, St. Thomas Aquinas from Aristotle, Martin
Luther King from Mahatma Gandhi. Each gained much from
his mentor and then added his own unique flavor to provide
the distillation which was his own particular brand of genius.

Even those infamous and notorious figures whose black
deeds besmirch the pages of history have exercised an almost hypnotic attraction for readers of all ages. For frequently evil is so repulsive that it does exercise a hypnotic
appeal. Again, though, there is much to be learned from the
villains of history. Often, too, as history unfolds, the villains
of a period are shown to be not quite the scoundrels they
had been thought for so long. We shall return to this point
a bit further along.

This then is the province of biography—the telling of the
events of a person's life in a manner which will present that
individual in his full dimensions. And how is that achieved?
Or, put another way, what is a good biography?

There are certain ingredients that all good biographical
works possess in common. First and most important, the author must have a thorough knowledge of his subject and a
complete understanding of the period in which he lived. No
author can do a thorough job in presenting his figure if he
is not thoroughly immersed in this essential background material. All men are products of their times, and to understand
them and to know them one must know intimately the
nuances of the culture, events, peoples and civilization in
which they lived out their lives.

Next, a most necessary attribute of the biographer is a

degree of objectivity. You will note we have carefully qualified this aspect of a biographer's character by stating he
must have a "degree of objectivity" not that he must be
"completely objective." No one is completely objective. The
very fact that an author has chosen a particular figure to
depict indicates a certain degree of involvement at the outset. And some of the best biographies ever written are the
products of an author's enthusiasm for his subject. But that
enthusiasm must not be so overwhelming that it beclouds
the author's judgment; otherwise, the work emerges as a
panegyric rather than as a biography. (The biographers of
churchly figures are the worst offenders on this score. Until
quite recently, for example, most biographies of American
ecclesiastical figures were monuments to the most flagrant
abuses of this nature—presenting their subjects as perfect,
flawless men which they most assuredly were not.) But the
point is that even when a biographer has the greatest admiration for his subject he must always present the full picture—the flaws and errors and faults as well as the virtues
and great accomplishments.

On the other hand, the opposite holds equally true—a biographer must not present only the negative side of a subject.
Many reputations have been ruined by biased, prejudiced,
distorted biographies which emphasized all the flaws in char
acter, weaknesses and mistakes of a subject while completely
eliminating either the favorable aspects of a man's career or
the extenuating circumstances which may have justified particular actions. To cite one example: until fairly recently, all
Catholic biographies of Martin Luther depicted him as nothing less than a depraved monster who wrecked Christendom;
and all Protestant biographers presented him as the flawless
knight who saved mankind. Only now, four centuries later, is
a true picture beginning to emerge as passions and prejudices
die down and the truth is allowed to emerge.

As with every other kind of writer, the biographer should
have a writing style with an accompanying felicity of expression which allows him to get across his message to the
reader. If a biography is worth writing, it is worth writing in
prose which can be read. Frequently, biographies contain all
the essential ingredients of a fine work except that they are

written so badly or in such a dull, lackluster style that the reader is repelled rather than attracted to the book.

Many biographies have been called the "definitive biography"—such a misused phrase!—when in reality their only claim to definitiveness is that they contain every available bit of information on the subject. Definitive it may be in this sense; but great or good it is not. For to the qualities of a good biographer must be added a sense of selectivity—the ability to select material that is relevant and appropriate and above all to present this selected material in such a way that it does not result in a distorted, one-sided presentation.

And finally, as a basic attribute of any good biography, the author must have caught the essence of his subject and conveyed it to the reader. If the biographer has not succeeded in making his subject come alive for the reader, then the biography has failed. This is the indefinable stamp of the truly great biography, which is immediately apparent to the reader and is not measured by length or time or language. Thousands of voluminous volumes, for example, have been written about St. Thomas Aquinas; yet, so eminent an authority as the noted philosopher Etienne Gilson has said of G. K. Chesterton's slim *Saint Thomas Aquinas* that it is the finest introduction to Aquinas he has ever read. On the other hand, who would deny that Meriol Trevor's massive two-volume life of Cardinal Newman is a monumentally great biography of the famous nineteenth-century English churchman? These are extreme examples, since they are such different books; but both Chesterton and Trevor have admirably succeeded in their assigned tasks of making their subjects real to their readers.

A special form of biography is the autobiography in which the author himself is the subject of the work. Much that we have said about the biographical form of literature is equally applicable to autobiography, but there are other aspects of this literary form of which the reader should be cognizant.

The first point which should be considered is the fact that, unlike our ideal biography, the appeal of the autobiography lies of its very nature in the fact that the author *is* biased. An autobiography is the author's own account of what has happened to him. It must then be a prejudiced account,

since perforce the events recounted are told from the special
viewpoint of the author. In this fact is the strength and the
weakness of the autobiography: it is written from a special
viewpoint—and human nature being what it is it is the rare
author who does not tend to justify his own actions in his
autobiography. But if this tendency is not so pronounced that
it ends up as sheer self-aggrandizement, it may also be the
strength of the autobiography. For here, right from the
source, is the depiction of a man's life and actions and the
justification for these acts. In the case of famous personages,
it is of inestimable value for future scholars and readers to
have that person's own explanation or defense of his actions.
Frequently, such explanations—sometimes unwittingly on the
author's part—shed light on matters which would never be
clear unless so revealed. Often, too, an autobiography will
shed light on a facet of its subject's character which would
otherwise have remained purely a matter of conjecture.

In the case of famous people, an autobiography can be a
most important footnote to history. But even an autobiography of one not in the public eye can be a source of great
pleasure, solace, or instruction to the reader. For the best
of autobiography offers an insight into the mind and heart
and soul of a man which is unequalled by any other literary
form. How could St. Augustine's *Confessions* have been
written except as an autobiography? Could Newman's *Apologia pro vita sua* have had its same impact if it were anything other than autobiographical? Is not the effect of St.
Thérèse's *Story of a Soul* due in large measure to its revelation of the Little Flower's most intimate association with God?
It is precisely because these and other great autobiographies
bring the reader into the very mind of the author that they
represent that unrivaled method of communication that is the
characteristic of the great autobiography.

In short, as is true of biography also, the autobiography as
a literary form can bring to the reader a portrait of its subject unattainable in any other form. At the same time, it
must be emphasized that again, as with biographies, the author's intent and purpose are all-important. If he honestly
wishes to share his life and experiences with the reader and
has the requisite literary skill, his autobiography can be an

outstanding adventure for the reader. If he wishes merely to produce a panegyric to himself, denouncing his critics and opponents and setting himself up as a paragon of virtue, then his efforts will come to naught and defeat the very purpose of his book. Obviously, an autobiography will contain some element of self-praise however muted it may be. If a man did not believe he had acted righteously and correctly in the majority of instances in his lifetime, he would certainly be guilty of lack of conviction without which no individual in the public eye can long function. Indeed, such belief in one's abilities is essential to greatness in any area of human activity; and this must be reflected in one's autobiography. But with this must go an integrity of purpose wherein the author does honestly, though with conviction, reveal himself to his reader. When he does, the autobiography is bound to reveal the inner man—which is what a good autobiography must always do.

On the list of books chosen for inclusion in this section of the *Guide* are represented all types of biographies and autobiographies; in general, we feel that they are representative of the criteria we have discussed above. Since this is a guide to Catholic reading, we have included mainly Catholic figures. However, there are also included a few biographies of key figures who are necessary to an understanding of events in key periods of Catholic history. For instance one must know something of Martin Luther if one is to understand the Reformation. Fortunately Catholic scholarship has developed to such a state that we are able to include a biography which presents him without the usual distortions that have characterized so many earlier biographies. For such figures, we have felt it essential to include biographies of this nature, where they exist. Unfortunately, however, many such important figures will not be represented since there is no adequate biography available according to the standards we have set up. On the other hand, we do feel that you will find a biography of merit for most of the major Catholic figures in this listing.

Finally, may we point out that through these lives you can gain an unparalleled insight into all of human life and human relations. For, in the final analysis, the destiny of mankind has been molded and shaped by the actions of men—though these actions are inexorably affected by divine intervention in history and by the consequences of that intervention. History and all the appurtenances of culture and civilization are the product of men, wrought through their actions and their thinking. How better, then, to know of man and his life on earth than through the lives of the outstanding men and women of all ages who have shaped history, literature, the arts, and the sciences?

COLLECTIONS

BELLOC, HILAIRE. *Characters of the Reformation.* Image, 1958. 200 p. pa. 85¢.

This is a series of biographical sketches of twenty-three of the most important characters of the Reformation. Among the subjects are Henry VIII, Richelieu, James I, Cromwell, Louis XIV, Thomas More, Clement, and Anne Boleyn. By a judicious choice of his subjects, the author manages to convey to the reader an historical concept of the entire era.

DELANEY, JOHN J. and JAMES E. TOBIN. *Dictionary of Catholic Biography.* Doubleday, 1961. xi, 1245 p., appendices. $18.50 (thumb-indexed, $19.95).

This work contains, in alphabetical order, concise but comprehensive biographies of some 13,000 important figures of Catholic history, exclusive of living persons. The material is intelligently arranged, clearly written with abundant cross-references, and includes suggestions for further reading on many subjects. This is an indispensable reference work for both Catholic and general libraries.

KITTLER, GLENN. *The Wings of Eagles.* Doubleday, 1966. 216 p. $4.50.

These popularly written biographies of six modern Catholics reveal how their common faith molded their thinking and their lives, which in turn shaped the course of history or eased men's spiritual and temporal sufferings. The figures discussed are Pope John XXIII, President John F. Kennedy,

Father John LaFarge, Father Teilhard de Chardin, Mother Katherine Drexel, and Doctor Tom Dooley.

MAYNARD, THEODORE. *Great Catholics in American History.* All Saints, 1962. xiii, 209 p., bibliography. pa. 50¢.

Twenty-one notable American Catholics are portrayed in what, because of the author's attention to background, is actually a survey of the history of the Catholic Church in the U.S. Among the subjects are Père Marquette, Junípero Serra, John Carroll, Mother Seton, Prince Gallitzin, Father Becker, Mother Cabrini, and Alfred E. Smith.

NEILL, THOMAS P. *They Lived the Faith.* Bruce, 1951. x, 388 p., bibliographies, index. $4.50.

Professor Neill has written short biographies of thirteen of the great lay religious leaders of modern times. His subjects are: Daniel O'Connor, Charles de Montalembert, Ludwig Windthorst, Garcia Moreno, Pauline Jaricot, Frederic Ozanam, Albert de Mun, Joseph de Maistre, Joseph Gorres, Donoso Cortes, Orestes Brownson, Louis Veuillot, and Wilfred Ward.

O'BRIEN, JOHN A. *The First Martyrs of North America.* Notre Dame, 1960. 310 p., maps, bibliography. $3.50.

This work (first published in 1953 under the title of *American Martyrs*) is the story of six priests and two laymen who worked to win for Christianity and civilization the whole Indian population of seventeenth-century Canada, and who were eventually martyred for their faith. The eight are: Isaac Jogues, Rene Goupil, Jean de Lalande, Jean de Brebeuf, Gabriel Lalemant, Antoine Daniel, Charles Garnier, and Noel Chabanel.

O'BRIEN, JOHN A. *Giants of the Faith.* Doubleday, 1957. 358 p. $3.75. Image, 1960. pa. 95¢.

These are very readable biographical sketches of six notable converts who have had an important influence on the Church: John Henry Newman, Gilbert Keith Chesterton, Orestes Brownson, Isaac Hecker, St. Paul, and St. Augustine. The ways in which each of these "giants of the faith" were led to Catholicism, and their lives in the Church, were varied, and their contributions to the Church are clearly outlined. The book may be recommended to the young as well as to adults.

INDIVIDUAL BIOGRAPHIES

[Abelard, Peter] WADDELL, HELEN. *Peter Abelard.* Illustrations by Laszlo Matulay. Peter Smith, 1959. 277 p., notes, bibliography. $5.00. Compass, 1959. pa. $1.45.

This is the story of one of the most fascinating figures of the Middle Ages, Peter Abelard, who is remembered today for two things: he loved Heloise, and he hated St. Bernard of Clairvaux. Miss Waddell, a non-Catholic, takes us into the man himself and shows us that, indeed, there was much good in him, that he was one of the greatest intellects of his time, and that he has had an enormous and lasting effect upon European civilization. It is an enthralling story, told by one of the most expert writers and respected historians of our time.

[Alfred] DUCKETT, ELEANOR S. *Alfred the Great.* University of Chicago, 1956. 220 p., bibliography, index. $3.75. Phoenix, 1958. pa. $1.50.

Alfred, England's king in the late ninth century, is the only English monarch to be called "the Great"; yet the story about Alfred and the burnt cakes is the only thing commonly known about him. Miss Duckett, a non-Catholic and one of the most polished historical writers of our times, tells the story of the man who was as concerned about the well-being of the Church in England as he was about the material welfare of his people and who accomplished wonders in both fields.

[Augustine] AUGUSTINE OF HIPPO, SAINT. *Confessions.* Translated by Frank J. Sheed. Sheed, 1946. 429 p., notes, bibliography, index. $3.50. Image, 1960 (translated by John K. Ryan). pa. $1.35. Washington Square, n.d. (translated by Edward B. Pusey). pa. 45¢.

By common consent, the work known as the *Confessions* holds a special place among the world's great books. Although it is autobiographical in character, it is not a story of the author's life; yet, no other book has ever gone more deeply into the author's character and deeds, expressed more incisive judgments about the inner man, or revealed its author more fully. The book is not only a penetrating psychological study of man in search of God, but a unique document for understanding the spiritual life and a treasure house of thought for the philosopher and the theologian. After fifteen hundred years, the book still attracts countless readers, from the professional theologian to the student of literature, from the expert in philosophy to the general reader. It is recommended to all readers of whatever category as an indispensable work for the educated Christian. (Of the three translations listed above, Frank Sheed's is a very readable rendition; that of Msgr. Ryan, in addition to being quite modern and flowing, has excellent explanatory notes; Edward Pusey's translation is regarded as a classic rendition in English, and is stately yet, occasionally, rather hard to read with complete understanding.)

[Belloc, Hilaire] SPEAIGHT, ROBERT. *The Life of Hilaire Belloc.* Farrar, 1956. xv, 552 p., bibliography, index. $6.50.

This biography of Hilaire Belloc, famous Catholic historian, essayist, and man of letters, by one of his friends who is himself an eminent man of letters, is a well written, generally sympathetic, and informative work. Its value as objective biography is somewhat hampered by Mr. Speaight's adulation of Belloc, but the book is interesting as the account of a great man in a great era of Catholic literature.

[Campion, Edmund] WAUGH, EVELYN. *Edmund Campion.* Image, 1956. 196 p., appendix. pa. 75¢.

The biography of the Jesuit priest-scholar who was martyred in Tudor England for his loyalty to Catholicism, this is an absorbing and colorful story told by one of the greatest writers of the twentieth century.

[Catherine of Aragon] MATTINGLY, GARRET. *Catherine of Aragon.* Vintage, 1960. viii, 415 p., tables, index. pa. $1.45.

Catherine of Aragon is the superb biography of the Spanish princess, daughter of Ferdinand of Aragon and Isabelle of Castille, who became Henry VIII's first wife. It is undoubtedly the most authoritative study of Catherine as a person, and her most readable biography.

[Catherine Thomas, Mother] CATHERINE THOMAS (MOTHER). *My Beloved.* McGraw, 1955. 239 p. $3.50. Image, 1959. pa. 85¢.

In this autobiography of a Carmelite nun who has spent three decades behind the walls of a strictly cloistered Car-

melite monastery, she describes in detail her entrance into
Carmel, her daily life in the convent, and the discipline of
mind and body attained through prayer and penance. A
charmingly written book, joyful and humorous.

[Columbus, Christopher] MORISON, SAMUEL ELIOT. *Christopher Columbus, Mariner.* Little, 1955. x, 224 p., maps,
index. $3.75.

Morison is regarded as the author of Columbus' definitive
biography (*Admiral of the Ocean Sea,* Little, 1942, two
volumes), of which this is a one-volume abridgment. This
volume begins with a study of Columbus' origins, his family
and his childhood, then analyzes the mature man, the origin
of his conviction that he could reach the Far East by sailing
West, his approaches to the sovereigns of Europe for support,
his eventual commissioning by Isabelle and Ferdinand of
Spain, his adventures in the New World, and, finally, his
death in relative obscurity. This is a work of scholarship,
beautifully written, by one of the great modern historians.

[Cushing, Richard] FENTON, JOHN H. *Salt of the Earth.*
Coward, 1965. xi, 242 p., illustrations. $5.00. Echo, 1966.
pa. 95¢.

This is a biography of Richard Cardinal Cushing, Archbishop of Boston, one of the most beloved, and one of the
most colorful, members of the American hierarchy. The book
covers the Cardinal's boyhood, his not always smooth career
in the seminary, his first years as a priest, and his rise in the
Church to his present position. The author's style is fast-moving and journalistic, and there are numerous amusing
and touching anecdotes about the Cardinal.

[de Foucauld, Charles] PREMINGER, MARION MILL. *The
Sands of Tamanrasset.* Hawthorn, 1961. 261 p. $5.00. Image,
1963. pa. 85¢.

This is the biography of Charles de Foucauld—playboy,
soldier, patriot, explorer, hermit, and, above all, lover of God.
A well written and exciting true story about a charming sinner who became a heroic saint.

[de Medici, Catherine] HERITIER, JEAN. *Catherine de
Medici.* Translated by Charlotte Haldane. St. Martin's, 1963.
469 p., plates, notes, index. $7.95.

Catherine de Medici's name has become almost a synonym

for "ruthless and unscrupulous politician." It is Jean Heritier's contention in this biography, however, that she was in fact the greatest and most capable Queen of France—a ruler who played the same role in France as did Isabella in Spain, Elizabeth in England, and Catherine in Russia. Although this is a work of scholarship and is highly detailed, it is an extremely readable book and it is probably the best and most objective portrayal we have of the queen who played such a decisive role in the political and religious life of sixteenth-century Europe.

[de Smet, Jean] TERRELL, JOHN UPTON. *Black Robe: The Life of Pierre Jean de Smet.* Doubleday, 1964. 381 p., maps. $4.95. Echo, 1966. pa. 95¢.

Father de Smet, the subject of this biography, was a Jesuit priest and one of the pioneers of the West in the nineteenth century. He is remarkable for the enormous influence which he was able to exercise over the Indians, who regarded him as a father and leader. The author provides an abundance of Western-frontier flavor and color in this lively and popularly written narrative.

[De Veuster, Damien] FARROW, JOHN. *Damien the Leper.* Image, 1957. 232 p., bibliography, index. pa. 85¢.

Mr. Farrow's book is the highly popular biography of Father Damien de Veuster, the priest who chose to live in the leper colony of Molokai to care for the spiritual and medical needs of the lepers, and who, as a result of his choice, himself contracted leprosy. It is a beautifully written work of almost classic stature.

[Dooley, Tom] MONAHAN, JAMES, Editor. *Before I Sleep.* Farrar, 1961. x, 275 p. $4.50. Signet, 1963. pa. 60¢.

The editor has pieced together the story of Dr. Tom Dooley's last days, from his cancer operation in 1959 to his death in 1961. The account was written largely by Dr. Dooley's associates, and furnishes a moving account of the final phase in the career of the man who had made the care of the poor of Laos his life's work.

[Dooley, Tom] DOOLEY, THOMAS ANTHONY. *Dr. Tom Dooley's Three Great Books.* Farrar, 1960. 383 p., illustrations. $5.00.

The three complete works contained in this book are Dr.

Dooley's *Deliver Us from Evil, The Edge of Tomorrow,* and *The Night They Burned the Mountain.* The author is a young doctor who was inspired by the example of Albert Schweitzer to devote his life to caring for the sick in lands beyond the reach of modern medical science. The three books cover various phases of his much publicized work in Laos, including his discovery that he was dying of cancer. One reason for the enormous popularity of Dr. Dooley's books is his ability to describe vividly specific medical problems, the niceties of political brutality, and the problems of a world of incredible ignorance and poverty. These books are highly recommended to everyone. (These three books are also available individually in paperback, Signet, at 50¢ each.)

[Dorcy, Sister Mary Jean] DORCY, SISTER MARY JEAN. *Shepherd's Tartan.* Sheed, 1953. xi, 179 p. $2.50. All Saints, 1961. pa. 50¢.

The author of this book is a young nun who sees religious life as an earnest, though sometimes amusing, lifelong adventure. Her work is an explanation and illustration of her view and, while there are many humorous incidents to demonstrate the "fun" of convent life, the basic message of the book is that joy and peace can be found only in a life of dedication—whether within or without convent walls. This is recommended reading for all who are interested in convent life.

[Eleanor of Aquitaine] KELLY, AMY RUTH. *Eleanor of Aquitaine and the Four Kings.* Harvard, 1950. xii, 431 p., maps, bibliography, index. $5.00.

This is the biography of one of the most mysterious and controversial figures of the Middle Ages. When Eleanor was divorced by King Louis VII of France, she took a classic revenge by marrying the man who was to become King Henry II of England—and taking half of France with her as her dowry. Though history has shown Eleanor to be a highly frivolous and stubborn woman, she has been invested through the ages with an unearned glamour; the author of this work presents a clear and correct picture of her, and an excellent survey of the history of France and England in the twelfth century.

[Erasmus] HUIZINGA, JOHAN. *Erasmus and the Age of Reformation.* Translated by F. Hopman and Barbara Flowers.

Torchbooks, 1957. xiv, 259 p., illustrations, index. pa. $1.50.

This is a critical, and quite likely the best, biography of Erasmus of Rotterdam. It studies not only his life, but integrates into that aspect his works, his religious beliefs, his personal attitudes, and his psychological constitution. Despite the title, the book is not particularly concerned with Erasmus' role in the Reformation. It is, however, an extremely well written biography, by one of the great non-Catholic scholars of the period.

[Galileo] BRODRICK, JAMES (s.j.). *Galileo: The Man, His Work, His Misfortune.* Harper, 1965. 120 p., bibliography, index. $3.50.

Father Brodrick, a respected biographer and historian, re-examines one of the greatest men of science and one of the most famous scandals of the Church. Early in the seventeenth century, Galileo published a work asserting that the earth (and, by implication, man) was not the center of the universe. The Holy Office promptly condemned the theory and confined the theorizer to his quarters. Father Brodrick reviews the circumstances of the trial, the implications of Galileo's theories, describes the situation of the Church in history, and concludes that the Church's action had its cause in political expediency as well as in the fact that the reigning pope, Urban VIII, was not, on the whole, an intellectual giant.

[Gerard, John] GERARD, JOHN (s.j.). *The Autobiography of a Hunted Priest.* Translated by Philip Caraman, s.j. Image, 1955. 318 p., notes, appendices, index. pa. 95¢.

Father Gerard, the author, was a French priest who worked in Elizabethan England and who, disguised as a country gentleman, traveled about the country saying Mass, preaching, and administering the sacraments—always in danger of his life. It is an accurate and exciting picture of an England where to be a Catholic priest was an act of treason.

[Gibbons, James] BOUCHER, ARLINE and JOHN TEHAN. *Prince of Democracy.* Doubleday, 1962. 308 p., bibliography. $4.95. Image, 1966. pa. 95¢.

In this biography of James Cardinal Gibbons, the authors re-create a formative period in American social, religious, and economic history (1834–1921). Gibbons was one of the most colorful and dynamic figures of American Catholicism—as well as one of the most loved, by Catholics as well as by non-Catholics. An understanding of Gibbons is essential to an understanding of the history of American Catholicism, and this biography is recommended as a well written and witty chapter in that history and as the stimulating biography of an important churchman.

[Gibbons, James] ELLIS, JOHN TRACY. *The Life of James Cardinal Gibbons*. Bruce, 1952. Vol. I: xix, 707 p. Vol. II: vii, 735 p., bibliography, plates, index. $17.50 boxed set.

This is the definitive biography of Cardinal Gibbons, Bishop of Baltimore from 1877 to 1921, who was famous for his defense of the "American theory" of separation of Church and State against conservative elements of the Vatican Curia. The history of Cardinal Gibbons is very much the history of the Catholic Church in America over a span of almost fifty years, and this well documented biography is recommended to the scholar and the student of Church history.

[Hawthorne, Rose] BURTON, KATHERINE. *Sorrow Built a Bridge*. Image, 1956. 274 p., bibliography, index. pa. 75¢.

This is the story of Rose Hawthorne Lathrop, a daughter of Nathaniel Hawthorne, who became Mother Alphonsa, a Dominican nun, and foundress of a religious order of women, the Servants of Relief for Incurable Cancer. The title to the contrary, this is not a book of sorrows, but a charming volume about how Mother Alphonsa used a personal sorrow to find happiness in serving the sick and the poor.

[Hecker, Isaac] HOLDEN, VINCENT F. *The Yankee Paul*. Foreword by Archbishop Richard J. Cushing. Bruce, 1958. xx, 508 p., bibliography, index. $6.95.

This is the first book of a projected two-volume biography of Father Isaac Thomas Hecker, founder of the Congregation of the Missionary Priests of St. Paul the Apostle, an organization popularly known as the "Paulist fathers." Father Hecker's life, of which this volume covers only the earlier part, is as colorful and exciting as any novel and, although the work may be rather too detailed and long for the casual reader, it is recommended to the informed reader as an important chapter in the history of the American Church.

[John, King] WARREN, WILFRED LEWIS. *King John*. Norton, 1961. xi, 340 p., maps, illustrations, tables, appendices. $6.50.

This biography of King John of England is a reappraisal of the ill-reputed ruler who was forced to sign the Magna Carta in 1215. Professor Warren's prose is clear and concise, and his work is the sort of biography which is colorful and fast-moving enough to be enjoyable reading for its own sake. It is recommended to the amateur as well as to the professional historian.

[Hopkins, Gerard Manley] PICK, JOHN. *Gerard Manley Hopkins: Priest and Poet.* Foreword by Martin Cyril D'Arcy, S.J. Galaxy, 1966. 179 p., plates, bibliography, index. pa. $1.35.

This unusual biography has as its subject Gerard Manley Hopkins, English Jesuit priest and poet. In addition to a treatment of Hopkins' life and career, the author devotes much space to an interpretation of Hopkins' work, and integrates into his text many quotations from the Jesuit's poetry, letters, and notebooks. This is probably the best introduction to the work of Hopkins available today.

[John XXIII, Pope] JOHN XXIII, POPE. *Journal of a Soul.* Translated by Dorothy White. McGraw, 1965. 453 p., illustrations, bibliography. $7.95.

This posthumous publication of Pope John's consists of his notes, in diary form, kept from his fourteenth year until the year before his death. Most of the material is in the form of simple spiritual reflections, but there are also a few letters, his spiritual testament to the Roncalli family, and his will. Since this is primarily a spiritual journal, there are few references to John's public life, but the book is useful in understanding the reasons and intentions of Pope John in undertaking to up-date the Church.

[John XXIII, Pope] HATCH, ALDEN. *A Man Named John.* Hawthorn, 1963. 237 p., illustrations, index. $4.95. Image, 1965. pa. 95¢.

This is a popularly written biography of Pope John XXIII, covering his life from his childhood through his career as a Vatican diplomat and as a bishop to his brief but revolutionary reign as pope. It is an excellent introduction to the man and to the changes he brought about in the Church and in the world.

[Knox, Ronald] WAUGH, EVELYN. *Monsignor Ronald Knox.* Little, 1959. 358 p., bibliography, index. $5.00.

This biography of Monsignor Knox was written as a study of the man as a literary figure rather than as a priest, since, as the author concedes, it was in the former capacity that he knew Knox. From that standpoint, it is hardly a definitive biography of the famous translator of the Bible who also was a writer of mystery stories, but it is well worth the reading both as a piece of literature in its own right and as a study of one facet of a great man.

[LaFarge, John] LAFARGE, JOHN (s.j.). *The Manner is Ordinary.* Harcourt, 1954. viii, 408 p., illustrations, map, index. $4.75. Image, 1957. pa. 95¢.

Father LaFarge was one of the most highly regarded American Catholic figures of the twentieth century, both for his ability as a man of letters and for his work in the field of social justice. This autobiography tells the story of his childhood, his student years at Harvard and Innsbruck, his entry into the Society of Jesus, his work in the missions of Maryland, and his twenty-five years with *America* magazine. It is a beautifully written and fascinating story, recommended without reservation to all readers.

[Luther, Martin] TODD, JOHN MURRAY. *Martin Luther: A Biographical Study.* Newman, 1964. xix, 290 p., illustrations, facsimiles, portraits, bibliography, appendices, index. $5.75.

It is likely that this is the first complete biography of Martin Luther that is more concerned with presenting historical truth than with defending either a Protestant or a Catholic position. Mr. Todd covers the whole life of the Great Reformer and analyzes his role in the Protestant schism as well as the quality of the reforms he proposed, demonstrating that the latter were, for the most part, the same reforms that had been proposed by many of the fathers and doctors of the Church before the Reformation, and by many of the theologians and saints after it. This is a remarkable work of original scholarship, written in a readily understandable style, and recommended without reservation.

[Madeleva, Sister] MADELEVA, SISTER (c.s.c.). *My First Seventy Years.* Macmillan, 1959. 191 p. $3.50. Macmillan, 1962. pa. $1.45.

Sister Madeleva, one of the most widely read of contemporary American poets, tells the story of her life as a woman and as a nun. It is a charming book, and often a moving one, filled with good humor, whimsey, and spiritual wisdom.

[Marie of the Ursulines] REPPLIER, AGNES. *Mere Marie of the Ursulines*. Foreword by Frances Parkinson Keyes. Sheed, 1957. xvi, 314 p., index. $3.00.

This is the biography of the Venerable Mother Marie of the Incarnation who, after becoming a nun in France, came to Quebec to teach the children of the French colonials and to convert the Indians to Catholicism. Mother Marie had a life of almost incredible hardship and disappointment, but it was an extremely useful life and one to which the author does full justice.

MARITAIN, RAÏSSA. *We Have Been Friends Together* and *Adventures in Grace*. Translated by Julie Kernan. Image, 1961. 392 p., notes. pa. $1.25.

These are the memoirs of Raïssa Maritain, wife of Jacques Maritain. The author recounts her memories of such gifted personalities as Charles Peguy, Leon Bloy, Georges Roualt, Jean Cocteau, and others who were "friends together" and who shared those "adventures in grace" which flowered into a brilliant intellectual and spiritual renaissance in modern France. From the author's first meeting with Jacques Maritain, when both were students at the Sorbonne, she tells of the spiritual and intellectual search of two gifted individuals for the meaning of existence—a search which took them eventually to the Church.

[Maryanna, Sister] MARYANNA, SISTER (O.P.). *With Love and Laughter*. Doubleday, 1960. 199 p. $3.50. Image, 1964. pa. 95¢.

The autobiography of an American girl who became a Dominican nun. In the author's words, her story is "a love letter to the world—the reflections of one Sister looking back gratefully with love and laughter." She recalls her life from the time when, at eighteen, she left home to enter the convent despite her friends' warning that she would be "buried alive" and her father's admonition to "work your way up, now, Mary" through the trials and joys of convent life and the purgatory of student theatricals, to the serenity of Lourdes. There is much good humor and wit, and a life's story sure to dispel any notions about nuns being "buried alive."

[Merton, Thomas] MERTON, THOMAS. *The Seven Storey Mountain.* Harcourt, 1948. 429 p., index. $3.95.

This famous work is the autobiography of Thomas Merton, covering the period from his birth in 1915 to the end of World War II. Essentially, it narrates the spiritual odyssey of a modern American man with little religious background through the philosophical isms until he finally finds an intellectual and spiritual home in the Church.

[Michelangelo] MICHELANGELO BUONAROTTI. *I, Michelangelo, Sculptor.* Edited, with introduction and notes, by Irving and Jean Stone. Doubleday, 1962. 283 p., introduction, notes, index. $4.95.

The letters of Michelangelo are so arranged in this volume as to present an autobiographically chronological picture of the great Renaissance artist. The entries begin in 1496, when he was twenty-one years old, and continue into 1563, shortly before his death. The letters, divided into sections according to their places of origin, are connected by background material provided by the editors. Some of Michelangelo's sonnets are included at appropriate points. Despite some rather naïve editorial tampering with the letters' contents, the book provides an adequate, if only partial, idea of Michelangelo and his times.

[Michelangelo] BRANDES, GEORG. *Michelangelo: His Life, His Times, His Era.* Translated with a foreword by Heinz Norden. Ungar, 1963. 428 p., notes, genealogical table. $8.50.

A biography of Michelangelo Buonarotti, this work is popularly written, imaginative, and filled with interesting anecdotes about the great artist and his contemporaries—although many of the stories are regarded, quite rightly, as apocryphal. The book does provide a colorful and exciting account of Michelangelo's trials and accomplishments, not only as a sculptor and painter but also as a poet and writer.

[Montessori, Maria] STANDING, E. MORTIMER. *Maria Montessori: Her Life and Work.* Academy Library, 1957. 354 p. $5.95.

This is an authoritative account of the lifework of a great Catholic educator, the founder of the controversial Montessori Method according to which children are provided with certain materials and, with no attempt at formal training, are encouraged to exercise their initiative; the teacher acts as a

guide rather than as an instructor. It is an interesting book
about a woman who has had an enormous influence on
modern educational theories.

[Newman, John Henry] NEWMAN, JOHN HENRY CARDINAL.
Apologia Pro Vita Sua. Modern Library, n.d. 439 p. $1.95.
Image, 1956 (Introduction by Philip Hughes). pa. $1.35.

The most famous of Newman's works, the *Apologia* is an
explanation of his changes of religious opinion from his childhood until, after years of study, he entered the Catholic
Church "in perfect peace and contentment." This undoubtedly is one of the great spiritual and literary classics of modern times, and it is recognized as one of the great autobiographies of the English language.

[Newman, John Henry] TREVOR, MERIOD. *Newman: The
Pillar of the Cloud* (Vol. I) and *Newman: Light in Winter*
(Vol. II). Doubleday, 1962–1963. Vol. I: xiv, 649 p., illustrations, portraits, bibliography. Vol. II: 652 p., illustrations,
portraits, bibliography, index. $7.95 ea.

These two volumes comprise the definitive biography of
John Henry Cardinal Newman, the leader of the nineteenth-
century Oxford movement who was converted to Catholicism and became one of the most extraordinary and endur-
ingly influential religious thinkers of modern times. Volume I
covers Newman's early life, ending in 1853 with his conviction for libel. Volume II treats of the period from 1853 until
his death in 1890. The work is unreservedly recommended.

[Paul VI, Pope] BARRETT, WILLIAM E. *Shepherd of Mankind.* Doubleday, 1964. 288 p., illustrations. $4.95.

The biography, by the author of *Lilies of the Field*, of
Pope Paul VI, this work begins with the future pope's childhood and ends with his coronation in 1963. In addition to a
comprehensive chronological treatment of Paul's life and
career, the author presents a wealth of interesting personal
details and anecdotes. The pace is lively, and Mr. Barrett's
style is entertaining as well as instructive.

[Paul VI, Pope] CLANCY, JOHN G. (MSGR.). *Apostle for Our
Time: Pope Paul VI.* Kenedy, 1963. 238 p., notes, plates, appendices, bibliography, index. $4.95.

The author of this biography worked under Pope Paul,
then Monsignor Montini, when the latter was in the Vatican

Secretariat of State. In the book, he tells of Paul's early years, his career as a Vatican diplomat, his appointment to the archbishopric of Milan, his election to the papacy, and his reign as pope up to August 1963. Despite some obvious failings in historical objectivity, Clancy's book is easily readable, contains numerous anecdotes about Paul VI, and gives a clear, if slightly larger-than-life, picture of the reigning pontiff.

[Philip II] WALSH, WILLIAM THOMAS. *Philip II*. Farrar, 1953. xiii, 770 p., notes, index. $7.00.

Philip II, King of Spain, was the son of the Emperor Charles V. He was ruler of the most powerful and influential country of Europe during the Reformation's latter phases, and the history of that period is incomprehensible without an understanding of this prince who was a devout Catholic, working not only for the benefit of his subjects but consciously for the glory of God as he understood it. Unfortunately, a definitive biography of Philip has not yet been written. The present work has many faults, not the least of them being the author's obvious Catholic bias, but it will suffice to give the reader a generally accurate picture of a fascinating and enormously influential historical figure.

[Savonarola, Girolamo] RIDOLFI, ROBERTO. *The Life of Girolamo Savonarola*. Translated by Cecil Grayson. Knopf, 1959. x, 326 p., index. $7.50.

Savonarola, the subject of this biography, is one of the most enigmatic and colorful figures in history. His attempts to reform Florence (and the Church) in the late fifteenth century met with temporary success and he, a Dominican monk, was for a time the ruler of that city. In attempting to extend his reforms to Rome, however, he ran afoul of Pope Alexander VI, was excommunicated, and eventually was put to death. In the eyes of many he was, and is, a saint; to others, he was a criminal fanatic. In the light of history, he seems simply to have been born several centuries before his time. This compassionate work of Ridolfi's is recommended as an excellent and popular portrayal.

[Serra, Junipero] REPPLIER, AGNES. *Junipero Serra*. All Saints, 1962. v, 184 p. pa. 50¢.

A biography of the first Jesuit missionary to California, Miss Repplier's work tells the story of Junipero Serra's abandonment of his promising career as a teacher and theologian to work for the conversion of the Indians in the New World. She depicts his extraordinary adventures in California, the political and military intrigues of the settlers and colonists there, and Father Serra's heroic resistance to all efforts to subordinate the spiritual good of his flock to the cause of temporal expediency. The book is as lively as an historical novel, and presents an accurate picture of the sixteenth-century West.

[Seton, Elizabeth Bayley] MELVILLE, ANNABELLE. *Elizabeth Bayley Seton*. Scribner, 1951. xix, 411 p., illustrations. $4.95.

Dr. Melville's work is a biography of the young New York widow who became a convert to Catholicism and, in 1809, founded the first native religious community for women. Her Sisters of Charity became the original source of teachers for the American parochial school system. This book is an excellent work of scholarship, and the author writes smoothly and enthusiastically of her subject.

[Spellman, Francis X.] GANNON, ROBERT I. (s.J.). *The Cardinal Spellman Story*. Doubleday, 1962. vi, 447 p., plates, portraits, notes, index. $5.95. Pocket Books, 1964. pa. 75¢.

This is the first full length biography of Francis Cardinal Spellman, Archbishop of New York and one of the most influential churchmen of the twentieth century. It covers the Cardinal's life in detail from his childhood until 1961. Occasionally, there is a certain apologetic tendency and a consequent lack of scholarly objectivity, but the author's flowing style and long acquaintance with Spellman have enabled him to produce an interesting and readable book.

[Teilhard de Chardin, Pierre] TEILHARD DE CHARDIN, PIERRE (s.J.). *Letters From Egypt*. Translated, with foreword by Henri de Lubac. Herder & Herder, 1965. 216 p. $4.95.

As a young man, Teilhard de Chardin was a high school teacher in Cairo, Egypt. This book is a collection of his letters, written during that period (1905–08), to his family. Although they are not so revelatory of the personality and bent of the man as are his later letters, the present collection shows the strong religious views of the young Teilhard and presage his intense interest in paleontology.

[Teilhard de Chardin, Pierre] LUBAC, HENRI DE (s.j.).
Teilhard de Chardin: The Man and His Meaning. Translated
by René Hague. Hawthorn, 1965. 203 p., notes, index. $4.95.

Father de Lubac has written a penetrating analysis of
Teilhard de Chardin as a man and as a Catholic. He describes
Teilhard's childhood and family background, his training as
a Jesuit, preparation for a scientific career, and his attain-
ment of intellectual maturity in the trenches of World War I
as well as his subsequent career as a scientist and philosopher.
There is an excellent summary of Teilhard's thought on
matters of religious doctrine and dogma and an able and convincing demonstration that nothing that Teilhard wrote or
thought was outside the framework of Catholic teaching but
that, on the contrary, the great Jesuit's work was predicated
on his intense belief in the Church.

[Trapp, Maria Augusta] TRAPP, MARIA AUGUSTA and RUTH
T. MURDOCH. *A Family on Wheels.* Lippincott, 1959. 199 p.
$4.50. Image, 1965. pa. 75¢.

The true story of the adventures of the famous Trapp
Family Singers on tour in America, Europe, and the Far
East, from the exotic cities of South America to the leper
colony of Molokai in Hawaii. This is a sequel to *The Story of
the Trapp Family Singers,* written in the same light vein
and entertaining style as that famous book.

[Trapp, Maria Augusta] TRAPP, MARIA AUGUSTA. *The
Story of the Trapp Family Singers.* Lippincott, 1949. 312 p.
$4.95. Image, 1957. pa. 95¢.

The famous story—later made into the musical comedy,
The Sound of Music—of Baron and Baroness von Trapp
and their seven children. It is a thoroughly enjoyable story,
simply written, with much humor and some pathos, and
should be enjoyed by anyone with a taste for autobiography.

[Tudor, Mary] PRESCOTT, H. M. F. *Mary Tudor,* revised
edition. Macmillan, 1962. xiii, 439 p., illustrations, bibliography, index. $5.00. Macmillan, 1962. pa. $1.95.

This is far and away the best biography of Mary Tudor,
daughter of Henry VIII and Queen of England. As Henry's
daughter by Catherine of Aragon, she was a staunch Catholic
who refused to abandon her religion even when she believed
that her life depended upon making at least a show of accepting Protestantism. Her one ambition was to re-establish

Catholicism in England, and her efforts to do so by means of the sword, the fire, and the gallows, have earned her the sobriquet of "Bloody Mary." Miss Prescott's work is highly recommended as fascinating reading and as sound history. (This book was first published under the title of *Bloody Mary*, in 1953.)

[Verot, Augustin] GANNON, MICHAEL V. *Rebel Bishop*. Bruce, 1964. xvii, 267 p., plates, portraits, notes, bibliography. $4.95.

The "rebel bishop" of the title is Augustin Verot, Bishop of St. Augustine, Florida, in the last quarter of the nineteenth century, and one of the most interesting and controversial figures of modern ecclesiastical history. This biography brings Verot to life as the *enfant terrible* of the First Vatican Council and as the center of a political storm in the U.S. when he dared to defend the property rights of Southern slave-owners. Although the author obviously is in sympathy with his subject, his material is historically sound, well written, and entertainingly instructive.

[Ward, Maisie] WARD, MAISIE. *Unfinished Business*. Sheed, 1964. viii, 374 p. $5.95.

This is the autobiography of Miss Ward, author and lecturer, covering seventy-five years of her intensely active life. It is also a portrait of her famous husband, Frank Sheed, and a history of the publishing firm of Sheed & Ward founded by them in 1926. There are many interesting sidelights on modern Catholic intellectual history and, although the book is badly organized and rather wordy, it will make interesting reading for the mature Catholic.

[Waugh, Evelyn] WAUGH, EVELYN. *A Little Learning*. Little, 1964. 234 p., index. $5.00.

This is the first book in a projected three-volume autobiography of the eminent Catholic novelist and wit. The present work covers Mr. Waugh's heredity, environment, education, and religious opinions as a young man. The author writes, as always, with the most polished simplicity and grace.

[Wolsey, Thomas Cardinal] FERGUSON, CHARLES WRIGHT. *Naked to Mine Enemies*. Little, 1958. 543 p., notes, bibliography, index. $6.75. Little, 1960. pa. $2.45.

Thomas Wolsey was born the son of a prosperous butcher

in fifteenth-century England. Through a combination of native intelligence and ambition, he rose rapidly through the ranks of the clergy to become eventually Archbishop of York, then of Durham, cardinal, and Chancellor of England under King Henry VIII. During Henry's early reign, Wolsey's power was so great that he was in effect the ruler of England, and aspired—almost with success—to the papal throne. He eventually lost his power, mostly through his handling of Henry's divorce from Catherine of Aragon, and was accused of treason but conveniently died before the trial. This dramatic presentation of Wolsey's life and time recreates the color of Henry's court and the enigmatic character of Wolsey himself with accuracy and skill. It is undoubtedly the best, and certainly the most readable, such biography of recent years.

4. THE CATHOLIC RELIGION

Probably no institution in all recorded history has been the object of such intense study, controversy, adulation, and hatred as the Catholic Church. Men have died to give evidence of their complete commitment to her teachings; on the other hand, many have been subjected to severe persecution for disagreeing with them. But whether one agrees with or opposes the religion which the Catholic Church asserts is the faithful teaching of Christ, few will dispute that this religion is worthy of close scrutiny.

What the Church proclaims has such far-reaching consequences for all mankind that to ignore her claims would be the height of folly for any thinking person. For, simply put, the Church states she was founded by Jesus Christ, the third Person of the Blessed Trinity, God, who entrusted to her alone the task and authority to spread his message—a message of salvation which provides the means by which one can achieve eternal life and happiness. One can either accept that claim or reject it; but to ignore it is unthinkable, and only by knowing the teaching of the Church can one come to an intelligent decision about it. It thus becomes a matter of the utmost importance for anyone concerned with the ultimate purpose of life to consider the astonishing offer the Church makes—that through her teaching one can gain immortality with God.

For the average person brought up in the Catholic faith, it is difficult to realize the depth and complexity of the Church's teaching. So many of the intricacies of the faith have been inculcated into us since early childhood that we do not realize how carefully structured and complex is the edifice of Catholic teaching. But even the "cradle Catholic" who studies his Church's teachings is constantly impressed by the scope and depth of the knowledge accumulated by the doctors and fathers and scholars of Catholic belief. To one coming to this study for the first time, therefore, the ramifications of the Church's teaching are apt to be awe-inspiring.

And yet, when all is said and done, this whole majestic structure of reason and faith stems from the teaching of Christ and from God's revelation as unfolded in the Bible. Of all the great teachers of men, none have taught the profound truths in such simple phrases and with such ordinary illustrations as did our Lord. He clothed the profundity of his teaching in simple parables readily understandable even to children; and yet, when scholars come to study them, the implications abound in concepts far beyond human understanding. For Christ's teachings may be approached from two angles: from that of faith, or from that of human reason. It is this basic fact that has so often puzzled great thinkers. How can a religion have such deep appeal for the simplest intellect—for children, peasants, the uneducated—and at the same time provide an unsurpassed way of life for the scholar, the intellectual, the university professor? For faith opens vistas that intellect cannot attain and yet intellect can open up even greater realms for faith to illumine. The combination, then, of faith with the fullest use of human reason is the method *par excellence* to achieve the fullest knowledge of the Catholic religion.

Many people find difficulty in understanding how the teachings of God, so simply expounded by Christ, could be developed into the seemingly overwhelming body of knowledge which is the deposit of faith so carefully guarded by the Church. So complex has the Church become that it sometimes seems she is involved in matters far beyond the scope of her proper function, which is to spread Christ's word. How can a church of half a billion people, with thousands of bishops, elaborate rituals, and a complex world-wide organization, be the same as the primitive church of 2000 years ago with a handful of believers, 12 apostles and no organization, in an obscure province of the Roman Empire? And yet, no one has any difficulty in understanding that a small seed can grow into the 300-foot tall redwood tree of California, or that a tiny microscopic sperm and egg can unite to produce the most complex organism on earth—the human being. The most involved mechanisms of modern society—

airplanes, steamships, locomotives, computers, cities—all are the complicated products of man's labor, but all evolved from simple, primitive, easy-to-understand beginnings. Applying this same reasoning to the Church, it becomes clear that indeed this Church today can very well be the same as that of twenty centuries ago.

All of the above comparison is of an external nature. Numbers of believers, complexity of structure, geographic area, profusion of buildings—all these are simply a matter of growth and proliferation. The essence of the matter is whether the teaching has been transmitted pure and unchanged through the centuries. Is the elaborate structure we know as the Catholic Church teaching to millions the same truths, through modern means of communication—books, magazines, newspapers, TV, radio, motion pictures, as Christ taught by word of mouth to the few thousands who listened to him? Here is the crux of the whole question of the Church's validity today: is she teaching the truths Christ entrusted to her?

Any Catholic scholar will answer that the Church has faithfully lived up to her mission through the centuries. But, to understand why the answer is so emphatically affirmative, two factors must be understood. The first of these is the development of dogma so brilliantly discussed in Newman's *Essay on the Development of Christian Doctrine*. This proposition is simply that, through the history of the Church, certain teachings of Christ have developed as men's understanding of these teachings developed but that *the basic dogma has remained constant and unchanging*. An appropriate concept to demonstrate this statement is the papacy. Christ appointed Peter the leader of the apostles when he said: "Thou art Peter, and upon this rock I will build my Church, and the gates of Hell shall not prevail against it" (Matt. 16:18–19). At the time, Peter was the leader of a small band of twelve men. Today Pope Paul VI, Peter's successor, is the head of half a billion Catholics. Obviously the problems faced by Paul are inestimably more complex and far-reaching than those of Peter, and obviously the papacy over twenty centuries has had to adjust to meet problems posed by the growth of the Church. But though Paul faces different and more difficult problems than those with which Peter wrestled, the basic concept of the papacy is the same for Paul as it was for Peter. Only the externals and ramifications have changed.

So, too, have many dogmas of the Church been developed in the past and will be developed in the future. The deposit of the faith was revealed in full by the time of the death of the last apostle. But the understanding and development of the tenets of that deposit is far from complete. Nor will it ever be; for this is the revealed knowledge of God and only union with him will reveal to humans the full scope of that knowledge. But men must constantly study that deposit and apply their whole intellectual energies to the problems of that deposit in order to achieve, within known limits, the full measure of God's revelations to us.

The second factor which must be understood is precisely this point: man's knowledge is constantly increasing. As he applies this knowledge, things previously beclouded become clear. For example, man has always dreamed of flying, and yet it was not until the twentieth century that he acquired sufficient knowledge to construct a device which would fly in the air. And fifty years after his first awkward flight in the air he is reaching for the stars.

So also in the field of religious truths, as man grows in wisdom and knowledge, so does his understanding of God's teaching become clearer as he applies to that thinking the accumulated knowledge and wisdom of mankind. It is this fact that requires such painful periods of renewal as we are presently undergoing in the Church. At intervals, the Church must apply the knowledge her scholars have developed to the actual practices of the Church so as to bring her people in line with the new discoveries and inventions and knowledge of the period. But always the basic teaching is constant. The externals, the structures, the façades can and must be rebuilt at regular intervals but the dogma given the Church by Christ is unchangeable. Truth is not variable. Only the method in which it is presented changes.

And so, while it is always desirable for the faithful to know the tenets of the Catholic religion, in a time of change it is absolutely essential that they have a thorough knowledge of the teaching of the Church. Indeed, one of the problems besetting many today is that, too frequently, people have confused the changeable externals with the basic dogmas, so that, when changes in externals are made to update the Church, they believe the very foundation of the Church is being ripped apart.

From the above, it is obvious why a thorough knowledge of the Church's teaching is so important. Knowing one's religion is a prime requisite for any Catholic—and never before is such a knowledge needed as today. In the books described below, the general reader will find the teachings of the Church discussed from many angles. Since this is a time of change, some of the books listed may reveal their age in not being completely in accord with some of the recent changes and practices; but they have been included in this list because they are outstanding in their treatment of the special areas with which they are concerned. Even such books, which are few in number and clearly labeled, are orthodox and correct on basic teaching. Only in external matters are they dated in some particular. Generally speaking, the authors of this *Guide* believe you will find the books in this section to be accurate and dependable considerations of one of the most fascinating subjects known to man—the Catholic religion.

ADAM, KARL. *The Spirit of Catholicism.* Translated by Justin McCann, O.S.B. Image, 1954. 260 p., notes, index. pa. 85¢.

Dr. Adam's book is a study of the fundamental concepts of the Catholic faith—its tenets, its historical development, and the role of the Church in world society—by one of the world's most distinguished Christian philosophers. This is probably the best, and certainly the most famous, analysis of the motive power of the Church written in modern times. It requires rather slow reading, for the author compresses many ideas into comparatively few words; but it will be time well spent. (The paperback edition cited above is the revised edition, translated by Justin McCann, O.S.B.)

ARADI, ZSOLT. *The Book of Miracles.* Preface by Agostino Gemelli, O.F.M. Farrar, 1956. 375 p. $5.00. Monarch, 1963. pa. 50¢.

The purpose of this work is to explore and interpret the recorded miracles of history for which there can be no natural explanation. Mr. Aradi, a former Hungarian diplomat accredited to the Holy See, writes for the general reader, avoiding the intricacies of theological terminology. His commonsense approach to supernatural phenomena will make this work of interest to the skeptic as well as to the believer.

BRUNINI, JOHN G. *Whereon to Stand*, revised edition. Introduction by Francis Cardinal Spellman. Chapel, 1961. 351 p., index. pa. 50¢.

Brunini explains what the beliefs and practices of the Catholic Church are, and why the Church believes and practices what it does. The book is written in a simple style, and does not presume any foregoing knowledge of Church doctrine; for that reason, it is an ideal choice of books for non-Catholics interested in the Church. What the author writes is not in any way controversial, and there is nothing in the book that will offend non-Catholics.

BULLOUGH, SEBASTIAN. *Roman Catholicism*. Penguin, 1964. 330 p. pa. $1.25.

The author gives a comprehensive survey of the faith and the practices of the Church, explaining not only what the Church teaches but also the reasons for teaching it and showing how those beliefs are logically applied in the area of practice. The book is an excellent work for the home and for students.

CHESTERTON, GILBERT KEITH. *Orthodoxy*. Dodd, 1924. 160 p. $3.00. Image, 1959. pa. 75¢.

Generally regarded as *the* masterpiece of a man who has written many such, *Orthodoxy* is Chesterton's personal statement of his faith. His approach is to demonstrate that only Christianity can satisfy the longing of man for wonder, love, happiness—everything that is embodied in that much misused word, *romance*. This is thoroughly enjoyable reading, and the best possible introduction to Chesterton's originality of style and brilliance of intellect.

CONWAY, BERTRAND L. *The Question Box*, third edition. Introduction by Francis Cardinal Spellman. Paulist, 1961. 448 p., bibliographies. pa. $1.95.

This is a completely revised and updated edition of a well

known and popular work of explanation of what the Church believes. The work is arranged by subject, in question-and-answer format, and provides information on hundreds of points of Catholic dogmatic and moral beliefs.

CONWAY, JAMES D. (MSGR.). *Facts of the Faith.* All Saints, 1961. ix, 371 p. pa. 75¢.

Monsignor Conway tells the story of the foundation and organization of the Church, and then explains such things as the sacraments, the commandments of God and of the Church, as well as such often misunderstood doctrines as "outside the Church there is no salvation." He writes for three groups of people: for Catholics who would like to know more about their Church, for those who might like to become Catholics, and for those who are simply curious about the Church. For each of those audiences, this book will provide a clear and factual presentation of all the information they could ask.

DOUILLET, JACQUES. *What Is a Saint?* Translated by Donald Attwater. Hawthorn, 1958. 124 p., bibliography. $3.50.

This is a popular explanation of what the word "saint" means. The author traces the use of the word from the primitive Church, when all Christians were called "saints," to the time when sainthood was conferred by popular acclamation, and then to the eventual codification of the process of canonization in the Middle Ages. There is a lucid discussion of the process of canonization, of relics, of what is meant by "the communion of saints," and of a few outstanding saints to illustrate the other material. The book is a valuable source of information for the general reader and for libraries.

HILDEBRAND, DIETRICH VON. *In Defense of Purity.* Helicon, 1963. 175 p. $3.50.

This is a famous theologian's analysis of the meaning for Catholics of the concepts of sex, purity, and virginity. In this small book the author outlines Catholic teachings, shows the Biblical, psychological and physiological bases for those teachings, and demonstrates that it is within the intention of Catholic doctrine that man be able to find true fulfillment of his emotional needs. Despite the author's reputation as a scholar, this is not a scholarly book; it is rather a popular presentation of a difficult subject.

KNOX, RONALD (MSGR.). *The Belief of Catholics*. Image, 1958. 198 p. pa. 75¢.

Msgr. Knox presents the beliefs of the Catholic Church on basic questions: Is there a God? Does he care about us? Has he ever revealed himself? Can we *prove* that he established a Church? What does that Church teach? What is its spirit? Does it make any claim on our allegiance? There is a wealth of information for both Catholics and non-Catholics —and Knox's justly famed beauty of style is a bonus for the reader.

KNOX, RONALD (MSGR.). *The Hidden Stream*. Sheed, 1953. 197 p. $3.00. Image, 1964. pa. 75¢.

This is a collection of essays in which the author examines some of the fundamental precepts of the Catholic faith in relation to some modern challenges to those precepts. Among the issues discussed are the meaning of religion, the miracles of Christ, salvation "outside the Church," sin and forgiveness, and the Christian concept of marriage. As in all of Knox's books, his literary brilliance and wit will entrance any reader.

LUBAC, HENRI DE (S.J.). *Catholicism*. Translated by Lancelot D. Sheppard. Sheed, 1958. xiv, 283 p. $4.00. Mentor-Omega, 1964. pa. 95¢.

Catholicism is a study of Catholic points of dogma in relation to what the author conceives as the corporate destiny of mankind, and it emphasizes the essentially social, or community, character of the Church. Father de Lubac is one of the most gifted, and one of the most controversial, theologians of our time. A particular point of controversy has been emphasized in this book; i.e., his theory of the supernatural destiny of man. As original and interesting as his work is, it is heavy reading for any but specialists.

NEWMAN, JOHN HENRY CARDINAL. *An Essay on the Development of Christian Doctrine*. Foreword by Gustave Weigel, S.J. Image, 1960, 434 p., notes, index. pa. $1.35.

Basically a history of the evolution of theological beliefs, this work's primary objective is to distinguish true "development" from mere corruption or decay. Within that framework, he considers the growth of doctrine from the time of the Apostles until the early nineteenth century. This is one of Newman's most important works, and is still one of the best available histories of theological thought. It presupposes no background in theology, but requires attentive reading; the clarity of style, however, keeps difficulties to a minimum, and an excellent introduction by Gustave Weigel will help the reader to view Newman's work in its historical perspective.

O'BRIEN, JOHN A. *Truths Men Live By: A Philosophy of Religion and Life.* Macmillan, 1946. xii, 427 p., diagrams, bibliography, index. $5.95. Macmillan, 1955. pa. $1.95.

Father O'Brien explores the basic truths of Christianity as well as a few of the more striking points of controversy that constantly recur in discussions of Catholicism. The book has five parts: (1) the existence and nature of God; (2) the origins and nature of religious belief; (3) the nature and qualities of the human soul; (4) creation and evolution; (5) Christ as Son of God and savior. Some of the proofs adduced for the existence of God and the author's views on evolution are dated, but generally the book still is valid as an exposition of what the Church teaches on particular points.

PEGIS, ANTON C., Editor. *The Wisdom of Catholicism.* Modern Library, 1960. 988 p., bibliography. $2.95.

This is a compilation of the best writings of Catholic authors through the ages, beginning with St. Augustine's classic *City of God* and ending in the twentieth century with G. K. Chesterton's essay "The World Inside Out." There is hardly an important work of the past fifteen centuries of Catholicism that is not represented, and the particular usefulness of this volume lies in the fact that many such works are not easily available individually in English translations. The book as a whole is also an outstanding introduction to the entire structure of Catholic tenets, doctrines, and dogmas.

SHEED, FRANCIS J. *The Map of Life.* Sheed, 1939. 147 p., study club outline, index. $2.00.

Mr. Sheed manages, in a few pages, to cover just about every point of Catholic dogma, from what we believe about God, Christ, and the Church, to what we believe about man's place in creation. He accomplishes his task with a wit and literary finesse seldom found in books of this sort. For all its age, *Map of Life* is still one of the most concise, comprehensive, exact—and certainly the most enjoyable—such exposition on the market.

SMITH, GEORGE D., Editor. *The Teaching of the Catholic Church.* Macmillan, 1949. Vol. I: 658 p., notes; Vol. II: 658 p., notes, index. $12.50 set.

These two volumes comprise a summary of Catholic doctrine. The first volume contains introductory chapters on the nature of faith and a comprehensive summary of the whole of Catholic doctrine, while subsequent chapters deal with specific subjects, as God, the Trinity, Mary, Jesus Christ, Man, Grace, and the Virtues. Volume II discusses the Church, the Sacraments both individually and as a whole, and the Four Last Things. Although, in several respects, this work is outdated because of the changes that have come about since Vatican II, on the whole it is one of the most comprehensive and detailed such works of value to the informed layman.

THOMAS AQUINAS, SAINT. *On the Truth of the Catholic Faith.* Translated by Charles J. O'Neil, Anton C. Pegis, James F. Anderson, and Vernon J. Bourke. Image, 1955. 5 volumes, introductions, notes, indices. pa. 95¢ ea.

This is a translation of Aquinas' *Summa contra gentiles* (also called the *Summa philosophica*). In this work, Thomas attempts to explain, by reason alone, the truth of the Catholic faith. It is, then, basically a book of apologetics, and the source from which all later such works have been drawn. The work is divided into four books, or parts: the first, "God," treats of the existence and nature of God; the second, "Creation," deals with the notion of creation and with the interrelationship of creator and creatures; the third book, "Providence," examines the concept of God as the final good and end of all creatures, and studies the role of free will and of grace in that context; the fourth section examines the meaning of salvation and the ways of attaining it, such as the Church, the sacraments, etc., and is entitled "Salvation." The book does not presume a deep knowledge of philosophy, but its depth and closeness of logic recommend it only to the serious reader.

TRESE, LEO J. *Wisdom Shall Enter.* Fides, 1960. 144 p. pa. 95¢.

The purpose of this small volume is to provide ready answers to questions asked by Catholics and non-Catholics about the Catholic faith. Basically, it is a book of apologetics, and provides the traditional answers, in easily understandable

and convincing language, to questions about the existence
and nature of God, the presence of evil in the world, the
structure of the Church, etc.

VAN DOORNIK, N. C. M.: S. JELSMA, and A. VAN DE LISDONK.
A Handbook of the Catholic Faith. Edited with an introduction by John Greenwood. Image, 1956. $1.55. (Hard-
bound title: *The Triptych of the Kingdom.* Newman, 1954.
440 p. $4.75.)

A presentation of the basic beliefs of the Catholic Church,
the book begins by examining the fundamental idea of the
existence of God and his relationship to man. Part One then
explains the antecedents of Christianity, with particular emphasis on the Hebrews as the Chosen People and the Old
Testament prophecies concerning the Messias, and investigates the historical reliability of the gospels and the founding
of the Church as revealed in the gospels. Part Two deals
with the teachings of the Church, starting with its papal and
episcopal foundations and working its way through the
various doctrines in logical order. Part Three explains the
Catholic principles of life in the Church by means of the
liturgy, moral law, and the spiritual life. Part Four studies
the "last things"—death, judgment, hell, purgatory, heaven,
and the resurrection of the body. This is a well organized
popular work; it explains the Catholic position on just about
every point of belief that might be of interest.

WALSH, JOHN (S.J.). *This Is Catholicism.* Image, 1959. 398
p., notes, index. pa. $1.25.

This is a complete catechism, in question-and-answer
form, of Catholic teachings. The book begins with the basic
problems about which questions most frequently arise—existence, pain, evil, death—and goes on to outline, in simple
language, the whole structure of Church doctrine. The book
was designed both to instruct Catholics in the essentials of
their faith, and to provide information on the Church to
non-Catholics.

WILLIAMS, MICHAEL. *The Catholic Church in Action,* revised edition. Written in collaboration with Julie Kernan,
completely revised by Zsolt Aradi. Kenedy, 1957. xvii, 350
p., bibliography, index. $5.75.

A descriptive portrait of the Catholic Church, this well
researched book explains how the Church is organized, how

it works, through whom it works, and what its purpose is for doing what it does. The author outlines the history, role, and function of the papal office, the Roman curial offices, the episcopacy, and the diocesan system down to the parish level, as well as the activities of the Church in the mission lands where the formal diocesan structures have not been established.

5. CHURCH AND STATE

The exact relationship between Church and state has agitated men's minds from the earliest days of human history. Man is a member of the society in which he lives, and at the same time has a supernatural allegiance to his God which transcends any obligation he has to a purely human society. The grounds for conflict were sown when man's reason had developed to the extent that he had cognizance of a supernatural destiny and the ability to organize himself into a society with laws and rules governing his conduct.

In ancient civilizations, the problem often was resolved by the deification of the ruler. If the temporal ruler is also the god of his state, obviously there can be no conflict. But as soon as any civilization realized the fallacy of the concept of a human ruler acting as a god, separation of the human and the divine was inevitable and the relationship between Church and state became a problem.

As human political and ecclesiastical institutions developed and became more complex, a real separation between political ruling groups and priestly groups developed apace, though their interests often overlapped. In ancient Israel, the rulers were frequently berated by a group of men, called the prophets, who denounced any worldly activities that they felt were in conflict with the teaching of God. Their authority was from purely spiritual sources, but arrogant indeed was the king or ruler who ignored them. These prophets were widely recognized as God's minions and king and subject alike paid them heed. Not even the most powerful rulers of Israel dared continue sinful practices in the face of the wrathful denunciations of this group of men whose very power came from the holiness of their calling and from their complete scorn of earthly honors and possessions.

The question of Church-state relations was early thrust at the Church when a group of priests and scribes seeking to trap Christ said to him, "Is it lawful for us to give tribute to Caesar, or not?" (Luke 20:22). Christ's answer of course

completely thwarted their purpose; but, even more signifi-
cantly, it set the basic philosophy for Church-state relations:
"Render to Caesar the things that are Caesar's and to God the
things that are God's" (Luke 20:25). But, though most people would agree that this concept is a sound basis for any
theory of Church-state relationship, the problem arises when
one attempts to discern what is Caesar's and what is God's.
There are certain areas where there is a clear-cut demarca-
tion; in others, the line separating the two allegiances becomes blurred.

Just a few of the areas in modern life which cause problems may be cited to illustrate the complexities and difficulties involved. Marriage is a Christian sacrament and the
Church has always claimed jurisdiction; yet, marriage involves civil considerations since income, property, legal
technicalities caused by offspring, marital relationships, all
have legal and social repercussions on secular society. Christian education has for centuries been propounded by the
Church as her prerogative; yet, as society became more industrialized and complex, a proper education for its people
was absolutely essential to the well-being of the modern
state. During the Middle Ages, ecclesiastical courts were organized to try cases in which clerics were involved; yet,
these clerics were individuals who were also members of the
state and could commit crimes in violation of statutes which
were legitimate laws of the state.

There are real differences between honest men in many
of these areas, and it is these difficult areas which provide
the often vexing problem of Church-state difficulties.

Our Lord laid down the basis for Church-state relations,
but men had to work out the details of the relationships.
And as Christianity grew in numbers and spread throughout
the Roman world, human weaknesses and foibles added their
dimensions to a basically difficult relationship.

The key to the whole development of Church-state relations is to be found in the fact that Christianity developed
in a decaying state—the Roman Empire. As the Empire de-
cayed and withered, Christianity grew and the Church waxed
strong. Scientists have a theorem to the effect that nature
abhors a vacuum. No less do men. As the authority of secular

Rome relaxed, the authority and prestige of ecclesiastical Rome grew, and as time went on the Church began to fulfill the functions of the fading civil authority by utilizing the political structure and legal mores of the stricken giant. It was no mere accident that Pope Leo the Great sallied forth from Rome to dissuade Attila and his Huns from attacking the city. There was no other Roman authority left to face the invader. Only the Pope was there, and his action had enormous implications. In time, all over Europe, it was to ecclesiastical authorities that the people turned for protection and for justice. In the absence of any effective civil authority, the Church began to assume the burdens of civil rule.

As time went on, Church rulers became secular rulers as well, so that in one person was vested both the civil and the ecclesiastical power and authority. Indeed, many of the bishops were more secular rulers than priestly shepherds. In a modified form, the ancient world's combination of the worldly and the spiritual in one ruler was revived.

The apex of this ecclesiastical domination was reached in the person of Pope Innocent III, who put into full effect his own theory of Church-state relations. Simply put, this theory was that, since the spiritual was always to take precedence over the material, the Church was superior to any human institution; hence, earthly rulers were subject to the Church in all things. The pope, as head of the Church, was not only an ecclesiastical ruler, but all secular monarchs were subject to him; there was no area of human activity in which the Church should not be active. By sheer force of his own will and personality, he was able to impose this doctrine on all of Europe, and the repercussions of his theory were to be felt for centuries.

With the passage of time, though, rulers who were wholly secular became stronger and more powerful. Inevitably, disputes arose; and all too frequently an ecclesiastical ruler would attempt to employ his priestly authority to overcome his opponent in strictly secular concerns. Indeed it was not unusual for prince-bishops to quarrel among themselves over strictly secular matters and to threaten each other with the whole arsenal of Church censures. It was inevitable that, sooner or later, thinking men would demand an end to the dual role of many of the bishops and insist on a separation of Church and state. With the rise of nationalism and modern states, the process was accelerated. To many rulers the Reformation was an invaluable aid in diminishing the power of the Church and increasing their own. In many of the European nations the Reformation developed along national lines and it was used to enhance the power of the princes.

But even while this struggle was at its height, the protagonists were, in a sense, on the same side of the political fence, for the prevailing form of rule for centuries throughout Europe was monarchical. The dispute was between men determined to hold or gain power, not over the guise in which that power was to be wielded. Even such extremists as the Emperor Joseph II of Austria agreed that Church and state should be closely allied. He simply wanted to make certain he, as Emperor, had the ultimate authority. On the other hand, popes too accepted as a basic fact that Church and state should be allied; their concern was that *their* opinions of what was Caesar's and what was God's be the accepted concept. In short, the underlying theory was that the Church should be supported and aided by the state; the state, in turn, conceived of the Church as a buttress for the state.

With the American and the French Revolutions, a new concept of government was introduced: democracy. The theory that governments were responsible to the people was nothing short of a catastrophe for rulers who had argued that they ruled by divine right. And among the basic tenets of this radical new form of government was the idea that religion should be shorn of governmental favor—that Church and state could and should co-exist, but as separate entities. No longer was the Church to be dependent on the state for its existence; henceforth, it must depend on its people and on their voluntary support. It was a concept that immediately met fierce and unrelenting opposition from the monarchs and monarchists who had ruled Europe for centuries. In the middle of this maelstrom and on the side of the monarchists was the overwhelming bulk of the Catholic prelates, for they had for centuries been dependent on state support and were in effect committed to monarchy as the only form of government. Further, the Pope was himself a secular ruler of the

Papal States and as much an absolutist as any other ruler in Europe.

The result is now history. The Church committed herself, generally speaking, to the monarchical form of government, lost all her dominions in 1870, and under Pope Pius IX, in protest against the excesses of the times, practically withdrew from the world.

But Catholics are part of the world, and slowly but inevitably the Church began to reconcile her position with the political, social, economic, and scientific developments of the modern world. Beginning with Pope Leo XIII and culminating in Popes John XXIII and Paul VI, she began to reexamine many of her long-held positions, to distinguish between basic dogmatic stands which are unchangeable and external forms and disciplines which must be adjusted to meet changing times and conditions.

Foremost in this re-examination has been the crucial and all important area of Church-state relations culminating in the declaration of religious freedom promulgated at the fourth session of Vatican Council II. For the relation between Church and state is so far-reaching in its consequences that it is an essential cornerstone of the structure of the Church. It has caused strife and controversy for centuries and obviously will not now be finally settled. What is taking place today is a thorough re-examination of the Church's traditional position, a modification of many previous positions, and the erection of a whole new, far-reaching theory of Church and state.

This new development is so important that it cannot be overstressed. Particularly in a pluralistic society, is it necessary that Catholics understand this significant modification of traditional Catholic positions. Further, from a world view, it must be thoroughly formulated and understood by all Catholics, for the Catholics of the world are a minority of the world's population. If ever the Church is to live up to her Founder's charge to convert all nations, she must have a concept of Church-state relations which will enable her to live amicably in non-Christian nations while she teaches the Word. Understanding this background will make clear why we have placed such stress on this section.

ABBO, JOHN A. (MSGR.). *Political Thought: Men and Ideas.* Newman, 1960. xv, 452 p., appendix, bibliography. $5.75.

Monsignor Abbo traces the main lines of the history of political theory in the West from antiquity to mid-twentieth century, from Plato and Aristotle to Hitler and Lenin. The book is, in effect, a survey of the great political books of the Western world, with special treatments of American thought, Fascism, etc. The appendix offers, in short article form, the main lines of Catholic political principles. The book is particularly recommended for its excellent treatment of the problem of Church-state relations.

EHLER, SIDNEY Z. and JOHN B. MORRALL, Editors. *Church and State Through the Centuries.* Newman, 1954. xiv, 625 p., index. $6.75.

The editors of this unusual collection have assembled what is in effect a panoramic documentary view of the relationship between Church and state from the beginnings of the Middle Ages to the mid-twentieth century. The book is a compilation of documents, both ecclesiastical and secular, on the subject; they are arranged chronologically, and tell the step-by-step story of Church-state relations in the words of the men who were involved in the making of those relations. There are commentaries giving the historical context of the documents and explaining their individual places in the over-all picture.

GRAHAM, ROBERT A. (S.J.). *Vatican Diplomacy.* Princeton, 1959. xii, 442 p., bibliography, index. $7.50.

This work is, in effect, a study of Church-state relations on the international level. The author traces the history of Vatican diplomacy through history, with particular attention to the relations of the Holy See as an independent temporal power with modern secular governments. This is the best such work available on the subject, but it requires a certain background in history and careful reading.

KERWIN, JEROME G. *The Catholic Viewpoint on Church and State.* Introduction by John J. Delaney. Doubleday, 1960. 192 p. $3.50.

An outstanding Catholic political scientist presents a thoroughgoing analysis of the relationship between Church and state. The book opens with an historical survey of the problem during the early Christian era, during the Middle Ages, and during modern times, with particular attention to the situation in the United States since colonial days. The author then considers the state of law in this area, noting the existence of many conflicting Supreme Court decisions, and summarizes the problem of non-Catholic attitudes toward things Catholic as well as that of Catholic resentments toward those attitudes. The book concludes with reflections and suggestions for improving the religious atmosphere in the United States.

LOVE, THOMAS T. *John Courtney Murray: Contemporary Church-State Theory.* Doubleday, 1965. 239 p., notes, bibliography, index. $4.95.

Father John Courtney Murray, s.j., is the foremost spokesman for, and to a large extent the official formulator of, the "progressive" or liberal school of thought on Church-state relations. This excellent work presents a synthesis and evaluation of Murray's thought on this important question and on such subsidiary issues as freedom of conscience, the "rights of truth," etc. The book does not presuppose a familiarity with Father Murray's works, but does require attentive reading.

MACHIAVELLI, NICCOLO. *The Prince.* Translated by Luigi Ricci. Oxford, 1906. 178 p. $2.25. Penguin, 1961. pa. 95¢.

This is the classic handbook, written in 1513, on the acquisition, use, and maintenance of political power. Rules are established for governing through various forms of monarchy, for the maintenance of military strength, and for the personal deportment of the prince with respect to the public and his ministers. The author was one of the first and the most articular proponent of political realism, and his work has had an immense influence upon the history of the Western world. It is indispensable reading for the educated man.

MARITAIN, JACQUES. *Man and the State.* Introduction by Jerome Kerwin. University of Chicago, 1951. xi, 219 p., index. $4.00. Phoenix, 1956. pa. $1.75.

Mr. Maritain in this work examines the idea of a democratic charter by which men must live in peace and by virtue of which they will arrive finally at a state of political and spiritual harmony. The book is valuable in that it is essentially a statement of Maritain's political philosophy and of his concept of a world state. It is free of professional jargon, but requires careful reading.

MARITAIN, JACQUES. *Scholasticism and Politics.* Translation edited by Mortimer J. Adler. Macmillan, 1940. viii, 248 p. $3.50. Image, 1960. pa. 95¢.

This collection of essays contains nine pieces by the world-famous philosopher on the human person—what he is, what is the basis of his human dignity, what is true human freedom, and what is the ultimate purpose of human life. Within that context, there are especially pertinent and authoritative treatments of the relation between democracy and authority and of Catholic Action in the political life of the community.

MARITAIN, JACQUES. *The Social and Political Philosophy of Jacques Maritain.* Edited, with notes and introduction, by Joseph W. Evans and Leo R. Ward. Scribner, 1955. 364 p., notes, index. Image, 1965. pa. $1.45.

These are selected readings from the social and political thought of the greatest Catholic philosopher of modern times. There are selections from Maritain's writings on the nature of the human person and his rights, man in relation to political society, human society in relation to Christianity, and a concluding section on the place of Christianity in the New Society of the twentieth century. The book is not easy reading, but the logical ordering of ideas and the brevity of the chapters reduce the difficulty; it is well worth the extra effort.

MURRAY, JOHN COURTNEY (S.J.). *We Hold These Truths.* Sheed, 1960. 317 p., notes. $5.00. Image, 1964. pa. $1.25.

In these reflections on the American Proposition, Father Murray examines the position of Catholicism in American society, and the welfare of the United States in general. There are two principal themes: Can the "American Proposition," i.e., that body of generally held self-evident truths which gives our nation its unique character, be compatible with Catholic tradition; and, is it possible to arrive at an American consensus—i.e., agreement within one political community comprised of groups with different religious beliefs? The author answers both questions affirmatively in demonstrating that the American way of life and Catholic tradition both emanate from one fundamental source. The philosophical aspects of the author's position make this rather serious reading at times, but the reward is worth the effort.

STURZO, LUIGI. *Church and State*. Translated by Barbara B. Carter. Notre Dame, 1962. 584 p., bibliography, index. $5.75. Notre Dame, 1962. (2 vols.), pa. $2.25 ea.

This is a study of the relations between Church and state as the result of social phenomena occurring from the earliest days of the Church until the establishment of the totalitarian governments of Germany, Italy, Russia, and Spain in the twentieth century. The author combines scholarly acumen with first-hand experience in diplomacy. Although time has, to a large extent, dulled the urgency of Sturzo's message, the book still makes for interesting and informative reading.

WOODRUFF, DOUGLAS. *Church and State*. Hawthorn, 1961. 128 p., bibliography. $3.50.

This survey of Church-state relations is a history of the relations, both ideal and actual, aimed at or attained, between the Church and civil governments through history, from the fourth century Roman Empire through the great contests of the Middle Ages, into modern times and the twentieth century. In relating the history of Church-state relations, the author provides also an informative summary of the Church's principles in that field. This is a recommended introduction to an understanding of a sensitive modern issue. (Volume 89 of the *Twentieth Century Encyclopedia of Catholicism*.)

6. THE CHURCH IN THE
MODERN WORLD

1. Vatican Council II and its Effects

The ecumenical or general council has always been a most important element in the life of the Church. Such councils are called to cope with particular crises that pose a grave threat to the Church and her teaching. Always the effects of a council are felt for decades and even centuries after it has adjourned. For from the very first general council, convened at Nicaea in 325, everyone in the Church has recognized their importance and accepted their decisions as the authentic and authoritative voice of the Church.

What is an ecumenical council and how does it come into being? An ecumenical or general council is a gathering of the bishops of the Church and others entitled to vote therein (cardinals, abbots, prelates nullius, the superior generals of religious orders—all those designated by Church law), convened by the Holy See to discuss a serious problem or problems confronting the Church. Its decrees have no binding authority until promulgated by the pope, but when these decrees are so confirmed they are infallible when concerned with matters pertaining directly to faith and morals. A council's decisions promulgated by the pope represent the highest magisterium of the Church and demand the respect and attention of all Catholics.

Vatican Council II is the twenty-first general council of the Church. The first eight were held in Asia Minor or Eastern Europe and the following thirteen in Western Europe. Councils are held at no regular interval, but are convened when deemed necessary by the Holy See. They have covered a vast range of topics and, until Vatican Council II, were always called to deal with a specific threat to the Church. For example, the first general council, held at Nicaea in 325, was called to meet the challenge of Arianism which taught Christ was "a pure creature" and not really divine. From it came the Nicene Creed and the denunciation of Arianism. The Council of Trent, convened in 1545 (it was to last eighteen years), was intended to chart the course of the Church in view of the challenges presented by the Reformation.

Many of the Councils were stormy affairs and often some of the participants were bitterly opposed to the reigning pontiff's suggestions or policies. But no general council has ever questioned the primacy of the Holy See nor has any general council ever suggested replacing the Bishop of Rome with some other bishop. The general councils have always recognized the primacy of the pope, though it was not until Vatican Council I, in 1870, that the dogma of papal infallibility was formally proclaimed.

Generally speaking then, the ecumenical or general council, acting in concert with the pope, is the most important instrument the Church possesses to register the mind of the Church and to indicate the course of action she should pursue in the light of the problems and crises of the times. Always their impact on the activities of the Church has been far reaching. And Vatican Council II has been no exception.

Interestingly enough, unlike all the other general councils of the Church, Vatican Council II was not called to meet a particular threat. As a matter of fact, Pope John's call for a general council came as a complete surprise to the whole Church. The announcement of his decision to convoke a general council was made to a group of cardinals at St. Paul-Outside-the-Walls in Rome on January 25, 1959, and it astounded them. Indeed, as he delighted in recounting, his own original decision came suddenly and unexpectedly. He said many times that his sudden decision was inspired by the Holy Spirit, and, as he so colorfully phrased it, it "sprang up within us like the first flower of an early spring." The purpose he assigned to the Council was to bring the Church up to date and to promote unity among all Christian peoples. His call set in motion forces in the Church which were to affect drastically every single one of the half billion Catholics in the world; and as the sessions of the Council unfolded, it became clear that not only the Catholic world but all Christendom and indeed all mankind were to feel the effects of the deliberations of the 2500 prelates who first assembled in Rome that momentous fall of 1962. When John died in 1963, one of the first acts of the new pontiff, Pope Paul VI, was to reconvene Vatican Council II in September of that year. Enthusiastically, he endorsed the aims of his predecessor and then added his own individual stamp to John's *aggiornamento*.

And so it can come as no surprise to anyone that Vatican Council II became the most important religious event of the twentieth century. In view of its significance and the revolution it is effecting in the Church, the compilers of this *Guide* felt a special section should be devoted to it and its effects. We have therefore provided a list of books describing what occurred during each of the sessions of Vatican Council II. This Council was the best-covered council in the history of the Church. No sooner had Pope John announced the convocation than the unrivaled news-covering facilities of the modern press, radio, and television immediately grasped the importance of this event and treated it as a news event of unique interest for the entire world. Thousands of newsmen from every section of the earth poured into Rome at the opening session of the Council and covered every move made by the bishops, periti, and observers. The coverage was fantastic and—though much nonsense was written, as might be expected—few events of our times have produced such a noteworthy collection of articles and books as Vatican Council II. We have selected those we believe to be outstanding in the first sub-section of this section.

Though descriptions of the happenings, debates, and decisions are helpful for the reader to know what is going on in the Church, the implementation and putting into effect of those decisions are of the utmost importance to each individual. In general, we feel that these effects can be grouped under three general headings: the reform and renewal of the Church; the ecumenical movement; and the Church's involvement in the social problems of the modern world. Each of these areas is of such vast scope and profound effect that we have devoted a separate sub-head to each of them with a list of books under each heading.

A final word before turning to each of these sections. We

have stressed in many sections of this *Guide* how important
it was for the Catholic reader to read books in this or that
category. At the risk of being repetitious, may we stress that
it is imperative that the Catholic, and the non-Catholic too,
know what the Church is doing in the subject areas. A
whole new spirit is abroad in the Catholic Church and its
full impact is yet to be felt. Seldom in its history has the
Church undergone such profound changes—and, most important of all, the events described and the actions taken are
the history of past centuries but are taking place right now
and are having a direct effect on us and our children. We are
living through a real revolution as the Church adjusts her
whole life to the challenges of the nuclear age and to the
problems and needs of all mankind. What is taking place in
the Catholic Church today may well affect the future of all
mankind. The early Christians knew they were going to
change the world and they did. No less is the Catholic
Church today seeking to do what the early Christians did
so well—to persuade modern Catholics to live their faith
and by so doing to change the world. If the reader will
pause for a moment to ponder on what is at stake, we feel
sure he will appreciate the urgency in our appeal to each
of you to learn and know what is going on. What is involved
is your Church and your mission on earth.

ABBOTT, WALTER M. (s.j.), Editor. *The Documents of
Vatican II.* Translated under the direction of Monsignor
Joseph Gallagher. Introduction by Lawrence Cardinal Shehan.
Herder & Herder, 1966. 816 p., index. $10.00. Guild, 1966.
pa. 95¢.

This is the first complete collection of all sixteen of the
documents of Vatican II in English. There are informative
introductions and extensive commentaries by Council Fathers
and experts for each of the documents, as well as essays of
appraisal by Protestant and Orthodox leaders. Among the
contributors of commentaries and essays are Avery Dulles,
s.j., R. A. F. MacKenzie, s.j., Donald Campion, s.j., Dr.
Robert McAfee Brown, Dr. Jaroslav Pelikan, Archbishop Paul
Hallinan, Bishop Fred Pierce Corson, Dr. John C. Bennett,

and John Courtney Murray, s.j. This compilation of all of the Constitutions, Decrees, and Declarations, and the commentaries and essays, will be an indispensable reference work for libraries, study groups, and for the informed Catholic reader.

ABBOTT, WALTER M. (s.j.). *Twelve Council Fathers.* Macmillan, 1963. 176 p. $3.50.

After the first session of Vatican II, the author interviewed twelve major participants in the Council on the subject of what they hoped the Council would accomplish. This book is a compilation of the material from those interviews, and covers such subjects as the necessity for a common Bible, liturgical reform, the reform of canon law, and a revision of marriage laws. Among those interviewed were Cardinals Léger, Cushing, Suenens, Koenig, and Alfrink. Their comments are, for the most part, quite candid, and provide an interesting cross-section of current trends in the Church.

BROWN, ROBERT McAFEE. *Observer in Rome.* Doubleday, 1964. 276 p. $4.95.

The author of this book on the second session of Vatican II is a Presbyterian, and was an "observer in Rome" throughout the Council. As such, he had access to secret documents, attended all meetings, socialized with the Fathers, and then wrote down his observations and reflections on the events of the Council, the personalities of the participants, and the significance of what he saw and heard. The result is a sympathetic and good-humored book covering the second session, which may well be the best work in English on that session.

CAPORALE, ROCK (s.j.). *Vatican II: Last of the Councils.* Foreword by Bishop John J. Wright. Helicon, 1964. 192 p. $4.95.

During the first session of Vatican II, Father Caporale interviewed almost a hundred of the principal Fathers on their ideas about the purpose, agenda, and eventual effects of the Council. This work brings together the results of those interviews and gives a general and informative view of early reactions to many of the most controversial problems faced by the Council. The author's style is readably journalistic and, despite the rather limited chronological scope of the book, his work is valuable background reading for an understanding of Vatican II's accomplishments.

KAISER, ROBERT. *Pope, Council and World.* Macmillan, 1963. 266 p., index. $4.95.

The author of this book was *Time* magazine's correspondent in Rome during the first session of the Council. In a journalistic style, he describes the events and personalities of that session. The book differs from most of the works on this session in several respects: by the sweeping view it affords of the entire movement of up-dating in the Church, by the very detailed treatment it gives to some of the issues involved and, less fortunately, by the author's extremely partisan view of the progressive-conservative tensions in Rome (Pius XII, for instance, is described as "a small-town aristocrat" for what the author considers his conservative influence). On the whole, this is an excellent treatment of the opening session, but the reader will find it necessary to overlook some of the author's editorializing.

KÜNG, HANS (s.j.). *The Council, Reform, and Reunion.* Translated by Cecily Hastings. Sheed, 1961. 200 p., notes, appendices, index. $3.95. Image, 1965 (with a new introduction by the author). pa. 85¢.

When this book was first published just before the opening of Vatican II, it caused a sensation because it said in print for the first time exactly what Pope John had meant by *aggiornamento* and it speculated on the consequences of putting *aggiornamento* into practice. The book has three basic parts: a consideration of the reawakening of a Christlike spirit in the Church by the convocation of the Council; an examination of the need for reform within the Church; an appraisal of the need for reunion among the Christian Churches. Father Küng's book, a prophetic work before the Council, continues to be a guide to understanding the issues confronting the Church today.

KÜNG, HANS. *The Council in Action.* Translated by Cecily Hastings. Sheed, 1963. 276 p., bibliographical notes. $4.50.

The author of this work was a theological adviser to the Second Vatican Council and is one of the most important of the "new theologians" in the Church today. His book comprises lectures and statements made by him, during the first session of the Council, to meetings of bishops, press conferences, radio broadcasts, etc., explaining and commenting on the events and implications of that session. It is not, however, a complete record of the session so much as an insight into some of the complex problems that confronted the Fathers, and its value lies in the theological perspective that it gives the reader.

NOVAK, MICHAEL. *The Open Church.* Macmillan, 1964. xiii, 370 p. $6.50.

Using Vatican I as a point of beginning, the author tells the story of the second session of Vatican II. He examines the "conservative" forces who opposed John XXIII's ideal of the "open Church" and, in the light of his conclusions, describes the events of the session itself. It is a well-written and intelligent book which will be useful to the general reader, although the author too often identifies himself with the progressive majority of the Council to an extent that precludes an objective reporting of events.

RYNNE, XAVIER. *Letters from Vatican City.* Farrar, 1963. 273 p., appendices, index. $3.95. Image, 1964. pa. 95¢.

This book consists of a series of letters describing the first session of Vatican Council II. The controversies of that session are clearly explained and the importance of the issues involved is discussed. An unusual feature of the book is its objective and frank reporting of the clashes of ideas and of personalities that occurred during the session. The controversial work is undoubtedly the most concise and realistic—and certainly the most entertaining—report available on the first session of Vatican II.

RYNNE, XAVIER. *The Second Session.* Farrar, 1964. xxiii, 390 p., facsimiles. $4.95.

With this book Rynne continues the job of reporting on Vatican II begun with the preceding volume. The present work covers the activities of the second session, from its opening on September 29 to its closing on December 4, 1963, and includes the full texts of three major addresses by Pope Paul VI as well as a draft of the Declaration on the Jews. Although there is complete coverage of the session, the style of this work lacks the flavor and fast-moving narration of the author's first volume, and it must be read for the sake of information alone.

RYNNE, XAVIER. *The Third Session.* Farrar, 1965. 300 p., tables, index, appendices. $4.95.

This third volume in the pseudonymous Rynne's series covers chronologically the events of the third session of Vatican II. Among the subjects treated in detail are the questions of the Church in the modern world, the role of bishops in the Church, the Declaration on Religious Liberty, the Declaration on the Jews, and the Decree on Ecumenism. The author's style is flowingly journalistic, witty, and, to a large extent, his approach is objective. His book undoubtedly is the best work yet available on the third session.

RYNNE, XAVIER. *The Fourth Session.* Farrar, 1966. 320 p., illustrations, index. $4.95.

This final volume in Xavier Rynne's coverage of Vatican II discusses the activities, events, accomplishments and personalities of the fourth session. Like the other volumes, it gives a day-by-day account of the negotiation both of unanimously accepted and of controversial matters—including, in the latter category, the Declaration on the Jews and the schema on religious liberty. Although the final session held little of the suspense engendered by earlier sessions, Rynne's present work is of particular interest for his post-conciliar summing up of the significance of the Council.

WILTGEN, RALPH M. (S.V.D.). *Vatican II.* Hawthorn, 1966. 320 p., index. $5.95.

This is an account of the whole of Vatican II—its aims, its achievements, and its personalities. Father Wiltgen first discusses the Council in its historical context, relating it particularly to the First Vatican Council of 1869–70. He then describes Vatican II as the Church's response to the challenges of the modern world, showing why Pope John's *aggiornamento* opened the way for long-needed reforms and gave a strong impulse to the movement for Christian unity. The great debates and documents of the Council, the tension between the progressives and the conservatives, the behind-the-scenes negotiations, and role of John XXIII, of Paul VI, and of the American bishops, are described and analyzed.

II. RENEWAL AND REFORM

Long before the dramatic announcement by Pope John XXIII of his intention to convoke a general council, many Catholics had had an uneasy feeling that all was not well in the Church. On the surface, the Church was in a flourishing condition, especially in the affluent western nations and the United States where schools, churches, convents, rectories, hospitals, homes, and orphanages had been built in amazing numbers; Church membership was at an all-time high; and in general Catholics were in a much better position socially, economically, and politically than they had been for centuries. And it was this air of satisfaction and general affluence which alarmed students of these matters in the Church. They were concerned that the spirit of Catholicism, given to the Church by Christ and cherished through the centuries by the saints and all dedicated Christians, was in danger of being smothered under the material and secular aspects of a society seemingly concerned solely with the ephemeral pleasures of this world. An affluent society posed a threat to the Church unlike anything she had ever faced before.

Churches were thronged; and yet there was a lack of a feeling of oneness at the most sacred liturgical ceremony—the Mass. To many, a barrier had been erected by the altar rail, with the priest on one side and the laity on the other. A formalization of the ceremonies and of the structure of the Church threatened to conceal the eternal, living word of God by means of a meaningless façade which, though impressive, was devoid of substance. The whole function of the Church seemed to have hardened into an immutable mold and form which preserved outwardly the structure, but seemed inwardly to lack the spirit of love and compassion and Christian charity which are the hallmarks of the Christian message.

In certain areas even more alarming portents were clearly discernible. In South America, for instance, the Church seemed to be losing her people. In Italy, apathy gripped vast segments of the populace and Communism made such incredible inroads that the largest Communist party in the world outside of Russia is in Italy—a country that for centuries has been completely Catholic. Missions in Asia and Africa were fighting a losing battle. Leakage of members was seldom referred to in public, but was reaching sizable proportions. Increasingly, the conviction grew in many Catholic minds that the Church had lost contact, that her people were either drifting away or had become indifferent to her message.

And finally, to many thinking men, the real problem was that the Church was out of step with the twentieth century —that many of her critics were right in asserting her structure and approach to atomic-age problems to be steeped in an outdated and outmoded medieval concept. Grave problems were crying for solution—race, overpopulation, war, nuclear weapons, poverty, world concepts, space—and the Church was offering only token understanding of the problems and doing little to effect a solution.

Some of the above may sound like a drastic description of the situation, but there is much truth in this short analysis —enough certainly to warrant the conclusion that the Church, to say the least, was not using to the full the resources at her command to apply Christian principles and love, her precious commodities, to solve these problems.

But many dedicated men had been devoting themselves to these matters for years. Often maligned and attacked and despised, they doggedly persisted and gradually built up a following that saw the danger to the Church and worked to alleviate the situation in crucial areas. The influence of these leaders had been growing as the realization spread that they were pointing the direction in which the Church should turn.

When Pope John announced plans for the Council and emphasized he was calling it to renew and reform the Church, the pent-up energy and enthusiasm of those who had anticipated such a turn of events burst the dams. A veritable flood of articles and books, plans and suggestions, approaches and courses of action was released. When the bishops from all over the world assembled in Rome for the Council, they soon realized that they were in overwhelming agreement and Pope John's longed-for *aggiornamento* became a reality.

Even though the final forms of the reform and renewal are not yet entirely clear, it is evident what the general outlines are and where they will lead. The policies which will last for decades and centuries are being postulated now. Fortunately the architects of these plans have been most articulate, and we have suggested below a selection of books which will make these developments clear to any reader.

BALDUCCI, ERNESTO. *John: The Transitional Pope.* McGraw, 1965. 352 p. $7.50.

This is not a biography of John XXIII, but an assessment and appreciation both of the man and of his accomplishments. The book has two parts: Part I is an examination of John's background, his character, and his attitude toward the Church and the world; Part II treats of John's pontificate and its significance, and traces the outlines of the new epoch launched by his election. The author envisions the Church, in a movement begun by John and continued by his successor, as newly responsive to the total needs of the whole world —religious, social, cultural, and economic.

CALLAHAN, DANIEL J. *Honesty in the Church.* Scribner, 1965. 188 p. $3.95.

The author examines the place of honesty in the public and private lives both of the Church itself and of the individual Catholic. Among the topics he discusses are current emphasis on the "public image" of the Church, the growing acceptability of forms of public dishonesty, the Church's approach to honest doubt on the part of Catholics, and the relationship between the Church's teaching authority and the rights of the individual conscience. The book is moderate in tone, well reasoned, and usefully constructive.

CALLAHAN, DANIEL J. *The Mind of the Catholic Layman.* Scribner, 1963. 208 p., bibliography, index. $3.95. Scribner, 1965. pa. $1.45.

The author presents an historical survey of the layman in America, demonstrating that the Catholic layman is heir to a double tradition: that of his Church, and that of democracy. He concludes that the present demand for greater lay participation in the work of the Church is founded on the layman's response to his country's pluralistic constitution and on his social, economic, and educational progress, and that the entire renewal-reform movement in the Church may well be in vain unless those circumstances are taken into account.

CONGAR, YVES-MARIE (O.P.). *Lay People in the Church.* Translated by Donald Attwater; foreword by Bishop Robert J. Dwyer. Newman, 1957. xxxvi, 447 p. $6.75. Newman, 1959. pa. $3.50.

In the late 1930s, when the notion of the layman as a vital, integral part of God's Church was still regarded with suspicion by most priests, Father Congar had already sketched out and, to a large extent, filled in, the main lines of what was to become a most important part of the spirit of renewal in the modern Church. *Lay People in the Church* is the work in which Congar put forward his then-revolutionary thesis that to regard lay people as less-favored members of the Mystical Body was not only without foundation in the Bible and in the teachings of the Fathers and Doctors of the Church, but that it was in fact contrary to the whole spirit of Catholicism. Despite its age, this book is probably still the single most authoritative work on the subject, and the one on which all later works have been based.

HALES, E. E. Y. *Pope John and His Revolution.* Doubleday, 1965. xv, 222 p., bibliography, index. $4.95. Image, 1966. pa. 85¢.

This is an account of the personality and accomplishments of John XXIII and of the effects that his ideas have had and are likely to have on the modern Church. The first section examines the development of John's thought on the mission of the Church; the second is an assessment of his teachings, and the third appraises the revolution set in motion by Pope John and predicts the directions in which it will move. This is probably the best and most readable evaluation of Pope John and his work yet available.

KÜNG, HANS. *Structures of the Church.* Translated by Salvator Attanasio. Nelson, 1964. 394 p., notes, bibliography. $7.50.

Father Küng, one of the foremost young theologians of the Church, examines the role and form of the Church with respect both to its place in the modern world and to its historical development. His thesis is that the Church itself is like one vast ecumenical council convoked by God, and he regards the interrelationships of Church, council, and people from the viewpoint of its Catholic and Protestant composition. The book is very rewarding in its contribution to ecumenism and to renewal, but it requires careful reading.

MEYERS, SISTER BERTRANDE (D.C.). *Sisters for the Twenty-First Century*. Introduction by Joseph Cardinal Ritter. Sheed, 1965. 364 p., index. $5.00.

The subject of this book is the process of growth, development, and adaptation by the women of religious orders to meet the demands of life in the modern world. The author treats of such controversial subjects as the relationship between conscience and the vow of obedience, the educational formation of teaching nuns, and the advisability of nuns undertaking an active apostolate in the world. The position throughout is one of moderate liberalism, and the book may be read with profit by anyone interested in the role of women religious in the Church.

RAHNER, KARL (S.J.). *The Christian Commitment*. Translated by Cecily Hastings. Sheed, 1963. 218 p., bibliographical notes. $4.50.

Father Rahner's work consists of seven essays on Christian life in the modern world. Among the topics discussed are the present situation of Catholics in a secular world, the significance of the individual member of the Church, the relationship between Mary and the apostolate, and the Mass and television. Father Rahner's style, as always, tends to be rather philosophical, but his work remains an important source of new ideas for informed Catholics.

TAVARD, GEORGE H. (A.A.). *The Church Tomorrow*. Herder & Herder, 1965. 190 p. $3.95. Image, 1966. pa. 85¢.

Father Tavard, an outstanding theologian, ecumenist, and historian, points out the dangers to be avoided and the possibilities to be considered in the modern renewal of the Church. He proceeds by describing the situation of the Church today, and then discusses the principles of renewal as envisioned by Vatican II, particularly with reference to liturgical reform, approaches to Christian unity, and the missionary function of the Church. This highly readable work will be useful in helping the Catholic layman to see where his Church is going and what his own role will be in the Church of tomorrow.

THORMAN, DONALD J. *The Emerging Layman.* Doubleday,
1957. 238 p., bibliography. $3.95. Image, 1965. pa. 85¢.

An analysis of the role of the Catholic layman in America,
as the link between the Church and civil society. This is a
down-to-earth, reasonable and responsible discussion of such
controversial topics as clergy-lay relations, the function of
the Catholic in the civic community, Catholics and democracy, Catholics and their relations with non-Catholics, the
racial issue, censorship, and peace. Especially recommended.

III. THE ECUMENICAL MOVEMENT

One of the unhappiest features of the Christian world in this
twentieth century is the fragmentation of Christendom into
many sects and churches in direct contradiction of our Lord's
explicit direction that "there shall be one flock and one
shepherd." The two great splits of Christendom are traced
back to the eleventh century, when the final break between
the Christians of the East and those of the West took place,
and the sixteenth century, when the Protestant Reformation
split Western Christianity into two bitterly opposed and hos-
tile groups.

The consequences of this latter division particularly are
felt to the present day. To most Catholics of the Latin rite
the Eastern churches are remote. Centered geographically in
the Near East and Russia, they seldom come into the consciousness of the Western Catholic. In the case of Protestantism, the exact opposite is true. Whereas the Eastern churches
were geographically contained, the Reformation split nations,
cities, towns, and even families, so that practically all Christians had direct contact and experience with Christians of
other denominations. The division of the sixteenth century
soon often developed into that most dreadful of human dis-
sensions, fratricidal warfare. After a century of destructive
conflict, Catholic Christianity and Protestant Christianity
came to a truce of sorts, for it had become evident by the
seventeenth century that the strength of each faction was
such that the other could not wipe it out. Also, as the forces
of nationalism set in motion the characteristic tendencies of

the modern period, religion no longer was the sole motivating force in men's lives. Open religious warfare was abandoned to be supplanted by widespread but mostly non-violent hostility; but a *modus vivendi* had been worked out. By the twentieth century many individuals, both Catholics and Protestants, began to query the need for continued hostility; increasingly, scholars began to close gaps by their scholarly researches and cooperation; men and women in the democratic societies of the new countries worked, studied, and played together and began to break down old prejudices and rivalries by their associations and friendships. By the mid-twentieth century a real trend toward ecumenism had set in. In various countries, theologians began dialogues and exchanged learned papers; common interests often found men of differing religious views on the same side; organizations dedicated to Christian unity, such as the Franciscan Friars of the Atonement in the United States, sprang up. The soil was fertile for a full-fledged ecumenical movement when Vatican Council II was called.

And then a remarkable demonstration began. Protestant and Orthodox observers for the first time were invited to a Catholic ecumenical council. The invitations were accepted with alacrity and the Protestants who attended were overwhelmed by the sincerity of their hosts and their obvious desire to learn their opinions. A desire to explore with Protestants the problems causing the rift in Christianity swept the council and quickly spread all over the Catholic world; on the other hand, Protestants, at first wary, quickly realized the genuineness and sincerity in the Catholic approach and responded in kind. Soon the movement was in full bloom, with dialoging going on in seminaries and colleges, with Catholic bishops appearing with their Protestant brethren, and each often attending the other's services; and there was a growing conviction that there were many unrealized points of agreement between Protestant and Catholic that should be developed and implemented to help close the gap between them.

Lest the above be construed as a feeling on the authors' part that the reconciliation of the Christian churches is at hand, let us dissipate any such feeling at once. There are grave differences and innumerable stumbling blocks to be surmounted; they will take years, perhaps decades, and possibly centuries to resolve. But, for the first time since the Reformation, there is a serious, concerted effort to study the differences separating the church and there is a body of men dedicated to that study.

Unquestionably, the whole ecumenical movement is a unique feature of our times. It received its impetus from Vatican Council II which propelled it to the fore of religious considerations today. It is only a question of time before it will reach the parish level (indeed it already has in many areas) and involve large numbers in the movement. It is well, then, that both Catholic and Protestant participants in the dialogue have written wisely and well of the whole ecumenical phenomenon—for it is nothing less.

We have included books in our selection from both Catholic and Protestant sources; after all this section must not only be on the ecumenical movement, it must be ecumenical as well. One thing the reader will find in all these books is the feeling of good will and Christian brotherhood exhibited by all the authors represented. Well do they reflect in their approach the remark of Pope John which he suggested for the guidance of the Council: "Stress that which unites rather than that which divides."

BEA, AUGUSTIN CARDINAL (s.j.). *The Unity of Christians.* Edited by Bernard Leeming; introduction by Gerald P. O'Hara. Herder & Co., 1963. 231 p., bibliography. $4.95.

Cardinal Bea, head of the Secretariat for the Promotion of Christian Unity, outlines briefly the obstacles and problems in attaining unity among the Christian Churches, the feasible means of reaching unity and possible solutions to some of the problems, and St. Paul's ideal of Christian unity as manifested in his teachings on the Mystical Body of Christ. The book is not difficult reading, though the last section (on St. Paul) requires the reader's full attention.

BOYER, CHARLES (s.j.). *Christian Unity.* Translated by Jill Dean. Hawthorn, 1962. 131 p., bibliography. $3.50.

This work, by a famous French theologian, is Volume 138 of the *Twentieth Century Encyclopedia of Catholicism*. In addition to discussing the situation of the ecumenical movement on the eve of Vatican II and expressing the hopes of Catholic and Protestant theologians for a giant step forward during the Council, Father Boyer provides an excellent survey of the history of ecumenism in modern times. Though the book does not take into account the progress made during Vatican II and since, it will give the reader, in an easily understandable form, valuable background for an understanding of later developments.

BROWN, ROBERT MCAFEE and GUSTAVE WEIGEL (s.J.). *An American Dialogue*. Anchor, 1960. 216 p. pa. 95¢.

Professor Brown and Father Weigel, spokesmen for America's two major religious groups, Protestantism and Catholicism, respectively, deal with aspects of existing tensions between their Churches. The authors consider secular matters as well as religious principles, treating all questions with a frankness and an honesty that is as refreshing as it is rare. Even today, when "ecumenism" is a household word, this book will be an eyeopener for most readers.

LEEMING, BERNARD (s.J.). *The Churches and the Church*. Newman, 1960. x, 340 p. $6.50.

Father Leeming's book is a study of the principles and practice of ecumenism. He approaches his subject by tracing the historical development and attitudes of Catholics and non-Catholics toward each other's Churches, discussing the evolution of the spirit of ecumenism on both sides, and indicating candidly the causes of friction between Catholics and other Christians. Finally, he cites the general principles which must govern the Catholic ecumenical movement. A background knowledge of history and theology is helpful, but not essential, for an intelligent understanding of the book.

NELSON, CLAUDE D. *The Vatican Council and All Christians*. Foreword by Roswell P. Barnes; epilogue by Edward Duff, s.J. Association Press, 1962. 126 p. $3.00.

The author of this book, a non-Catholic, is a specialist in the field of Protestant-Catholic relations. The book discusses the significance for non-Catholics of the agenda of Vatican II and of Pope John's "open door" policy toward

Protestants and Eastern Orthodox Catholics. It is an interesting presentation of the reactions of non-Catholics to Catholic progress in ecumenism, and a graphic description of the importance of Vatican II in that same field.

O'NEILL, CHARLES (S.J.), Editor. *Ecumenism and Vatican II.* Foreword by Vincent T. O'Keefe, S.J. Bruce, 1964. xii, 146 p. $3.75.

The purpose of this book is to record the impressions of representatives of the Christian and Jewish churches concerning the future of the ecumenical movement in the light of the accomplishments of Vatican II. Among the contributors are Bernard Cook, S.J., Rabbi Reuven Siegel, Rev. John Meyendorff, Francis Canavan, S.J., and Otto Karrer. The various essays represent varying degrees of optimism and of pessimism. The collection may be recommended as a candid sampling of reactions to the movement toward Christian unity.

SHEERIN, JOHN B. *Christian Reunion.* Hawthorn, 1966. 272 p. $4.95.

Father Sheerin's work is a study of the significance for American Catholics of the ecumenical movement. First, the traditional attitudes of Catholic leaders and theologians toward other religious beliefs are explained; then there is a study of the growth of the spirit of ecumenism among Protestants, Orthodox, and Catholics in modern times, showing how Pope John's attitude opened up new possibilities in the field. The author discusses what effects these new developments can be expected to have on relations between American Catholics and non-Catholics. The book is a solid, earnest study of the state of ecumenism today and what its prospects are for the future.

TAVARD, GEORGE H. (A.A.). *Two Centuries of Ecumenism.* Translated by Royce W. Hughes. Mentor-Omega, 1962. xi, 239 p., bibliographies. pa. 95¢.

An historical survey of the ecumenical movement, Father Tavard's work traces the evolution of the spirit of reunion from its early manifestations in the nineteenth century to the beginning of the Second Vatican Council. The book is written for a general audience, and it is valuable as background material for a proper understanding of current trends in Catholic thinking.

WEIGEL, GUSTAVE (S.J.). *A Catholic Primer on the Ecumenical Movement.* Preface by Joseph F. Murphy, S.J. Newman, 1957. pa. 95¢.

This small book, by one of the spokesmen of the modern ecumenical movement, presents in a clear, concise manner the essential facts on that movement from the non-Catholic and Catholic viewpoints. Although much has happened within the movement since this book was written, it is still interesting and worthwhile reading for the principles that it outlines as well as for the historical background that it offers.

IV. OTHER RELIGIONS

To participate fully and intelligently in the ecumenical movement a Catholic must have an understanding of other religions. The books below will provide information which is indispensable for the ecumenical movement to progress—knowledge of the other man's religious beliefs.

BOUYER, LOUIS (C. OR.). *The Spirit and Form of Protestantism.* Preface by G. de Broglie, S.J. Newman, 1956. xii, 234 p. $3.75.

This is probably the best and most comprehensive presentation to date of the origins, beliefs, and practices of the Protestant Churches that is available in English. Father Bouyer traces the roots of Protestantism to the Catholic abuses of the fourteenth and fifteenth centuries, describes the theological and philosophical differences that led to a final break with Rome, and analyzes present-day points of difference between the Protestant and Catholic faiths. The book requires, in addition to a basic knowledge of philosophy and theology, very careful reading, for the author often sacrifices simplicity to clarity; yet, it remains indispensable for an understanding of the obstacles to, and of the possibilities of, Christian unity.

DALMAIS, IRENEE-HENRI (O.P.). *Eastern Liturgies.* Translated by Donald Attwater. Hawthorn, 1960. 141 p., bibliography. $2.95.

The rites of the Eastern Orthodox Churches—i.e., of those who do not recognize the authority of the pope—are so different from those in common use in the West as to be both mysterious, attractive, and intriguing to the Roman Catholic. The purpose of this volume (number 112 of the *Twentieth Century Encyclopedia of Catholicism*) is to explain to the layman how those oriental liturgies came into being, how they differ from those of the West, and how they are, in all essential respects, the same. There is also a comprehensive historical survey of the origins of the Eastern Orthodox Churches.

HARDON, JOHN A. (s.j.). *The Protestant Churches of America.* Newman, 1956. xxiii, 365 p., bibliography, index. $5.00. Newman, 1961. pa. $1.75.

Basing himself on the official publications and writings of leaders of the various Protestant denominations, Father Hardon outlines the history, beliefs, ritual, government, and organization of each of the major American Protestant Churches. The work is suitable for the general reader, and it is particularly timely now, when the ecumenical spirit requires an understanding of the teachings of our "separated brethren."

HARDON, JOHN A. (s.j.). *Religions of the World.* Newman, 1963. 539 p., bibliography, index. $7.50.

The purpose of this work is to review the beliefs and practices of the various religious systems which prevail in different parts of the world. Father Hardon writes for the general reader, and his account of the religions of the East is particularly clear, while his description of those of the West is instructive and objective. Although not more than a dozen major religious systems are studied, the author's approach is sufficiently general to make the book of much value to those interested in the possibilities of ecumenism.

WEIGEL, GUSTAVE (s.j.). *Churches in North America.* Helicon, 1961. 152 p. $3.95.

Each of the thirty chapters of this work gives a brief description of the thirty major non-Catholic Churches in America and their beliefs. The presentation is popular and lucid, and the book is an excellent source of information for Catholics on Protestant doctrines and organization.

v. The Social Involvement of the Church

In his opening address to the Council Fathers assembled for the second session of Vatican Council II, Pope Paul VI cited, as the objectives of the Council, renewal, reform, and complete and universal ecumenicity. He then went on to add a fourth goal: "Finally the council will build a bridge toward the contemporary world." He told the Fathers that they themselves had determined "to treat no longer of your own limited affairs but rather of those of the world; no longer to conduct a dialogue among yourselves but rather to open one with the world," and then continued with this significant paragraph: "The Church looks at the world with profound understanding, with sincere admiration, and with the sincere intention not of conquering it, but of serving it; not of despising it, but of appreciating it; not of condemning it, but of strengthening and saving it." And so, formally, the Supreme Pontiff committed the Catholic Church to direct involvement in the pressing problems of mankind in this most distraught age.

The Church has, of course, always been involved in helping assuage the physical ills and miseries of mankind. Through the centuries where the Catholic Church was there too one would find hospitals, orphanages, foundling homes, homes for the aged and infirm. Whole orders of nuns, priests, and brothers were devoted to the corporal works of mercy. In community after community one could search in vain for such institutions were it not for the omnipresent Catholic foundation staffed by zealously dedicated men and women freely giving of themselves to help their fellow men. Typically, any mission almost automatically had attached to it a clinic or dispensary where medical aid was rendered to those in need of it.

There is nothing unusual about the Church's concern for mankind. But the complexity of modern life has added new dimensions to the problems plaguing men. Hospitals and homes and orphanages are still needed, and desperately so in many areas of the globe; but, in addition, the over-all social problems of the world are demanding attention as problems of such dimensions that a whole new philosophy is desperately needed to solve them. In the past the Church has been concerned with treating symptoms and results. Now she is determined to attack the causes. Treating a child from the rat-ridden slums of Harlem in a hospital does no more than help the child recover; what is needed is to eliminate the slums and what created them. The rat bite is a result; the cause is poverty. By the same token, providing a shelter for a child whose parents have been killed in a racial demonstration is necessary for the welfare of the child; but the welfare of humanity demands that equal justice be extended to all men by eliminating racial discrimination. Shipping surplus food to starving peoples of a foreign country will ward off starvation; but the real solution is to turn the "have-not" nations into "have" nations. That is the Christian way. That is the social commitment of the Catholic Church in the modern world.

No longer is the Church to be apart from the world and aloof from its concerns; it is to be in it. The whole broad spectrum of human problems of whatever coloration and dimension is now the concern of the Church. But this involvement is not to be merely a formal statement of policy by Church officials. It is to be the personal concern of every individual Catholic who must involve himself wholeheartedly in every area of human concern where injustice prevails. Social justice is no longer to be a textbook phrase and the concern of a few enlightened persons who have been heeding the pleas and strictures of every modern pope from Leo XIII to Paul VI. No longer are the papal social encyclicals to be regarded as the prerogatives of study groups as they have been for so long. Their precepts and exhortations are to be assiduously embraced by every Catholic and their principles translated into a living reality. Racial prejudice, poverty, injustice, "have-not" nations—all of these and a host of other modern plagues are no longer to be regarded as evils that are inevitable and necessary. Rather they are to be viewed as mockeries of the mercy and justice of God and are to be attacked again and again until they are eliminated.

The consequences of this commitment of the pope and

the Council Fathers are staggering to contemplate. Imagine the effect of the determined application of Christian principles to the burdens of the world if pursued resolutely and unflinchingly by millions and millions of Catholics. Inexorably applied, such pressure would lead to a new age reminiscent at least of the atmosphere prevailing in the early Christian communities where astonished pagans could only exclaim admiringly "See how these Christians love one another" (Tertullian, *Apologetics* ch. 39, sec. 7).

The challenge formulated by the Church can be described graphically as her demand to her children that they live the name they bear—that they truly be followers of Christ. Too often one's Christian duty has been obscured by the immensity and complexity of the instrumentalities created by modern man. No longer can that be an excuse, as repeatedly and with increasing urgency the Church points the way for all to follow to make Christianity the living, dynamic force it should be in the affairs of men.

Few of the effects of the Council will have the tremendous impact of this commitment of the Church to the affairs of the world—Pope Paul's "other dialogue." Few of the Council's decisions will place such a responsibility on the individual Catholic as this involvement in the modern world. As in so many areas of Church affairs, fortunately, outstanding men have been laboring in the field for many years. Once the voices "crying in the wilderness," these men are finally revealed for what they are—prophets of righteousness. Many of them have committed their thoughts and plans to paper so there is a large literature available, broad in scope, decisive in approach, and representative of the Church's commitment. Those are the books you will find in this section.

ABELL, AARON. *American Catholicism and Social Action.* Notre Dame, 1964. 306 p., notes, bibliography, index. pa. $1.95.

Dr. Abell, professor of history at Notre Dame University, presents a comprehensive study of the Catholic social movement in the United States. Beginning with the period immediately following the Civil War, he traces every social movement in which the Church participated until 1950. Though the book was designed more for the social-science student than for the general reader, the author's presentation should be readily intelligible to the mature reader.

HALES, E. E. Y. *The Catholic Church in the Modern World*. Image, 1960. 314 p., notes, tables, bibliography, index. pa. 95¢.

Mr. Hales' book is a survey of Church history from the French Revolution to the present, covering the period with emphasis on the impact of personalities, ideologies, and events upon the exterior life of the Church—from the guillotines of the French Revolution to the Russian tanks in Budapest during the Hungarian revolt. It is a colorful presentation of an exciting era, written for the general reader.

HOUTART, FRANCOIS. *The Challenge to Change*. Translated by Mary Anne Chouteau. Sheed, 1964. xi, 212 p. $4.50.

Father Houtart, one of the best known of the progressive theologians, examines the nature of our modern civilization with respect to the Church's place in it. The book deals with many of the problems that are widely debated today, such as the role of the Church vis-à-vis social problems, the function of Christian poverty in a world of affluence, etc. The book is written in a readable style, and it will be of interest to the informed layman.

HUGHES, PHILIP (MSGR.). *The Popes' New Order*. New Directions, 1965. viii, 331 p., index. $5.75.

This collection of papal documents contains, in synopsis form, all of the important social encyclicals, letters, and addresses of the modern popes, from Leo XIII to Pius XII's early years as pope—the period 1878–1941. In some cases, the pope's words are given, while in others there is a synopsis of the encyclical, letter, or address. The documents are divided into nine sections, by subject, covering such questions of social importance as international relations, the extent and limitations of political authority, education, society, labor, etc. The most unusual feature of the book, and that one which most commends it to the reader, is the minutely detailed subject index which, for the period covered, will furnish a complete guide to papal pronouncements on subjects of social interest.

LEO XIII, POPE. *The Church Speaks to the Modern World.* Edited, with an introduction and notes, by Etienne Gilson. Image, 1954. 348 p., notes, bibliography, index. pa. $1.25.

This is a collection of the writings of Pope Leo XIII on social problems. The basic encyclicals of that pope are arranged in the order which he himself expressly indicated: *Aeterni Patris* (On Christian Philosophy); *Libertas praestantissimum* (On Human Liberty); *Arcanum divinae sapientiae* (On Christian Marriage); *Humanum genus* (On Freemasonry); *Diuturnum* (On Civil Government); *Immortale Dei* (On the Christian Constitution of States); *Quod apostolici muneris* (On Socialism); *Rerum novarum* (On the Rights and Duties of Capital and Labor); *Sapientiae Christianae* (On Christian Citizenship); *Inscrutabili* (On the Evils Affecting Modern Society); *In plurimis* (On Slavery); *Graves de communi* (On Christian Democracy). The editor provides historical perspective for each document in the introductory sections, and explanatory notes and summaries of each encyclical.

LEONARD, JOSEPH T. *Theology and Race Relations.* Foreword by Archbishop Patrick A. O'Boyle. Bruce, 1963. 316 p., bibliography. $5.00.

The author discusses the problem of race relations in America within the framework of Catholic theology, with emphasis on Negro-white relations. Among the specific questions discussed are: the Negro and organized labor, the obligations of property owners, Catholic Negroes and the parochial school system, and the morality of sit-in demonstrations and of freedom marches. The author presents a Christian sociological point of view, in a popularly written style. The book is recommended as a forthright expression of Catholic principles.

MASSE, BENJAMIN. *Justice For All.* Bruce, 1964. 196 p., bibliography. $3.95.

This small work is an introduction to the social teachings of the Church on problems of current importance in the United States. The author explains the Church's principles, especially as enunciated in modern papal encyclicals, as applied to such problems as: property rights, just wages, labor unions, industrial relations, distribution of wealth, and the obligations of rich nations to poor nations. There is also an excellent survey of the evolution of Catholic social thought in modern times.

O'DEA, THOMAS F. *American Catholic Dilemma.* Foreword by Gustave Weigel, s.j. Mentor-Omega, 1962. xiv, 140 p., notes. pa. 60¢.

In this provocative book a Catholic sociologist examines such questions as the quality of Catholic schools, the contribution of Catholics to the arts and sciences, the effect of censorship on intellectual growth, and the problem of conformity among American Catholics. Professor O'Dea finds the American Church particularly backward in its attitudes toward the intellectual life, and he outlines a program for re-awakening the American Catholic to the joys and rewards of that life. Although some of the author's data are outdated (the book first was published in 1958), his book will still furnish much worthwhile information on Catholic contributions and attitudes to American culture.

PAUL VI, POPE. *The Christian in the Material World.* Translated by Michael M. McManus. Helicon, 1964. 71 p. pa. $1.95.

These essays were written by the present pope when he was Cardinal Archbishop of Milan; they contain his thoughts on the proper relationship between Christian poverty and material affluence in the modern world. Individual essays discuss the virtues of gratitude, charity, and the spirit of poverty. The material is written simply and clearly, and the book is suitable for use in meditation or spiritual reading.

PIUS XI, POPE. *The Church and the Reconstruction of the Modern World.* Introduction, with notes and commentary, by Terence P. McLaughlin, c.s.p. Image, 1957. 433 p., notes, bibliography, index. pa. $1.25.

This collection of the social encyclicals of Pius XI contains the following documents: *Ubi arcano* (On the Peace of Christ in the Reign of Christ); *Quas primas* (On the Kingship of Christ); *Divini illius Magistri* (On the Christian Education of Youth); *Casti connubii* (On Christian Marriage); *Ad Catholici sacerdotii* (On the Priesthood); *Quadragesimo anno* (On the Reconstruction of the Social Order); *Caritate Christi* (On the Present Distress of the Human Race); *Non abbiamo bisogno* (On the Apostolate of the Laity); *Mit brennender Sorge* (On the Church in Germany); *Divini Re-*

demptoris (On Atheistic Communism); *Firmissimam constantiam* (On the Religious Situation in Mexico). The editor furnishes, for each encyclical, an introduction, a summary, and explanatory notes.

RAHNER, KARL (s.j.). *The Christian Commitment*. Translated by Cecily Hastings. Sheed, 1963. 218 p., bibliographical notes. $4.50.

Father Rahner's work consists of seven essays on Christian life in the modern world. Among the topics discussed are the present situation of Catholics in a secular world, the significance of the individual member of the Church, the relationship between Mary and the apostolate, and the Mass and television. Father Rahner's style, as always, tends to be rather philosophical, but his work remains an important source of new ideas for informed Catholics.

7. CONVERSION

There are few experiences so capable of stirring a man to the depths of his being as his conscious, deliberate, reasoned decision to change his method of worshiping God—possibly excepting the realization of the atheist or the agnostic that there is indeed a God. In each case, there is a period of sheer agony while the individual weighs the new claims and their effect on his spiritual allegiance. Those who have undergone such an emotional and spiritual experience have given vivid testimony that few events in life can compare with one's mental turmoil as one contemplates the dimensions of the drastic step that will inexorably change the whole course of one's life.

To those who have never endured doubts of sufficient intensity to lead them to consider another mode of spiritual life, the story of a conversion is always a thrilling one. For the Catholic, convert stories have always had an irresistible appeal as dramatic proof that his Church is at work on her divinely ordered mission to teach all nations.

This fascination with the reasons men have decided to enter the Catholic Church is as old as the Church herself. Though the apostles may be considered the first converts, theirs was an exceptional case indeed, since they were chosen by God himself to abandon all else and follow him. The first conversion in the modern sense may well be considered that of St. Paul, and Paul endured the ordeal that so many later converts were to suffer—ostracism by his former comrades and skepticism on the part of his new brethren. But it was with good reason the Christians of Paul's day questioned his sincerity, for Paul, as Saul, had been the ruthless, untiring persecutor of the early Church so much so that his name had become synonymous with those who would have suppressed the Christian sect at any cost and by whatever means. Small wonder that they had difficulty believing that overnight he had been converted to Christian belief.

Though most conversions have not been so spectacular as Paul's—God does not usually intervene in a blinding flash of light as he did with Paul—all are characterized by the bestowal of God's grace on the men and women involved. It is through his grace that these men and women over the centuries have been enabled to see the light which led them into the Catholic Church.

But that grace is never forced on an unwilling subject. The individual involved must of his own free will embrace Catholicism. His thirst must be such that he must dedicate his whole being to studying every aspect of the religion he is considering. Many non-Catholics are puzzled by the seeming reluctance of the Church to accept converts, insisting as she does on long periods of study and prayer before she will welcome them to the visible Body of Christ on earth. Wisely, the Church demands that the prospective convert literally stop, look, and listen before taking such a momentous step with such eternal implications. In her eyes, such a move is the most important any man can make. To allow anyone to take the step without full cognizance of its significance would be a serious breach of the Church's obligation in such matters. Once she is convinced of the applicant's sincerity and knowledge of what he is doing, then she lovingly and wholeheartedly welcomes the new convert.

One of the most fascinating aspects of conversion stories is the wide variety of roads that lead to conversion. Some, like St. Paul, have had a blinding flash of inspiration. Others, like Cardinal Newman, came to Catholicism after years of intense study and deep meditation and prayer. Some come into the Church as the result of some dramatic incident in their lives. Others have been inspired by a Catholic acquaintance. Some have been brought in by the work of some great Catholic figure, as witness the conversions of so many highly placed figures by Bishop Fulton Sheen. Others have heard the word as a result of formal convert drives such as were so successfully staged in the 1950s by Father John A. O'Brien, often called "the convert-maker." Some came from places of prominence and importance, others from lowly stations in life. For the Church's appeal is to all, regardless of worldly rank or material possessions. Christ called for all to come to him and so does his Church. By the same token the paths men can take are as varied as the intellects of men.

And what a magnificent contribution these converts have made in and to the Church! From every field of human activity, they have put their multitudinous talents at the disposal of their new spiritual mother and have enriched her immeasurably. Time and again they have provided new insights, fresh approaches, and sparkling vigor to matters and areas of the Church which had been neglected or overlooked by Catholics accustomed to the Church from childhood. Again and again they have set in motion fresh currents which have re-invigorated and helped renew the Church, from St. Paul in the first century to Cardinal Newman and G. K. Chesterton in the nineteenth and twentieth centuries.

All too often the sacrifices these men and women have had to make are overlooked. Frequently they have been cut off from life-time friends and associations. A man like Newman—raised, educated, and occupying a respected place in the Church of England—literally cut himself adrift from all he held dear, emotionally, socially, and intellectually. And, unfortunately, too often the controversial convert is looked on with suspicion by his new religious compatriots especially if he has been prominent in a movement inimical to the Church, as was the case with such individuals as Louis Budenz and Bella Dodd who, after their disillusionment with Communism, embraced Catholicism. All Catholics should be aware of what converts have given to the Church and sympathetic to the suffering and anguish they have endured to become Catholics. Their courage and fortitude are worthy of admiration.

In recent times there has been an attempt in some Catholic circles to de-emphasize conversion activity in an attempt to advance the ecumenical movement. Indeed, some astute observers of conversion techniques believe the whole ecumenical drive has been responsible for the drop in conversions in the past few years. Obviously, the very idea of conversion to the Catholic Church is repugnant to some of the Protestant sects, just as the idea of Catholics becoming converted to a Protestant church would be distasteful to many Catholics. But ecumenism does not and should not mean that one should water down one's own faith to meaninglessness so as to dialogue with another religious group. Actually, strong commitment to one's own faith is just as desirable today as it ever was and the Church has never lifted her condemnation of indifferentism. Further, the whole concept of freedom of conscience and of the free choice by the individual of his religious affiliation militates against any effort to dilute one's faith. Catholics should always be interested in bringing a fellow human into the Church. Catholicism is a missionary religion, and Christ did say the Church should convert *all* nations.

The books included in this section encompass the whole scope of conversion activities. The most thrilling, of course, are the personal stories of outstanding and well known individuals who have been irresistably attracted to the Church. But every conversion is thrilling, regardless of the convert's worldly position; so there are also included books by men and women who are not so prominently in the public eye, but whose conversions are unusual and well described. There are books on techniques to be employed to effect conversions by men and women who have been eminently successful in the field of conversions. There are books describing the difficulties in the way of a conversion and offering help to one seriously interested in the Church and her beliefs. In short, we have tried to give representation to all aspects of this most important area of Catholic activity.

In closing, we would utter one word of caution. As Catholics, we should all be interested in being potential convert-makers. But the most effective technique for impressing any prospective convert is by good example. We do not all have the ability to propound the truths of the Church in such a manner as to convert our neighbor. Nor should many of us try. For when one becomes involved in explaining the intricacies of the Catholic faith to a non-Catholic, one should be certain one has the knowledge and the training to do so. Usually at this stage, the inquirer had best be turned over to an expert skilled in this type of apostolate—a priest. But all Catholics can be potential convert-makers by the example they set for their non-Catholic associates. There is no better

way of impressing the full meaning of Catholicism on anyone than by living the Catholic religion as the Church
teaches it. Probably more conversions are made by good
example than anyone realizes. It is one area of life where a
Catholic can do the bidding of his Master, bring incalculable
benefits to his neighbor, and do so much for himself.

AUGUSTINE OF HIPPO, SAINT. *Confessions.* Translated by
Frank J. Sheed. Sheed, 1946. 429 p., notes, bibliography,
index. $3.50. Image, 1960 (translated by John K. Ryan). pa.
$1.35. Washington Square, n.d. (translated by Edward B.
Pusey). pa. 45¢.

By common consent, the work known as the *Confessions*
holds a special place among the world's great books. Although it is autobiographical in character, it is not a story
of the author's life; yet, no other book has ever gone more
deeply into the author's character and deeds, expressed
more incisive judgments about the inner man, or revealed its
author more fully. The book is not only a penetrating
psychological study of man in search of God, but a unique
document for understanding the spiritual life and a treasure
house of thought for the philosopher and the theologian.
After a thousand five-hundred years, the book still attracts
countless readers, from the professional theologian to the
student of literature, from the expert in philosophy to the
general reader. It is recommended to all readers of whatever
category as an indispensable work for the educated Christian.
(Of the three translations listed above, Frank Sheed's is a
very readable rendition; that of Msgr. Ryan, in addition to
being quite modern and flowing, has excellent explanatory
notes; Edward Pusey's translation is regarded as the classic
rendition in English, and is stately yet, occasionally, rather
hard to read with complete understanding.)

CHESTERTON, GILBERT KEITH. *The Catholic Church and Conversion.* Foreword by Hilaire Belloc. Macmillan, 1936. v,
115 p. $2.95. Macmillan, 1956. pa. 95¢.

A common-sense look at the problems of conversion to
Catholicism, both from the standpoint of the Church and
from that of the convert, this book discusses the mistakes that
can be made in judging the pro's and con's of changing one's

religion, what to do about one's family and friends, and how to look upon one's former church as well as one's new church. Like much of Chesterton's writings, this work is a marvel of insight and literary brilliance. Some of the problems discussed may seem a little "dated" today; still, they remain problems, and the solutions given, particularly with respect to the convert's own attitudes, are as valid as they ever were.

DULLES, AVERY (s.j.). *A Testimonial to Grace*. Sheed, 1946. 121 p. $2.50.

The author of this book is the much (and unwillingly) publicized son of the late John Foster Dulles, Secretary of State. He writes the story of his conversion to Catholicism from the Presbyterian Church. While a student at Harvard, the future Father Dulles met and defeated "the three monsters, skepticism, materialism, and liberalism, which hold almost unchallenged sway in our secular universities," as he says. In this brief book, he describes his experiences in that battle, his own spiritual crisis, and his ultimate victory.

GILL, ERIC. *Autobiography*. Introduction by Beatrice Warde. Dufour, 1963 (reprint). xv, 326 p. $3.50.

This is the autobiography of a convert to Catholicism who was also a renowned sculptor, engraver, and painter. There are several rather explicit paragraphs on sex which were thought quite daring for a Catholic autobiography when the book first was published (1941), but which will not offend today's adult reader. This book will be of particular interest to Catholics interested in the arts; it demonstrates a complete integration of Gill's qualities as an artist with his life as a Catholic.

HOLDEN, VINCENT F. *The Yankee Paul*. Foreword by Archbishop Richard J. Cushing. Bruce, 1958. xx, 508 p., bibliography, index. $6.95.

This is the first book of a projected two-volume biography of Father Isaac Thomas Hecker, founder of the Congregation of the Missionary Priests of St. Paul the Apostle, an organization popularly known as the "Paulist fathers." Father Hecker's life, of which this volume covers only the earlier part, is as colorful and exciting a story of conversion—both the subject's and that of others—as any tale of adventure, and although it is rather too detailed for the casual reader, it may be recommended to the serious reader as an important chapter in the history of the American Church.

MERTON, THOMAS. *The Seven Storey Mountain.* Harcourt, 1948. 429 p., index. $3.95.
This famous work is the autobiography of Thomas Merton, covering the period from his birth in 1915 to the end of World War II. Essentially, it narrates the spiritual odyssey of a modern American man with little religious background through the various philosophical isms until he finally finds an intellectual and spiritual haven in the Church.

NEWMAN, JOHN HENRY CARDINAL. *Apologia Pro Vita Sua.* Modern Library, n.d. 439 p. $1.95. Image, 1956 (Introduction by Philip Hughes). pa. $1.35.
The most famous of Newman's works, the *Apologia* is an explanation of the author's changes of religious opinion from his childhood until, after years of study, he entered the Catholic Church "in perfect peace and contentment." This undoubtedly is one of the great spiritual and literary classics of modern times, and it is recognized as one of the great autobiographies of the English language.

O'BRIEN, JOHN A. *Giants of the Faith.* Doubleday, 1957. 358 p. $3.75. Image, 1960. pa. 95¢.
These are the stories of six conversions which have changed the world, covering the lives and works of St. Paul, St. Augustine, Cardinal Newman, G. K. Chesterton, Orestes Brownson, Isaac Hecker. Of particular interest are Brownson—author, editor, and probably the most important Catholic thinker to appear in America—and Father Hecker, the founder of the Paulist Fathers.

O'BRIEN, JOHN A., Editor. *The Road to Damascus.* Image, 1955. 228 p. pa. 85¢.
A collection of the personal accounts of fifteen notable converts to Catholicism, in which they tell of the spiritual experience which led them to the Church. Among those represented are: Clare Boothe Luce, Robert F. Wagner, Frances Parkinson Keyes, Evelyn Waugh, and Fulton Oursler.

SIMON, M. RAPHAEL (O.C.S.O.). *The Glory of Thy People.* Preface by Fulton Sheen. Macmillan, 1954. xvii, 139 p. pa. $1.25.

The author of this spiritual autobiography was a brilliant young Jewish psychiatrist who was converted to Catholicism and eventually became a Trappist monk. In a completely candid and moving style, he tells of his conversion and of his abandonment of a lucrative and highly promising career to enter the strictest monastic order of the Catholic Church.

STERN, KARL. *The Pillar of Fire*. Harcourt, 1951. 278 p., index. $3.50. Image, 1959, pa. 85¢.

The story of the conversion to Catholicism of an eminent Jewish psychiatrist, Dr. Stern's book begins with his childhood in a Jewish community in Germany, and covers his years as a medical student in pre-Hitlerian Germany, his work in the German slums, his return to Jewish orthodoxy, and his eventual transition to Catholicism. This is a work of unusual beauty, well written, and evoking a great variety of experiences. Since the author's religious anxieties and problems were primarily of an intellectual nature, this book is not "popular" in the sense that it will have universal appeal. For the intellectual or scientist with problems of his own, however, it will provide new insights and solutions.

8. EDUCATION

The problems of education have been the concern of men of all civilizations. Thinking men have always realized that one of the most vital tasks of any society is to transmit from one generation to another the knowledge accumulated by themselves and by previous generations. If this knowledge were to be blotted out today, mankind would revert to the primitiveness of an aboriginal society. This has always been true, but never so much as in today's complex and machine-dominated culture. Knowledge has reached such a state of complexity, and our way of life has become so dependent on the tools we have created, that civilization would perish overnight if the knowledge to create and operate the mechanisms on which we are so dependent were suddenly to be wiped out.

This is so obvious from a technological viewpoint as to require no further commentary, but it is equally true for every aspect of our culture. Through the centuries, men have struggled to better themselves intellectually and spiritually as well as in the material advantages which have provided for our creature comforts. How impoverished we would be, then, if the teachings and philosophies of the great men of all centuries were denied our generation. It is the transmission of the knowledge of our predecessors that constitutes the very fabric of our society. A nation which fails in education, therefore, is doomed to extinction.

What is true of nations and civilizations is just as true of religions. If the teaching of Christ had ended with the generation he knew, then there would be no Catholic religion or anything that we associate with it. But our Lord charged his apostles with the task of spreading the Word he had taught them, and that charge must perforce take the form of some educational process.

Obviously, the process can be as varied as the imagination of men. At the beginning of the Christian era, the apostles used the centuries-old methods of their Jewish forebears—

word-of-mouth preaching supplemented by letters (the Epistles of the New Testament). From the time of Abraham
that had been the traditional method of passing the Jewish
heritage from one generation to the next, and it is still the
method most widely used in simple primitive societies.

As the Church grew geographically and numerically, and
as the doctrine entrusted to her began to grow when scholars
and theologians began to develop the various aspects and
implications of Christ's often deceivingly simple statements,
more and more attention was devoted to arranging this body
of knowledge and information in forms relatively easy to
handle for transmission from one generation to another. Increasingly formal methods of presenting the teachings of the
Church were developed, and over the centuries many kinds
of schools began to spring up. In many instances, such schools
were patterned after the schools of antiquity, but with the
passage of time entirely new concepts were developed to
replace the educational institutions which had outgrown
their usefulness or had ceased to exist with the collapse of
Rome and the barbarian invasions of the Empire.

As Roman civilization faded, in many areas the savagery
and crudeness of the barbarians replaced it. In the centuries
required for the transformation of a tired, faded civilization
and an energetic, barbaric vitality into a new dynamic civilization, all learning was threatened with complete extinction.
It was under these conditions that the Church assumed a role
and performed a function which should earn her the gratitude
of all future generations of mankind. For with the extirpation
of secular learning, the monasteries and later cathedral
schools assumed the burden not only of teaching the faith
but of transmitting all human knowledge. It is always rather
fruitless to speculate on the "ifs" of history, but certainly
one of the more fascinating of such speculations is how many
more centuries it would have taken Western man to reach
his present state if the Church had not kept the flickering
torch of knowledge alive through so many centuries.

Later, when the amalgam had jelled and a new civilization
had emerged, it was the Church that founded or sponsored the great centers of learning which have provided so
many of the great universities of today. Practically every

great university of Europe and many of the leading universities in the United States were founded and developed under Church auspices.

The Catholic Church, then, has always had a great interest in education. She has retained that interest in the modern era, and in more recent times that concern has been intensified. For, with the tremendous growth in secular knowledge, there was an increased tendency to disassociate the knowledge from a religious orientation or commitment. More and more, emphasis on secular and empirical knowledge has been stressed with a concomitant tendency to slight any religious involvement in the processes of learning. Also, as a consequence of the Reformation, even those schools with religious affiliations stressed their own type of religious commitment and tended to exclude all others.

In the United States, both of these tendencies led to particular educational problems for Catholics. In the first half of the nineteenth century, the United States developed a school system dedicated to a hitherto unheard-of principle in education—that all of the citizens of the nation were to be educated. In pursuit of this laudable ideal, a public school system, unlike anything ever devised by man, came into being. It was supported by the state, which compelled by law its citizens to attend for stipulated periods of time. Theoretically open to all, the public school system rapidly developed into what was in effect a Protestant school system. The whole orientation was Protestant, mainly because at the time the system was developing the nation was overwhelmingly Protestant and the teachers automatically taught Protestant tenets along with the 3Rs—readin', 'ritin', and 'rithmetic. Trouble inevitably broke out when millions of immigrant Catholics, most of them too poor to provide for their own education, began to attend public schools and were subjected to Protestant religious teaching.

After fruitlessly protesting for decades, the American Catholic hierarchy decided, at the Third Plenary Council of Baltimore in 1884, to establish a Catholic parochial school system which would provide the education required by the state, but would at the same time instruct the children in their Catholic faith. That the bishops were successful is attested by the fact that today more than 7,000,000 Catholics attend these Catholic schools which number in the thousands, ranging from kindergartens to universities.

But, as so often happens, the solution of one problem often creates another. Despite attacks on the legality of its existence and because of great sacrifices by the Catholic community, the parochial school system by the middle of the twentieth century was widely accepted as an integral part of the American educational system, though still regarded with misgivings by some of the professional teaching fraternity. Two developments, sometimes closely related, brought on a new crisis which still confronts the Church and threatens to continue for years to come.

The first of these is simply a matter of economics. As the parochial school system expanded, it became more and more expensive to maintain it. As taxes rose higher and higher, it became increasingly a problem for the Catholic parent who had to foot the bill to pay taxes for public education and then had to contribute again to education by maintaining the Catholic school. With the tremendous proliferation of knowledge requiring more and more costly educational facilities and tools, the inflationary trend in which the nation is currently involved, the need for more lay teachers at a far higher cost than the religious teachers who had hitherto staffed Catholic schools, the Church was caught in a financial vise which threatened the whole structure.

In 1965 a new element was added to education with the passage of the first federal-aid-to-education bill. Formerly the sole concern of local governmental units, the soaring costs of education led to the entry of the federal government into the educational picture in the form of direct grants to the cities and states. After a bitter struggle, minor concessions were made to private and parochial education. Inevitably, this arrangement is but the forerunner of massive federal aid to come. If this is to be of any real assistance to private schools, the pittance offered them in this first bill will need to be greatly increased. All are aware of the crisis, but a full solution will not be forthcoming until there is a concerted effort to solve the problem by all those affected.

In the midst of this financial crisis, and partly as a result of it, frequently critical studies of the Catholic school system were launched by Catholics themselves to determine just how effective the parochial school was as an instrument for educating Catholics and for preserving and spreading the Faith. The inquiries are directed at every level of Catholic education and it is evident that the full answer will not be forthcoming for years to come. It is even more evident that the whole structure and purpose of Catholic education is at a critical stage in the United States.

From all we have said above, it is evident that the Church has always had a great interest in education, an interest that continues unabated to the present day. For the Catholic in the United States, the Catholic commitment to education is close to the primary function of the Church, to spread the Word of God. Few subjects should engage his attention as does this all-important area of Church activity, for the Church in the United States in this generation is the product of that decision taken at Baltimore by the American bishops in 1884. What Catholic education will be for future generations will be the result of decisions made in the next few years, and few subjects involving the Church will so intimately affect the average Catholic as will the whole question of Catholic education. It is an area in which no Catholic can afford to be uninformed.

Fortunately, in recent years, much has been written on every aspect of Catholic education, from learned treatises on technical curriculum considerations and on the over-all policy of the Church to the state of the individual Catholic in the whole field of Catholic education. Increasingly, the lay Catholic will be involved in Catholic education on the working level as teacher, on the policy levels as more laymen are appointed to diocesan boards of education, and above all as Catholic parents with a direct concern in what happens to Catholic schools. Here is one area where the individual Catholic has a particular obligation to be an informed Catholic.

BLUM, VIRGIL (s.j.). *Freedom in Education.* Doubleday, 1965. 235 p. $4.95.

Here is a statement of the argument in favor of federal aid to private education. Father Blum maintains not only that it is indeed constitutional for the federal government to grant funds to all educational institutions, but also that it is *un*-constitutional for it to refuse funds to *any* school. There is a thoroughgoing analysis of the financial aspects of the question, an examination of legal precedents, and a survey of the situation in countries where government funds are granted to all schools.

BUCKLEY, WILLIAM F. *God and Man at Yale.* Introduction by John Chamberlain. Regnery, 1951. 240 p., notes, bibliography. pa. $2.00.

Mr. Buckley reflects on the "superstitions of academic freedom" at Yale University. He considers specifically the role of religion at that university, the place of individualism, the relationship of alumni to the school, and what is meant —and what should be meant—by "academic freedom." The author combines wit with erudition and insight and, whether the reader's bias be conservative or liberal, the author's insights into the nature of academic freedom warrant consideration.

CALLAHAN, DANIEL J., Editor. *Federal Aid and Catholic Schools.* Helicon, 1964. 160 p., appendix. $3.95.

A collection of ten essays, this work presents varying opinions, both Catholic and non-Catholic, on the question of the propriety of federal aid to Catholic schools. The contributors include Virgil Blum, s.j., Robert Francoeur, s.j., Dean M. Kelley of the National Council of the Church of Christ, and Milton Himmelfarb of *Commentary* magazine. An appendix contains brief summaries of the solutions applied in Britain, Germany, Canada, and Italy.

CULLAR, A. DWIGHT. *The Imperial Intellect.* Yale, 1955. 340 p., bibliography. $6.00.

Cardinal Newman's concept of education was essentially that instruction had only one purpose: to provide the student with a universal view of creation, an all-inclusive knowledge made up of many parts, with each part ordered in relation to the whole. In this work, the author traces the genesis and evolution of Newman's theory, and the practical means by which the cardinal proposed for the realization of his ideal.

The book is, in practice, an excellent synthesis of Newman's thought on education.

DAWSON, CHRISTOPHER. *The Crisis of Western Education.* Program outlines by John J. Mulloy and John P. Gleason. Sheed, 1961. vi, 246 p. $3.95. Image, 1965. pa. 95¢.

In the first part of this work, Dawson traces the history of education and shows the eighteenth-century break with the religious and classical tradition as a break in the cultural continuity of Western man. The second part treats mainly of the theory and practice of education in American schools. The author's thesis is that Catholics now are in a position to combat the de-spiritualization of Western culture by re-establishing the Christian orientation of education. The book requires careful reading.

MARITAIN, JACQUES. *Education at the Crossroads.* Yale, 1943. x, 120 p. $4.00. Yale, 1960. pa. $1.25.

An eminent Catholic philosopher discusses the crisis of modern education. Among the aspects treated are the aims of modern education, the dynamics of education, and the current difficulties in which the American educational system finds itself. While this work is not always easy reading, the reader will be amply repaid for his effort.

MARITAIN, JACQUES. *The Education of Man.* Edited with an introduction by Donald and Idella Gallagher. Doubleday, 1962. 191 p., bibliography, index. $3.95.

This anthology of Maritain's writings on the philosophy of education and the status of Christian instruction includes selections on the nature of Christian education, Thomistic views on education, the place of the humanities in education, the importance of moral and spiritual values, the education of women, and the role of freedom in education. The selections give a comprehensive view of the great philosopher's thought on the nature of education, and they presuppose no particular background in philosophy on the reader's part.

McCLUSKEY, NEIL G. (S.J.). *Catholic Viewpoint on Education,* revised edition. Image, 1962. 189 p., notes, index. pa. 75¢.

Father McCluskey, an authority on American Catholic education, explains the Catholic position on federal and state aid to parochial and other church-affiliated schools. He places that position in its historical perspective, and accurately details the rationale on which it is based. This is probably the best popular exposition of this controversial issue.

NEWMAN, JOHN HENRY (CARDINAL). *The Idea of a University*. Introduction by George N. Shuster. Image, 1959. 477 p., notes, index. pa. $1.45.

This is Cardinal Newman's classic work on the ideal of Christian education. The first part of the book is a thorough study of the role of the divine sciences in relation to knowledge, and of the role of knowledge in relation to religion. The second part deals with specific branches of learning at the university level and in the elementary schools, and the last part treats of the physical sciences. This work grows in importance as it grows in age and it is indispensable reading for anyone involved or interested in the philosophy of education.

NEWMAN, JOHN HENRY (CARDINAL). *University Sketches*. Edited with notes and introduction by Michael Tierney. Alba, 1963. xvii, 314 p. $4.95.

These essays by Cardinal Newman, published during his tenure as rector of the Catholic University of Ireland, contain an important part of his educational doctrine. The introduction and notes by Mr. Tierney are lucid and helpful, placing the essays in their proper historical setting, and relating them to the thoughts on education expressed in Newman's other writings.

RAMBUSCH, NANCY M. *Learning How to Learn*. Foreword by George N. Shuster; bibliography compiled by Gilbert E. Donahue. Helicon, 1962. x, 180 p., notes, appendices, bibliography, index. $4.50.

This is a discussion of the ideas of Maria Montessori, founder of the "Montessori Method" and pioneer in the fields of psychiatry, child development, and education. The book treats specifically of Dr. Montessori's beliefs on the importance for the child of social and educational environment, the roles of parent and of teacher, and the nature of the "new school" conceived by Montessori.

RYAN, MARY PERKINS. *Are Parochial Schools the Answer?* Foreword by Bishop Ernest J. Primeau. Holt, 1964. ix, 176 p. $4.00. Angelus, 1965. pa. 50¢.

The author of this controversial study examines the Catholic educational system in America and reaches some startling conclusions. Her thesis may be summed up by stating that, under present circumstances, it is not possible for the continuance or extension of the Catholic parochial school system to be anything but an obstacle to the Christian obligation to participate in, and thus apply Christian principles to, the cares of the world. This is a lively and provocative book, well worth reading, no matter what one's own views on the value of a specifically Catholic education.

STANDING, E. MORTIMER. *Maria Montessori: Her Life and Work.* Academy Library, 1957. 354 p. $5.95.

This is an authoritative account of the lifework of a great Catholic educator, the founder of the controversial Montessori Method according to which children are provided with certain materials and, with no attempt at formal training, are encouraged to exercise their initiative; the teacher acts as a guide rather than as an instructor. It is an interesting book about a woman who has had an enormous influence on modern educational theories.

9. FICTION

Of all the forms of literature, none has achieved the pre-eminence enjoyed by the novel in the twentieth century. A comparative newcomer on the literary scene (the first book recognized as a novel by modern definition was Samuel Richardson's *Pamela; or, Virtue Rewarded* published in 1740) it soon attracted an enormous following and, in the first half of the twentieth century, was the undisputed popular monarch of all literature in English-speaking countries. Its golden age was reached in the 'twenties and 'thirties and, though its popularity has waned in recent years (for reasons we shall mention later in this essay), it still constitutes an integral and important segment of the world of books.

The reasons for the popularity of the novel are many and varied. To some, it is an ideal escape mechanism; for others, it is a sugar-coated learning method; for still others, it provides entertainment. But the serious novel, though it may be all of these things, is far more than a mere vehicle of pleasure and/or amusement. The novel can provide a more searching examination and more deeply penetrating study of any aspect of human experience than any other type of literature. And it is when it is engaged in a serious consideration of man and of his life on earth and of his human aspirations that the novel must become involved with the basic questions of human existence: where did man come from, what motivates his actions, what is his ultimate destiny—above all, what of man's relationship to God which, in one way or another, is the single most important factor in any man's life. There is no other literary form that can illuminate these areas of the human spirit with such impact and insight as the novel.

It should be made clear, though, that this does not mean that the novel is merely a sociological or theological or any other kind of tract. Indeed, the novel-tracts that are considered great novels are few and far between. For the writing of a novel is a craft and a great novel is a work of art. The author of a fictional work is a craftsman and, of course, he must have a knowledge of that about which he is writing. But above all he is a creator. From his own imagination he must create characters and events that are real to the reader. A great novelist has the ability to make his reader associate with his characters to the point where the reader feels he is a part of the book and suffers and exhilarates, is defeated and triumphs, rises and falls with the characters, and is a participant in the scenes and events in the book. A great novelist achieves these ends so perfectly that his book transcends time and space, nationality and class, religion and race, and has a universal appeal and message that is timeless and placeless. So, we find a French novelist who appeals just as strongly to the Briton, the German, the Russian, the Italian, the Japanese, as he does to his countrymen. When a novelist achieves universality, he is truly a great novelist.

It is only when he is dealing with the fundamental problems of human existence that an author of fiction can really achieve greatness, and no problem is as basic in the human scheme of things as the relation of man to God and the hereafter. The fundamental questions we raised earlier—what is man, whence did he come, where is he going—for believers, at least, can all be traced to the most fundamental of all man's dilemmas, his relationship to a supernatural being.

For the Christian, then, plot, characterization, style, all the devices of a novel are significant elements in the structuring and creation of a novel, but of overwhelming importance is the fact that in one way or another the novel must concern itself with fundamental considerations. It is this concern with the primary purposes of man's existence which has characterized the great novels of the past. One of the reasons the novel has declined to its present state must certainly be that too many modern authors have lost sight of the fact that overshadowing all the other concerns of human persons must be the question of man's ultimate destiny. No novelist can achieve true greatness who does not keep this fact clearly in mind.

There are, of course, other factors involved in the decline in popularity of the novel. Not least of these causes has been the incredible, real-life happenings of the past few decades.

Formerly a novelist drew on his imagination for his people and plots, and usually his imagination was so much more varied and colorful than that of his readers that they were swept up by the events and characters he set loose on paper. But the events of our times have far outdistanced the most vivid and bizarre events concocted by the imagination of any novelist. People have actually experienced events and been involved in episodes which would have caused any reputable author to be laughed out of business a few short decades ago if he had written of them in his novels. Actual events have completely surpassed in reality anything that the novelist could have conceived.

Perhaps an even more telling reason can be laid at the door of a whole school of novelists. In their eagerness to provide realism, many writers have simply gone beyond the bounds of what most people consider decency. No person can quarrel with the efforts of an author to depict a scene realistically when such treatment is necessary for the development of a character or the theme of his book. Unfortunately, too many untalented authors attracted attention by sheer shock—the use in profusion of four-letter words, explicit descriptions of sexual incidents, and the exploitation of sexual aberrations, perversion, and the like.

At first, a ready audience for this type of writing was available. To many, this new realism was a symbol of revolt against the dead hand of the past. For others, it was simply an opportunity to indulge in vicarious experiences, and they eagerly seized upon such books as a means of titillation in the respectable guise of keeping abreast of the new trends. As more and more such books appeared, with each reaching for more sensationalism to stimulate and arouse tastes jaded by previous such attempts, the shock values and sensational qualities became less as their novelty wore off. A reaction set in, for after all the vocabulary of vulgarity is limited and repetition inevitably wears down shock value. Readers began to demand again the qualities of writing in a novel essential to any piece of writing—not least of which are the basic tools of the novelist's trade: the ability to write, to structure a novel, to construct a plot, to create believable characters, to depict a scene. The tide began to turn against the sloppily written, badly presented novel which depended solely on shock treatment to hold its audience.

Hopefully such a reaction from a sizable segment of the reading audience, coupled with the large audience which had remained steadfast in its adherence to fine writing as a requisite for any literary form, will re-focus attention on the many fine and the comparatively few great novels which are available.

Before listing and describing our selection of such books, we should like to discuss briefly in a general way the titles we have included. All of them, without exception, may be identified as "Catholic books." We use the term with full realization of the fact that many discerning Catholic critics contend there is no such thing as a Catholic novel. For our part, we can simply reiterate our belief that there is such an animal, and that to describe a book as a Catholic novel is merely a convenient term to describe a particular kind of book which really does exist.

Perhaps this is the place to define what we mean by a Catholic book. Our own definition is broad but, we think, justified. A Catholic book is one which is in accord with Catholic precepts and culture in the treatment of its theme and in the author's approach. With such a definition I think we are completely justified in describing the books below as Catholic books.

One further point on this matter of the Catholic novel is the fact that our definition permits the inclusion of books by non-Catholics; in fact we have done exactly this. Willa Cather was not a Catholic, but her *Shadows on the Rock* and *Death Comes for the Archbishop* are Catholic through and through. There is a Catholic feeling from first page to last and not a single false note is sounded. The same thing is true of such a book as H. F. M. Prescott's *The Man on a Donkey*, surely one of the outstanding novels of our times. And though it is not a novel, who would deny that Cardinal Newman's *Essay on the Development of Christian Doctrine* is Catholic? And yet he wrote this work before he formally entered the Catholic Church. With such examples, it seems to us indisputable that some books written by non-Catholics must be included in any list of Catholic books.

Finally, a word about the books we have selected for inclusion in this section. There is a wide variety of novels listed for all tastes, ranging from such light novels as Bruce Marshall's *Father Malachy's Miracle* and Myles Connolly's *Mr. Blue* to Sigrid Undset's magnificent *Kristin Lavransdatter* and François Mauriac's bleak *Viper's Tangle,* but all fit well within the definition above. And, most important of all, each of the books listed, whether light entertainment or a serious study of a character or period, treats, in one way or another, of the most important thing in any man's life—his ultimate destiny.

BARRETT, WILLIAM E. *The Lilies of the Field.* Drawings by Burt Silverman. Doubleday, 1962. 92 p. $2.50. Popular, 1964. pa. 40¢.
Lilies is the heart-warmingly whimsical story of a good-natured but rather cynical Negro youth who is "conned" into becoming the handyman of a poverty-stricken convent in the Southwest. The novel basically is the record of conflict between materialistic and spiritual values, but it contains, in addition to its important message, a good deal of subtle and gently ironic humor.

BERNANOS, GEORGES. *The Diary of a Country Priest.* Translated by Pamela Morris. Macmillan, 1937. $3.50. Macmillan, 1962. pa. $1.95.
This award-winning novel records the aspirations, struggles, failures and accomplishments of a French country priest. The book is in diary form, recounting the writer's impressions of the people with whom he is working, of the workings of human nature and divine grace—for the priest, Father Donessan, has the extraordinary gift of being able to see the souls of men as God sees them. This novel is required reading for the informed Catholic.

CATHER, WILLA. *Death Comes for the Archbishop.* Knopf, 1927. 303 p. $3.95.
This novel concerns the Church and its missionary endeavors in the deserts of New Mexico. It is essentially a collection of episodes hinging upon the personality and life of Jean Latour, Archbishop of Santa Fe, and upon his relation-

ship with his assistant, Father Vaillant. This is Miss Cather's most famous work. It has become a classic of American letters, and the book is as enjoyable as it is important.

CATHER, WILLA. *Shadows on the Rock.* Knopf, 1931. 301 p. $3.95.
This novel is about the closing days of the life of the Governor of Quebec, the Count de Frontenac, in French colonial days. The heroine, through whose eyes the reader views the rather romantic plot of the book, is an engaging young woman named Cecile Auclair. Upon the death of Frontenac, Cecile marries a fur-trader, whose characterization is one of the highlights of the book. Although this book does not enjoy the fame of Miss Cather's *Death Comes for the Archbishop*, it is a major work in its own right.

CHESTERTON, GILBERT KEITH. *The Amazing Adventures of Father Brown.* Dell, 1959. 192 p. pa. 40¢.
This is a collection of ten of Chesterton's famous stories about the bumblingly effective detective-priest, Father Brown, including such old favorites as "The Blue Cross" and "Eye of Apollo."

CHESTERTON, GILBERT KEITH. *Father Brown Omnibus.* Dodd, 1933. 1037 p. $5.00.
This collection of Chesterton's celebrated "Father Brown stories" includes: *The Innocence of Father Brown, The Wisdom of Father Brown, The Incredulity of Father Brown,* and *The Secret of Father Brown.* The hero of all these stories was drawn from a real priest who was a friend of the author and who, like Father Brown, "had a face as round as a Norfolk dumpling, eyes as empty as the North Sea," and who was constantly grappling with large brown parcels and umbrellas. The Father Brown tales, to a large extent, are responsible for the present respectability of detective fiction and themselves have become classics of that *genre.* They possess a whimsical humor and an inexhaustible ingenuity that will appeal to all readers.

CONNOLLY, MYLES. *Mr. Blue.* Macmillan, 1928. 119 p. $2.50. Image, 1954. pa. 65¢.
A touching novel about the incredible Mr. Blue—mystic, spendthrift, maker of gloriously impossible plans, preacher of love, and resident of a large packing box. The book essen-

tially is a satire on contemporary values, but like its hero it is a happy book. It is recommended to everyone who wants to be happy—but it is guaranteed to offend the pompous, the rigidly conventional, and the Babbitts.

CRONIN, A. J. *The Keys of the Kingdom.* Little, 1941. 283 p. $3.00. Bantam, 1962. pa. 75¢.

This is the famous novel about Father Francis Chisholm, a spirited young Scottish priest who is sent to China as a missionary and who, in his simple, plodding way, manages to win the respect and admiration of the Chinese people if not that of his ecclesiastical superiors. It is a well written, engrossing, and sometimes inspiring story, and it is recommended to any adult reader.

DE WOHL, LOUIS. *The Quiet Light.* Lippincott, 1950. 319 p. $2.95. Image, 1958. pa. 95¢.

In this novel about St. Thomas Aquinas and his times, the Emperor Frederick II is terrorizing Italy, burning churches, making war on the pope, and fighting the Italian nobility—including Thomas' own family. How the family of Aquinas is saved because of the love of an English knight for his beautiful sister makes a colorful story. Interwoven with the plot are passages that highlight Thomas' key thoughts in simple language.

DE WOHL, LOUIS. *The Spear.* Lippincott, 1955. 383 p. $5.95. Popular Library, 1957. pa. 75¢.

Mr. De Wohl's novel reconstructs quite plausibly the lives of some of the Roman soldiers and officials who were involved in the life of Christ. The account is fictional, of course, but it bases itself closely on the Gospel accounts, particularly when dealing with the public life of Christ and his mission. The story is entertaining and gives some unusual historical background for an understanding of Jesus' time.

DUGGAN, ALFRED. *The Cunning of the Dove.* Pantheon, 1960. 254 p. $3.50. Image, 1966. pa. 85¢.

This is a novelized version of the life and times of Edward the Confessor, saint, King of England, and builder of Westminster Abbey. Edward died in the year of the Norman Conquest of England (1066), and, to a certain extent, may be said to have paved the way for the Normans. He is probably the least understood of the important English rulers, both through lack of material in his life and because of certain apparent paradoxes in his personality. Mr. Duggan, basing himself upon historical fact, provides a believable characterization and tells an exciting story with wit and charm.

DUGGAN, ALFRED. *Count Bohemond.* Preface by Evelyn Waugh. Pantheon, 1965. 281 p. $4.95.

This is a fictionalized biography of Bohemond, Prince of Antioch, who was one of the leaders of the First Crusade in the eleventh century. The story as told by Duggan is colorful, often humorous, and gives a picture of the Crusades in general and of their spirit which is accurate and entertaining. Evelyn Waugh's preface is a tribute to Mr. Duggan, whose last book this was before his death.

GIRONELLA, JOSE MARIA. *The Cypresses Believe in God.* Translated by Harriet de Onis. Knopf, 1955. 1010 p. $6.50.

This is the first work in a trilogy on the Spanish Civil War. The author, a Spaniard who was himself involved in that conflict, has set out to depict the tragedy of violence in civil war, where one finds brother fighting brother, and where families are separated not only by war but also by hatred. This first volume deals with the period from 1931, when the Spanish Republic was founded, until the beginning of the Civil War in 1936. It was acclaimed as one of the outstanding novels of modern times.

GREENE, GRAHAM. *The End of the Affair.* Viking, 1951. 240 p. $4.95. Compass, 1961. pa. $1.25.

One of Mr. Greene's most popular novels, *The End of the Affair* is the story of an adulterous love affair and of how it changed from love to hate, and then from hate to divine love. The book is a beautiful and moving example of Catholic writing at its best, and it is recommended to the adult reader.

GREENE, GRAHAM. *The Heart of the Matter.* Viking, 1948. viii, 306 p. $3.50. Compass, 1960. pa. $1.45.

This is one of the most widely acclaimed and enduring novels written in the last quarter-century. It concerns the fate of an English police officer, a Catholic, who is assigned to duty in an African port city and who allows his compassion for mankind to lead him into lies, debauchery, sacrilege

and, finally, suicide. The book is well on its way to becoming
a modern classic.

GREENE, GRAHAM. *The Power and the Glory.* Viking, 1946.
301 p. $3.75. Compass, 1958. pa. $1.45.
Originally published under the title of *Labyrinthine Ways,*
this novel tells the story of a Mexican priest who administers
the sacraments during an acute phase of the religious persecutions in his country. Under the pressure of anxiety, the
priest turns to drink and becomes a sort of sacerdotal tramp
—but continues to minister to his flock. Eventually, he finds
the courage, once captured, to give up his life for his faith.
This is a strong drama of sin, salvation, and humanity, and
one of Greene's most famous works.

GUARESCHI, GIOVANNI. *Comrade Don Camillo.* Translated by
Frances Frenaye. Farrar, 1964. 212 p. $3.95. Pocket Books,
1965. pa. 50¢.
Another volume in the series about the friendly war between Don Camillo, the imperturbable and resourceful
Italian pastor, and Peppone, the hot-tempered Communist
mayor of Don Camillo's village, this novel takes the good
pastor on an hilarious journey to the Soviet Union disguised
as a fanatic Communist. All very good-natured fun, the book
is highly recommended for young and old.

GUARESCHI, GIOVANNI. *The Little World of Don Camillo.*
Translated by Una V. Troubridge. Farrar, 1951. 205 p.
$3.00. Pocket Books, 1961. pa. 50¢.
Don Camillo has become famous the world over as the
desperately sincere and unintentionally humorous, but wholly
engaging, pastor of a Communist-dominated village in Italy.
His friend and antagonist is the Communist mayor, Peppone,
and the pair clash wits and ideologies on every conceivable
occasion. The third major character is Christ on the crucifix
in the parish church, with whom Don Camillo talks over his
problems. Some of the best lines in the book are reserved to
the Lord who, so far as the good priest is concerned, is
wholly unpredictable. This is a thoroughly enjoyable novel,
from every standpoint.

HEMON, LOUIS. *Maria Chapdelaine.* Translated by W. H.
Blake. Macmillan, 1921. 198 p. $3.50. Image, 1956. pa. 75¢.
A simple, direct folk tale which has become a little classic,

this is the story of a young French Canadian woman and her final, heroic sacrifice. An unusual piece of writing, idealistic and moving, and well worth the reading.

HORGAN, PAUL. *Things As They Are*. Farrar, 1964. 239 p. $4.50.

In this novel about a boy's journey from innocence to reality, Paul Horgan explores the awakening of the mind of his hero, Richard, to the facts of human weakness, selfishness, and depravity. The thesis of the story seems to be that the road to maturity is really a process of gradual disillusionment with life and with people. Whether or not the reader agrees with the story's moral lesson, the book is deeply introspective and beautifully written, and will provide hours of reading pleasure.

HULME, KATHRYN C. *The Nun's Story*. Little, 1956. 339 p. $4.50. Pocket Books, 1962. pa. 50¢.

This book, widely acclaimed at its publication, is a story of convent life that holds up for inspection the meaning of a nun's life—its grandeur, as well as its occasional pettiness and human faults. The author writes with polished style and compassion, and the book, in addition to being excellent entertainment for adults, will provide an accurate picture of life within convent walls.

KENT, MICHAEL. *The Mass of Brother Michel*. All Saints, 1961. 275 p. pa. 75¢.

This well known dramatic novel about sixteenth-century France concerns young Michel de Guillemont who, having been crippled in a hunting accident, leaves his fiancee to his brother and takes refuge in a monastery, where he develops an overpowering love of the Mass and, although not a priest, is consumed with the desire to say a Mass. How Michel finally attains his ambition forms the climax of this absorbing story.

MANNIN, ETHEL. *Late Have I Loved Thee*. Putnam, 1948. 359 p. $3.00. Image, 1962. pa. 95¢.

This is a novel about a twentieth-century St. Augustine who, after a youth misspent in the glittering literary set of Paris and London in the 1920s, and crushed under the weight of tormenting guilt, feels the hand of God write an astonishing message on his soul.

MANZONI, ALESSANDRO. *The Betrothed.* Translated by Archibald Colquhond. Everyman, n.d. $1.95. Dutton, n.d. pa. $2.15.

The Betrothed (*I Promessi Sposi*), written in 1825, is generally considered to be the great Italian novel of modern times and holds a place in literature comparable to that of *War and Peace.* The story takes place in seventeenth-century Lombardy, and concerns the love of Renzo and Lucia for one another. Although the novel is set against an historical background, it rises above historical limits and is considered a literary masterpiece because of the beauty of its style and the greatness of its conception.

MARSHALL, BRUCE. *Father Malachy's Miracle.* Image, 1955. 198 p. pa. 75¢.

The famous novel of a priest who did not believe that the Age of Miracles was over—and proved his point by performing a miracle of his own. A hilarious satire on irreligion and skepticism, for everyone with a sense of humor.

MARSHALL, BRUCE. *The World, the Flesh and Father Smith.* Image, 1957. 196 p. pa. 75¢.

Father Smith's career as a priest in an anti-Catholic parish, a chaplain in World War I, and a post-war pastor are related with all the skill for which Mr. Marshall is so well known. It is one of the wisest and funniest books ever written about the life of a priest, and will appeal to every taste.

MARY CATHERINE, SISTER. *Brother Petroc's Return.* Little, 1937. 160 p. $2.00. Image, 1955. pa. 85¢.

A novel which has become a little classic. It is 1949, and a community of monks is rebuilding a chapel destroyed during the Reformation. In order to make way for the new construction, they open a grave marked "Brother Petroc—died 1549," and find within the perfectly preserved body of a young monk. The community stares in awe at the "corpse"— and Brother Petroc heaves a sigh, opens his eyes and stares back. A beautiful tale, told with charming simplicity.

MAURIAC, FRANÇOIS. *Viper's Tangle.* Translated by Warren B. Wells. 159 p. $3.00. Image, 1957. pa. 75¢.

Mauriac's novel is about the struggle between despair and hope, love and lust, in the soul of a wretchedly unhappy millionaire. This work has been acclaimed as the greatest novel of the Nobel Prize winner.

MAURIAC, FRANÇOIS. *Woman of the Pharisees*. Translated by Gerard Manley Hopkins, s.j. Noonday, 1964. pa. $2.25.

This novel concerns the struggle between the spirit and the flesh, and man's extraordinary gift for overcoming evil. The "woman" of the title is Brigitte Pian—a "good" woman who believes herself to be rational and noble but who, in reality, is spiritually degenerate, domineering, and narrow-minded; she is a masterful study in self-love at its most vindictive. François Mauriac is considered to be one of the great writers of the twentieth century, and this is perhaps his greatest novel. The work is superbly translated.

O'CONNOR, EDWIN. *The Edge of Sadness*. Little, 1961. 460 p. $5.00. Bantam, 1963. pa. 75¢.

This 1962 Pulitzer Prize-winning novel tells the story of Father Hugh Kennedy who, after being cured of alcoholism, is assigned to a slum parish where his one ambition is to avoid becoming involved with the personal lives of his parishioners. Despite his resolutions, however, he is drawn into the confusing, and thoroughly amusing, Carmody family problems. This book is an unusually moving and satisfying novel, and it is recommended to adult readers.

O'CONNOR, EDWIN. *The Last Hurrah*. Little, 1956. 427 p. $5.00. Bantam, 1964. pa. 75¢.

This famous novel is the fictionalized study of political intrigue in a large eastern city. Its hero is a hard-fighting Irishman, beloved by the poor of his city for his "pork-barrel" approach to vote-gathering. The strength of the book lies in its richly authentic characterization and its flamboyant color. It is a moving and rewarding story, well worth the reading.

POWERS, J. F. *Morte d'Urban*. Doubleday, 1962. 336 p. $4.50. Popular, 1965. pa. 60¢.

This best-selling novel tells the story of Father Urban, a priest whose commitment basically is to the world rather than to the spirit, and whose field of apostolic activity is the golf course. The book is a satire on a certain clerical type and on the pettiness of ecclesiastical jealousies, but it is clearly aimed at the human, rather than at the divine element in the Church. As such, it is highly recommended, both for its content and for its literary style.

PRESCOTT, HILDA F. M. *The Man on a Donkey.* Macmillan, 1952. 631 p. $5.00. Macmillan, 1962. pa. $2.50.

The author, a non-Catholic and a popular historical writer, tells in chronicle form the story of the beginnings of the Protestant Reformation in England. The story moves around the characters of Henry VIII, his chancellor Cardinal Wolsey, and Thomas Cromwell. Miss Prescott is one of the most polished writers of popular history, and her work is recommended to every reader.

ROBINSON, HENRY MORTON. *The Cardinal.* Pocket Books, 1963. x, 579 p. pa. 75¢.

Robinson's famous novel deals with the life of a young man who becomes successively a priest, bishop, and eventually a cardinal. It is an expertly told story, from a literary standpoint, and although it may leave something to be desired in depth of characterization, it represents a fund of exact information on the inner workings of the machinery of the Church as well as being a fascinating story.

SIENKIEWICZ, HENRYK. *Quo Vadis?* Dodd, 1955. 541 p. $1.98. Bantam, 1961. pa. 75¢.

This famous novel is based on the life of the early Christians in Rome during the reign of the Emperor Nero. The plot concerns the love of Ligia, a Christian, for Vinicius, a pagan. Eventually, Vinicius is converted, but he and Ligia, along with other Christians, are caught up in the persecutions and condemned to die in the arena. Because of a remarkable display of strength and skill on the part of Ligia's slave, Ursus (who plays a large part in the story), the Christians are set free and Ligia and Vinicius are reunited. There are many thrilling scenes conveying the color and splendor of Imperial Rome, and the novel shows a rare combination of historical erudition and narrative skill.

UNDSET, SIGRID. *Kristin Lavransdatter.* Translated by A. G. Chater. Knopf, 1935. 1065 p. $6.50.

This modern classic is a novel trilogy comprising *The Bridal Wreath* which relates the love story of Erlend Nikulaussön and Kristin Lavransdatter, ending with their marriage; *The Mistress of Husaby*, telling the story of the protagonists' fifteen years of married happiness and political troubles at their estate of Husaby; *The Cross,* describing the misfortunes by which Kristin and her husband lose their fortune and the ways in which each character faces the crises thus presented. *Kristin Lavransdatter* is set in medieval Scandinavia, and is recognized as one of the great historical novels of this, or any other, age. For it, the author, a convert to Catholicism, received the Nobel Prize for Literature.

UNDSET, SIGRID. *The Master of Hestviken.* Translated by A. G. Chater. Knopf, 1934. 1065 p. $6.95.

The Master of Hestviken comprises four novels: *The Axe, The Snake Pit, In the Wilderness, The Son Avenger.* The story developed in those four books concerns the life of Olav, the hero, as played out in thirteenth-century Norway. Olav marries his foster sister, eventually kills two men (one for seducing his wife), and takes refuge as the vassal of a powerful nobleman, in whose service he eventually dies a tragic death. (These novels are available individually in paperback from Pocket Books, at 50¢ ea.)

WAUGH, EVELYN. *Brideshead Revisited.* Dell, 1956. 351 p. pa. 75¢.

This is probably the most widely read of the great English Catholic novelist's books. It is the story of Charles Ryder, an English youth who is raised to a life of ease and pleasure only to find himself caught up in World War II and forced to accept the responsibilities of being a human being. Though the story has a serious message, it is filled with wit and subtle humor, with splendid characterizations, and with hilarious situations. The book is highly recommended to adults as the best work of one of the best of contemporary authors.

WERFEL, FRANZ. *The Song of Bernadette.* Translated by Ludwig Lewissohn. Compass, 1956. xiii, 466 p. pa. $1.65.

Of all the books on Bernadette and Lourdes, this is by far the most popular and the most gratifying to read. The author, a Jew, presents Bernadette Soubirous as a person who became a saint, not as an unearthly, unhuman saint who was born already canonized. The translation is flowing and highly readable, and this is a "must" book for anyone who has not yet read it.

WEST, MORRIS. *The Devil's Advocate.* Morrow, 1959. 319 p. $3.95. Dell, 1962. pa. 60¢.

Morris West's best-selling novel is the story of a priest of the Roman Curia who is assigned to investigate the case of an Italian layman who is being considered for canonization. The priest's position is that of "devil's advocate"— that is, he is responsible for turning up any reasons why the man should not be declared a saint. The book is not always complimentary to the men or methods of Rome, but if it is read as a study of the ways in which both holiness and silliness may manifest themselves in human beings, instead of as an evaluation of ecclesiastical bureaucracy, it makes exciting and suspenseful reading.

WEST, MORRIS. *The Shoes of the Fisherman.* Morrow, 1963. 374 p. $4.95. Dell, 1964. pa. 75¢.

Morris West, author of the best-selling *Devil's Advocate,* writes a novel about the Church of the near future, when a Russian Eastern-Rite bishop is elected pope and is faced with the problem of averting nuclear war between his native country and the United States. There are several subplots, posing problems in the morality of politics, social justice, ecclesiastical censorship, etc. A fascinating tale, this is the most popular of West's novels.

THE SHORT STORY

A word about the particular type of fiction known as the short story should be included in this section. Basically, the short story, as its name implies, is a shortened version of the novel. To the extent that the short story is fiction, that it involves characters in one or a series of incidents, that it draws on all human experience for material, the analogy is true. But the short story has been developed to such a state that it is a unique literary form worthy of at least special treatment under the general heading of fiction. It is more compact than the novel (about 10,000 words is usually considered its limit; anything in excess is a "novella" which is a long short story or a short novel depending on the reader's—or author's —viewpoint); its characters and incidents are fewer and more scantily treated and developed than in the novel; and above all it concerns itself with a particular effect usually revealed in a dramatic climax. There is a particular approach, a special flavor, and a unique craftsmanship in the structure and form of the short story, so that only in its particular form could the story being told exert the appeal it does.

For example, J. F. Powers is considered to be one of the finest short story writers of our times, a master of that form. You are aware of his mastery from the first word of any of his short stories. And yet, when one finishes one of Powers' short stories, it would be impossible to envisage it in any other form than the short story. Slightly longer in length is Paul Horgan's *Devil in the Desert*, one of the greatest works in the whole of American literature, a perfect gem. It is perfection as it is; a complete literary entity. It just could not be anything else but a long short story. If it were, it would not be the masterpiece that it is.

It is interesting to note that the modern form of the short story is of comparatively recent origin, dating back only to the mid-nineteenth century. Perhaps more than any other author, Edgar Allan Poe was responsible for the interest in the short story both because of stories which came from his pen and popularized this form and because his critical theories of this literary form have shaped our modern concept of the short story.

It is also a curious fact, not easily explained, that Catholics have excelled in short story writing. The names of J. F. Powers, Paul Horgan, Flannery O'Connor, Frank O'Connor, Sean O'Faolain immediately spring to mind, and it seems more than mere coincidence that these authors, among the greatest short-story writers on the contemporary scene, are all Catholic. If you add to this list those short-story writers who have had a Catholic background, the result is a *Who's Who* of today's leading short-story writers.

However, we do not wish to belabor these points, nor enter into any prolonged discussion as to what technical aspects of the short story give it its unique flavor. This we leave for the textbooks on the short story. Suffice it to say that it is a genuine literary form, that we are blessed with a fine group of short-story writers, and that the short story has much to offer to any reader. For further proof, we refer you to the following list of short stories which offer something of great value for each individual reading taste.

CONNOLLY, F. X. and BRUNINI, J. G., Editors. *Stories of Our Century by Catholic Authors*. Image, 1955. 317 p. pa. 95¢.

A collection of twenty-five of the best short stories of our time written by Catholic authors. The writers represented are, among others: G. K. Chesterton, Heywood Broun, Graham Greene, Bruce Marshall, J. F. Powers, Evelyn Waugh. The stories themselves run the gamut from character studies and action stories to tales of mystery.

FREMANTLE, ANNE, Editor. *The Greatest Bible Stories*. Stephen Daye, 1951. 239 p. $3.50. Image, 1957. pa. 85¢.

This is a world anthology of Catholic fiction. All the selections have in common that they take the Bible as the basis of their stories. The stories themselves—by such writers as François Mauriac, Ronald Knox, and Paul Claudel—are so arranged that the life of Christ unfolds chronologically.

GARRITY, DEVIN ADAIR, Editor. *44 Irish Short Stories*. Devin Adair, 1955. 500 p. $5.00.

The editor has assembled a collection of stories having to do with Ireland and things Irish, written by Irish authors. The stories are, for the most part, well written and interesting, and are not available elsewhere. The book is excellent material for light reading.

GREENE, GRAHAM. *21 Stories*. Viking, 1962, 245 p. Compass, 1962. pa. $1.25.

This collection of Graham Greene's short stories contains some of the finest fiction of this best-selling author. Among the stories are: "The Basement Room," "I Spy," "When Greek Meets Greek," "The Hint of an Explanation," and "A Chance for Mr. Lever." Many of these stories, like most of Mr. Greene's writings, are intended for, and highly recommended to, an adult audience.

HERR, DAN and WELLS, JOEL, Editors. *Blithe Spirits*. Doubleday, 1962. 236 p. $4.50. Image, 1963. pa. 95¢.

Catholics have always suspected that, beneath the topsoil of profound truths and liturgical solemnity, there lay a rich vein of humor. This book is a collection of that humor as recorded by many of the great names of modern letters: G. K. Chesterton, Jean Kerr, Cornelia Otis Skinner, Phyllis McGinley, Evelyn Waugh, etc. Highly entertaining.

O'CONNOR, FLANNERY. *Everything That Rises Must Converge*. Farrar, 1965. 269 p. $4.95.
This best-selling collection of short stories is by an author who is widely recognized as one of the major literary talents of our time. The stories, almost all of which are situated in the South, are concerned with man's search for identity and self-knowledge. The action is consistently violent: a young boy's suicide, a mother's heart attack, a murderous fight between a grandfather and his nine-year-old granddaughter. As with all of Miss O'Connor's writings, these stories are intended for a mature and discriminating audience.

O'CONNOR, FLANNERY. *Three*. Signet, 1964. 476 p. pa. 95¢.
This volume is a composite of some of Miss O'Connor's short stories and novels, and reproduces in full *A Good Man Is Hard to Find* (short stories), *Wise Blood,* and *The Violent Bear It Away* (novels). Both the novels and the short stories are set in the South of the U.S., and deal mostly with the problems and circumstances of lower-middle and lower class citizens. These works are gems of literary technique, but many readers will find some situations too gruesome for their taste. In any case, Miss O'Connor's work can be recommended only to the discriminating adult reader.

O'CONNOR, FRANK. *The Stories of Frank O'Connor*. Knopf, 1952. vi, 367 p. $4.95. Vintage, 1958. pa. $1.45.
This is a collection of twenty-seven short stories by one of today's best storytellers, all the stories reflecting some phase of life in Ireland. They are amusing, compassionate, and told with extraordinary warmth and skill. Among the pieces in this collection are: "My Oedipus Complex," "Old Fellows," "The Pretender," "News for the Church," "Legal Aid," and "The Holy Door." (Frank O'Connor is a pseudonym for Michael O'Donovan; under the latter name, the author is well known in this country as a critic and lecturer.)

O'FAOLAIN, SEAN. *The Finest Stories of Sean O'Faolain*. Little, 1957. xvi, 385 p. $4.75.
A compilation of short stories, this work is a representative

collection of some of the best work of one of Ireland's most accomplished fiction writers. Among the twenty-seven selections—all of them about Ireland and things Irish—are "Midsummer Night Madness," "Fugue," "A Born Genius," "The Judas Touch," "End of the Record," and "An Enduring Friendship."

POWERS, J. F. *The Presence of Grace.* Atheneum, 1960. 191 p. pa. $1.25.

One of the great short-story writers of our times has composed these tales with one purpose: to show that human weaknesses are always able to be countered by unsuspected human greatnesses. Without exception, these stories are remarkable for their understanding and love of humanity, and they will provide outstanding reading for every type of reader.

POWERS, J. F. *Prince of Darkness.* Image, 1958. 189 p. pa. 85¢.

This is a collection of short stories by a writer whose craftsmanship has been widely and loudly praised. Powers writes about baseball and jazz, old people and children, boxers and Negroes; but above all he writes about priests, and he does it with rather frightening insight. Clever writing, entertaining, and recommended for all tastes. There isn't a plaster saint in the book.

WAUGH, EVELYN. *The World of Evelyn Waugh.* Selected and edited by Charles J. Rolo. Little, 1958. xvii, 411 p. $6.50.

This volume is a collected sampling of Evelyn Waugh's work, comprising short stories, the complete text of his novel *The Loved One,* and excerpts from eight other novels (including the second part of *Brideshead Revisited*). An introduction by the editor furnishes biographical and critical information.

10. HISTORY

Since the dawn of civilization, man has always been interested in recording the events of his life on earth. What man
has done and the effect of his actions on other men have
been the source of a tremendous literature which we label
"history."

As time went by and the numbers of men increased and
spread all over the earth, the record of his activities of necessity became more specialized to cope with the magnitude of
his interests and his many activities. In modern times, as
society has become increasingly complex, the compartmen-
talization of various aspects of history has become essential
if the incredible varieties of man's activities are to be recorded with some measure of order and thoroughness. Consequently, we have histories and historians concerned solely
with the economic aspects of history; or the social; or the
political; or the intellectual.

But in addition to specialized treatment of general history,
another type of specialization has come into being. This is the
treatment of a particular segment of history. For example,
Egyptology is now a very exact branch of history, limited,
within well-defined chronological boundaries, to a study of
ancient Egyptian culture. The study of individual dynasties
of ancient China is a similar particularized study. Such disciplines, of course, are confined to a single era in the history
of mankind and are concerned with civilizations long since
passed from the immediate and direct concerns of modern
man.

But there is another type of specialized history which concerns itself with man in a particular guise which *is* very much
in the thoughts of men today as they struggle with the
overwhelming problem of a nuclear age; it is the study of
the Christian Church, certainly the most unique and unusual
organization of all human history. As Lord Macaulay so elo-
quently put it:

"There is not and there never was on this earth, a work of human policy so well deserving of examination as the Roman Catholic Church . . . She saw the commencement of all the governments and of all the ecclesiastical establishments that now exist in the world; and we feel no assurance that she is not destined to see the end of them all. She was great and respected before the Saxon had set foot on Britain, before the Frank had passed the Rhine, when Grecian eloquence still flourished in Antioch, when idols were still worshipped in the temple of Mecca. And she may still exist in undiminished vigour when some traveller from New Zealand shall, in the midst of a vast solitude, take his stand on a broken arch of London Bridge to sketch the ruins of St. Paul's."

Though the study of Church history is a specialized area of historical interest, it is in a sense as broad as the history of all mankind during the past two millennia. Indeed, for the thousand years of the Middle Ages, the story of the Church *was* the story of Western civilization, so deeply did Catholic principles permeate every nook and cranny of society. But even in the centuries before Christianity and the Church became the life of medieval man, the Church had deeply affected human history. As Christianity spread through the known world in the first four centuries of the Christian era, emperors and rulers everywhere had to reckon with this new religion. At first, opposition and suppression were the order of the day. But suppression and persecution only accelerated its spread, until finally Christianity conquered and ultimately became the dominant force in all Europe and the Middle East. With the dawn of the modern era powerful forces arose which aligned themselves against the Church and, in the nineteenth century, many learned men were convinced the days of the Church were numbered. Indeed, Napoleon in 1798 boasted that the French had "destroyed the Pope." And if the papacy ceases to exist, so too does the Catholic Church.

But despite all such dire predictions, the Church in the third quarter of the twentieth century numbers half a billion adherents and is in an unparalleled period of renewal. Few events of our times have so attracted the attention of Catholics and non-Catholics alike as the deliberations and decisions of Vatican Council II. The effect of the decisions reached there will be felt by all men of whatever religious persuasion. Such is the impact of the Catholic Church in our times.

And it is exactly this last point that makes a perusal of Church history so meaningful and important. Whatever happens in and to the Catholic Church has an impact not only on Catholics but on all men. It was true at the time Christ founded his Church. It was true when his religion was spreading through the Roman Empire. It was true when the rationalists attempted to destroy the Church in the eighteenth and nineteenth century. And it is true today when the Church is adjusting to the needs of modern man and in the process is affecting millions in Europe, in Asia, in Africa, in the Americas.

In short, no student of history can really understand the history of man without a knowledge of the Church, since the influence she has exerted in every area of human activity in the past twenty centuries has always been enormous. By the same token, no Christian can afford not to know something of the history of the Catholic Church. Today, as seldom if ever in her history, the Church is emphasizing the role of *all* her members in Church worship and activities. Such full participation requires an understanding of what the Church has been for a real appreciation of what she is. Further, the Church is vitally alive to the problems of today's world and wants her children to become deeply involved in these problems, bringing to bear Christian principles in their solution. To understand any living institution, one must know something of her background. In the case of the Church, a knowledge of her tradition and history is essential to an understanding of many of the developments of doctrine she is undergoing.

One final point should be made about Church history. Few human concerns can arouse human passions as do differences of opinion about religion. In the case of Christianity, the traumas of the Reformation are still clearly discernible even now, four centuries later. One of the most lamentable results of the Reformation is that much of the writing of Church history of these past four centuries has been polemical in nature. Historians all too frequently were more concerned with asserting sectarian viewpoints than in writing objective history. Happily, at long last, this unfortunate state of affairs is beginning to give way to the pressures of dedicated scholars of all denominations who are seeking the truth rather than defending a position or buttressing a belief. This development is resulting in a wholesale re-evaluation of historical personalities and conflicts in Church affairs. Most important of all, it is responsible for an unbiased and objective approach by historians which will help clear up many of the misconceptions and prejudices that arose from the prejudiced writings which attained widespread circulation in a time of fierce passions and which have filtered down to our times as factual presentations. In fact, all too frequently the positions so painstakingly constructed were founded on gross distortions and deliberate misrepresentations.

In the books described in this section we have made every effort to select those which conform to modern critical standards of scholarship, objectivity, and research. In a few cases, certain books are deliberately included which do somewhat carry over the old feuds and approaches. These are included in this listing because they are unrivaled on the subjects they cover, despite their weaknesses, or are the only works on those subjects; in all such cases the authors of this *Guide* have clearly labeled the shortcomings.

I. General

DANIEL-ROPS, HENRI. *The History of the Church of Christ.*

A series covering the history of the Catholic Church from its beginnings to the present day. Critics both secular and religious have been unanimous in their praise of the work. It is the first popular study of the Catholic Church which looks at the history of the Church in the context of the great events which have occurred in the history of total Western civilization. The following volumes of the series are available: *The Church of Apostles and Martyrs, The Church in the Dark Ages, Cathedral and Crusade, The Protestant Reformation, The Catholic Reformation, The Church in the Seventeenth Century, The Church in the Eighteenth Century, The Church in an Age of Revolution.* Highly recommended for all readers.

Descriptions of individual volumes will be found in their proper historical section.

DANIELOU, JEAN (s.j.). *The Lord of History*. Translated by Nigel Abercrombie. Regnery, 1958. viii, 375 p., index. $6.00.

Father Danielou, one of the great biblical scholars of modern times, examines what he calls "the inner meaning" of history. He is concerned, not with the events that are commonly called "history," but with the significance that such events have in God's plan for human salvation. His basic theme is that history consists of the works of God and the sacramental activity of the Church, together foreshadowing and preparing the events of the end of the world. The book presupposes a knowledge of theological terminology.

DAWSON, CHRISTOPHER. *The Dynamics of World History*. Edited by John J. Mulloy. Sheed, 1956. xiv, 489 p., index. $6.00. Mentor-Omega, 1962. pa. 95¢.

One of the greatest scholars of Catholicism examines in this work the relationship between religion and civilization, and shows Christianity as the basic dynamic force in man's progress through history. His approach is to analyze the four vital forces of society: biology, geography, economy, and religion, and to demonstrate their mutual interaction. The result is a synthesis that harmonizes the basic data of each of those disciplines into a modern Christian philosophy of history.

DAWSON, CHRISTOPHER. *Religion and the Rise of Western Culture*. Sheed, 1950. 242 p., notes, index. $3.50. Image, 1958. pa. 85¢.

The thesis inherent in all of Dawson's writings is that religion is the key to history. In this work, he applies that thesis to the case of Western culture, considering particularly the genesis of that civilization during the Dark Ages and its flowering in the High Middle Ages. This is a book for beginners as well as for students of medieval history; it is clearly written, and tells a fascinating story about the world in which we live.

GRANDI, DOMENICO and ANTONIO GALLI. *The Story of the Church*, revised edition. Translated and edited by John Chapin. Doubleday, 1960. 358 p., appendix, tables, index. $4.95. Image, 1966. pa. $1.25.

Beginning with the spread of the Church in the Roman

Empire, the authors record the years of persecutions, the struggles against heresy, the Church's profound influence on civilization during the Middle Ages and the Renaissance, the turmoil of the Reformation, the struggle for social justice during the Industrial Revolution, and Catholicism's present emergence into the twentieth century under the reign of Paul VI. The book is a fine piece of concise writing, and may be highly recommended as a survey of Church history.

HUGHES, PHILIP (MSGR.). *The History of the Church.* Sheed, 1934–1947. Vol. I: 405 p., maps; Vol. II: xvi, 517 p.; Vol. III: xvi, 556 p., appendices, bibliography, index. $15.00 set.

This is probably the best available comprehensive treatment of the whole of Church history from the time of the Apostles to the Protestant Reformation. The work is divided into three parts, each part forming one volume in the series. Part I deals with the founding of the Church, its early internal and external struggles, and its eventual triumph as the dominant religion of the Roman Empire. Part II considers the Church during the Middle Ages, from the time of Augustine to that of Aquinas. Part III brings the narrative to the events of the Reformation. The size of the work may make it appear forbidding, but the reader will find Msgr. Hughes' writing as entertaining as any novel.

HUGHES, PHILIP (MSGR.). *A Popular History of the Catholic Church.* Macmillan, 1962, 320 p., tables, bibliography. pa. $1.95.

Msgr. Hughes' well known work is probably the best popular presentation of the history of the Catholic Church from the time of its founding to mid-twentieth century. It is well organized, skillfully written, and gives a superlative over-all view of the development of the Church through the ages.

McKENNA, MARIAN. *A Pictorial History of Catholicism.* Philosophical Library, 1961. 318 p., notes, illustrations. $12.50.

Professor McKenna's work is essentially a collection of illustrations tied together by a short, but accurate and comprehensive, text. The two elements together comprise an enjoyable survey of twenty centuries of Catholic history. The illustrations alone are worth the price of the book; in themselves, they constitute an unusual and enlightening survey of Christian art—painting, architecture, and sculpture.

MEADOWS, DENIS. *A Short History of the Catholic Church.*
Devin, 1959. 246 p. $4.50. All Saints, 1960. pa. 60¢.

As the title indicates, this is a popular survey of twenty
centuries of Church history. Given the amount of material
which the author has had to compress into comparatively few
pages, the work covers comprehensively and adequately the
broad lines of Church history, and it will provide satisfactory
background in the subject for the general reader.

NEILL, THOMAS P., Editor. *The Building of the Human City.*
Peter Smith, 1963. 377 p. $3.50. Anchor, 1963. pa. 50¢.

This compilation of historical documents is so arranged as
to form a record of Western civilization from about 2000 B.C.
to the present. There are ninety-seven such documents, beginning with the laws of Hammurabi (c. 1950 B.C.) and including the most important historical sources of Greece and
Rome, the Middle Ages, the Renaissance, and modern times
up to the United Nations Charter. There are introductions to
the individual documents, establishing their context and their
historical importance.

WARD, BARBARA. *Faith and Freedom.* Norton, 1954. 313 p.
$5.00. Image, 1958. pa. 95¢.

The author's theme is that faith and freedom are the twin
pillars of Western civilization, and that the West cannot sur-
vive unless both of these concepts flourish. She traces the development of supernatural faith and human freedom since the
beginnings of our civilization, noting the crises that they have
faced and are facing: the growth of the omnicompetent state,
Communism, the emergence of Asia and Africa, the deper-
sonalization of society, the demand for higher standards of
living. Miss Ward advocates a mixed economy in which both
government and free enterprise would play roles and which
would support an Atlantic Union as a practical means of
strengthening the West.

II. THE ANCIENT WORLD

DANIEL-ROPS, HENRI. *Israel and the Ancient World.* Translated by K. Madge. Image, 1964. 435 p., notes, index. pa.
$1.35.

This is a history of the Jewish people from the time of
Abraham to the birth of Christ. The author places the events

of the Old Testament narrative in their proper relation to the histories of the other civilizations and peoples of the ancient world. An especially interesting treatment is accorded to the borrowing of traditions by the Israelites from the Babylonians, Egyptians, Hittites, Assyrians, Persians, and Greeks—a borrowing which allowed elements of those civilizations to pass, by way of the Bible, into the consciousness of Western civilization. The book is not "light" reading, but it is indispensable for a proper understanding of the Old Testament, and very helpful in understanding the New. (Originally published under the title of *Sacred History*.)

RICCIOTTI, GIUSEPPE. *The History of Israel*. Translated by Clement della Penta, O.P., and Richard T. A. Murphy, O.P. Bruce, 1955. 2 volumes, notes, maps, bibliography, index. $15.00 set.

A famous scholar and writer narrates the history of the Chosen People from the beginnings of their recorded history until their final dispersion. The first volume covers the period to the Babylonian Exile, and the second ends with the final fall of Jerusalem to the Romans in A.D. 135. The author's approach is popular, his narrative clear, and his style polished.

III. THE EARLY CHRISTIAN ERA

AUGUSTINE OF HIPPO, SAINT. *The City of God*. Introduction by Thomas Merton. Modern Library, 1950. xxxii, 676 p. index. $2.95. Image, 1958 (abridged version). pa. $1.55.

As St. Augustine's most important work, *The City of God* was for a thousand years one of the most influential books of Christendom. Its purpose was originally to win over to Christianity those cultivated pagans who were looking for an explanation of the collapse of the Roman Empire. The work is divided into twenty-two books: Books I–V argue against the pagan belief that polytheism is necessary to happiness; Books VI–X consider pagan concepts of life after death; Books XI–XIV examine in detail the "two cities, the City of God and the city of the world"; Books XV–XVIII explain the stage of development attained by each of the two cities; Books XIX–XXII treat of the purposes and ends of each of the cities. This work represents the first human attempt to arrive at a consistent and systematic philosophy of history.

It is not always easy reading, but it is a wholly indispensable book for the educated Christian. (The paper-bound edition cited above is taken from the three-volume edition of the *Fathers of the Church* series published by Catholic University Press.)

BEDE THE VENERABLE, SAINT. *Ecclesiastical History of the English Nation.* Translated by John Stevenson, revised with notes by L. C. Jane, introduction by Dom David Knowles, O.S.B. Everyman, 1954. xxiii, 382 p., bibliography. $1.98. Penguin, 1955 (*A History of the English Church and People*) translated by Leo Sherley-Price. pa. $1.45.

It is generally agreed that the Venerable Bede (672–735) was one of the ablest of the medieval historians. His *History* provides us with our only thorough and reliable record of the establishment of Christianity in England. After a general introduction, the work begins with the coming of Augustine in 597, and continues until 731. It gives not only an account of early English Christianity but also a history of the fusion of Anglo-Saxon culture with native British elements. The book is regarded as indispensable reading for the cultivated Christian.

COCHRANE, CHARLES NORRIS. *Christianity and Classical Culture.* Oxford, 1944. xii, 516 p., notes, index. Galaxy, 1957. pa. $2.45.

The theme of this work is the revolution in thought and action which took place during the first four centuries of the Christian era through the impact of Christianity upon the Graeco-Roman world. The first part describes the pre-Christian pagan culture of the Empire; the second studies the establishment of Christianity as the official religion of the Roman world; the third part gives an account of the formation of a specifically Christian culture, a blend of pagan learning and Christian ideals. The book closes with a masterly analysis of Augustine's *City of God.*

DANIEL-ROPS, HENRI. *The Church of Apostles and Martyrs.* Translated by Audrey Butler. Dutton, 1960. 758 p., notes, tables, bibliography, index. $10.00. Image, 1962 (2 vols.). pa. $1.35 ea.

This first volume of Daniel-Rops monumental *History of the Church of Christ* studies the establishment of Christianity in its beginnings. There is an historical account of the Gospel narratives, and a survey of the infant Church in the Roman Empire—the persecutions, Christian life in the catacombs—and of its final establishment by the Emperor Constantine first as an accepted religion within the Empire, and later as the official religion of Rome. The book includes an excellent account of early Christian, or patristic, literature, and a clear explanation of such early heresies as Donatism, Arianism, and Manichaeism.

DANIEL-ROPS, HENRI. *Daily Life in the Time of Jesus.* Translated by Patrick O'Brien. 512 p., maps, tables, bibliography. $6.00. Mentor-Omega, 1962. pa. 95¢.

This is a companion volume to this author's *Jesus and His Times,* providing a comprehensive and rather detailed account of the people, the social, cultural, religious, and political life, of ancient Israel at the time of Christ. It is well written, and is an excellent work either for independent reading or for use, with its companion volume, as an introductory study of the Christ of the Gospels.

EUSEBIUS PAMPHILI. *Ecclesiastical History.* Translated with an introduction by Roy J. Deferrari. Fathers of the Church, 1953 and 1955. Vol. I: xv, 347 p.; Vol. II: 325 p., index. $10.00 set.

Eusebius Pamphili, Bishop of Caesaria, was the foremost of the early historians of the Church, and his *Ecclesiastical History* is the most important source of information on the Church in the time prior to the Council of Nicaea (325). The work is divided into ten "books" or chapters, beginning with the life of Christ and ending with the final victory of the Emperor Constantine over his rival Licinius (324).

FREMANTLE, ANNE, Editor. *A Treasury of Early Christianity.* Mentor-Omega, 1954. xiv, 625 p., bibliography, index. pa. 75¢.

This is a collection of writings from the works of the early Christian fathers; that is, from the period of the first to the fifth centuries. The selections treat of various subjects, from Church history to theology and philosophy to spirituality, and are taken from the works of such men as Jerome, Tertullian, Eusebius, Chrysostom, Clement of Alexandria, and Augustine of Hippo. Miss Fremantle's introduction describes the historical position of the Church in the subject era.

OURSLER, FULTON and APRIL OURSLER ARMSTRONG. *The Greatest Faith Ever Known.* Doubleday, 1953. 383 p., end-paper maps. $3.95. Perma, 1960. pa. 35¢.

In a fast-moving, lucid and colorful narrative, the authors tell the story of the apostles and early martyrs, beginning a few hours after the death of Christ and ending with the cruci-fixion of St. Peter and the decapitation of St. Paul. It is a highly readable work, instructive as well as entertaining.

RICCIOTTI, GIUSEPPE. *The Age of Martyrs.* Translated by Anthony Bull. Bruce, 1959. viii, 305 p., bibliography, maps, index. $4.95.

The "age of martyrs" covered by this work begins with the great persecution of the Emperor Diocletian and ends with the accession of Constantine, roughly including the pe-riod 284–324. The author, a distinguished historian and bibli-cal scholar, has written what is essentially a history of the Church during an era that saw the last and greatest of the persecutions and the final establishment of Christianity as the dominant religion of the Western world.

TAYLOR, HENRY OSBORN. *The Emergence of Christian Cul-ture in the West.* Introduction and bibliography by Kenneth M. Seton. Torchbooks, 1958. xx, 358 p., notes, bibliography, index. pa. $1.75.

This important work goes back into classical Greece and Rome and forward into the Middle Ages, but its primary con-cern is the transitional period of the fourth through the sev-enth centuries. The author shows how pagan and Christian ideals met and mingled, and how each was changed as a re-sult into something specifically different and new: Christian culture. An eminently readable book by a great scholar, this will be as useful to the general reader as to the student. (Originally published under the title, *The Classical Heritage of the Middle Ages.*)

IV. THE MIDDLE AGES

ADAMS, HENRY. *Mont-Saint-Michel and Chartres.* Anchor, 1959. xiv, 422 p., index. pa. $1.45.

Henry Adams was renowned during his lifetime as an au-thority on American History. It is ironic, perhaps, that since his death he is best remembered for this great contribution to an understanding of the mind and faith of the Middle Ages. Essentially, the book is an examination of the faith that brought into being the great Gothic cathedrals, and one of its primary concerns is architecture as a manifestation of religious faith; but it is also concerned with such matters as the literature of the period, the earthly queens and the Heavenly Queen, and with such churchmen as Abelard, Francis of Assisi, and Aquinas. This work is a modern classic, and a brilliant interpretation of the Middle Ages for the twentieth-century reader.

DANIEL-ROPS, HENRI. *The Church in the Dark Ages.* Translated by Audrey Butler. Dutton, 1960. 868 p., notes, bibliography, index. $10.00. Image, 1962 (2 vols.). pa. $1.35 ea.

The history of the Church from the end of the fourth century to the middle of the eleventh, treating such events as the end of the Roman Empire in the West, the barbarian invasions, the conversion of the barbarians, the Eastern schism, the rise of Mohammedanism, and Charlemagne's attempt to re-establish the Empire in a Christian form.

DANIEL-ROPS, HENRI. *Cathedral and Crusade.* Translated by John Warrington. Dutton, 1957. 722 p., notes, bibliography, index. $10.00. Image, 1963 (2 vols.). pa. $1.35 ea.

A survey of the late Middle Ages, from 1050 to 1350—a period which saw the rise of the great Gothic cathedrals, the Crusades, the Inquisition, the abortive union of Church and State, the intellectual rebirth of Christianity, and the clashes between temporal and spiritual rulers.

DUCKETT, ELEANOR SHIPLEY. *The Gateway to the Middle Ages.* Ann Arbor, 1960. Vol. I: 212 p.; Vol. II: 145 p.; Vol. III: 255 p., notes, bibliographies, indices. pa. $1.75 ea.

This work, published originally in a single volume, gives an account of the civilization which arose from the ruins of the Roman Empire. The first volume is entitled *Italy,* and is the story of Italy at the opening of the Dark Ages. The second, *France and Britain,* deals with the early medieval centuries in those countries, and portrays an age when Christianity was just beginning to tame the Franks and Britons and to establish a modicum of civilization in those lands. The third volume, *Monasticism,* is an excellent description of monasticism as it developed under such figures as Benedict, Columban, and Gregory the Great. The present work, by a non-Catholic historian, is a popularly written classic, and an outstanding introduction to an understanding of the Middle Ages.

DUGGAN, ALFRED. *The Story of the Crusades*. Illustrations by C. Walter Hodges. Pantheon, 1964. 263 p., maps, notes, indices. $4.95. Image, 1966. pa. 95¢.

This is a popular history of the Crusades, from the time of Pope Urban's famous exhortation in 1095 to the fall of Acre in 1291. Well known as one of the twentieth century's great historical novelists, the author brings scholarship as well as colorful writing to this account of one of the most important movements in the Middle Ages. The book is highly recommended to students as well as to the general reader.

FROISSART, JEAN. *The Chronicles of England, France, and Spain*. Translated by Thomas Johnes; edited by H. P. Dunster; introduction by C. W. Dunn. Everyman, 1961. xxi, 616 p., tables, maps. pa. $2.15.

Jean Froissart long was regarded as one of the leading historians of the late Middle Ages (the "age of chivalry"). The content of this work is apparent from the full title: *The Chronicles of England, France, Spain and the Adjoining Countries, from the Latter Part of the Reign of Edward II to the Coronation of Henry IV*. Although Froissart is not accepted today as an historian so much as a weaver of historical tales, his work still is a valuable source of information on feudal life and manners.

GANSHOF, F. L. *Feudalism*. Torchbooks, 1961. xxxi, 170 p., notes, bibliography. pa. $1.65.

This slender work is an authoritative exposition of that social, economic, political, and military structuring of the Middle Ages known as *feudalism*. The author's style is clear and quite readable, and he presents an excellent account of a system which, to a large extent, was responsible for the making of the Middle Ages into what they were.

HASKINS, CHARLES HOMER. *The Renaissance of the Twelfth Century*. Meridian, 1957. x, 396 p., notes, bibliography, index. pa. $1.65.

The Italian Renaissance of the fifteenth century was preceded, structured, and, to a certain extent, determined by a less famous revival of learning in the twelfth century. In this work, one of the greatest American scholars of the medieval period explores that initial renaissance which manifested itself in the beginnings of Gothic art, the emergence of vernacular languages as literary media, the revival of Latin classics, poetry and Roman law, the recovery of Greek science and of much of Greek philosophy, and the origins of universities, towns, and sovereign states. The book is a literary as well as a historical classic.

HEER, FRIEDRICH. *The Medieval World*. Translated by J. Sondheimer. World, 1962. xiii, 305 p., illustrations, bibliography, index. $7.50. Mentor, 1963. pa. 95¢.

This is a social, economic, cultural, and political history of Europe from the twelfth to the fourteenth centuries. The author describes how the fluid society of the twelfth century crystallized into the medieval world of religious and intellectual rigorism, fortified frontiers, and nationalistic states. This is an excellent introduction to the later Middle Ages, by one of the great Catholic scholars of the twentieth century.

JOINVILLE, JEAN DE. *The Memoirs of the Crusades*. Translated with introduction by Sir Frank T. Marziola. Everyman, 1958. xli, 340 p., notes, bibliographies, index. pa. $1.35.

The Sieur de Joinville accompanied King Louis IX (Saint Louis) on a crusade to the Holy Land in 1248, and his work is an account of the adventures of six years' traveling and fighting among the Muslims. Book I describes the saintly Louis IX, and Book II continues the same theme, and also gives the feudal history of Champagne. The remainder of the book concerns the exploits and mishaps of the crusaders, and the account is filled with personal observations and current gossip, with colorful detail and interesting sidelights on notable personalities. The book is a valuable source of information about medieval mores, and makes for fascinating, if occasionally unintentionally amusing, reading. (This edition also contains Geoffrey Villehardouin's *Memoirs of the Crusades*.)

KNOWLES, DAVID (O.S.B.). *The Evolution of Medieval Thought*. Helicon, 1962. ix, 356 p., reading list. $5.95. Vintage, 1964. pa. $1.95.

Dom David Knowles, a leading English historian, in this work describes the main currents of medieval thought and outlines the events which gave rise to the intellectual life peculiar to the Middle Ages. Among the questions he discusses are: the place of pagan learning in the Middle Ages, the renaissance of the twelfth century, the founding of the universities, the rediscovery of Aristotle, and the achievements of the thirteenth century. The book is highly recommended as a comprehensive survey of medieval intellectual accomplishments.

POWER, EILEEN. *Medieval People*, revised edition. Barnes & Noble, 1963. 216 p., notes, bibliography, index. $4.50. Barnes & Noble, 1964. pa. $1.75.

In this modern classic of social history, Dr. Power describes the lives of six people of the Middle Ages: a Frankish peasant of the time of Charlemagne, Marco Polo, Madame Eglentyne ("the prioress" of Chaucer's *Canterbury Tales*), the young wife of a fourteenth-century Paris merchant, and two English merchants of the fifteenth century. The book is outstanding both for its literary worth and for the insight it gives into everyday life during the medieval period; it requires no particular historical preparation on the reader's part, and is recommended to everyone.

PRESCOTT, HILDA F. M. *Friar Felix at Large*. Yale, 1950. x, 254 p., notes, index. $3.75. Yale, 1960. pa. $1.25.

In 1480, one Friar Felix, a German monk, set out for a pilgrimage to the Holy Land. Basing herself on Friar Felix's journals, Miss Prescott gives a vivid picture of life in the fifteenth century by means of Felix's recounting of gossip, jokes, observations on human nature, and on how it was in the Age of Faith to enter the Holy City with all its symbols and meanings. When the friar's journal is vague, the author fills in with excerpts from other contemporary authors. The book is filled with good humor, compassion, and wit; it is an excellent piece of literature as well.

ROSS, JAMES BRUCE and MARY M. McLAUGHLIN. *The Portable Medieval Reader*. Viking, 1946. xiv, 690 p., chronological tables, bibliography. $2.95. Viking, 1950. pa. $1.65.

The aim of the editors is to give, by means of selections from contemporary documents, a picture of the whole social, political, and religious spectrum of the medieval era. They have made use, wherever possible, of sources that are not generally available, and those sources have been translated into modern English. There is an excellent introduction situating contributors and contributions within the historical framework of the Middle Ages. This is an excellent, and often delightful, initiation into the life and thought of the Middle Ages.

RUNCIMAN, STEPHEN. *History of the Crusades.* Cambridge, 1951–54. Three volumes, notes, appendices, bibliographies, indices. Torchbooks, 1964–66, 3 vols. pa. $2.25 ea.

This is undoubtedly the finest and most authoritative study of the Crusades ever to be published, from the standpoint both of literary worth and historical value. It is divided into three sections, each occupying one volume. The first part deals with the First Crusade and the foundation of the Latin Kingdom of Jerusalem; the second, with the history of that kingdom and with the crusades of the twelfth century; the third, with the history of the Kingdom of Acre and the later Crusades. The work is an indispensable addition to libraries, and will be of immense value to students of history as well as to the informed general reader.

TAYLOR, HENRY OSBORN. *The Medieval Mind,* fourth edition. Harvard, 1949. Vol. I: xx, 603 p., notes; Vol. II: viii, 589 p., notes, index. $10.00 set.

The Medieval Mind is a history of the development of thought and emotion in the Middle Ages, and it is probably the single most important work on medieval civilization to be published in modern times. It comprises seven parts: the influence of late Antiquity and of the Fathers on medieval civilization, the early Middle Ages, a comparison between the ideal and the actual accomplishments of the medieval mind, the saints, medieval society, medieval symbolism in art and architecture, medieval education, and medieval scholasticism. The concluding chapter is a superb analysis of Dante as the embodiment of the medieval synthesis.

WADDELL, HELEN. *The Wandering Scholars,* revised edition. Barnes & Noble, 1949. xxxiii, 299 p., notes, appendices, bibliography, index. $3.50. Barnes & Noble, 1956. pa. $1.75.

The priests and monks of the Middle Ages were not always engaged in writing pious lives of the saints, nor in practicing the great Christian virtues. Occasionally, they left their monasteries and schools and took to the roads to celebrate the pleasures of God's earth in verse and song. These "wandering scholars" and their works are the subject of Miss Waddell's book; she describes their life and their poetry, and gives a representative selection—the Latin text as well as an excellent translation—of their accomplishments. This is a thoroughly delightful work, well written, and enormously informative.

v. THE RENAISSANCE AND THE REFORMATION

ADAM, KARL. *Roots of the Reformation*. Translated by Cecily Hastings. Sheed, 1957. 95 p. pa. 95¢.

This is a concise introduction to the causes of the Protestant Reformation, to its actual events, and to its theological implications. For all its brevity, the book succeeds in conveying to the reader an accurate, though necessarily general, idea of the most critical period in the history of the Church.

BELLOC, HILAIRE. *Characters of the Reformation*. Image, 1958. 200 p. pa. 85¢.

This well known book, by one of the most popular Catholic historians of the twentieth century, comprises a series of biographical sketches of twenty-three of the most important personalities of the Reformation. Among the subjects are Henry VIII, Catherine of Aragon, Mary Tudor, Thomas More, Richelieu, Henry of Navarre, and Oliver Cromwell. By a judicious choice of subjects, the author manages to convey a comprehensive picture of the whole of Europe during the Reformation.

BELLOC, HILAIRE. *How the Reformation Happened*. Apollo, 1961. 290 p. pa. $1.95.

Rather than a chronological narrative, this is an analysis of the causes, course, and effects of the Protestant Reformation. Belloc, an eminent twentieth-century Catholic historian and literary figure, describes the abuses which made the Reformation not only possible but inevitable, the events of the actual schism, and the far-reaching effects of both the Reformation and the Counter-Reformation.

BOUYER, LOUIS (s.j.). *Erasmus and His Times*. Translated by Francis X. Murphy. Newman, 1959. 220 p. $3.75.

This collection of five essays treats of the Catholic experiment with humanism at the time of the Renaissance. Within that context, the book discusses the attitude of the papacy toward the revival of pagan learning, the significance of "humanist theology," the role of Erasmus in the Renaissance, the theology of Erasmus, and the final stages of humanistic theologizing. Despite a rather awkward translation, this is probably one of the best introductions, for the general reader, to the significance of the Renaissance with respect to Catholic theology.

BURCHARDT, JACOB. *The Civilization of the Renaissance.* Translated by S. G. C. Middlemore; introduction by Benjamin Nelson and Charles Trinkaus. Torchbooks, 1963. Vol. I: xxxv, 278 p.; Vol. II: xv, 238 p., notes, indices. pa. $1.35 ea.

Burchardt's work, long accepted as the standard, and well nigh definitive, work on the Italian Renaissance, still is regarded as the point of departure for modern historians of the Renaissance. Burchardt's work is divided into six parts, treating of the Renaissance's political philosophy, humanism, revival of interest in antiquity, science, social situation, and religious spirit. The author combines incredible erudition with a delightful style, and this work, probably the single most important book on the Renaissance, is required reading for the cultivated man.

DANIEL-ROPS, HENRI. *The Catholic Reformation.* Translated by John Warrington. Dutton, 1962. 640 p., notes, tables, bibliography, index. $10.00. Image, 1964 (2 vols.). pa. $1.25 ea.

This is an account of the reawakening of the true spirit of Catholicism which was brought about, to a large extent, as a result of the shock of the Protestant Reformation. The author studies that counter-reformation as epitomized in the work of Ignatius of Loyola and the Jesuits. Then follows a summary of the Council of Trent and of the history of Europe under such rulers as Philip II, Elizabeth of England, and Henri IV, in a time when religion, and not nationality, was the basis of war and peace.

DANIEL-ROPS, HENRI. *The Protestant Reformation.* Translated by Audrey Butler. Dutton, 1961. 763 p., notes, tables, bibliography, index. $10.00. Image, 1963 (2 vols.). pa. $1.35 ea.

This volume covers the period 1350 to 1564, and investigates the causes—the spiritual, disciplinary, and intellectual crises of the fourteenth and fifteenth centuries—of the storm of Protestant revolt which broke in 1517. Later chapters examine in detail the development of Protestantism from its beginnings to its final establishment as a separate church.

DAWSON, CHRISTOPHER. *The Dividing of Christendom.* Foreword by Douglas Horton. Sheed, 1965. 289 p., notes, index. $5.95.

The author studies the development of Catholic and Protestant cultures in modern times and considers most of the religious and political personalities of importance from the fourteenth through eighteenth centuries. Mr. Dawson's thesis is that the divisions in Christendom are primarily cultural, not theological, and he demonstrates his conclusion by an analysis of the military, political, diplomatic, and literary events of the period under consideration.

DOLAN, JOHN P. (C.S.C.). *History of the Reformation.* Desclee, 1965. 407 p., notes, bibliography, index. $6.75.

This excellent general history of the Reformation traces the beginnings of the revolt against papal authority to the late Middle Ages, when, as the author points out, the Church had "lost the desire to reform herself." Having established the remote causes of the Protestant schism, Father Dolan records the event itself, and the belated Catholic Reformation or Counter-Reformation which culminated in and was formalized by the Council of Trent. An objective and candid narrative, concerned with historical fact rather than with polemics, this work is highly recommended.

HUGHES, PHILIP (MSGR.). *A Popular History of the Reformation.* Doubleday, 1957. 313 p., notes, index. $4.00. Image, 1960, revised edition. pa. 95¢.

A popularly written survey of the Protestant Reformation. The author treats of the causes of the Reformation—i.e., the laxity and corruption widespread in the clergy—and studies the religious, social, and cultural circumstances of each country affected by the Reformation. Of particular interest are his analyses of the major characters of the movement: Luther, Zwingli, Henry VIII, Erasmus, Cromwell, Thomas More, Calvin, etc. The book closes with an explanation of the Council of Trent which finally achieved a reform of the Church from within.

LORTZ, JOSEPH. *How the Reformation Came.* Translated by Otto M. Knab. Herder & Herder, 1964. 115 p. $2.95.

This short work re-examines the causes of the Protestant Reformation. Avoiding the traditional pitfall of putting the entire blame either on Luther's ambition or on Rome's intransigence, Father Lortz shows how basic discontent with the clergy, lack of strong theological principles, and an underlying weakness of faith finally destroyed what, by the time of the Reformation, was really only the mere appearance of Christian unity. The present work is recommended as an historically sound and objective appraisal of a controversial historical question.

PLUMB, J. H. *The Horizon Book of the Renaissance.* Edited by Richard M. Ketchum; biographical essays by Morris Bishop et al. American Heritage, 1961. 431 p., illustrations, maps. $17.50.

This is a comprehensive and copiously illustrated picture history of the Renaissance in its artistic, social, cultural, and political aspects. The narrative supplied by Professor Plumb —one of the world's leading authorities on the Renaissance —is supplemented by nine biographical sketches on the leading figures of the period: Beatrice and Isabella d'Este, Foscari, Leonardo da Vinci, Machiavelli, Lorenzo de' Medici, Michelangelo, Montefeltro, Petrarch, and Pius II. The book is an unusual combination of artistic beauty and excellent historical presentation.

VI. THE MODERN PERIOD

ACTON, JOHN EMERICH, BARON. *Lectures on Modern History.* Introduction by Hugh Trevor-Roper. St. Martin's, 1960. 319 p. $3.75. Meridian, 1961. pa. $1.45.

Lord Acton, an eminent nineteenth-century Catholic historian, discusses such topics as the origins of the modern state, the Renaissance, the Reformations (Protestant and Catholic), Philip II, Henry VIII, and the American Revolution. The essays are non-technical in style, interesting in content, and, for the most part, factually accurate in the light of twentieth-century historical critical methods.

BELLOC, HILAIRE. *The French Revolution.* Oxford, 1960. 205 p., illustrations, maps. pa. $1.40.

Belloc presents a Catholic interpretation of the French Revolution, analyzing the chief characters of the Revolution, their motives, and concentrating on events as they affected the circumstances of the Church in France and the relations between Church and State. There is some evidence that Mr. Belloc allowed his personal convictions to influence his historical judgment on certain points—for instance, in not taking into account sufficiently the undeniable corruption of the higher French clergy as one of the causes of the vehement anti-religious sentiment of the Revolution—yet, on the whole, the book presents a fairly objective portrayal of events.

DANIEL-ROPS, HENRI. *The Church in the Seventeenth Century.* Translated by J. J. Buckingham. Dutton, 1963. 638 p., notes, tables, bibliography, index. $10.00. Image, 1965 (2 vols.). pa. $1.25 ea.

The sixth volume of the series has as its subject a century dominated by two forces: the growth of national consciousness, and the resurgence of the spirit and ideals of Catholicism. The France of Louis XIV was the meeting place of those two forces, and as the battleground France dominated all of Europe at this time. It is through France, then, that the author studies the political, intellectual, spiritual and cultural state of the Church and of Europe in this all-important century.

DANIEL-ROPS, HENRI. *The Church in the Eighteenth Century.* Translation by John Warrington. Dutton, 1965. ix, 343 p., notes, tables, bibliography, index. $10.00. Image, 1965. pa. $1.45.

This seventh volume in the series begins with an account of the intellectual revolution that paved the way for the political revolutions of the late eighteenth and early nineteenth centuries. It includes excellent studies of the Galileo affair, Descartes, Voltaire, the Protestant origins of the United States, and the suppression of the Jesuits. The period studied here is critical in the history of the Church, for during it Rome was fighting a defensive war on many fronts and seemed to be about to lose not only the battles but the war as well.

DANIEL-ROPS, HENRI. *The Church in an Age of Revolution.* Translated by John Warrington. Dutton, 1965. x, 509 p., chronological tables, notes, bibliography, index. $10.00. Image, 1966 (2 vols.). pa. $1.25 ea.

This is the eighth volume in the series, *History of the Church of Christ*, and it covers the period from the beginnings of the French Revolution (1789) up to the fall of the Second French Empire in 1870 and, in the same year, the decisive session of Vatican I. Among the events covered in this critical era are the revolutionary upheavals in France, Napoleon's relations with the Vatican, the controversial policies of Pius XI, the Church's loss of temporal power, the effects of the Industrial Revolution, the First Vatican Council, and the apparitions at Lourdes and LaSalette.

DAWSON, CHRISTOPHER. *The Making of Europe.* Sheed, 1946. xxiv, 317 p., plates, maps, bibliography, index. $3.50.

Professor Dawson was an advocate of a united Europe long before the issue became a matter of public interest. In this early work—it was originally published in 1932—he explains the historical reasons for regarding European unification not only as possible but as a historically logical step. He shows that the fragmentation of Europe was only attained, and to a certain extent is only maintained, by ignoring the basic cultural, intellectual, social, and especially religious unity of Europe—a unity that was dissolved by the Reformation but which may be restored by recognizing the common heritage, in every field, of the countries of Europe. This is a work that, despite its age, is as solid historically as it was when first written, since it deals with historical fact and with principles. In addition to its value as a recognition of the cultural unity of the Western world and of its common Christian heritage, the book provides an excellent historical synthesis of modern European history before World War II.

DAWSON, CHRISTOPHER. *Understanding Europe.* Image, 1960. 238 p., index. pa. 95¢.

A study of three interrelated themes: that Europe is a society of peoples; that Europe is a spiritual unity; and that the modern "revolt" against the culture and traditions of Europe is the result of Europe's loss of common spiritual aims and the common system of moral values derived from the Christian tradition. Within the framework of those principles, the author studies the development and symptoms of the present crisis of Western culture; he concludes that Western civilization must choose between total secularization or a return to total Christian culture. Like all of Dawson's epoch-making works, this one requires an unusual effort on the part of the reader, but it is well worth the trouble.

ELLIOTT, JOHN H. *Imperial Spain.* St. Martin's, 1964. Illustrations, maps. 411 p. $7.95.

One of the most baffling phenomena of history was the rise of Spain in the fifteenth century from the position of an obscure, poor, and thoroughly second-rate power, to the level of the wealthiest, most powerful, and most extensive empire that the world had ever seen. Equally mysterious was its decline, two and one-half centuries later, to its original status. That period of the rise and decline of Spain, from 1469 to 1716, is the subject of this work, and it is an enthralling story which analyzes such figures as Ferdinand and Isabella, Charles V, the puzzling Philip II, and their progressively ineffectual successors. The author is an eminent scholar, but his work is as exciting as any historical novel.

HALES, E. E. Y. *The Catholic Church in the Modern World.* Image, 1960. 314 p., notes, tables, bibliography, index. pa. 95¢.

Mr. Hales' book is a survey of Church history from the French Revolution to the present, covering the period with emphasis on the impact of personalities, ideologies, and events upon the exterior life of the Church—from the guillotines of the French Revolution to the Russian tanks in Budapest during the Hungarian revolt. It is a colorful presentation of an exciting era, written for the general reader.

KNOX, RONALD A. (MSGR.). *Enthusiasm: A Chapter in the History of Religion.* Oxford, 1950. viii, 622 p., bibliography, index. Galaxy, 1958. pa. $2.95.

Although this book is intended primarily to explain and place in its proper historical perspective the religious movement known as *Quietism* (a seventeenth-century mystical system based on abstraction from worldly interest and on passive contemplation of God), it covers in effect a range of related movements from early Christianity to the present day. It might be described, therefore, as a history of unusual mystical movements within the Church.

McGurn, Barret. *A Reporter Looks at the Vatican.* Coward, 1962. x, 316 p., index. $5.00.

Mr. McGurn, a foreign correspondent for the New York *Herald Tribune,* examines the Vatican and its role today. The first two sections of the book are devoted, respectively, to critical evaluations of Pius XII and John XXIII, and the final portion reports on the activities of the Vatican in the years following World War II. This is a candid work, well written in a flowing journalistic style; it is highly recommended to the general reader.

Wedgwood, C. V. *The King's War.* Macmillan, 1959. 703 p., notes, portraits, bibliography, index. $7.50.

This is a description of the English Civil War of 1641–47, as seen through the eyes of King Charles I of England. Charles was always at the center of the action, so there emerges a subtle study of the character, ideals, policies, mistakes and misfortunes of that ill-fated monarch, as well as a vivid picture of the struggle itself. The book therefore is interesting both as historical narrative and as a biographical study.

Wedgwood, C. V. *Richelieu and the French Monarchy,* revised edition. Collier, 1962. 146 p., bibliography, index. pa. $1.50.

This short biography of Cardinal Richelieu is intended to be a study of the man as a statesman rather than as a churchman. As such, there is considerable emphasis on the policies and principles of Richelieu who, in the early seventeenth century, was almost absolute ruler of France and who laid the foundations for that splendid state which Louis XIV was to inherit. As the author readily acknowledges, however, Cardinal Richelieu's statesmanship was in fact inseparable from his Christianity; from that standpoint, this is a unique and well written study of one of history's most important, and most enigmatic, figures.

Wedgwood, C. V. *The Thirty Years War.* Anchor, 1961. 508 p., notes, tables, bibliography, index. pa. $1.45.

There is probably no era of history more confused than that of the first half of the seventeenth century, when the Wars of Religion were being fought. The Thirty Years War (1618–48)—a "war of religion"—was one of the decisive episodes of European history: it decided once and for all which parts of Europe were to be Protestant and which were to remain Catholic. Miss Wedgwood sets out clearly and understandably the events and implications of that war, with special attention to the personalities of the guiding spirits of the era. Highly recommended to anyone interested in history, religious or secular.

VII. THE COUNCILS OF THE CHURCH
(see the section on the Church and the Modern World for books on Vatican Council II)

GUITTON, JEAN. *Great Heresies and Church Councils.* Harper, 1965. 183 p., bibliography, index. $4.50.

Jean Guitton, the first Catholic appointed to act as lay observer at Vatican II, has drawn upon his experiences at the council to write an analysis of some of the major heresies that have occurred since the founding of the Church. His thesis is that heresy essentially is but the arbitrary stressing of one particular aspect of reality and that it is therefore not so much the lack of truth as the overemphasis of one facet of truth. The author proves his thesis by an examination of various heresies and of their relation to the body of Catholic dogma.

HENNESEY, JAMES (S.J.). *The First Council of the Vatican: The American Experience.* Herder & Herder, 1963. 341 p., notes, bibliography, index. $6.50.

This is an account of the participation of the American bishops in the First Vatican Council (1869–70). Although the author concentrates on the personalities and accomplishments of the American participants, his scope is sufficiently wide to provide a thorough account not only of the hierarchy's activities, but also a thorough account of an ecumenical council strikingly similar, in many ways, to Vatican II. It is a work of impressive scholarship, but not lacking in humor or in interesting anecdotal material.

HENZE, ANTON. *The Pope and the World.* Translated by Maurice Michael. Viking, 1965. 133 p., illustrations, maps. $8.50.

This volume is an illustrated history of the ecumenical councils of the Church, beginning with that of Nicaea in

325 and closing with the beginning of Vatican II. Each of the councils' reasons for convocation are described and their accomplishments recorded, while appropriate illustrations—modern photographs of the places where they were held as well as reproductions of contemporary paintings—furnish a colorful and realistic stage for the proceedings. The treatment of the councils is not profound, but the book is recommended as a well-written, beautifully illustrated survey of an important facet of Church history.

HUGHES, PHILIP. *The Church in Crisis.* Doubleday, 1961. 438 p., notes, index. $4.95. Image, 1964. pa. $1.25.

This is a detailed and popularly written account of the first twenty general, or ecumenical, councils of the Church, beginning with the Council of Nicaea in 325 and ending with the First Vatican Council in 1870. The author does an excellent and thoroughly comprehensive job of placing each council in its proper historical circumstances and of explaining the origins, functions, and accomplishments of each. Since an ecumenical council has always been the result of a great crisis in the Church, this book is an outstanding introduction to the study of Church history by way of emphasis on its most important events.

JEDIN, HUBERT. *Ecumenical Councils of the Catholic Church.* Translated by Ernest Graf. Herder & Herder, 1960. v, 253 p., chronological tables, bibliographies. $3.95.

Father Jedin discusses the great councils that defined and explained the teachings of Christ, the Bible, and the early Church. Beginning with the Council of Nicaea in 325, the author goes to the "papal councils" of the Middle Ages, the Council of Trent in the sixteenth century, and the First Vatican Council, discussing the circumstances which made each council necessary and outlining the accomplishments of each. The author's work is enhanced by his emphasis on the "human" factors present in each council and by his introduction of information about extraconciliar reactions and influences to conciliar actions.

VIII. THE CHURCH IN THE UNITED STATES

BOUCHER, ARLINE and JOHN TEHAN. *Prince of Democracy.* Doubleday, 1962. 308 p., bibliography. $4.95. Image, 1966. pa. 95¢.

In this biography of James Cardinal Gibbons, the authors re-create a formative period in American social, religious, and economic history (1834–1921). Gibbons was one of the most colorful and dynamic figures of American Catholicism —as well as one of the most loved, by Catholics and non-Catholics alike. An understanding of Gibbons is essential to an understanding to the history of American Catholicism, and this biography is recommended as a well written and witty chapter in that history and as the stimulating biography of an important churchman.

ELLIS, JOHN TRACY (MSGR.). *American Catholicism.* Preface by Daniel J. Boorstein. University of Chicago, 1956. xiii, 208 p., notes, bibliography, index. $3.00. Image, 1965. 85¢.

This is an excellent, short introduction to the history of the Catholic Church in America, written by one of the most eminent of American Catholic scholars. It is probably the best short work available on the subject, and it is recommended to the reader who has an interest in discovering the source of the present strengths and weaknesses of the Church in America.

ELLIS, JOHN TRACY (MSGR.), Editor. *Documents of American Church History,* second edition. Bruce, 1962. xxii, 667 p., notes, bibliography, index. $8.50.

Msgr. Ellis has collected the historical documents which he considers most important for the study of the Church in America. The period covered is 1493 to 1961. The book is an indispensable reference work for students of American Church history.

GANNON, MICHAEL V. *Rebel Bishop.* Bruce, 1964. xvii, 267 p., plates, portraits, notes, bibliography. $4.95.

The "rebel bishop" of the title is Augustin Verot, bishop of St. Augustine, Florida, in the last quarter of the nineteenth century and one of the most interesting and controversial figures in modern ecclesiastical history. This biography brings

Verot to life as the *enfant terrible* of the First Vatican Council, and as the center of a political storm in the U.S. when he dared to defend the property rights of Southern slaveowners. Although the author obviously is in sympathy with his subject, his material is historically sound, well presented, and entertainingly instructive.

GANNON, ROBERT I. (s.j.). *The Cardinal Spellman Story.* Doubleday, 1962. vi, 447 p., plates, portraits, notes, index. $5.95. Pocket Books, 1964. pa. 75¢.

This is the first full-length biography of Francis Cardinal Spellman, Archbishop of New York and one of the most influential churchmen of the twentieth century. It covers the cardinal's life in detail, from his childhood until 1961. Occasionally, there is a discernible apologetic tendency and a consequent lack of objectivity, but the author's flowing style and long acquaintance with the cardinal have enabled him to produce an interesting and readable book about a figure of the first importance for the history of the American Church.

HORGAN, PAUL. *Conquistadors in North American History.* Farrar, 1963. 303 p., bibliography, index. $5.50.

Mr. Horgan's work covers about 250 years of the early history of Central America and of the southern and southwestern portions of the present United States. It is an account of the early explorers, conquerors, missionaries, and soldiers of fortune who established Spanish civilization and religion in the New World, and all of the famous names are here— Columbus, Cortes, de Soto, Ponce de Léon, Cabeza de Vace, Diego de Vargas, etc. A special point of interest is the unusual amount of space devoted to quotations from Indian accounts of the Spanish conquests.

LAFARGE, JOHN (s.j.). *The Manner Is Ordinary.* Harcourt, 1954. viii, 408 p., illustrations, map, index. $4.75. Image, 1957. pa. 95¢.

Father John LaFarge was one of the most respected American Catholic figures of the twentieth century, both for his ability as a man of letters and for his work in the field of social justice. This autobiography tells the story of his childhood, his student years at Harvard and Innsbruck, his entry into the Society of Jesus, his work in the missions of Maryland, and his twenty-five years with *America* magazine. It is a beautifully written and fascinating story, furnishing many insights into the history of American Catholicism during the first half of this century, and it is recommended without reservation to all readers.

LALLY, FRANCIS J. (MSGR.). *The Catholic Church in a Changing America.* Little, 1962. 143 p. $3.75.

Monsignor Lally's purpose is to examine the "public image" of Catholicism in America today. He begins by a review of the past image of the Church in this country—from the public animosity of the colonial period to the open hostility of the mid-eighteenth century, and from the rehabilitation of that image after the Civil War to the affluent and influential American Church today. Monsignor Lally finds, however, that although the Catholic image is much improved, there are many areas in which Catholics must take more seriously their civic and religious responsibilities in order to be more authentically Catholic and more positively American. There is a good deal of wit, and much wisdom in this book. It is a book for the informed Catholic, and is highly recommended to that audience.

MAYNARD, THEODORE. *Great Catholics in American History.* All Saints, 1962. xiii, 209 p., bibliography. pa. 50¢.

Twenty-one notable American Catholics are portrayed in what, because of the author's attention to background, is actually a survey of the history of the Catholic Church in the U.S. Among the subjects are Père Marquette, Junípero Serra, John Carroll, Mother Seton, Prince Gallitzin, Father Becker, Mother Cabrini, and Alfred E. Smith.

MAYNARD, THEODORE. *The Story of American Catholicism.* Image, 1960. Vol. I: 320 p., notes; Vol. II: 273 p., notes, bibliography, index. pa. 95¢ ea.

Mr. Maynard, a well known writer of popular history, has written the story of the Catholic Church in the United States. He traces the development of Catholicism in this country from its original condition as a despised minority in colonial times, through the dark days of the "Know-Nothings," to its present status as an influential and affluent force in American society. This is probably the most popular history of the American Church available today.

MELVILLE, ANNABELLE. *Elizabeth Bayley Seton.* Scribner, 1951. xix, 411 p., illustrations. $4.95.

Dr. Melville's work is a biography of the young New York widow who became a convert to Catholicism and, in 1809, founded the first native religious community for women. Her Sisters of Charity became the official source of teachers for the American parochial school system. This book is a work of solid scholarship, but the author writes smoothly and enthusiastically of her subject.

TERRELL, JOHN UPTON. *Black Robe: The Life of Pierre Jean de Smet*. Doubleday, 1964. 381 p., maps. $4.95. Echo, 1966. pa. 95¢.

Father de Smet, the subject of this biography, was a Jesuit priest and one of the pioneers of the West in the nineteenth century. He is remarkable for the enormous influence which he was able to exercise over the Indians, who regarded him as a father and leader. The author provides an abundance of Western-frontier flavor and color in this lively and popularly written narrative.

11. LITERATURE

In this section will be listed and described that type of book so felicitously called *belles lettres*—poetry, essays, and the drama. Strictly speaking, of course, fiction should be included under the heading of literature, but because of the sheer number of novels and the great interest in that literary form, a separate section is devoted to works of fiction.

Of all the forms of literature, it is in the realm covered by the term *belles lettres* that the human imagination is most free to soar untrammeled by formal bounds. With the possible exception of mystical writing, no other literary form allows and actually encourages the human spirit to range far and wide, reflecting the mystery and sensitivity and delicate nuances of that complex creation which is the human person. Indeed, it is safe to say that no form of communication devised by man compares with poetry in its ability to express abstract and mystical concepts clothed with all the beauty and splendor of a language. It is interesting to note how frequently spiritual and mystical writing approaches the poetic form. As a matter of fact, that master of mysticism, St. John of the Cross, used poetry as the perfect medium to express his sublime spiritual flights. He then based his meditations on these short poems into which he had packed such tremendous meaning. And of course, the greatest praise of God ever created by man is the unmatched poetry of the Psalms, which express, as can no other form of expression, man's innermost feelings for the God of infinity and eternity.

Granted that poetry is the ultimate in man's efforts to clothe his most ethereal thoughts in the full beauty of a language, it is a pity how the reading of poetry has languished in our times. We have become so preoccupied with the mundane and practical things of the world that we no longer have time to sit down and savor the beauty and wisdom to be found in the great poetry of the ages. We are so beset with the myriad attractions of our civilization which occupy our attention—television, the movies, magazines, newspapers, sports, travel, etc.—that we are loath to spend the time necessary for the full appreciation of poetry. Occasionally, a reading on television by a noted actor or a particularly beautiful poem quoted in a book or magazine article reminds us of what we are losing by ignoring what should be a constant source of refreshment to the spirit.

Interestingly enough, the Catholic contribution to poetry is meager. Any list of the great poets of the past century will reveal how few of them are Catholic. One explanation advanced is that the radiant beauty and deep spiritual appeal of Catholicism suffice to fill man's hunger for the spiritual and the beautiful; it is of course an explanation that is often made by Catholics for the paucity of Catholic contribution in all areas of creative writing. If so, it is only in modern times that this is true, for certainly art is one of the great creative outlets of man's nature and the greatest art of all times was executed against the background of Catholic culture and civilization. Perhaps, though, there is some measure of truth in the explanation, and the fact that for centuries now, and particularly is this true—until the past decade—in the United States, that we have been too occupied with the defense of religion to devote the intellectual and creative effort necessary to produce great poetry.

And yet there is more good poetry being written today by Catholics in the English-speaking countries than ever before. Whether this is the beginning of an era of great Catholic poetry remains to be seen. But there are unmistakable signs that such a resurgence is under way. Time alone will tell how far it will go.

However, lest the above remarks dissuade the potential reader from indulging in poetry, we hasten to assure him there is available much excellent Catholic poetry, some of it unquestionably great, as he will see from the poetry we list and describe below. We urge the users of this *Guide* to sample at least some of this material. For some it will bring back memories of what glory there is in our language; for others it will be an introduction to a wonderful experience. For all it will be a draught of loveliness from fountains of beauty.

The essay, too, is a literary form which from a cursory examination, would seem to have fallen on difficult times.

But in reality, the essay is still very much alive. What has happened to it is that it has simply changed its form. No longer the formal literary form bound by strict standards of form and content, it has burst its bounds and is now found in practically every aspect of non-fiction writing: it is widely used as a vehicle for humor; historians constantly use it; a favorite type of essay is the spiritual meditation; essays on a particular religious point are common. The essay lends itself admirably to a particular aspect of a subject; in short, the main difficulty in preparing a list of essays is identifying an essay and then deciding it belongs in this section rather than in one of the more specialized areas into which we have divided this *Guide*.

This problem has resulted in our using a rather formal definition of the essay for the material listed under that section. Webster defines an essay as "A literary composition, analytical or interpretative, dealing with its subject from a more or less limited or personal standpoint." We have used this in general as our yardstick for including material. Occasionally we have felt it necessary to add an item arbitrarily, but even in such cases we feel there is adequate reason for inclusion.

Of all the creative forms of writing probably drama is the one in which a Catholic contribution is most notoriously lacking. The Catholic dramatists are few and far between and, in general, Catholic efforts in this area are pathetic. What makes this state of affairs so frustrating is the fact that drama as we know it today is a direct descendant of the miracle play, that medieval morality pageant devoted to depicting the struggle between good and evil. The miracle play was a product of the Middle Ages which was culturally the most Catholic epoch of history.

Today, when the same forces of good and evil are still confronting each other, the Catholic drama often is merely in essence the old morality play with good and evil depicted in simplistic concepts of white and black. That the complexities of modern life have produced a wide variety of grays— so that often the opting is no longer the black-white choice of a simpler age—seems to have eluded completely most modern Catholic dramatists.

But the more serious aspect of the whole matter is that

Catholics do not even attempt to enter the field of drama in the role of playwrights in any appreciable numbers. It is, bluntly, the area of modern literature where Catholics have made little or no impression.

There are, however, some small signs that there is hope for the future. The interest in the theater reflected by the growing number of serious Catholic theater groups, the increasing awareness of the theater as a vehicle for Catholic ideas (ironically emphasized by the controversial *The Deputy*, which revealed the theater as an unrealized showcase for bringing religious questions before the public), and those few Catholics, headed by Graham Greene, who are writing for the theater, all portend better things ahead. For the present, though, one can but report that the theater as a means of expression for Catholic ideas is largely unexploited.

Despite this pessimism, we should point out that there are some fine examples to light the way for future aspirants in this field. These plays we have listed, though few, are of top-notch quality. In the years to come, it is our fervent hope that this list can be greatly amplified.

1. LITERATURE

AUGUSTINE OF HIPPO, SAINT. *The City of God*. Introduction by Thomas Merton. Modern Library, 1950. xxxii, 676 p., index. $2.95. Image, 1958 (abridged version). pa. $1.55.

As St. Augustine's most important work, *The City of God* was for a thousand years one of the most influential books of Christendom. Its purpose was originally to win over to Christianity those cultivated pagans who were looking for an explanation of the collapse of the Roman Empire. The work is divided into twenty-two books: Books I–V argue against the pagan belief that polytheism is necessary to happiness; Books VI–X consider pagan concepts of life after death; Books XI–XIV examine in detail the "two cities, the City of God and the city of the world"; Books XV–XVIII explain the stage of development attained by each of the two cities; Books XIX–XXII treat of the purposes and ends of each of the cities. This work represents the first human attempt to arrive at a consistent and systematic philosophy of history. It is not always easy reading, but it is a wholly in-dispensable book for the educated Christian. (The hard-bound edition cited above is taken from the three-volume version in the *Fathers of the Church* series published by Catholic University Press.)

Augustine of Hippo, Saint. *Confessions.* Translated by Frank J. Sheed. Sheed, 1946. 429 p., notes, bibliography, in-dex. $3.50. Image, 1960 (translated by John K. Ryan). pa. $1.35. Washington Square, n.d. (translated by Edward B. Pusey). pa. 45¢.

By common consent, the work known as the *Confessions* holds a special place among the world's great books. Although it is autobiographical in character, it is not a story of the author's life; yet, no other book has ever gone more deeply into the author's character and deeds, expressed more in-cisive judgments about the inner man, or revealed its author more fully. The book is not only a penetrating psychological study of man in search of God, but a unique document for understanding the spiritual life and a treasure house of thought for the philosopher and the theologian. After a thou-sand five-hundred years, the book still attracts countless readers, from the professional theologian to the student of literature, from the expert in philosophy to the general reader. It is recommended to all readers of whatever category as an indispensable work for the educated Christian. (Of the three translations listed above, Frank Sheed's is a very read-able rendition; that of Msgr. Ryan, in addition to being quite modern and flowing, has excellent explanatory notes; Edward Pusey's translation is regarded as the classic rendition in Eng-lish, and is stately yet, occasionally, rather hard to read with complete understanding.)

Boëthius, Anicius Manlius Severinus. *On the Consolation of Philosophy.* Translated by Richard Green. Bobbs, 1962. 199 p. $3.00. Liberal Arts, 1962. pa. $1.25.

One of the great classics of philosophy as well as of liter-ature, this book was written early in the sixth century while its author awaited execution at the hands of Theodoric the Goth. It considers such subjects as the nature of Good, and shows that Good does not consist in power or wealth, but in the possession of God. The subject of free will is examined, and finally free will is reconciled with God's plan for man's salvation. Boëthius wrote before philosophy had developed an oppressive terminology, and his book requires no particular background in that discipline. It is required reading for the educated Christian.

CERVANTES, MIGUEL DE. *Don Quixote.* Translated by Samuel Putnam. Viking, 1954. xxx, 1043 p. $4.95. Everyman, n.d. (2 vols.). pa. $1.95 ea.

An old Spanish country squire has become quite mad over tales of knightly deeds—so much so that he imagines himself a knight errant and rides out into the world to protect the weak, defend noble ladies, and slay dragons. Sancho Panza, a good-natured peasant, acts as his squire, and together they fight windmills that look like giants, storm inns that might be castles, and attempt to free slaves whom they mistake for imprisoned gentlemen. Eventually, Don Quixote dies of old age; but, as it turns out, he is not to be regretted, for he expired with his illusions intact. The true hero has become Sancho Panza, with his clear view of the basic verities and his unfettered devotion to the old fool who was his master. Originally conceived as a satire, this work is, in fact, an unequaled description of Spanish life in the sixteenth century. It is regarded as one of the great literary masterpieces of all time.

CERVANTES, MIGUEL DE. *The Portable Cervantes.* Translated by Samuel Putnam, with introduction and notes. Viking, 1951. ix, 854 p., notes. pa. $2.50.

This excellent anthology of Cervantes' works includes substantially all of *Don Quixote* (omitted parts are covered by editorial summaries), two complete novels (*Rinconete and Cortadillo,* and *Man of Glass*), and the author's famous *Farewell to Life.* This collection uses the translation which, though not in idiomatic modern English, is regarded as a classic and is unsurpassed for beauty and intelligibility.

CHAUCER, GEOFFREY. *Canterbury Tales.* Translated by Frank E. Hill. McKay, 1960. 383 p. $2.25. Washington Square, 1960. pa. 60¢.

One of the most remarkable works of English literature, *Canterbury Tales* is Chaucer's greatest work. In the prologue, the author meets a group of twenty-nine pilgrims en route to the shrine of St. Thomas à Becket at Canterbury. The company agrees that each pilgrim should tell two stories during the trip to the shrine, and two on the way back. The work was not completed, however, and there are only twenty finished tales, two unfinished ones, and two interrupted ones, instead of the 120 called for by the original plan. The setting of *Canterbury Tales* is, of course, religious, but Chaucer wrote principally to amuse and to entertain. Some of the tales are humorous, some boisterous to the point of bawdiness, and a few are chivalrous. This is one of the few classics which is every bit as entertaining now as when it was written.

CHAUCER, GEOFFREY. *The Portable Chaucer*. Edited, with introduction and notes, by Theodore Morrison. viii, 600 p. Viking, 1949. pa. $2.50.

This collection comprises selections from *Canterbury Tales*, edited and translated into modern English. The editor's introduction gives valuable information on Chaucer's religious beliefs and on his style and rhetorical devices. The book is well suited to be used as an introductory study of one of the great classics of literature.

CHESTERTON, GILBERT KEITH. *The Man Who Was Chesterton*. Edited with an introduction by Raymond T. Bond. Image, 1960. 512 p. pa. $1.45.

This is a collection of Chesterton's best essays, stories, poems, and other writings. One volume could never contain all the thoughts of this literary giant, but the book presents a comprehensive and representative selection that dramatizes the many-faceted genius of Chesterton.

COLUM, PADRAIC, Editor. *A Treasury of Irish Folklore*. Crown, 1954. xx, 620 p., index, musical notation. $5.00.

Mr. Colum has collected here in one volume most of the best known and many of the less known stories, traditions, legends, humor, wisdom, ballads, and songs of the Irish people. The work is unique in that, using methods of sound scholarship, the editor has drawn upon both written and oral compositions and traditions.

DANTE ALIGHIERI. *The Divine Comedy*. Translated by M. B. Anderson; introduction by Arthur Livingston; drawings by William Blake. Heritage, 1944. 513 p., notes, illustrations. $5.00 (boxed). Galaxy, 1961. Translation and commentary by John D. Sinclair, with Italian text. 3 vols., pa. $2.50 ea.

The Divine Comedy is a tremendous monument of the Middle Ages, symbolizing the destiny of the human soul, which, once free from error and ignorance, can attain to the contemplation of God. The work is divided into three parts: *Inferno, Purgatorio,* and *Paradiso*—describing respectively the situations of souls in hell, purgatory, and heaven. Dante tells his story as an eyewitness, guided through hell and purgatory by the pagan poet, Virgil, and through heaven by his love, Beatrice. The work, one of the most famous ever written, sums up the essence of religion, philosophy, and theology in the Middle Ages. It is indispensable reading for every educated man.

ERASMUS, DESIDERIUS. *The Essential Erasmus.* Selected and translated, with introduction and commentary, by John P. Dolan. Mentor-Omega, 1964. 397 p. pa. 75¢.

Erasmus is one of the few writers of the sixteenth century who is still popular today. This selection from his works includes the full text of his famous *The Praise of Folly,* as well as substantial excerpts from his *Addages, Colloquies, Handbook for the Christian Soldier,* etc. Dr. Dolan's translation is smooth and readable, and this collection is highly recommended to all readers and students.

ERASMUS, DESIDERIUS. *The Praise of Folly.* Translated by Hoyt H. Hudson. Modern Library, 1962. xl, 165 p., illustrations. $1.95. Ann Arbor, 1958. Translated by John Wilson. pa. $1.35.

This is one of the most popular of the Renaissance classics, and probably the only one which is still widely read. Speaking in the name of Folly, Erasmus satirizes the institutions, mores, men, and beliefs of his age. The targets of his wit include self-love, war, ecclesiastical corruption, materialism, neglect of spiritual duties, the verbosity of lawyers, etc. The book is every bit as amusing and pertinent today as when it was written—and perhaps even more needed now than it was then.

FOSTER, JOSEPH R. *Contemporary Christian Writers.* Hawthorn, 1963. 160 p., bibliography. $3.50.

The author's definition of a Christian writer is one whose work provides a concrete literary form for the abstract truths of Christianity. This volume (number 117 in the *Twentieth Century Encyclopedia of Catholicism*) therefore is concerned solely with the imaginative literature of this century that interprets life in Christian terms. It considers the modern novelists, poets and dramatists who have shown the truths of Christianity through their choice of characters, plots, settings, and styles: Chesterton, Graham Greene, Morris West, Muriel Spark, Sigrid Undset, and many others.

GARDINER, HAROLD C. (S.J.). *Catholic Viewpoint on Censorship*, revised edition. Doubleday, 1958. 200 p., notes, appendices. $2.95. Image, 1961. pa. 75¢.

Father Gardiner makes a clear statement and explanation of the Catholic position on censorship. The book is divided into three parts: the first provides the background for the subject and discusses law and liberty, authority and coercion; the second examines the Legion of Decency, the current legal climate in the U.S., the role of the boycott and "pressure" groups; the third part documents the whole discussion by presenting as appendices the most cogent arguments both pro and con. Well and popularly written, this is the authoritative book on the subject.

GARDINER, HAROLD C. (S.J.). *Norms for the Novel*, revised edition. Doubleday, 1960. ix, 180 p. $2.95.

This is the definitive Catholic study of the bearing of morality on the art of the novel and on the objectives of that art. The first part of the book discusses five principles for arriving at a moral evaluation of a novel, and the second deals with the relationship between "realism" and morality, and with the function of literature. The concluding section deals with the creative challenge of literature with respect to the reader. This book, by the foremost American Catholic literary critic of our time, will be of special value to those who are often puzzled by the apparent contradiction between "bad books" and "good writing."

MAGILL, FRANK N.; THOMAS P. NEILL, and ROBERT CAPONIGRI, Editors. *Masterpieces of Catholic Literature*. Harper, 1965. 1200 p. $9.95.

This is a collection of three hundred essay-reviews of the most important Catholic literature produced from the time of the primitive Church until the reign of Paul VI. Among the approximately two hundred writers discussed are St. Jerome, Aquinas, St. Ignatius Loyola, John XXIII, Gerard Manley Hopkins, Jacques Maritain, Dante, Hans Küng, and Gabriel Marcel. It is an attractive and useful reference work for students, libraries, and literate Christians generally.

MALORY, SIR THOMAS. *Morte d'Arthur.* Everyman, n.d. (2 vols.). $1.95 ea. Mentor, 1962. pa. 95¢.

This famous work, in addition to being the best English prose of the fifteenth century, has been the immediate source, as well as the definitive account, of the legends of King Arthur and his court for such later writers as Spencer and Tennyson. The work traditionally is divided into twenty-one books, dealing successively with King Arthur's parents, his selection as king by his drawing of the magic sword from a stone, and his subsequent career as chief of the Knights of the Round Table. The other heroes and villains of Arthurian legend are well represented: Guinevere, Sir Gawain, Merlin the Magician, Sir Lancelot, Sir Tristram and King Mark and La Beale Isoud, Sir Galahad, Sir Mordred, etc. The work remains fascinating reading for all ages.

MORE, THOMAS, SAINT. *Utopia.* Edited, with an introduction, by Edward Surtz, S.J. Yale, 1965. 254 p., notes, bibliography, index. pa. $1.75.

This classic, written in 1516, is a satire on the evils of the world and the need for a republic founded upon reason, and describes in detail what the author envisages as the ideal commonwealth. Among the startling reforms proposed are religious freedom, monetary rewards for virtue, the introduction of euthanasia, and the banning of cosmetics. The editor's introduction sets the work in its historical context, and his notes serve to clarify and expand points of particular interest. *Utopia* is required reading for the educated Christian.

NEWMAN, JOHN HENRY CARDINAL. *Apologia Pro Vita Sua.* Modern Library, n.d. 439 p. $1.95. Image, 1956. pa. $1.35.

The most famous of Newman's works, the *Apologia* is an explanation of his changes of religious opinion from his childhood until, after years of study, he entered the Catholic Church "in perfect peace and contentment." This undoubtedly is one of the great spiritual and literary classics of modern times, and it is recognized as one of the great autobiographies of the English language.

NEWMAN, JOHN HENRY CARDINAL. *A Newman Reader.* Edited with introduction by Francis X. Connolly. Image, 1964. 478 p. pa. $1.45.

An anthology of the writings of John Henry Cardinal Newman, compiled by a well known authority on Newman. The book is designed to present the full range of the Cardinal's life and thought, and records his intellectual, spiritual, and emotional growth by grouping his writings—essays, poetry, sermons, letters, and excerpts from his books—into the major and critical periods of Newman's life. The editor has provided a lengthy and valuable introduction which situates Newman in time, in history, and points out the importance of Newman and the pertinence of his thought for modern times.

PASCAL, BLAISE. *Pensées*. Translated by M. Jarrett-Kerr. Allenson, 1959. 135 p. $2.50. Penguin, 1965. pa. 95¢.

This classic is a collection of random thoughts which were taken from Pascal's notes by his friends after his death. Essentially, the book constitutes an apologia for the Christian faith, addressed to a growing class of intellectual freethinkers among the French aristocracy in the seventeenth century. There is little doubt that Pascal was something of a fanatic, and not always an orthodox one. Because, however, of the lucidity and brilliance of his reflections on common moral as well as religious questions, the *Pensées* remain a source of guidance and information for those who wish to believe but are troubled by doubt, as well as a classic of modern literature.

ROSS, JAMES BRUCE and MARY M. McLAUGHLIN, Editors. *The Portable Medieval Reader*. Viking, 1946. xiv, 690 p., chronological tables, bibliography. $2.95. Viking, 1950. pa. $1.65.

The aim of the editors is to give, by means of selections from contemporary documents, a picture of the whole social, political, and religious spectrum of the medieval era. They have made use, wherever possible, of sources that are not generally available, and those sources have been translated into modern English. There is an excellent introduction situating contributors and contributions within the historical framework of the Middle Ages. This is an excellent, and often a delightful, initiation into the life and thought of the Middle Ages.

WADDELL, HELEN. *The Wandering Scholars*, revised edition. Barnes & Noble, 1949. xxxiii, 299 p., notes, appendices, bibliography, index. $3.50. Barnes & Noble, 1956. pa. $1.75.

The priests and monks of the Middle Ages were not always engaged in writing pious lives of the saints, nor in practicing the great Christian virtues. Occasionally the monks left their monasteries, and the students left their universities, and took to the roads to celebrate the pleasures of God's earth in verse and song. These "wandering scholars" and their works are the subject of Miss Waddell's book; she describes their life and their poetry, and gives a representative selection—the Latin text as well as an excellent translation—of their accomplishments. This is a thoroughly delightful work, well written and enormously informative.

II. POETRY

BERRIGAN, DANIEL (S.J.). *Time without Number*. Macmillan, 1957. 53 p. $3.50.

Father Berrigan is one of American Catholicism's most promising poets. This volume was awarded the Lamont Poetry Prize by the Academy of American Poets in 1957, and it contains some of his most polished work. Father Berrigan writes in blank verse, in a style that is simple and stark, yet subtle, on his favorite topics: the beauty and grandeur of Nature, and the longing of man for God.

CAMPBELL, ROY. *Talking Bronco*. Regnery, 1956. 91 p. $2.50.

Mr. Campbell was one of that vanishing breed, the action poet. His poems, as the title of this collection indicates, are poems of action; they are turbulent and occasionally violent, centering around the challenges of life as their theme. Campbell's work will appeal to young readers as well as to the mature, and this collection, the poet's last before his death in 1957, is especially interesting as being representative of the poet's best work.

CHESTERTON, GILBERT KEITH. *Collected Poems*. Dodd, 1932. 391 p. $5.00.

This book is an omnibus volume of all of Chesterton's poetry that had appeared before 1932. It includes the material of *The Ballad of St. Barbara; Poems; New Poems; Wine, Water, and Song; Ballad of the White Horse; The Wild Knight;* and *Miscellaneous Poems*. Although Chesterton is better known for his essays, histories, and novels than for his poetry, his poems are of a quality equal, and sometimes even superior, to his other works, and the reader who has yet to discover them will be pleasantly surprised.

HOPKINS, GERARD MANLEY (s.j.). *A Hopkins Reader.* Edited with an introduction by John Pick. Oxford, 1953. 440 p., illustrations, notes, bibliography, indices. $4.50. Image, 1966 (revised and enlarged edition). pa. $1.45.

Dr. Pick, the editor and a leading authority on Hopkins and his work, has collected in this book all of the great Jesuit poet's completed mature poems, as well as his letters, journals or "notebooks," essays, sermons, and occasional writings. For anyone—student, casual reader, teacher, librarian—wishing a thorough understanding of this famous poet's thought and work, there is no finer introduction to Hopkins' thought and work.

JENNINGS, ELIZABETH. *Christian Poetry.* Hawthorn, 1965. 191 p., bibliography. $3.50.

The aim of this volume is to show what English and American poets have contributed to Christianity, and how Christianity has been influenced by the poetry and critical writings of English and American poets. The author begins with a discussion of the nature of Christian poetry, emphasizing that such poetry does not always come from Christian poets. There is a short history of the development of English verse, from Anglo-Saxon times to the present, with particular attention to the writings of Eliot, Auden, Edwin Muir, and David Jones. (Volume 118 of the *Twentieth Century Encyclopedia of Catholicism.*)

JOHN OF THE CROSS, SAINT. *Poems.* Translated by Roy Campbell; preface by Martin C. D'Arcy, s.j. Pantheon, 1951. 90 p. $2.75.

St. John of the Cross is perhaps as famous for his burning poetry as for his mystical theology. In this volume, Roy Campbell—himself a well known poet—renders into modern English St. John's poetic works, among them "The Dark Night," "The Spiritual Canticle," "The Living Flame of Love," as well as the various "Stanzas," "Romances," and "Commentaries." The original Spanish text appears alongside Campbell's translation.

KILMER, (ALFRED) JOYCE. *Trees, and Other Poems.* Edited by Robert C. Holliday. Doubleday, 1934. 271 p. $2.50.

This is a collection of the great Catholic American poet's famous and less known poems, and presents a representative selection of his works. The editor has contributed a detailed, if rather idealistic, biography and critique of Kilmer's work.

McGINLEY, PHYLLIS. *The Love Letters of Phyllis McGinley.* Viking, 1954. ix, 116 p. $3.95. Compass, 1960. pa. 95¢.

This is a collection of light verse by a best-selling Catholic poet. The poems take an amusing, and sometimes touching, look at the faults and foibles of the author herself ("Why must I talk so much at parties?") and at the idiosyncrasies of her family, as in the tender "Ballade of Lost Objects." Miss McGinley writes clearly and simply, avoiding the cult of obscurity that is fashionable today; her poetry has one purpose: to delight. It does that.

McGINLEY, PHYLLIS. *Times Three.* Foreword by W. H. Auden. Viking, 1960. xvi, 304 p. $5.00.

This collection contains three hundred pieces of light verse, dealing with a variety of subjects and conveying a variety of moods: irony, satire, gaiety, compassion. Miss McGinley, a Pulitzer-Prize winner and probably the most widely read contemporary American poet, will entertain and enchant even the reader who does not like poetry.

MARITAIN, JACQUES. *Art and Poetry.* Translated by E. duP. Matthews. Philosophical Library, 1943. 104 p. $1.75.

This small work comprises three essays. The first treats of the work of three modern painters: Marc Chagall, Georges Roualt, and Gino Severini. The second essays, entitled "Dialogues," is concerned mostly with the relationship of art and morality in the novel, and within that context examines some of the work of Mauriac, Dostoevsky, and Gide. The third, "Freedom of Song," discusses music as an art in modern times, and deals with Stravinsky, Lourie, and Satie. The thesis throughout the book is that artistic greatness cannot exist unless the artist knows God and possesses humility, intelligence, and love. This work, despite its excellent translation, is not always easy reading, but it may be recommended as a brief but incisive statement of principles on the relation between artistic and spiritual beauty.

MARITAIN, JACQUES. *Creative Intuition in Art and Poetry.* Pantheon, 1953. viii, 423 p., notes, plates. $7.50. Meridian, 1955. pa. $1.55.

The most esteemed Catholic philosopher of modern times explains his concept of creative intuition as the mark of genius in art. He also applies that criterion to poetic values and to the evaluation of painting, illustrating his points by extensive quotations from famous poets and by the use of excellent reproductions of works of art. This book is, in effect, the synthesis of Maritain's thought on aesthetics. It is not easy reading, but it is highly recommended to those involved or interested in the literary or plastic arts.

MERTON, THOMAS. *Selected Poems*. Introduction by Mark Van Doren. New Directions, 1959. xvii, 139 p. pa. $1.35.

In this collection of Merton's poetry are included selections from five previously published volumes along with three new poems, and the essay "Poetry and Contemplation: A Reappraisal" discussing the author's views on the value of poetry in the contemplative life and the mutual influence of poetry and the monastic or contemplative life on one another. The poetry in this volume is probably the most representative selection available.

NOYES, ALFRED, Editor. *The Golden Book of Catholic Poetry*. Lippincott, 1946. Preface, xxix, 440 p., indices. $4.50.

This is a collection of the work of Catholic poets through the ages. Among the poets represented are Chaucer, Langland, Southwell, Crashaw, Pope, Dryden, Moore, Mangan, Patmore, Meynell, Thompson, Hopkins, Belloc, Chesterton, Colum, and Noyes, as well as many other major and minor figures. The editor has contributed an excellent introduction establishing the relationship between the Christian spirit and poetry. This is an excellent and thoroughly representative anthology of the best work of the best Catholic poets.

PÉGUY, CHARLES. *Basic Verities*. Translated by Anne and Julian Green. Pantheon, 1943. 282 p., notes. $2.75.

This is an assortment of excerpts from the writings of Péguy, one of the giants of modern Catholic letters. The collection includes some of the author's most moving passages on the people of France, on poverty, on politics and mysticism, on the Jews, and on Joan of Arc. This edition contains both the French texts and their English translation. There is a biographical introduction.

PICK, JOHN. *Gerard Manley Hopkins: Priest and Poet.* Foreword by Martin Cyril D'Arcy, s.j. Galaxy, 1966. 179 p., plates, bibliography, index. pa. $1.35.

This unusual biography has as its subject Gerard Manley Hopkins, English Jesuit priest and poet. In addition to a treatment of Hopkins' life and career, the author devotes much space to an interpretation of Hopkins' work, and integrates into his text many quotations from the Jesuit's poetry, letters, and notebooks. This is probably the best introduction to the work of Hopkins available today.

THOMPSON, FRANCIS. *The Hound of Heaven.* Dodd, n.d. 62 p. $1.75. Morehouse, 1953. pa. 40¢.

The Hound of Heaven is perhaps the most widely read poem of modern times. It depicts Divine Love as the "hound of heaven," pursuing unwilling Man who attempts to flee because he fears that, if he accepts God's love, he will have to give up everything else. Never has man's reluctance to submit to the inevitable been depicted with more power or more magnificent imagery than in this work.

THOMPSON, FRANCIS. *Poems of Francis Thompson,* revised edition. Edited, with biographical and textual notes by Terence L. Connolly, s.j. Appleton-Century-Crofts, 1947. xxiv, 587 p., bibliographies, indices. $4.50.

Francis Thompson is probably one of the most popular and best loved of modern English Catholic poets. Although he is best known for the imperishable "The Hound of Heaven," which has come to be recognized as a modern classic, several of his other works show the same depth of religious feeling and technical proficiency, e.g., his "Ode to the Setting Sun." This Thompson anthology contains all of Thompson's poetry, enhanced by an excellent and revealing set of notes by Father Connolly. It is probably the best such collection available, and it may be recommended to everyone interested in poetry.

VALÉRY, PAUL. *The Art of Poetry.* Translated by Denise Folliot; introduction by T. S. Eliot. Vintage, 1958. xxiv, 345 p., notes. pa. $1.45.

Paul Valéry was one of the giants of French letters in the twentieth century; he was famous as a poet, essayist, critic, and philosopher. In this work Valéry examines the nature of poetry, its form, its method, and its purpose. The book essentially is a work of literary criticism, and so its primary audience will be an academic one; it is not, however, an overly technical book, and will be useful to the general reader as well.

III. DRAMA

ANOUILH, JEAN. *Becket, or The Honor of God.* Translated by Lucienne Hill. Coward, 1961. 128 p. pa. 60¢.

A famous French playwright's drama in three acts about the arrest and trial of Thomas Becket, the friend, and finally the victim, of King Henry II of England, when he dared to oppose the latter in his attempt to take control of the Church in England. The play is highly recommended, both for reading and for viewing, for its literary, dramatic, and spiritual qualities.

BOLT, ROBERT. *A Man for All Seasons.* Random House, 1962. xxv, 163 p., illustrations. $3.95.

This is the award-winning Broadway play about St. Thomas More, the friend and chancellor of Henry VIII, who was disgraced and died a martyr's death because of his refusal to acknowledge the king's supremacy over the Church in England.

CLAUDEL, PAUL. *The Satin Slipper.* Translated by John O'Connor. Sheed, 1955. xxvii, 310 p. $3.50.

First published in 1929, this play was written while Claudel was French ambassador to the United States. At that time, it gained wide popularity here. The plot concerns the unfortunate love of Dona Prouheze for Don Rodrigo, and its theme is one that plays a large part in all of Claudel's writings: the salvation of the individual, and the responsibility of individuals for the salvation of one another. This is one of those plays which is more suited to reading than to viewing, and it was probably written as such. It is one of the author's most compelling pieces.

DUPREY, RICHARD A. *Just off the Aisle.* Newman, 1962. xiv, 209 p. $3.95.

The author, a teacher and drama critic, offers reflections on the state of contemporary theater. The subjects covered by these essays include the place of the Catholic critic in the modern theater, sex and morality in the theater, the place of modern comedy, and the role of drama in man's relations with God.

ELIOT, T. S. *Murder in the Cathedral.* Harper, 1935. 87 p. $2.75. Harcourt, 1965. pa. $1.25.

T. S. Eliot is generally considered the outstanding poet and critic of the modern English-speaking world. Among other distinctions, he received the Nobel Prize for Literature in 1948. *Murder in the Cathedral* is probably his best known and most enduring play. It recounts the struggle between Thomas à Becket, Archbishop of Canterbury, and King Henry II, over the respective rights of pope and prince in medieval England, culminating with the murder of Becket in 1170. The play is in rhymed as well as unrhymed verse, and is representative of Eliot at his best.

GREENE, GRAHAM. *The Potting Shed.* Viking, 1956. 123 p. $3.00. Compass, 1961. pa. 95¢.

A play in three acts by one of the twentieth century's most widely read Catholic writers, this work deals with religion and the faith of childhood years in an adult who is estranged from his family. As a literary work and as a study in human psychology, this religious drama is recommended reading.

ROSE, MARTIAL, Editor. *The Wakefield Mystery Plays.* Doubleday, 1962. 552 p. $5.95.

This is the complete acting version of the original text of the thirty-two plays of the Wakefield cycle. These pieces date back to the fourteenth and fifteenth centuries, and form part of the body of semiliturgical dramatic works, all dramatizing events from the Old and New Testaments, in common use before the advent of the modern theater. This edition of the plays contains notes on production and staging.

SPEAIGHT, ROBERT. *Christian Theatre.* Hawthorn, 1960. 140 p. $2.95.

Mr. Speaight, a British critic and an authority on the theater, traces the presence of Christianity in the more important sections of European drama during the past seven centuries. Beginning with the "miracle plays" of the Middle Ages, he continues on to the dramas of the Reformation and of the Renaissance, of Elizabethan England with particular attention to Shakespearean theater, of seventeenth century Spain in the person of Calderon, and of the classic French theater of Corneille and Racine. The concluding section considers the decline of Christian influence in the theater of the nineteenth century, and its renaissance in the twentieth century in the works of Claudel, Anouilh, Greene, etc. (This is volume 124 of the *Twentieth Century Encyclopedia of Catholicism*.)

12. THE LITURGY

The first important document approved by Vatican Council II was the *Constitution on the Liturgy* promulgated by Pope Paul VI at the closing of the Second Session on December 4, 1963. In view of the high hopes held by Catholics and non-Catholics alike for Vatican Council II, it came as a shock to many that the main result of the first two sessions of this Council was a paper on the liturgy. After all the weeks and months of work and debate and struggle, for the assembled bishops of Roman Catholicism to have issued a document which seemed merely to regulate the arrangement of various liturgical practices seemed somewhat akin to the mountain that labored and produced a mouse.

Now that so many of the changes recommended by the Constitution have been put into practice and the effects of these new practices have been studied, the wisdom of the Council Fathers effecting changes in the liturgy as the first definite contribution of the Council is clearly apparent. What most people did not realize was that the most minute change in the liturgy immediately affected practically every individual in the Church. This, of course, is especially true of the Mass. The slightest change in the Mass affects every Catholic who practices his faith, and when such drastic changes as substituting vernacular languages for the traditional Latin, and having people participate actively in the Mass—instead of, as had previously been the case, passively attending Mass —then indeed every individual is directly, immediately, and personally affected. No other method could have been devised which would so effectively bring home to the great masses of Catholics the fact that their Church is in the process of reform and renewal to meet the challenges of twentieth-century life.

Now that some of the changes have been put into widespread practice, it is evident that Catholics everywhere have become more deeply involved in the public worship of their Church, whether they be in favor of the changes, resolutely opposed to them, or taking a wait-and-see attitude; but affected and involved they are, as most of them have never been in their entire lives.

With her usual wisdom, the Church has been using the changes in the liturgy to drive home to her children a series of lessons. The first obviously is the benefit all Catholics derive from participating more actively and consciously in the public worship of the Church. No longer is the Mass to be considered a service to which an individual goes to lose himself in his own private worship and meditation. The Mass is a social function at which all the parishioners join together in the worship of God. If one remembers that the original concept of the Mass as instituted by Christ was that of a Eucharistic feast where his apostles gathered with him to break bread together and offer worship to God, then it is clear that these seemingly revolutionary changes are in reality simply a return to the basic forms of the Mass instituted by Christ and practiced by the early Christians. The Church has returned to this original and basic concept of the Eucharistic sacrifice as a communal act with all joining in.

There is a further more subtle benefit resulting from the greater active participation of the individual in the liturgy. Pope Paul and the Council Fathers have repeatedly indicated their desire for the Church and individual Catholics to become more involved in the great social issues facing the world today. Just as the individual Catholic is an integral part of the Church and must participate in the Church's worship and activities, so too he is a member of the family of man and must become more closely involved in helping to solve the problems of mankind. His involvement in the new liturgy on a communal basis, with his consequent realization that he is a participating member of a group, will undoubtedly increase his social consciousness by making him more cognizant of what membership in a group means. This increasing awareness of his social role in the community of his Church is of inestimable value as a training for his role in the community of man and for his increasing participation in attempts to solve the pressing social problems of our times.

Under the new liturgy, the Mass is divided into two parts: the Liturgy of the Word and the Liturgy of the Eucharist.

We have already mentioned above the Church's renewal of emphasis on the Liturgy of the Eucharist, but in the Mass the Liturgy of the Word precedes and leads up to the Liturgy of the Eucharist. In this part of the Mass the Church emphasizes the word of God as revealed through the Bible. Greater emphasis on Bible readings and on homilies based on the Bible has renewed the early Christian concept of the Bible as the word of God and the source of spiritual strength for the Christian. As time goes by and more perfect vernacular translation of the Epistles and Gospels are made available, this renewed emphasis on the word of God will have greater and wider effect on the faithful.

Above all, though, the whole point of the renewal of the liturgy has been to re-emphasize the fact that the liturgy is public worship and that public worship calls for participation by the public. And such participation by the individual can be most fully realized if one is aware of the meaning of the liturgy, how it developed and what the Church intends the new liturgy to do. The drastic changes that have been put into effect are all of recent origin, but the genesis of these changes is to be found in the studies that have been going on among liturgical specialists for many years.

For the average individual, such information can be found only in books on the subject. And fortunately, there is a wealth of such books explaining and describing in the fullest detail the new liturgy. As is true of each group of listings in this *Guide*, we have tried to avoid listing books on the liturgy which are obtuse or so scholarly as to be understandable only by the most experienced liturgist. But some of the subjects treated are rather difficult because of their very nature; where such books are foundation books, we have listed them and indicated they may be rather difficult.

In view of the relative newness of the liturgical reforms, the books listed and described below will mainly be of recent publication. However, we have included some of the older books which are still valid today and which will reveal the development of thinking in this area and will show how the labors of so many often-maligned liturgists have now come to fruition. We strongly urge any readers of these pages to dip deeply into the springs of liturgical writings and promise unreservedly that any efforts in this field will amply repay those who draw from their knowledge and wisdom.

BOUYER, LOUIS (C.O.). *Liturgical Piety.* Notre Dame, 1957. x, 284 p. $6.00.

Father Bouyer, an expert in matters liturgical as well as a well known writer on spiritual subjects, explains in this work what is meant by "liturgical piety" or "liturgical spirituality," as distinct from personal, or paraliturgical, spirituality. The central theme of the book is that nowhere can the Christian find more opportunity, or more help, for developing a truly Catholic interior life than within the framework of the liturgy of the Church. Despite the liturgical reforms of Vatican II, Father Bouyer's book remains the best available introduction to the spiritual uses of the liturgy, for he treats of unchanging principles. The book requires careful reading, but it may be highly recommended to the mature Catholic.

BOUYER, LOUIS (C.O.). *The Liturgy Revived.* Notre Dame, 1964. 107 p. pa. 95¢.

In this commentary on the 1963 "Constitution on the Sacred Liturgy," Father Bouyer explains the doctrinal implications of the document for the Church and for the individual Catholic. The book, like the Constitution, treats of the general principles of liturgical development and renewal, the mystery of the Eucharist, the Mass and con-celebration, the sacraments and sacramentals, the divine office, and liturgical cycle, sacred ornaments, sacred music, and sacred art. Although the subjects receive treatments of varying length, according to their over-all importance, the book is on the whole perhaps the most concise and comprehensive commentary on the Constitution yet to appear.

CATHERINE FREDERIC, SISTER. *The Handbook of Catholic Practices.* Foreword by Winfrid Herbst. Hawthorn, 1964. 319 p., glossary, appendix. $4.95.

This book is an explanation of the various Catholic devotions and symbols, of the Mass, and of the activities of the liturgical cycle and of various liturgical functions. The work is, in effect, a survey of liturgical practices in the Church, with clarifications on their nature, purpose, and proper use.

There is a glossary of common liturgical terms, and a list of recommended readings.

DIEKMANN, GODFREY L. (O.S.B.). *Come, Let Us Worship.* Helicon, 1961. 180 p., bibliography. $4.50. Image, 1966. pa. 85¢.

In this series of essays, Father Godfrey discusses, within the context of their liturgical significance, such subjects as the Sacraments, the Mass, the union of Christ with the Church, the liturgical year, and Christian life and worship. The author is an authority on matters liturgical, and he writes well and appositely.

ELLARD, GERALD (S.J.). *Christian Life and Worship,* revised edition. Preface by Joseph Husslein; illustrations by Ade de Bethune. Bruce, 1956. xxi, 420 p. $4.50.

This work explains the richness of means offered by the Church to develop the spirituality of the individual. Within that framework, Father Ellard analyzes the meaning of the priesthood, the ceremonies of the Church, sacred art, the sacramental system, the Mass, and, above all, the meaning of Christ for the Church. Although, in some respects, this book has been outdated by the liturgical reforms enacted by Vatican II, the substance of its message remains as valid as the unchanging realities symbolized by and enacted in the liturgy.

HILDEBRAND, DIETRICH VON. *Liturgy and Personality,* revised edition. Helicon, 1960. 131 p. $3.50.

This work stresses the exceptional strength of the liturgical life in forming the truly Christian personality. The liturgy, however, is not regarded as a pedagogical experience, but rather as a deep and organic form of development of the divine personality within us, a personality received in baptism through our participation in the life of God. This is a practical work, treating of concrete situations with deep psychological insight. It will be of particular use to those, such as priests and religious, who live the full liturgical life, but will be of much value also to the lay reader.

HOVDA, ROBERT, Editor. *Sunday Morning Crisis.* Helicon, 1963. 152 p. $3.95.

This is a collection of essays on the liturgical renewal in

Catholic worship. Among the contributors are Gerard Sloyan, Frederick R. McManus, and H. A. Reinhold. The purpose of the book is to make clear to the Catholic layman what effect the liturgical renewal, particularly in its application to the Mass, can have on his own spiritual life. This is an extraordinarily lively and informative collection.

HOWELL, CLIFFORD (S.J.). *Of Sacraments and Sacrifice.* Liturgical Press, 1952. 171 p., illustrations. $2.00.

One of the concepts traditionally associated with any interpretation of the meaning of the Mass in particular and of the sacraments in general is that of "sacrifice." In this work, Father Howell explains what is meant by that term, and develops that explanation into a study of the essentials of Mass and sacraments. His writing is clear and precise, and his approach is comprehensive enough to provide the reader with a valuable over-all view of the significance of the Eucharistic and sacramental rites.

HUME, PAUL. *Catholic Church Music.* Dodd, 1956. xiv, 259, appendices, index. $4.50.

This book is a practical and very readable guide to the proper use of music in Catholic churches. It contains advice on organizing choirs, training them, and "handling" them, on relations between pastors and choirs, and on the hundred-and-one problems, both personal and professional, that face the Catholic choirmaster. There are suggestions on repertoire for all occasions, as well as on liturgical music for weddings and on hymns, and there is a discussion of the teaching of sacred music in Catholic schools.

JUNGMANN, JOSEF ANDREAS (S.J.). *The Eucharistic Prayer,* revised edition. Dome, 1964. 93 p. pa. 75¢.

Father Jungmann, a liturgical and theological specialist who is regarded as one of the Church's foremost authorities on the development and significance of the Mass, in the present work studies the Canon of the Mass. The book is, in essence, a commentary on and an explanation of the liturgy of the Mass from the Offertory to the Communion. Despite the author's reputation for scholarship, his work is simply written and it will be very useful to the layman as well as to the priest.

LEFEBVRE, GASPAR (O.S.B.). *The Spirit of Worship*. Translated by Lancelot D. Sheppard. Hawthorn, 1959. 126 p., bibliography. $2.95.

The purpose of this work (Volume 108 of the *Twentieth Century Encyclopedia of Catholicism*) is to show how the Church, under the inspiration of the Holy Spirit, ensures the spiritual health of the faithful by requiring participation in her official worship of God. The largest part of the book is an explanation of the liturgical year, with emphasis on the role of the Holy Spirit and divine activity in certain prayers. There is also an analysis of the Holy Spirit's action in the liturgical rites of the administration of the sacraments. Dom Gaspar is one of the leading liturgists of the twentieth century; his work is a worthwhile and highly readable introduction to an understanding of the role and importance of the official liturgical worship of the Church.

McNASPY, C. J. (S.J.). *Our Changing Liturgy*. Hawthorn, 1966. 272 p., appendices. $4.95.

The purpose of this work, the first volume of the *Catholic Perspectives* series, is to help the troubled and confused layman attain some understanding of the changes that face him every time that he goes to church. The author explains first why the Church has undertaken a reform of the liturgy, discussing the historical, social, and pastoral reasons for that movement. Later chapters deal with the ecumenical implications of the new liturgy, liturgy and the arts, and the confusion—clerical as well as lay—concerning the purpose of liturgical reform. The appendices contain the text of Vatican II's "Constitution on the Sacred Liturgy" and other pertinent documents. This is a useful, well written, and very timely work. It is recommended to the priest as well as to the layman.

NEWLAND, MARY REED. *The Year and Our Children*. Kenedy, 1965. 314 p., appendices. $3.95. Image, 1964. pa. 95¢.

The Year and Our Children is, quite literally, a guidebook to Christian family living. It tells of the year and its seasons, their spirits, and suggests things for children to make and do to celebrate them. The book is designed to show Catholic parents how to initiate their children, in a simple and natural way, into the spirit of the liturgical year. The book is recommended to all Catholic parents.

REINHOLD, HANS A. *The Dynamics of Liturgy*. Foreword by Edward G. Murray. Macmillan, 1961. xii, 146 p. $4.75.

The author, a Catholic scholar who has lectured extensively on the modern liturgical movement, shows how lay participation in the liturgical year is related to the whole of life. Among the specific subjects treated are the historical background of the liturgical movement, the Christmas cycle, the relationship of liturgy to the arts, the place of the Eucharist in the liturgy, and liturgy as the work of the People of God. Although Father Reinhold's style tends to be somewhat didactic, the book holds much interest for the priest and the educated layman, and it is highly recommended to that audience.

ST. SEVERIN, COMMUNITY OF. *Christians Around the Altar*, revised edition. Translated by Margaret Clark. Dome, 1961. 159 p. pa. 95¢.

This is the up-dated edition of an excellent work on the significance of the Mass for Catholics as a community. The first part of the book takes up the Mass and its meaning, giving a brief survey of the theology of the Eucharist; the second part focuses this theology on the parish and the parishioners, explaining particularly how the Mass and its liturgy helps bring Christians back to an appreciation of what it means to worship together "around the altar."

ST. SEVERIN OF PARIS, SOCIETY OF, and SOCIETY OF ST. JOSEPH OF NICE. *The Liturgical Movement*. Translated by Lancelot Sheppard. Hawthorn, 1964. 139 p., bibliography. $3.50.

This volume tells the story of the liturgical reform or revival, tracing the reasons for its rise and growth and providing a clear picture of the events and personalities behind the movement. The book begins with a short survey of the history of the liturgical revival, and then goes on to show the development of its fundamental concepts. There is a discussion of the main features of the modern liturgical movement and their application to daily Christian life. The last part of the work is devoted to the principal advances in liturgical reform made in recent times, and there is a complete analysis of the Council's "Constitution on the Sacred Liturgy." (Volume 115 of the *Twentieth Century Encyclopedia of Catholicism*.)

SLOYAN, GERARD S. *Liturgy in Focus*. Deus, 1964. 112 p., bibliography. pa. 95¢.

Father Sloyan, a well known author and an authority on the liturgy, writes a brief and popular explanation of the principles of the "new liturgy" and of the practical norms that are being established. He discusses briefly such matters as the celebration of the Eucharist, the sacraments, and sacred music. The book is a recommended introduction to an understanding of current liturgical reform.

SLOYAN, GERARD S. *Worship in a New Key*. Herder & Herder, 1965. 190 p., index. $3.95. Echo, 1966. pa. 75¢.

Worship in a New Key, is the work of one of the foremost liturgical experts of the Church. It is a clearly explained, wide-ranging interpretation of and commentary on Vatican II's "Constitution on the Sacred Liturgy," and furnishes a comprehensive guide to the liturgical renewal and to an understanding of how Catholics may live a more complete spiritual life according to the norms of the Constitution. Father Sloyan writes for everybody; his work is one of the most practical, plain-spoken books yet to appear on what is going on in the liturgy.

WEISER, FRANCIS X. (s.J.). *A Handbook of Christian Feasts and Customs*. Preface by Bishop John Wright. Paulist Press, 1960. xviii, 366 p., index. pa. 95¢.

This work is an exposition of the "year of the Lord" considered both in the liturgy and in folklore. Father Weiser explains not only the approved major feasts of the liturgical year, but also the various Christian customs—many of which are sacramentals—and gives their historical origins. It is an instructive, entertaining work, and should find a place in Catholic homes and libraries.

13. LIVES OF THE SAINTS

Through the centuries the lives of the saints have served as a constant inspiration and source of edification for Christian men and women in all walks of life. The holiness, sanctity, and concern for their fellow men that have characterized the lives of these holy people have always been examples greatly admired by the commonalty of mankind. King and commoner alike realized that these individuals, in searching for that closer union with God which we should all be seeking, have reached degrees of spiritual perfection that we should all be striving to achieve. Since, in the final analysis, spiritual perfection through union with God should be the main purpose of our life on earth and the goal toward which we should be laboring, emulation of those who have achieved these laudable aims, within each individual's capacity, certainly is worthy of our every effort.

Though all are not so gifted as to reach the spiritual heights attained by the saints, most people appreciate true holiness in others. Often this holiness is not immediately apparent, and there are numerous instances of men and women achieving a sanctity which was not immediately apparent to their contemporaries. But once such holiness is recognized and becomes known, a legion of admirers spring up. And though most of us are fated never to become saints, practically all of us in the depths of our being realize the need for leading a holy life. Since there is this deep-rooted desire in all of us, we admire and put up for emulation those relatively few individuals who do lead a life of holiness.

Though it is freely admitted that we should all be trying to be saints, it is a curious phenomenon today that of all the writings in the religious field, hagiography (literature dealing with the lives and legends of the saints) has in the past few years suffered a serious decline in reading interest among the general public. While writings of a spiritual nature—meditations, inspirational works, spiritual reflections, etc.—have retained their popularity and are as well received as ever, generally speaking people no longer evince the intense interest they did as recently as a decade ago in books on the saints.

A moment's reflection will reveal some of the reasons for this decline in popularity. A leading cause is the fact that we live in a sophisticated age. In a more uncritical period, people were willing to accept as fact statements and incidents by mere hearsay which tended to become more exaggerated with each new telling. In bygone times, when learning was not so widespread as it is today, people often grasped at myths and unproved theses to explain certain naturally inexplicable phenomena. Today we are of a more skeptical nature and demand proof of allegations which often seemingly defy the laws of science and of nature. To add to this attitude of disbelief, it has too often been shown that fervid followers of certain individuals or causes have frequently seized upon events not apparently attributable to natural causes and exaggerated them to muster support for the person or cause. Frequently these distortions were so incredible that to moderns they became ridiculous. As modern scholarship unmasked many of these more obviously exaggerated and easily explainable, by natural means, happenings and labeled them for the myths and gross distortions that they obviously were, disillusionment set in. From this disillusioned attitude towards these unmasked claims, it was often but a step to view with skepticism perfectly legitimate claims of great happenings involving men and women of great personal holiness.

Furthermore, the harm caused by poorly written, over sentimentalized, pietistic biographies of good men and women can never be adequately assessed. The numerous attempts to gloss over the human faults present in all of us by overzealous writers trying to present their subjects as perfect in every respect has caused a reaction to set in against such impossibly saccharine and unworldly word portraits. Today we are experiencing the fruits of that reaction.

So, too, all too frequently, writers have not made their saints relevant for today's men and women. Every saint is a product of his times and takes on the coloring, customs and practices of his period, many of which have no appeal for today and often are actually repulsive. For instance, a few centuries back it was quite customary for a preacher to beat himself with a whip or chain until he was covered with blood. Bruised, bloodied, and semiconscious, he would preach a sermon. You can imagine the reaction of a congregation today if a priest staggered to the pulpit, exhausted and covered with blood, and tried to preach a sermon. Again, in the early Christian era, thousands of men and women fled to the deserts, lived in dirty ragged clothing, starved themselves, eating only insects for food, and presented an offensive, starved, emaciated appearance that would repel today's churchgoer.

In most of these cases, the times justified or even approved the drastic measures by these holy men and women. But too frequently authors either did not care or were unable to explain the background sufficiently so a modern reader could understand why these men and women acted as they did. In failing to get this explanation across to the reader, the author also failed to get across the essence of the universal appeal that the true saint has for all ages and all people.

For above all else, the true saint has achieved what we should all be seeking—a method of living which brings him closer to God and prepares him for life after death. And it is this aspect of saints' lives which does have as much meaning for us today as for people living in any other period of history. And this is the tragedy in the decline of interest in the lives of the saints—that men and women who have so much to offer are being rebuffed by the modern reader. In rejecting the pietistic, sentimentalized distortions which passed so often as saints' lives, the modern reader is at the same time ignoring those excellent biographies of the saints which by every exacting standard of modern scholarship are recognized as outstanding works. As scholarly knowledge grows by leaps and bounds, aided and abetted by modern scientific discoveries and inventions, the real scholar and author approaches his subject as does any biographer in other fields of human activity. Thanks to the unceasing efforts of scholars all over the world, led by that small intrepid group of Jesuit scholars, the Bollandists, organized early in the seventeenth century with the avowed purpose of sifting material on the lives of saints for veracity and accuracy, we now have a substantial body of hagiography which presents full-bodied pictures of its subject, realistically and honestly.

And there is so much for all of us to learn from the lives of the saints that it is high time that the average reader take another look at one of the most fascinating of all literary forms. For if the saints are really that, then they have so much to offer us that it would be the height of folly not to learn what they can teach us.

In the list we have collected below we have tried to include only those lives of the saints that meet the critical standards of modern biography: they provide a full-dimensioned portrait of their subject, the author must know his background and he able to re-create it in his book, he must reject out of hand incredible happenings which are obviously gross exaggerations, and he must label myths as such. Equally important is that at all times he approach his subject with an open mind so that he be willing to accept the miraculous when it is such, and above all that he himself have the knowledge to write on his chosen subject.

One last point. As always in these lists that we have prepared, we have books for every reading taste, so there is a variety of styles represented. We have labeled each book as we see it, so the reader can judge his interest. Included are some books that are quite scholarly or quite spiritual in approach. When such is the case we have listed them because they are, quite simply, the best book on that particular saint or because the approach the author has used is such that it is unique and must be included in any work on that saint if one is fully to understand him or her. There is a treasure to be found in these books, for here are the lives of the men and women whom history has confirmed as the light of the Church on earth.

COLLECTIONS

ATTWATER, DONALD A. *A Dictionary of Saints.* Kenedy, 1958. vii, 280 p. $4.50.

This is a one-volume revision of the standard authority on the lives and deeds of the saints, Butler's *Lives of the Saints.*

The better known saints are included in this volume, in alphabetical order, and the details of their lives and miracles are given in easily readable language. This work is indispensable for libraries who do not have Butler's multi-volume work, and it is a valuable reference work for the home.

Book of Saints, 4th edition, revised and enlarged. Edited by the Benedictine Monks of St. Augustine's Abbey. Macmillan, 1947. xvii, 708 p., bibliography, appendix. $7.50.

This is a collection of lives of the saints, extracted from the official and unofficial martyrologies of the Church. The entries are arranged in alphabetical order and give brief biographical sketches of each saint as well as information concerning their patronage of occupations, countries, etc., and their feast days. There is a calendar of saints, or liturgical calendar, showing the feast days of the saints in chronological order. This is a concise and comprehensive work of reference, ideal for use in the home as well as in libraries.

BUTLER, ALBAN. *Lives of the Saints.* Edited, revised, and supplemented by Herbert Thurston, s.j. and Donald Attwater. Foreword by Francis Cardinal Spellman. Kenedy, 1956. Vol. I: xxxii, 720 p.; Vol. II: xxii, 692 p.; Vol. III: xx, 705 p.; Vol. IV: xx, 707 p., bibliographies, indices. $39.50 (boxed).

Butler's classic work, written in the mid-eighteenth century, has long been regarded as the standard reference work on the saints of the Church. The editors have brought it up to date by including the names of saints canonized in modern times, revising Butler's material in the light of the discoveries of modern historical methods, and, where necessary, rephrasing the author's always elegant, but not always lucid, style into idiomatic modern English. This is the complete source of information on any saint, containing 2565 entries, and it is an indispensable reference book for Catholic libraries.

COULSON, JOHN. *The Saints: A Concise Biographical Dictionary.* Introduction by C. C. Martindale. Hawthorn, 1958. 496 p., bibliography. $12.95.

As the title indicates, this is an alphabetical listing of all of the better known saints to whom one might expect to find reference made either in the liturgy or in the history of the Church. There is a brief but comprehensive biography given of each saint, along with useful information concerning the particular saint's place in the liturgy.

DANIEL-ROPS, HENRI. *The Heroes of God.* Translated by Lawrence G. Blochman. Hawthorn, 1959. 226 p., index, maps. $3.95. Echo, 1965. pa. 75¢.

A famous historian and man of letters presents biographical studies of eleven Christian heroes: St. Paul, St. Martin of Tours, St. Francis Xavier, St. Isaac Jouges, Blessed Ramon Lull, Bishop Las Casas, Fra Junípero Serra, Mother Javouhey, Father de Foucauld, Father Damian, and Father Nussbaum. The individual biographies are short, and suitable for spiritual reading.

DUCKETT, ELEANOR. *Anglo-Saxon Saints and Scholars.* Macmillan, 1947. 498 p., bibliography, index. $5.00.

This is a collection of interpretative biographies of four prominent figures of the seventh and eighth centuries in England: Aldheim of Malmesbury, Wilfred of York, the Venerable Bede, and St. Boniface. The author, a non-Catholic, is an authoritative medieval scholar, but her prose is delightfully non-academic and her viewpoint is thoroughly objective.

DUCKETT, ELEANOR. *The Wandering Saints of the Early Middle Ages.* Norton, 1959. 319 p., bibliography, index, maps. $5.00. Norton, 1963. pa. $1.75.

Miss Duckett's subject essentially is the process by which Christianity spread through Western Europe. Her approach is biographical, tracing the Christian expansion by studying the lives of those apostles, such as Augustine of Canterbury and Boniface, who were chiefly responsible for the conversion of the barbarian nations. The author, a non-Catholic historian, writes with a happy combination of style and scholarship, and her work makes fascinating as well as instructive reading.

ENGLEBERT, OMER. *The Lives of the Saints.* Translated by Christopher and Anne Fremantle. McKay, 1951. 532 p., index, illustrations. $5.00.

This collection, by an eminent Catholic scholar and writer, narrates the lives of the saints in an easy-to-read and readable style. Included are all of the well known saints and many less known ones of particular interest, arranged chronologically according to feast days. The author, in selecting his material, has used modern historical methods of criticism, and his work is historically sound as well as inspirational and informative.

GHEON, HENRI. *Secrets of the Saints*. Translated by F. J. Sheed and Donald Attwater. Sheed, 1944. 395 p. $3.95. Image, 1963. $1.25.

This book contains four popularly written full-length biographies of saints, covering the lives and works of the Cure d'Ars, St. Thérèse of Lisieux, St. Margaret Mary Alacoque, and St. John Bosco. These are unusual studies by a famous literary figure and suitable for spiritual reading.

GOODIER, ALBAN (S.J.). *Saints for Sinners*. Image, 1959. 152 p. pa. 65¢.

Father Goodier has written brief biographies of nine saints who fought to overcome temptation and attain holiness: St. John of the Cross, St. Francis Xavier, St. Camillus de Lellis, St. Joseph of Cupertino, St. Margaret of Cortona, Blessed Claude da la Colombiere, St. Augustine of Hippo, St. John of God, and St. Benedict Joseph Labre. Each of the nine had a particular passion or a special sin that they were obliged to overcome; St. Margaret of Cortona, for example, was an extremely beautiful woman and a courtesan; St. Camillus was an ill-tempered and lazy professional soldier, addicted to gambling, and St. Joseph of Cupertino was incurably stupid.

HOMAN, HELEN W. *By Post to the Apostles*. McKay, 1952. xii, 260 p. $3.50. All Saints, 1962. pa. 50¢.

The author takes the twelve apostles, and St. Mark and St. Paul, and studies each one in the light of all scriptural references to them as well as of all the legends about them. Her method not only furnishes a clear picture of each apostle and evangelist, but it is also valuable as illustrating the immense amount of information available about them—some of it legendary, some apocryphal, and some well documented.

LUCE, CLAIR BOOTHE, Editor. *Saints for Now*. Sheed, 1952. 312 p., portraits. $3.50. All Saints, 1963. pa. 75¢.

The editor, a famous convert, requested twenty of her friends to depict the life of a saint who, in the opinion of each contributor, had a special message for the modern world. Among the contributors and their subjects are: Alfred Noyes on St. John the Evangelist; Evelyn Waugh on St. Helena; Whittaker Chambers on St. Benedict; Paul Gallico on St. Francis of Assisi; and Thomas Merton on St. John of the Cross.

MAYNARD, THEODORE. *Saints for Our Times.* Image, 1955. 304 p. pa. 95¢.

This is a collection of eighteen biographies of saints whose lives and achievements hold special meaning for modern man. Among those represented are: Francis of Assisi, Elizabeth of Hungary, Thomas Aquinas, Joan of Arc, Thomas More, Ignatius Loyola, Vincent de Paul, and Mother Cabrini. This is an interesting and unusual collection, written in Mr. Maynard's much admired and highly readable style; it will be enjoyed by those who are not normally given to reading the lives of saints.

NEWLAND, MARY REED. *The Saints and Our Children.* Kenedy, 1958. xv, 215 p. $3.95.

This is a work intended to help Catholic parents in the raising of Catholic families. It contains twenty "morality stories" or events taken from the lives of the saints which may be used by parents to impress their children with the importance of particular virtues. The material makes excellent ammunition for story-telling time, and Catholic mothers with children in the 4-to-8 age group will find it a useful book.

WADDELL, HELEN. *The Desert Fathers.* University of Michigan, 1957. 209 p., notes. pa. $1.45.

One of the most famous hagiographic works of the Middle Ages is the *Vitae Patrum*—the lives of the (desert) fathers—and from that work Miss Waddell has gathered together the words and deeds of those strange men who left wives, children, and civilization to live in the deserts of Egypt so as to overcome the flesh. The author has deliberately, as she says, "chosen that part of the desert teaching most alien to and most sovereign in a world that has to the ancient anarchs of cruelty and pride." Though much of the material has historic, rather than spiritual, interest, it makes for fascinating reading.

Individual Lives

[Augustine] POPE, HUGH (O.P.). *St. Augustine of Hippo.*
Newman, 1937. 439 p., notes, bibliography, index. $4.00.
Image, 1961. pa. $1.35.

A biography of Saint Augustine, this is undoubtedly the
best available survey of his contributions to literature, philosophy, and history. The author's unusual approach has been
to make Augustine relate, through his letters, spiritual and
social writings, the story of his rather odd character, his failings, his intellectual turmoil, and his struggle for perfection.

[Bellarmine, Robert] BRODRICK, JAMES (S.J.). *Robert Bellarmine,* revised edition. Newman, 1961. x, 430 p., notes,
bibliography, index. $5.75.

Cardinal Bellarmine, whose biography this is, was Catholicism's most learned defender during the Counter-Reformation. He was the friend and adviser of popes, princes, and
saints, and a man whose writings—particularly on Church-
State relations—profoundly influenced Catholic thought for
centuries. This work is regarded as the standard life of Bellarmine, and it is an excellent introduction to an understanding of the Church's role in the formation of the modern world.
(This is the one-volume revision of a two-volume work.)

[Benedict] McCANN, JUSTIN (O.S.B.). *Saint Benedict,* revised edition. Image, 1958. 233 p., notes, index. pa. 85¢.

The story of the life and work of Benedict of Nursia,
founder of the Benedictine Order and of western monasticism. This is perhaps the best biography of Benedict for modern readers, written by a noted Benedictine scholar.

[Bernard] JAMES, BRUNO S. *St. Bernard of Clairvaux.*
Harper, 1958. 192 p. $3.50.

This is a popularly written and comprehensive biography
of the man who was responsible for the great reformation of
the monastic orders during the Middle Ages and who was
one of the most influential figures of his time. As an important
adviser to popes, saints, kings and emperors, he played an
important role in history as well as in religion, and this brief
biographical study develops the man both as a saint and as
a historical figure.

[Catherine of Siena] UNDSET, SIGRID. *Catherine of Siena.* Translated by Kate Austin-Lund. Sheed, 1954. vii, 293 p. $3.50.

This is the biography of the fourteenth-century saint and mystic who was the adviser of popes and kings, written by a winner of the Nobel Prize for Literature. Though this is not a definitive biography of Catherine, it is undoubtedly the best written and historically the most accurate version to appear to date, and it is recommended as a literary accomplishment as well as for spiritual reading.

[Brebeuf, Jean de] TALBOT, FRANCIS X. (s.j.). *Saint Among the Hurons.* Image, 1955. 355 p., notes, index. pa. 95¢.

This is the story of the Jesuit priest, Jean de Brebeuf, who came to North America to work among the Indians and who died a martyr's death for his faith. The book is historically accurate, and provides an exciting and colorful picture of frontier life in pre-Revolutionary America.

[Bernadette] KEYES, FRANCES PARKINSON. *Bernadette of Lourdes,* revised edition. Hawthorn, 1953. 191 p., bibliography. $3.50. Echo, 1966. pa. 75¢.

First published under the title of *Sublime Shepherdess,* this book by one of the most popular novelists of our century tells the story of the little French shepherdess to whom the Virgin appeared in 1858. Avoiding the temptation to the melodramatic presented by the sufferings of Bernadette at the hands of skeptics, both within and without the Church, Mrs. Keyes tells a colorful and inspiring story accurately, simply, and interestingly. Although this is not the conventional "life of a saint," it is one of the most readable books about the great happenings at Lourdes.

[Cabrini, Frances Xavier] DI DONATO, PIETRO. *Immigrant Saint.* McGraw, 1960. 246 p., illustrations. $4.95.

This is a popularly written biography of St. Frances Xavier Cabrini, the immigrant Italian woman who became the first American citizen to be canonized. From her own experience, Mother Cabrini had a vivid knowledge of slum life in large cities, and her life was devoted to bettering the conditions of the poor; she founded a religious order for that purpose, the Missionary Sisters of the Sacred Heart, as well as hospitals, schools, homes, etc. for the poor. The story of her native enterprise and skill in raising money, in building, and in managing the affairs of her order makes for delightful reading, while her great love for people—a point emphasized in this work—is an inspiring example for all Christians.

[Dominic] JARRETT, BEDE (O.P.). *Life of St. Dominic.* Image, 1964. 160 p., notes. pa. 75¢.

St. Dominic's life was curiously modern. From a quiet and scholarly life in a monastery he was plunged, quite by accident, into the active and contentious life of a street-corner preacher. His life's work was to dispute with heretics who threatened the existence of the Church in the thirteenth century, and he found the vital inspiration for his mission in dedication to the intellect of Christ. Through the religious order he founded—the Dominicans—he not only defended the faith, but spread it throughout Christendom. This is by far the best English biography of St. Dominic.

[Francis of Assisi] CHESTERTON, G. K. *St. Francis of Assisi.* Image, 1957. 158 p. pa. 75¢.

The famous biography of the founder of the Franciscans, written by one of the outstanding authors and thinkers of our times. The utterly unusual personality of St. Francis depicted with Chestertonian incisiveness and wit makes for thoroughly enjoyable reading.

[Francis of Assisi] JÖRGENSEN, JOHANNES. *St. Francis of Assisi.* Translated by T. O'Conor Sloane. McKay, 1912. 354 p., notes, appendices, index. $4.00. Image, 1955. pa. 95¢.

A biography of St. Francis of Assisi, this work is more detailed and more scholarly in form than that of Chesterton described above. Yet, it is written in a lively and enjoyable fashion by a distinguished European author. The abundant notes to the text will be most helpful to serious students of St. Francis and of the Franciscan tradition.

[Francis Xavier] BRODRICK, JAMES (S.J.). *Saint Francis Xavier,* condensed version. Image, 1957. 359 p., notes, index. pa. 95¢.

The story of St. Francis Xavier, the astonishing missionary who took the Orient as his responsibility and had the most exciting adventures since the time of St. Paul. This book rejects the pious legends which have hitherto surrounded the figure of Francis and achieves an accurate portrait of the real man. It is full of wit, learning, and entertaining sidelights on life in the sixteenth century, and it is doubtless the best available popular biography of St. Francis Xavier.

[Ignatius Loyola] PURCELL, MARY. *The First Jesuit.* Foreword by John LaFarge, s.j. Newman, 1957. 433 p., notes, bibliography, index. $5.00. Image, 1965. pa. $1.35.

A biography of St. Ignatius Loyola, founder of the Jesuits. As the life of a saint, this book is unique in that it presents Ignatius essentially as a human being; it is not a "pious work." It also provides an interesting and colorful insight into the history of the Church in the critical sixteenth century. This is the best one-volume work of St. Ignatius to appear in modern times, and it is highly recommended.

[Joan of Arc] BEEVERS, JOHN. *St. Joan of Arc.* Image, 1962. 152 p. pa. 75¢.

This is a biography of the little French peasant who saved France from the armies of England and who was later burned at the stake as a witch. Clearly and popularly written, the book is enhanced by an intelligent and non-partisan analysis of the charges against Joan brought by an ecclesiastical court.

[Jogues, Isaac] TALBOT, FRANCIS (s.j.). *Saint Among Savages.* Image, 1961. 522 p., notes, bibliography, index. pa. $1.45.

Father Talbot has written the definitive biography of St. Isaac Jogues, the priest who devoted his life to Christianizing and civilizing the Indian nations of seventeenth-century America and who eventually suffered the death of a martyr. It is a colorful and exciting story, as well as an inspirational account of a life devoted to one's fellow men.

[John of the Cross] BRUNO DE JESUS-MARIE (o.c.d.). *St. John of the Cross.* Edited by Benedict Zimmerman, o.c.d.; introduction by Jacques Maritain. Sheed, 1957. xxxii, 495 p., notes, index. $6.00.

St. John of the Cross, Doctor of the Church and a friend of that great reformer of the Carmelites, St. Teresa of Avila, is known as the greatest mystical theologian of the Church. In this biography of the saint, Father Bruno brings out not only the importance of St. John's contribution to the Church and to spirituality in general, but also the color and excitement of life in sixteenth-century Spain where it was possible for a reformer monk, such as St. John, to be kidnapped and imprisoned by other monks who refused to be reformed. Despite the fact that this is basically a work of scholarship, well documented and thoroughly factual, the general reader will find it not only instructive but fascinating reading. The book is generally regarded as the standard biography of St. John of the Cross.

[Labouré, Catherine] DIRVIN, JOSEPH I. (C.M.). *St. Catherine Labouré of the Miraculous Medal.* Foreword by Joseph A. Skelly, C.M. Farrar, 1958. xv, 239 p., bibliography, index. $3.95. Echo, 1965. pa. 85¢.

This is a biography of the French peasant girl who, as a Sister of Charity of St. Vincent de Paul, had a series of visions from the Blessed Virgin and was entrusted with the task of promulgating devotion to the Immaculate Conception. From these visions came the medal known as "the miraculous medal." Father Dirvin writes simply and clearly, and his work is suitable for spiritual reading.

[More, Thomas] FARROW, JOHN V. *The Story of Thomas More.* Guild, 1965. 242 p., bibliography. pa. 95¢.

This is an interesting and factual biography of St. Thomas More, who was the Chancellor of King Henry VIII of England, the father of a family, the author of *Utopia* and one of the great humanists of the Renaissance. Mr. Farrow writes in a lively journalistic style, and his work is as interesting for its historical insight as for its spiritual treatment of More.

[Paul] RICCIOTTI, GIUSEPPE. *Paul the Apostle.* Translated by Alba I. Zizzamia. Bruce, 1961. xi, 540 p., bibliography, plates, maps, index. pa. $2.95.

This is probably the finest account, from the standpoint of historiography, biography, and hagiography, that is available of St. Paul. Along with a complete chronological treatment of the events of Paul's life, the author provides an excellent analysis of each of the Epistles. The work is highly recommended as biography, history, and spiritual reading.

[Teresa of Avila] AUCLAIR, MARCELLE. *Teresa of Avila.* Translated by Kathleen Pond. Image, 1959. 480 p., notes, index. pa. $1.45.

This is the biography of St. Teresa of Avila, the great reformer of the Carmelites and one of the great mystics of

Catholicism. An unusual feature of the book is the use made by the author of the unwritten traditions concerning St. Teresa, kept alive today in the monasteries founded by the saint.

[Teresa of Avila] TERESA OF AVILA, SAINT. *The Autobiography of St. Teresa of Avila.* Translated with notes by E. Allison Peers. Newman, 1962. 397 p., notes. $4.50. Image, 1960. pa. $1.25.

The autobiography of St. Teresa of Avila was written at the command of her confessors, to give an accurate and detailed account of her spiritual progress. The first part of the book is an autobiography in the ordinary sense, describing the author's family, education, and the beginnings of her spiritual life. The last part describes the spiritual trials and triumphs of the saint and the effects of them in her soul.

[Thérèse of Lisieux] BEEVERS, JOHN. *Storm of Glory.* Sheed, 1950. 199 p. $3.00. Image, 1955. pa. 75¢.

Probably no saint of modern times has captured the imagination of Catholics to the extent that St. Thérèse of Lisieux has. This popular biography of the "Little Flower" tells the story of her life, from her childhood in a middle-class French family to her death in a Carmelite monastery at the age of twenty-four.

[Thérèse of Lisieux] GOERRES, IDA FRIEDERIKE. *The Hidden Face.* Translated by Richard and Clara Winston. Pantheon, 1959. viii, 428 p., bibliography, index. $5.50.

The subtitle of this work is "A Study of St. Thérèse of Lisieux," and the book is exactly that—a study, and one in which the author examines St. Thérèse as a woman and as a human being rather than as the impossible model of all perfection into which she has so often been made by well intentioned, but misguided, biographers. The Thérèse who emerges from these pages is a thoroughly human and sympathetic figure who, by simply accepting life as it is as the expression of God's will, became a saint. This is probably the model of what hagiography should be, and so seldom is. It is recommended reading.

[Thérèse of Lisieux] THÉRÈSE OF LISIEUX, SAINT. *The Autobiography of St. Thérèse of Lisieux.* Translated by Ronald Knox; foreword by Vernon Johnson. Kenedy, 1958. 320 p., illustrations. $4.50. Image, 1957 (translated by John Beevers). pa. 75¢.

This is the famous life story of "The Little Flower"—the obscure Carmelite nun who has worked so deeply upon the imagination of modern man. The story is one of simplicity, and contains what is perhaps the most basic axiom for attaining spiritual perfection: Do what you are supposed to do. This is probably the most popular spiritual work to appear in modern times, and it is an inspiring book, unreservedly recommended for everyone.

[Thomas à Becket] DUGGAN, ALFRED. *My Life for My Sheep.* Coward, 1955. 341 p., illustrations, map. $5.00. Image, 1957. pa. 95¢.

Duggan writes a fictionalized history of St. Thomas à Becket, twelfth-century Archbishop of Canterbury. Becket was a hot-tempered youth who became head of the English Church and defended the rights of the Pope in England against the king. Eventually he was assassinated and is regarded as a martyr for the faith. This book follows historical fact closely; the author uses his imagination freely only in recounting minor events and reconstructing conversations.

14. MARRIAGE AND THE FAMILY

Of all the many facets of Catholic teaching, few have been subjected to the attacks that have been leveled against the Catholic concept of marriage and the family. The whole trend of modern times has been at variance with what the Church teaches in this vital area of society. Where the Church consistently stresses the indissolubility of marriage, the divorce rate has soared to such astronomical proportions that now 40% out of every 100 marriages in the United States ends in the divorce court. In a society that treats marriage pretty much as a contractual obligation, the Church teaches the sanctity of marriage and reaffirms the sacramental nature of that institution. Where broken homes are accepted as the norm of a sophisticated, blasé culture, the Church insists on the inviolability of family ties. Where children all too frequently are looked upon as a burden to one's "fulfillment in life," the Church emphasizes parental responsibility. Where defiance and disobedience are the order of the day in children's relations to their parents, the Church points to the fourth commandment as the criterion for all children.

It is only too obvious then that there is a basic conflict between the widespread practices of a secular society and the tenets governing family relationships which the Church has always proclaimed. Faced on every side by customs directly contradictory to Church pronouncements, it is essential that the Catholic be aware of his Church's teaching and of the logic behind it. Fortunately, there is no dearth of outstanding material readily available on every aspect of these contradictions between secular practices and sacred teaching. But in these ever-changing times, the Catholic must also be aware that the stress in Church teaching also has changed in many areas of marriage and family relationship. The fundamental teaching of the Church always remains constant in every area of Church activity. But one of the great strengths of the Church has been her ability to adjust to changing patterns of human practice. She has done this throughout the two thousand years of her history in order to bring her own practices into line with the new times and new outlooks, but always she retains the basic dogmas given her by her Founder. And so, in what is probably the most dynamic age of recorded history, the Church adjusts her non-essentials to update her own practices and teachings.

Thus, among the institutions which are undergoing searching scrutiny by eminent Church authorities is that of marriage. In fulfillment of her teaching role, the Church is examining family relationships in the light of the revolutionary changes which have swept the world in the past few decades and affected every aspect of life.

An example of this scrutiny may be seen in the whole matter of families and their size. All over the world, nations have been experiencing a tremendous population increase as science and medicine have decreased infant mortality, have cut the death rate by controlling or wiping out previously killer diseases, and have extended the life span. In many nations population growth has become *the* problem to be resolved if the great social ills of mankind are ever to be cured.

Many of the solutions proposed violate traditional Catholic teaching and are repugnant to Catholics. But the Church is aware of the problem and is working on it. One definite answer has been the rhythm method of family limitation by which the Church offers a solution to too large families and teaches that the husband and wife are the ones to decide in all conscience how large their family shall be. The Church teaches the primary purpose of marriage is the propagation of offspring, and the care and education of children; now, it is also *stressed* that besides having children, parents are equally obliged to provide for their welfare. They should have only as many children as they can adequately take care of, and to do otherwise is reckless and imprudent.

In this single illustration is revealed the point we made above, that the Church changes her stress to meet changing times, but at the same time retains the fundamentals of her policy. Children are still a primary purpose of marriage (which the Church has always taught), but in this complex world of today providing for them adequately has become

more difficult than ever before. Therefore the Church
stresses, in the light of modern conditions, more than ever
before, the second portion of the marriage purpose, which
also has always been present in her teaching but hitherto
has not needed the added emphasis the Church now gives
it.

So, too, in the whole area of sexuality, the Church has
relaxed some of her peripheral restrictions, while at the same
time retaining and emphasizing the basic teaching. For instance at one time priests were almost unanimous in denouncing all forms of dancing, as did St. Francis de Sales
in his spiritual classic *Introduction to the Devout Life;* today
churches everywhere sponsor dances. Present-day feminine
garb would cause saintly pastors of twenty-five years ago to
turn in their graves. Yet so commonplace have become scanty
bathing suits (and I do not mean such indecencies as topless
bathing suits), tight slacks, shorts, and the like that no one
really pays much attention to them unless they are quite
extreme. The Church objects to them only when they are
extreme, but at the same time reiterates her constant teaching that sex is a gift of God and must be treated with the
respect due a gift from Him.

And so it is with the whole range of family life from the
youngsters on their first date, to the young married couple
and their relations with each other, to their offspring and
their responsibility to them, to the youngsters' obligation to
their parents—in short the whole range of relationships and
responsibilities we cover by the expression "marriage and the
family relationship." There is a whole body of Catholic teaching and doctrine on every aspect and problem resulting from
the relationship between a man and a woman. Many topics
previously never mentioned in polite society are blazoned on
the front pages of our newspapers. Abortion, contraception,
birth control, promiscuity, sexual license, immorality, homo-
sexuality, conjugal relations—all these and a host of others are
facts of life which are now openly discussed, and the Church
has a stand on each of them. As Catholics it is essential to
our spiritual life to know what she does have to say on these
topics as opposed to the carelessly bandied-about jingoes so
widely prevalent.

Fortunately, there is a perfectly splendid body of writing covering every phase of this most basic of human drives. Catholic scholars and theologians have written profusely and well, so there is no excuse for not being well informed on any of these frequently controversial topics. And some of the areas are controversial with the answers still to come.

In our selection of titles we have made every effort to give the reader a wide variety of books on all aspects of marriage and the family. Included are books which have raised storms of protest in certain quarters. The authors of these works are honest and dedicated men and women who are involved in difficult and often unclear areas of Catholic teaching. We have included such books for those interested in knowing some of the controversial questions which are presently under consideration. In all such cases we have clearly labeled them for what they are. In general, though, the books on the list will be found to be informative and instructive rather than of such an exploratory nature that they are controversial.

More than in any other era, the twentieth century is witness to the challenging of beliefs fundamental to Catholicism. The whole area of marriage and of sexual relations seems to be the target for the most intensive of such efforts, so that more than in other sections of this *Guide* we do urge you to read widely here to absorb fully what the Church teaches.

BARBEAU, CLAYTON. *The Head of the Family.* Regnery, 1961. xv, 144 p. $3.75.

Mr. Barbeau defines the function of the Christian husband and father as covering seven major roles: creator, lover, Christ, priest, teacher, provider, and saint. He devotes one chapter to each activity, describing its purpose and its relationship to the concept of ideal fatherhood. The book is popularly written in a pleasing style and deals with situations rather than with theories.

DOYLE, CHARLES HUGO. *Cana Is Forever.* Image, 1958. 233 p. pa. 85¢.

This is a popular guide to the Catholic concept of marriage, for use both before and after marriage. The book covers such topics as the signs of true love, the qualities to look for in a mate, the honeymoon, the psychological differences between the sexes, the ways in which husbands and wives usually cause unhappiness to their spouses, etc. This is a practical, sympathetic, wise, and well-rounded book; the author's light style and sense of humor make it ideal reading for anyone.

FULLAM, RAYMOND B. (S.J.). *The Popes on Youth.* McKay, 1957. xvii, 442 p., bibliography, index. $5.00.

This is a collection of texts from papal pronouncements on the formation and guidance of youth, issued during the reigns of Leo XIII, Pius X, Benedict XV, Pius XI, and Pius XII. The work is divided into four parts: the first contains excerpts concerning the authority and responsibility of the popes toward youth, the second presents principles for the formation of youth, the third lists directives on adult responsibilities toward youth, and the fourth studies adverse influences in the formation of youth.

GEISSLER, EUGENE. *Family Man.* Fides, 1960. xii, 157 p., illustrations. pa. $1.00.

This work is a collection of reflections on the ideal of the Christian family as exemplified by the Holy Family. After introductory chapters describing what is known of the family life of Jesus, Mary, and Joseph, the author discusses what can be learned from their example about the family, about marriage, and about authority.

GIBERT, HENRI. *Love in Marriage.* Translated by André Humbert. Hawthorn, 1965. 224 p., charts. $4.95.

This is a guidebook to the meaning and practice of sexual love in Christian marriage. An authority in the field, the author writes with candor and reverence about the practices and problems of marital love. It is recommended to young adults as well as to spiritual and medical advisers.

GREELEY, ANDREW M. *Letters to Nancy.* Sheed, 1964. x, 182 p. $3.95.

The author counsels the young woman on various problems she may encounter of a moral, social, and vocational nature. There is particular emphasis on the role of the woman in family life, and on the problem of a career in relation to marriage. The book is in the form of a series of letters to a fictional Nancy, and the author's style and approach are informal and practical.

GREELEY, ANDREW M. *Strangers in the House.* Sheed, 1961. 179 p. $3.50.

In this study of Catholic youth in America, a well known priest-sociologist examines such problems as apathy among the young, loss of the "crusading spirit," the search for identity, drinking, cheating, and prolonged adolescence. Father Greeley writes clearly and to the point, analyzing the personal, social, religious, political, and economic causes of youthful discontent and the forms of that discontent. He concludes with a well formulated outline for a spiritual solution to the problem.

GREELEY, ANDREW M. *And Young Men Shall See Visions.* Sheed, 1964. xii, 177 p. $3.95.

Father Greeley's book is cast in the form of sixteen letters to his young friend, John. It is basically a book of spiritual counseling on problems peculiar to adolescents, but the author's approach emphasizes the promise and opportunities of youth rather than its negative aspects. Among the topics dealt with are questions of faith and religious observance, morality, education, love, and marriage. The author's advice is soundly practical and is delivered in a fresh, non-condescending manner, with humor and sympathy.

HALEY, JOSEPH E. *Accent on Purity.* Fides, 1960. 130 p., illustrations, index. pa. 95¢.

This slender volume is a manual of sex instruction for use by parents, teachers, priests, and by anyone engaged in dealing with young people's problems. The methods recommended and the material outlines in this work are easy to follow and to present, and the book is recommended for general use.

KELLY, GEORGE A. (MSGR.). *Birth Control and Catholics.* Doubleday, 1963. 246 p., charts, appendix, index. $4.95.

This thorough and authoritative guide to birth control covers every practical and theoretical aspect of the question: the morality involved, the particular problems of Catholics, and the Catholic approach to marriage and parenthood. There is a complete analysis of the traditionally acceptable methods of birth control based on periodic continence—the so-called "rhythm" methods—such as Calendar Method, Obvious Ovulation Method, Test-Tape Method, and Body Temperature Method. An appendix gives a list of suggested further readings.

KELLY, GEORGE A. (MSGR.). *The Catholic Family Handbook.* Foreword by Francis Cardinal Spellman. Image, 1965. 278 p., appendix, index. pa. 95¢.

This volume, as its title indicates, is a practical guide for Catholic parents. Among the subjects Msgr. Kelly discusses are happiness in the family, the job of being a parent, the moral training of a child, the role of Catholic schools in raising Catholic children, sex education, the "exceptional" child, motherhood and careers, handling teenagers, and preparation of children for marriage. Like all of Msgr. Kelly's writings, this work is practical and concrete, easily readable, and sure to be immensely valuable to Catholic couples.

KELLY, GEORGE A. (MSGR.). *The Catholic Marriage Manual.* Foreword by Francis Cardinal Spellman. Random, 1958. xvi, 240 p., bibliography, index. $4.95.

Msgr. Kelly provides a complete guide to the Church's teaching on the purpose, meaning, and responsibilities of the married state. This is probably one of the most concise and comprehensive such books available, and its down-to-earth approach will appeal to all who are, in any capacity, occupied in marriage counseling or instruction.

KELLY, GEORGE A. (MSGR.). *The Catholic Youth's Guide to Life and Love.* Random, 1960. xiv, 209 p. $3.95.

Msgr. Kelly, a specialist in youth guidance, has written what is in effect a comprehensive guide to the problems that are likely to be encountered in the period between the early teens and the age of marriage. Among such problems treated are dating, going steady, love and its meaning, engagement, and the preparation for marriage.

KELLY, GEORGE A. (MSGR.). *Dating for Young Catholics.* Doubleday, 1963. 135 p. $2.95. Echo, 1965. pa. 75¢.

This work is intended for Catholic youth still somewhat removed from the age at which one may become engaged, as well as for the parents of Catholic children in that category. It outlines the Catholic principles for dating, discussing such complementary topics as necking, drinking, fast driving, good and bad reputations, going steady, being in love, the nature of marriage, and many such related topics. Msgr. Kelly manages to answer most of the questions that young people of high-school age are likely to ask, and his work will be exceptionally useful.

LYNCH, WILLIAM A. *A Marriage Manual for Catholics.* Foreword by Richard Cardinal Cushing. Trident, 1964. xx, 359 p. $4.95.

The author of this book is a Catholic layman who is also an outstanding obstetrician and gynecologist. He presents a practical and realistic guide to the physical, emotional, and esthetic aspects of Christian marriage, treating in depth such problems as the emotional adjustments necessary in marriage and the importance of a satisfactory marital sex life. This is a highly satisfactory exposition of what a couple, individually and collectively, should bring to marriage and what they can expect from marriage.

MARY DE LOURDES, SISTER. *Baby Grows in Age and Grace.* Illustrations by Beatrice and Frederick Ryan. Image, 1960. 198 p., drawings, index. pa. 75¢.

Sister Mary de Lourdes is a specialist in the care of children in the pre-school age group, and she has written this practical and popular manual of child-care for the Catholic mother with children from one to seven years of age. She discusses thoroughly the main points of child care from the physical, mental, and spiritual standpoint, pointing out the objective to be aimed at and suggesting concrete methods for attaining maximum development in each area.

MESSENGER, ERNEST CHARLES. *Two in One Flesh.* Introduction by J. L. King, s.j. Newman, 1955. 368 p., bibliography, index. $4.00.

This study of Christian marriage has three basic parts. Part One is introductory and sets out the general principles governing sex and marriage; Part Two explains the evolution through the centuries of the Christian attitudes toward love and marriage; Part Three studies the modern Christian ideals on those matters. This work is of special importance for priests as a guide both in marriage-counseling and in preparing sermons on marriage, but it is by no means too specialized for the layman interested in the theology of marriage.

NEWLAND, MARY REED. *Our Children Grow Up*. Kenedy, 1965. 200 p. $4.50. Image, 1967. pa. 85¢.

Mrs. Newland deals with a problem of increasing complexity in the twentieth century: what to do about teenagers. She discusses the major problems that a parent may expect to face when children reach the 12-to-15-year-old level: spiritual sloth, sex, fads, reading matter, school, jobs, drinking, etc. She handles her subject with a good deal of wit and charm, and her common-sense advice will be of interest to all parents.

NEWLAND, MARY REED. *We and Our Children*. Kenedy, 1954. 273 p. $3.50. Image, 1961. pa. 85¢.

Mrs. Newland writes an informative manual on the raising of Catholic children in holiness, truth, and the Christian virtues. Virtually everything in a child's life—play, creative activity, work, school, family responsibilities, prayer, the sacraments, the liturgy—is demonstrated to be an occasion for impressing a spiritual outlook onto the developing mind of the child. This is an invaluable guide for Catholic parents with children in the 3-to-10 age group.

ODENWALD, ROBERT (M.D.). *Your Child's World*. Random House, 1958. 194 p. $3.95. Image, 1963. pa. 85¢.

A guide to the emotional interrelations between parent and child from birth through adolescence, popularly written by an eminent child psychiatrist. The author begins with an explanation of the child's basic needs, and goes on to discuss the problems of the first two years of the child's life, the appearance of individuality in the child, the pre-adolescent personality, and the storms of adolescence. This is a clear and practical manual, enthusiastically recommended by educators and by parents.

ORAISON, MARC. *Love or Constraint?* Translated by Una Morrissy. Deus, 1961. xv, 286 p. pa. 95¢.

The author treats of some of the psychological aspects of Christian education, including such subjects as the examination of the "unconscious" of parents, the emotional evolution of man, the relationship between the superego and morals, and the evolution of religious sentiment in the young. The book is written with a minimum of technical terminology, although a profitable reading does require a general knowledge of psychological and pedagogical principles.

SATTLER, HENRY V. (c.ss.r.). *Parents, Children and the Facts of Life.* St. Anthony's Guild, 1953. 237 p., notes, bibliography, index. $3.00. Image, 1956. pa. 85¢.

This is a text on sex education for parents and for those engaged in working with parents. For Catholics, "sex education" means more than the mere passing on of biological facts; it signifies primarily the training of boys and girls in the ways of purity and of a worth-while marriage. This volume tells parents (and teachers) what to tell their children, when and how to tell it, and what to avoid. It is popularly written, frank, and sensible.

SUENENS, LEON JOSEPH CARDINAL. *Love and Control.* Translated by George J. Robinson. Newman, 1961. 200 p. pa. 95¢.

Cardinal Suenens' work is intended for those who are involved in sex education—parents, teachers, counsellors. He discusses the need for sexual control both within and before marriage, the means for attaining that control, and he outlines a program of sex education for the use of priests, doctors, teachers, and Catholic social organizations. The book is not a sex manual as such, but rather a pedagogic guide dealing with principles.

THOMAS, JOHN L. (s.j.). *The Catholic Viewpoint on Marriage and the Family.* Introduction by John J. Delaney. Hanover, 1958. 191 p. $3.50. Image, 1965. pa. 85¢.

This volume of the "Catholic Viewpoint Series" considers straightforwardly such controversial issues as divorce, mixed marriages, birth control, artificial insemination, the rhythm method, and abortion. Father Thomas explains in each case what is the Church's position and gives the reasons for that position. Like the other books in this series, this treatment was written for the non-specialist and it will be of interest to anyone concerned about the Church's teaching on marriage.

WERTH, ALVIN (o.f.m. cap.) and CLEMENT S. MIHANOVICH. *Papal Pronouncements on Marriage and the Family.* Bruce, 1955. xiii, 189 p., index. $3.50.

This is a compilation of papal documents on the subject of

marriage and the family issued during the reigns of Leo XIII, Pius X, Benedict XIV, Pius XI, and Pius XII—the period from 1878 to 1954. The material is arranged chronologically, and includes all of the most important papal pronouncements on marriage issued in modern times.

15. MISCELLANEOUS

A section with this heading should well cause any good librarian to shake her head in wonderment. Aside from the fact that this *Guide* is designed for the general reader and not specifically for the librarian, there is an excellent reason for this catch-all section. There is a limit to the number of categories we can treat in a volume of this size. Obviously, if we had unlimited space, a special category could be devised for every book in this *Guide*. However, we were obliged to limit the sections and the 26 subject categories we have set up cover the great bulk of the books we would recommend for the general reader. Yet there are some few books of great merit which cannot be classified under any one of these sections. We have therefore resolved upon this strictly unorthodox but highly utilitarian device of a *Miscellaneous* section. Our apologies to the dedicated classifiers—but I am sure even they will approve of the fine volumes listed here which might not otherwise have been included. To the general reader, we suggest you will find a wealth of excellent reading material below.

BELLOC, HILAIRE. *The Path to Rome*. Image, 1956. 270 p., drawings. pa. 85¢.

In form, this book is exactly what the title suggests—the description of a journey on foot from the Franco-German border to Rome. But, in fact, it is far more than a travelogue, for the author's wanderings give him frequently the opportunity to reflect on the exciting Christian tradition of European civilization. It is filled with interesting observations on such unusual items as the influence of windows upon civilization, the particular value of morning Mass, reflections on folk singing, etc., all written in the sparkling style which has made Belloc one of the great literary figures of the twentieth century.

FAHERTY, WILLIAM B. (s.J.). *Living Alone: A Guide for the Single Woman.* Sheed, 1964. xiv, 162 p. $3.95.

Father Faherty discusses the problems peculiar to the single woman in America, from a social, spiritual, and economic standpoint. Although the work is sociological in nature, basing itself upon answers to questionnaires and in-depth interviews, it is non-technical in approach and in style.

FENNER, KAY T. *American Catholic Etiquette.* Newman, 1961. xxiii, 402 p. $5.95. Newman, 1963. pa. $1.95.

An unusual and useful book for all Catholics, this guide to proper social behavior concentrates on situations in which Catholics, as such, are most likely to find themselves. Among the subjects discussed are baptisms, the administration of the last sacraments, funerals and mourning, the duties of the parishioner, manners for children, etc.

JOHN XXIII, POPE. *The Wit and Wisdom of Good Pope John.* Edited by Henri Fesquet; translated by Salvator Attanasio. Kenedy, 1964. 192 p. $3.95. Signet, 1965. pa. 50¢.

Pope John XXIII was well known for his love of gaiety and laughter, for his native wit and for his ability to express profound and eternal truths in a simple and human way. Mr. Fesquet has collected in this book all the available material on John's humor—his epigrams, comments, etc.—as well as a group of quotations expressing his views on life, man, the world, and the spirit. The book is often amusing, moving, and always good reading.

KERR, JEAN. *Please Don't Eat the Daisies.* Doubleday, 1957. 143 p., illustrations. $3.50. Crest, 1962. pa. 35¢.

This best-selling work is a collection of delightfully humorous essays on the perils of being a wife and mother. It is filled with gentle irony and good-natured commentary on the foibles of modern living, and is highly recommended for light reading.

KERR, JEAN. *The Snake Has All the Lines.* Doubleday, 1960. 168 p., drawings. $3.50. Crest, 1963. pa. 35¢.

This book is a sequel to the author's best-selling *Please Don't Eat the Daisies,* and, like its predecessor, contains a series of essays on her experiences as a wife and mother in suburbia. Mrs. Kerr gives an hilarious account of her trip to the beach with her five children, discusses the vagaries of deportment at table among young people, and describes her own role as one-time Queen of the May at age thirteen.

KLINGER, KURT. *A Pope Laughs.* Translated by Sally Mc-Devitt Cuneen. Holt, 1964. 158 p., portraits. $3.95.

This is a collection of the amusing, and often touching, stories of Pope John XXIII, skillfully translated and well arranged.

LAFARGE, JOHN (S.J.). *Reflections on Growing Old.* Doubleday, 1963. 137 p., bibliographical notes. $2.95.

These wise and practical thoughts on turning old age into the best years of one's life are written by an eminent Jesuit author, columnist, and leader in the fight for racial justice. Father LaFarge expresses a positive point of view: he explores what old age has to say to us in the light of our faith and of our personal experience. He provides an answer to the question, "What is the purpose of our suffering, deprivation, and eventual death?" And he emphasizes the absolute necessity, above all in old age, for the twin virtues of patience and love.

McGINLEY, PHYLLIS. *The Province of the Heart.* Viking, 1959. 181 p. $3.50.

Miss McGinley, best known as a poet, presents here a group of essays in defense of life in suburbia. She divides her essays into three groups: Unorthodoxies ("The Consolations of Illiteracy"), Frivolities ("Against Gardens"), and From My Terrace ("Suburbia, of Thee I Sing"). The chapters are mostly about children, husbands, and especially about the joys of being a woman, a mother, and a wife. It is a witty, compassionate book.

McGINLEY, PHYLLIS. *Sixpence in Her Shoe.* Macmillan, 1964. 281 p. $4.95.

This best-selling collection of essays comprises a series of brightly amusing, and sometimes startingly germane, chapters on the tribulations and rewards of motherhood and housewifery in the twentieth century.

McNASPY, C. J. (S.J.). *A Guide to Christian Europe.* Hawthorn, 1963. 255 p., glossary, bibliography, index. $3.95.

The author designed this book as a personal, informal set of hints for the person planning a first trip to Europe. He deals with all of the major countries of the western part of Europe, with the exception of those of Scandinavia, describing in detail the cities, cathedrals, shrines, and art, to be found in each, and taking into account the historical background and religious significance of the places described.

MARITAIN, JACQUES. *Reflections on America*. Scribner, 1958. 119 p., notes, index. $3.50. Image, 1964. pa. 75¢.

A series of essays in which Maritain analyzes the social, economic, and political philosophies of America. Among the subjects treated are "The Old Tag of American Materialism," "The Race Question," "American Modesty," "Some American Illusions," "Work and Leisure." Surprisingly, here is a Maritain book which is lucid and non-technical; it is recommended for anyone who wants to stand back and take a searching and objective look at his country.

MORTON, H. V., and FULTON J. SHEEN. *This Is the Holy Land*. Hawthorn, 1960. 160 p., illustrations, index. $4.95. Image, 1962. pa. 95¢.

A pilgrimage in words and pictures to the Holy Land, conducted by Bishop Sheen, described by H. V. Morton, and photographed by Yousuf Karsh. There are descriptions, and superb photographs, of all the Holy Places in Palestine, with notes on the history of each of the shrines. A very useful book either for the pilgrim who needs a guidebook, or for the non-traveler who wants a graphic picture of the Holy Land.

MORTON, H. V. and FULTON J. SHEEN. *This Is Rome*. Photographs by Yousuf Karsh. Hawthorn, 1959. 154 p., illustrations, notes. $4.95. Image, 1961. pa. 95¢.

This is a verbal and photographic tour of the major religious and historic places of interest in Rome, conducted by Bishop Sheen and described by H. V. Morton. There are many unusual and striking photographs by Yousuf Karsh. It is an excellent introduction to the beauties of Rome for the persons who have never been there, and a comprehensive source of memories for those who have.

MORTON, HENRY V. *A Traveller in Italy*. Dodd, 1964. 636 p., illustrations, maps, bibliography. $10.00.

A distinguished traveller and writer describes a journey through Italy, pointing out, by means of words and illustrations, the great cathedrals and churches, the works of art, the shrines, and the places of historical interest. The book makes entertaining and instructive reading as well as an ideal companion for the reader's own tour of Italy.

SERTILLANGES, A. D. (O.P.). *The Intellectual Life*. Newman, 1948. xxiii, 260 p., notes, index. pa. $1.50.

This work has come to be recognized as the standard guidebook for those engaged in intellectual work. The author provides an account of the nature and dignity of the intellectual vocation, but for the most part confines himself to practical considerations, discussing such matters as the organization of one's time, the relation of one's specialty to the whole of human knowledge, one's choice of reading matter, the use of memory, taking of notes, etc. Father Sertillanges regards the intellectual life as a vocation in the strict sense: as a calling from God which carries with it sufficient talent and grace to enable the intellectual to fulfill the role that God has planned for him.

SUMMERS, MONTAGUE (REV.). *The History of Witchcraft*. Foreword by Felix Morrow. University Books, 1956. xxiii, 313 p., notes, bibliography, index. $6.00.

The History of Witchcraft examines the general principles of witchcraft and demonology from earliest times to the present day, considering the religious and social implication of witchcraft, diabolical possession, modern spiritism, and the place of the witch in dramatic literature. When Father Summers' book first appeared (1927) it caused a sensation and became a "best seller." Since that time, it has come to be accepted as an extraordinarily erudite and polished Catholic version of the place of witchcraft in history. Whatever one's personal views on witchcraft and demonology, the reader will find Father Summers' book lively and informative.

THURSTON, HERBERT. *Ghosts and Poltergeists*. Gateway, 1959. 210 p. pa. $1.25.

Mr. Thurston has assembled a file of astonishing instances of poltergeist and ghostly activities which occurred from medieval times up to the twentieth century. The material is taken from all over the world—England, Ireland, America, Asia—and the author gives a "straight" presentation of it, without attempting to convince the reader one way or another. Whether one views unexplained physical phenomena as amusing, puzzling, or terrifying, this book will provide many hours of entertainment.

TRESE, LEO. *Vessel of Clay.* Sheed, 1950. 113 p. $2.50. Image, 1959. pa. 65¢.

This is the story of a day in the life of a parish priest. The author takes the reader through the day with him, from early Mass, visiting sick parishioners, greeting school children, hearing confessions, instructing converts, preparing a sermon, attending a teenage dance in the parish hall, to his last—if vain—hope for an uninterrupted night of sleep. There is much humor and wisdom in this book; it will satisfy the layman's curiosity about what priests do "with all that free time," and will entertain the reader who wants something different.

16. MISSIONARIES AND MISSIONARY ACTIVITIES

When our Lord said to his apostles "Go, therefore, and make disciples of all nations" (Matt. 28:19) he charged his Church with a responsibility that has been accepted and acted upon for 2000 years. During these twenty centuries missionaries have gone to every corner of the earth in response to his command. From the missionary journeys of St. Paul in the first century to the far-flung activities of the missionary priests, nuns, and laymen of the twentieth century, there is a wide gap of time and method, but the motivating force is always the same—to bring to all peoples the word of God.

How successful these activities have been is attested by the fact that half a billion men, women, and children all over the world are Catholics. The measure of failure is in the stark statistic that more than 2½ billions are not Catholics, and of this huge number more than 2 billions are not even Christians. And in these comparative figures may be found the glory and the failure of the missionary activity of the Catholic Church.

Interestingly enough, Christianity has been most successful with Western man and with primitive peoples. Though launched in Palestine, the center of Christianity early was located in Rome and soon made great inroads in the Roman Empire and among nations on its periphery. As the Empire declined, Christianity grew in strength and numbers, offering as it did a way of salvation which strongly appealed to men and women disenchanted with what remained of Roman civilization. Gradually, Christians began to occupy positions of importance and, as civil authority diminished, the authority of the Church moved into the vacuum providing a sorely needed focal point for confidence and belief.

As the barbarians infiltrated and then flooded the civilized Western world, they came into contact with the Church and, as time passed, were Christianized and absorbed into the

Church. The Church, true to the commands of her Divine Founder, was not satisfied with converting the barbarians who came within the old Empire boundaries, and began sending missionaries to the tribes beyond the civilized world. Soon, Christian missionaries were to be found as far north as the Scandinavian countries, west to England and Ireland, and east to what is now Poland, the Baltic nations and Russia. By 1000, all Europe was Christian and Christ's command had been realized in the Western world. Meanwhile the Eastern Church had spread all along the rim of northern Africa and Asia Minor but when the Roman Empire broke into East and West, the Christian Church of the East had about reached its height and its missionary activities had just about ceased. When the Eastern Church finally broke completely with Rome in 1054, it also, to all intents and purposes, abandoned any real missionary activity.

As the European powers began to spread over the world at the beginning of the modern era, their explorers, fighting men, and settlers brought with them the religion of their home country. South America became the territory of Spain and Portugal and was Catholic. In North America, Canada was settled by the French and was Catholic; the southeast and west of the United States were explored and settled by Spaniards from Mexico who brought their friars and Catholic faith with them; the eastern United States eventually became British territory, and by that time the Reformation had added England to its roster of nations, and the English brought their versions of Christianity. By the same token Australia became largely Protestant and the Philippines Catholic.

The point to all of the above is that wherever he went the European brought his religion with him and since, with few exceptions, the natives in all these areas were in a primitive state of culture, they were overcome and eventually absorbed into the faith of their conquerors. Often this acceptance was the result of long, faithful, persevering effort on the part of heroic missionaries sent with the avowed purpose of converting these savages. Indeed, there is no more glorious page in the history of the Church than that recounting the deeds of the heroic men and women who so freely gave of their efforts and often lives to bring the teaching of the Church to their reluctant brothers.

But if the Church was successful in these efforts, only failure attended her efforts among the peoples of established cultures. The most notable examples, of course, are India, China, and the nations of central Asia. As far back as the time of the apostles, missionary activity was carried on in India. As a matter of fact there is a strong tradition among Catholic Indians that St. Thomas, the apostle, preached and taught in India and died there, and that his disciples had penetrated central Asia.

But though spasmodic missionary activities were directed to these parts of the earth, it was not until modern times that real efforts were undertaken. Even such efforts had little impact until the nineteenth and twentieth century. An effort was made in the sixteenth century headed by the famed Jesuit Matteo Ricci, but it foundered when the Chinese Rites controversy flared in Rome. Ricci had been lenient in allowing the Chinese to retain Chinese rites and customs when they became Catholics on the sound theory that Catholicism was a universal, not only a western religion. He was accused of introducing pagan concepts into Catholicism and in the ensuing controversy in Rome the whole Eastern missionary effort was dealt a blow from which it was not to recover for centuries when missionaries were strictly enjoined from permitting the use of any pagan practices in Catholic rites and ceremonies. The natives of these countries quickly associated Catholicism with the nationality of the foreigner and the full effect of this association was felt in the twentieth century when the rising forces of nationalism began to be felt. Catholicism (as was all Christianity) was labeled the tool of the foreign invader and became the first target of any nationalist uprising.

This inability of the Church to convince peoples of other than Western culture nations that Catholicism is not a national or even single culture religion but is universal and above nationalism, has been the root cause of the failure of the missionary effort among some of the most populous nations in the world. Invariably, when a national uprising drove out the hated foreigner it drove out with him his religion.

So when China drove out all foreigners, she unleased a savage, all-out attack on Christianity. Despite the years of sacrifice and devoted service by all Christian missionaries, the people still considered Christianity a foreign religion. For all intents and purposes, Christianity no longer exists in China. It is true that Communism played a large role in this tragic development; but compare the situation in Poland where Communism has also taken over. The difference is that for Poles, Catholicism is not something foreign but an actual part of Poland and the Polish character. In China, Christianity is dead; in Poland it is very much alive and flourishing, despite every contrary effort by the government.

All of these shortcomings of the past are realized among missionary authorities and new methods are constantly being tested. As in every other area of Church activity, there is a ferment in missionary circles as all labor to meet the challenges of these new and trying times.

It is evident that all of the points made above are of concern to those involved in over-all policy formulation. The effects are felt down to the poorest mission in the most desolate area. A change in policy and direction will have the most far-reaching effects in this most important work of the Church.

Having stated this fact, though, it must be added that tho basic effort remains as it always has through the centuries. The missionary must go to "all nations" teaching the word of God and bringing the message of salvation. Usually, he labors among the poorest, most neglected, and most pitiful of God's creatures. He must heal them and feed them and clothe and house them if he is to succeed. A starving man is in no mood to hear of the life hereafter when the pangs of hunger have so enervated him that his sole concern is food. An ill person is not particularly receptive to words. These things missionaries of all ages have known. A French Jesuit preaching to the savage Indian of French Canada in the seventeenth century would be right at home with the Franciscan of the twentieth century in some poverty-ridden South American village or with a Tom Dooley in the steaming jungles of Vietnam.

And what a heroic group these men and women of the missions have been through the centuries! No other group in the Church has suffered as have they. No other group has struggled against such overwhelming odds. No other group has contributed so much to suffering mankind. And no other group has so freely offered of their all as have these men and women—so much so that who can disagree with the dictum "the blood of martyrs is the seed of the Church"? What a noble rollcall it would make to list the names of those who have given so much to the Church.

Authors, fortunately, have always been attracted to this noble group and have written stirringly and well of their deeds. There is a fine literature telling of their exploits from the time of St. Paul to the year in which you are reading these words. It is no accident that missionaries are everywhere and are always in the midst of great events. The Church has always had missionaries and always will. It is the command of her Founder. It would be a pity if their heroic deeds and accomplishments were to be ignored when good books are available about the men and women, working under every conceivable difficulty, who are fulfilling that divine command "Go, therefore, and make disciples of all nations, baptizing them in the name of the Father, and of the Son, and of the Holy Spirit."

BURKE, THOMAS J., Editor. *Catholic Missions: Four Great Missionary Encyclicals.* Fordham, 1957. 83 p., appendix, index. pa. $1.50.

This collection contains the missionary encyclical letters of popes Benedict XV ("On Spreading the Catholic Faith Throughout the World"), Pius XI ("On Fostering Missionary Zeal"), and Pius XII ("On Intensifying Missionary Effort" and "The Gift of Faith"). There are study plans for each encyclical.

DANIELOU, JEAN (S.J.). *The Advent of Salvation.* Translated by Rosemary Sheed. Deus, 1962. 192 p., notes. pa. 95¢.

A comparative study of non-Christian religions and Christianity, this work views all religions from the standpoint of the missionary function of the Church and of the universal implications of Christ's death. Father Danielou, writing for the priest and for the educated layman, discusses within that context the remote and proximate precursors of Christianity, particularly within the ancient Hebrew religion.

DANIELOU, JEAN (S.J.). *The Salvation of Nations.* Translated by Angeline Bouchard. Notre Dame, 1962. ix, 118 p., notes. pa. $1.75.

This is an explanation of the Church's missionary role in God's plan to gather all peoples into the unity of the Mystical Body. The author considers such subjects as the universal nature of the Church's missionary function, the universal implications of the incarnation, the spiritual significance of the Second Coming, and the Holy Spirit's mission. This is an excellent guide to the theology of missionary activity within the Church, though the nature of the author's approach presupposes in the reader at least a general background in theology.

HANLEY, BONIFACE (O.F.M.) and SALVATOR FINK (O.F.M.). *The Franciscans: Love At Work.* St. Anthony's Guild, 1962. 240 p., illustrations. $6.50. Image, 1966. pa. 95¢.

This is a pictorial essay describing the Franciscan Order. With 103 full-page photographs, the book tells the life of St. Francis, explains the application of his spirit in the twentieth century, and shows how that spirit is put to work today through mission work, teaching, preaching, and other activities in which the Franciscans are presently engaged.

KITTLER, GLENN D. *The White Fathers.* Introduction by Laurian Cardinal Rugambwa. Image, 1961. 318 p. pa. 95¢.

The religious congregation known popularly as the "White Fathers" was established in 1868, as the Society of Missionaries of Africa, by Cardinal C. M. A. Lavigerie. The purpose of the Society is to work for the African missions, particularly among the Arabs. They are bound to live as much like the natives as possible, and their dress closely resembles the flowing tunic and burnoose of the Arabs. Mr. Kittler tells in this book the story of the founding of the Society, and of their activities until the middle of the present century. The book is as interesting as any story of adventure, and it is well and colorfully written in a journalistic style.

MARIA DEL REY, SISTER (C.M.). *No Two Alike.* Dodd, 1965. x, 240 p., illustrations. $5.00. Echo, 1966. pa. 85¢.

These biographical "profiles" of Maryknoll nuns are in-

tended to do away with the quaint notion that all Sisters,
like all West Pointers, look alike, talk alike, and act alike. In
a fast-moving narrative, the author tells the story of Sister
Patrice who worked among the lepers of Hawaii; of Mother
Mary who went on horseback into the jungles of Central
America to found a hospital; of Sister Martin, a Negro social
worker in Oregon; of Sister Magdalena and her life in China
and Manchuria—and of a dozen others who resemble each
other only in their dedication to God and in their love of
humanity.

MILLOT, RENE-PIERRE. *Missions in the World Today.* Translated by J. Holland Smith. Hawthorn, 1961. 139 p., bibliography. $3.50.

Father Millot discusses the special characteristics of modern missionary activity, recent papal teachings on the missions, and the role of missionary activity in the over-all
apostolate of the Church. He explains the organization and
activities of the missions, and conducts a brief survey of
missions around the world in mid-twentieth century. The
closing chapter discusses future prospects of the missions.

VAULX, BERNARD DE. *History of the Missions.* Translated by
Reginald F. Trevett. Hawthorn, 1961. 191 p., bibliography.
$3.50.

Father de Vaulx has written a history of the most exciting
and dangerous work of the Church over the past two thousand years. The book is divided into two parts; the first section treats of missionary activity from the first to the nineteenth centuries; the second—about one-third of the work
—is devoted to the nineteenth and twentieth centuries. Only
the broad lines of missionary history are sketched, yet attention is given to some of the more colorful figures in missionary work; e.g., de Nobili and Ricci in the Far East.
(Volume 99 of the *Twentieth Century Encyclopedia of
Catholicism.*)

17. OUR LADY

From the earliest days of the Christian era Mary has been the object of great popular veneration. Although little is actually known of her life beyond the relatively few references to her in the New Testament, a whole literature on the woman who was the mother of the Lord has been written. Indeed it is safe to say that through the centuries more has been written about her and her role in Catholic life than about any other human being who ever lived. What was lacking about her in recorded fact has been amply supplied by a rich heritage of tradition and by the insights and imaginations of scholars and authors in every area of literature. Mary rightly occupies a leading role in any consideration of the great truths of Christianity. As Eve by her actions in the Garden of Eden caused the downfall of mankind so Mary by her act of giving birth to the Redeemer provided the means of salvation for us all.

Created by God with no stain of original sin, she lived a life of immaculate purity and has ever since been the ideal for all women. As the mother of Christ, she has always been regarded as the mother of the Catholic Church and as the mother of all Catholics. As the devoted spouse of St. Joseph she is all that any wife could hope to be. As the sorrowing mother at the foot of the Cross she is the epitome of the all-encompassing love that mothers have always had for their children. The recipient of God's tender love as revealed through her bodily assumption into heaven, she is the queen of heaven and a mediatrix before God for all men. God showered on her all of his blessings and graces as he clearly indicated she was the most perfect of all his human creatures.

All these things have passed into Catholic tradition, teaching, or dogma. And yet, in the past few years many feel that our Lady's role has been slighted and relegated to an inferior position. In view of this "downgrading" it is worth pausing to consider a few aspects of this recent change of attitude on the part of some, if there really is a change, and the reasons for it.

At the outset it should be pointed out that many theologians have long felt that some of the enthusiasts of our Lady were going too far in their veneration of Mary and that such veneration often seemed to border on worship which, of course, is reserved only for God. Though all Marian devotees would deny any such allegations, it is true that many Marian practices and claims put forth for Mary gave this impression. An example of this was the increasing tendency to consider our Lady as co-redemptrix of the human race. When it was pointed out that only Christ could be called Redeemer, these adherents readily admitted this fact and pointed out that they never meant to put Mary on an equal plane with her Son. And yet the prefix "co-" definitely gave that very impression. Indeed one of the stumbling blocks for many non-Catholics to understanding Catholicism was their belief that Catholics worshiped our Lady. They waved aside any denials and pointed to the many Marian devotions in the Church which to them indicated that the Catholic attitude toward Mary was indeed worship rather than, as all Catholics emphasized, veneration, respect, admiration, and love.

So widespread was this feeling among non-Catholics that as the overtones of Vatican Council II became more ecumenical, there was a tendency in many Catholic quarters to play down the Marian aspect of Catholicism. As the ecumenical movement gained momentum many Catholics felt Mary had been cast aside to lessen the differences between many of the non-Catholic churches and Catholicism. Whether this criticism is correct or not is a matter of conjecture; what is a fact is that there was a drastic falling off in magazine articles, books, and devotions to our Lady in the years immediately following the first session of Vatican Council II.

Regardless of who was right in this controversy, the inescapable fact is that Mary has occupied an important position in Catholic life for centuries and will continue to do so for as long as the Church endures. For she is the object of dogmatic statements by the Church as to her virginity, her freedom from the stain of original sin, her bodily assumption into heaven. And far overshadowing all else is the overwhelming fact that the Blessed Virgin Mary is the mother of God, Jesus Christ the second Person of the Blessed Trinity—that it was in her body that the Word became incarnate. From this stems all the reverence and veneration and love that Catholics have poured forth to her through the centuries. And well they might, for Mary's role as mother of Eternity in time is so dazzling that the very thought of it must leave one breathless. It is small wonder that whole libraries have been written about her and that even now great scholars are, as they have been in past centuries, expanding the doctrine of Mary's role in the Church as new minds bring new solutions to various aspects of that role. The wonder of it all fully justifies the most minute exploration of every facet of the most wondrous of all human creatures, her effect on us, and the relationship she exerts between God and man.

Just as she is of the utmost importance to the theologian and scholar, so too it behooves all of us to know more about her. And what a wonderful literature there is on the Virgin of Galilee. Great authors have written on Mary, and the fruits of their research, genius and inspiration are readily at hand. We have selected those books which we feel are most appropriate for the modern reader and readily admit that this is but a modicum. Nevertheless, we feel the books we describe below will give any reader a fine and varied introduction to the woman of whom the Constitution on the Church defined by the Council Fathers at the third session of Vatican Council II and promulgated by Pope Paul VI on November 21, 1964, said: "The Virgin Mary . . . is acknowledged and honored as the Mother of God and Mother of the Redeemer . . . The Catholic Church, taught by the Holy Spirit, honors her with filial affection and piety as a most beloved mother."

ATTWATER, DONALD. *A Dictionary of Mary*. Kenedy, 1956. viii, 312 p. $6.50.

This was the first, and it still is the best, book in English which brings together all of the assorted bits of information and historical facts about the Virgin. The book is in dictionary format, listing and explaining, in alphabetical order, the facts of Mary's life, her privileges, the theology of Mary, her feasts, her shrines, etc. It is a valuable reference work for home and library.

DANIEL-ROPS, HENRI. *The Book of Mary.* Translated by Alastair Guinan. Hawthorn, 1960. 189 p., notes, bibliography. $4.95. Image, 1963. pa. 75¢.

Mr. Daniel-Rops, one of Catholicism's most popular historians, has collected in one book all the data that are known about the life of our Lady. After an examination of the Scriptures, the author turns to the apocryphal writings and to the works of the Church Fathers, and through such texts he traces the development of the Marian tradition in the Church. This is a popularly written book, but one founded on sound scholarship.

DOHENRY, WILLIAM J. (C.S.C.) and JOSEPH P. KELLY, Editors. *Papal Documents on Mary.* Bruce, 1954. x, 270 p. $4.50.

This is a compilation of thirty-seven papal documents, beginning with the *Ubi primum* of Pius IX, by which the doctrine of the Immaculate Conception was promulgated, and ending with Pius XII's "Prayer for the Marian Year"—a span of approximately seventy-five years—and including the full texts of all pertinent encyclicals as well as papal addresses and public statements on our Lady. This is a valuable work of reference for Marian studies.

LYNCH, JOHN W. *A Woman Wrapped in Silence.* Macmillan, 1941. vi, 277 p., bibliography. $3.95.

This is the life of the Virgin Mary told in verse. The poet-author, however, has allowed himself no poetic license with respect to fact, but bases himself solidly on the New Testament recitals. Whatever the individual reader may think of Father Lynch's poetry, there is no doubt that his work furnishes many unusual reflections on Mary and her role in the salvation of man.

MOST, WILLIAM G. *Mary in Our Life.* Kenedy, 1959. 358 p., notes, bibliography, appendix, index. $4.50. Image, 1963. pa. 95¢.

The theme of this book is the belief that God gave to Mary an essential place in the work of the redemption of mankind, and, therefore, that we should give to Mary a correspondingly essential place in our lives. The author shows how to achieve a synthesis of God-centered and Mary-guided spirituality, and draws on the Scriptures, the writings of the Fathers and the Doctors of the Church, and papal pronouncements on the role of Mary.

SHEED, FRANK J., Editor. *The Mary Book.* Sheed, 1950. xii, 411 p., plates. $4.00.

Mr. Sheed's purpose in this collection has been to assemble together contributions by modern authors which would cover every aspect of modern Mariology. Thus, the selections, arranged by subject, deal with Mary's position in Catholic thought from the standpoint not only of doctrine and devotion, but also of poetry and art.

SHEEN, FULTON, BISHOP. *The World's First Love.* Image, 1956. 237 p. pa. 85¢.

Bishop Sheen tells the story of the Blessed Virgin and the beliefs which have been attached to her from the Immaculate Conception to the apparition at Fatima. He presents a loving and reverent portrayal of her whole life, from the Annunciation, through the boyhood of Jesus, the public life of her Son and his passion and death, up to her assumption into heaven. Clearly and logically written, and based on a solid foundation of history, philosophy, and theology, this book is probably the most eloquent popular portrayal available on the Mother of God.

WEIGER, JOSEF. *Mary: Mother of Faith.* Translated by Ruth Bethell. Regnery, 1959. 267 p. $5.00. Image, 1962. pa. 85¢.

A biography of the Virgin Mary. The work is divided into three parts. First, it examines the life of Mary as known from the Gospels: the Annunciation, the birth of Christ, the flight into Egypt, and the crucifixion of Christ. Then Mary is considered as she appears in the writings of the prophets and saints. Finally, Mary is studied as the mother of mankind, revealed through meditations on the rosary.

THE APPARITIONS

During the past century or so, a series of events took place with such frequency they caused many people to dub the modern era "The Marian Age." These unusual occurrences consisted of the repeated appearances of our Lady usually to children or simple people of poor background in isolated areas.

Now there have been recorded in past centuries numerous instances of the appearance of our Lady. What characterized the present apparitions was the tremendous impact they had and the fact that they were all subjected to the most intensive investigations—in many cases by scoffers and non-believers. Despite the humble background of the visionaries and despite every pressure brought to bear on them, no one was able to break their stories or catch them in contradictions. Add to this the actual detailed records which have been kept of the so-called miracles which have taken place at many of the sites at which our Lady reputedly appeared, and the reality of our Lady's actual appearance perforce becomes more than mere conjecture. And finally when one considers the effect of Lourdes, Fatima, La Salette, Guadalupe—to mention just a few—on millions and millions of people, it must be obvious that those who believe our Lady was intervening in human affairs are not indulging in wishful thinking. The evidence is much too overwhelming and impressive to dismiss as the vaporings of shepherd children or illiterate peasants. There is a solid body of factual evidence to support the proposition that something of great significance did take place at these now great pilgrimage sites.

Fortunately authors of note were early attracted to these unusual occurrences and we have a fine body of literature on the appearances of our Lady. It is interesting to note that many of the outstanding writings on the apparitions are by non-Catholics. So powerful has been the effect of our Lady's intervention in the world that her message has been heard by men and women of all creeds and beliefs. Perhaps the finest book on Lourdes is *The Song of Bernadette* by Franz Werfel, a Jew; and *Miracle of Lourdes* by Ruth Cranston can hardly be accused of Catholic predisposition, since Miss Cranston is a Protestant; and these are just two of many such works.

At any rate the apparitions of our Lady are a noteworthy aspect of Marian literature which deserves special notice. We call them to your attention through the following books and assure you there is a thrill in store for those who do not know of these great apparitions and added knowledge for those who would know more of them.

DELANEY, JOHN J., Editor. *A Woman Clothed with the Sun.* Doubleday, 1960. 274 p. $3.95. Image, 1961. pa. 85¢.

This book describes eight famous appearances of our Lady. Seven of these took place in the last century: Lourdes, La Salette, Beauraing, Fatima, Miraculous Medal, Knock, and Banneux; the eighth, Guadalupe, which occurred in the sixteenth century, is included because of its profound message for Americans. The contributors to this anthology include Frances Parkinson Keyes, Mary Purcell, Msgr. William Mc-Grath, Ethel Cook Eliot, and Msgr. John S. Kennedy. In his introductory chapter, the editor traces the relationships between the apparitions and provides an analysis of their significance. This is an unusual collection, especially valuable because of the explanations of the apparitions in relation to one another.

KENNEDY, JOHN S. *Light on the Mountain.* Farrar, Straus, 1954. 192 p. $3.00. Image, 1956, pa. 75¢.

The story of the apparitions of the Virgin Mary at La Salette. During the past century, Mary has appeared several times—Lourdes, La Salette, Fatima, etc.—and, of the major apparitions, only La Salette has failed to receive the public attention and fame that it deserves. This book is intended to popularize that vision by giving a vivid and popular account of Mary's appearance and of the message she communicated at La Salette.

[Bernadette] SAINT-PIERRE, MICHEL DE. *Bernadette and Lourdes.* Translated by Edward Fitzgerald. Image, 1955. 266 p. pa. 95¢.

The whole remarkable story of the little shepherdess who saw the Virgin Mary in the grotto at Lourdes, the miracles and cures that take place there, and the eventual canonization of Bernadette. There is an interesting epilogue on the miraculous cures, and an appendix which gives incidental information on the family and home of Bernadette, the visions, letters of Bernadette, etc.

SHARKEY, DONALD. *The Woman Shall Conquer.* All Saints, 1961. 306 p., bibliography, index. pa. 50¢.

The author relates, in a smoothly journalistic style, the story of Mary's apparitions in modern times, and of their effect upon the world. There is emphasis, of course, on such famous instances as the apparitions at Lourdes and at Fatima, but also covered are such less known manifestations as those of La Salette and Guadalupe. This is not the account of a critical observer or of a historian, but of a believer; the book, therefore, is suitable for spiritual reading.

WALSH, WILLIAM THOMAS. *Our Lady of Fatima.* Macmillan, 1947. 229 p. $3.50. Image, 1954. pa. 75¢.

The greatest miracle of modern times took place on October 13, 1917, as, in the presence of 70,000 people, the sun whirled like a gigantic wheel of fire and plunged toward the earth. This was the culmination of a series of events occurring in a small Portuguese village where the Mother of God had appeared to three children and predicted World War II, the rise of Communism, and the present world chaos. This is the whole story, told simply and with reverence. Highly recommended for everyone.

WERFEL, FRANZ. *The Song of Bernadette.* Translated by Ludwig Lewissohn. Compass, 1956. xiii, 466 p. pa. $1.65.

Of all the books on Bernadette and Lourdes, this although a novel, is by far the most popular and the most gratifying to read. The author, a Jew, presents Bernadette Soubirous as a person who became a saint, not as an unearthly, unhuman saint who was born already canonized. The translation is flowing and highly readable, and this is a "must" book for anyone who has not yet read it.

18. OUR LORD

There have been more books written about Jesus Christ than about any other figure in history. And this is only appropriate. For if Christ was a faker, then he perpetrated the biggest fraud ever conceived on all mankind and much should be written about him to unmask him. If, on the other hand, as all Catholics believe, he is truly the Second Person of the Blessed Trinity, the Word made flesh, the Incarnation, then he should be the main preoccupation of writers of every generation for he is the Eternal God entered into time, infinity in the form of a man, the means of salvation for mankind, the hope of the world. Small wonder that he is the object of countless books from the time of the apostles to the present. Next to the Bible, a good life of our Lord must perforce be basic reading for any Catholic.

Note though that we said "next to the Bible." For the gospels of the four Evangelists are the story of Christ, his mission on earth, and his teaching. They are the authentic accounts of his life on which any life of Christ must be based, for they are the sole contemporary source of information about him. All writers, in writing of Christ, use the Gospels as the starting point for their narratives.

However, this does not mean that the Gospels contain the only early references to Christ's life on earth. Aside from the Gospels there are enough references in Roman and Jewish works of the first and second centuries to insure the historical reality of Christ aside from his supernatural characteristics. For example, about 112 the author Pliny the Younger in a letter to the Emperor Trajan tells of the many Christians in the province of Bithynia of which he was governor who were "accustomed to gather before daybreak and sing hymns to Christ as if he were a god." Written just before 117, the *Annales* of Tacitus reported that Emperor Nero foisted the blame on the Christians for the burning of Rome in 64 and "presented as the guilty ones and visited with the most refined punishments those whom the populace, hating them for

their crimes, called *Crestiani.* The author of this denomina-
tion, one Crestus, in the reign of Tiberias, had been condemned to death by Pontius Pilate; but, though checked for
the moment, the deadly superstition broke out afresh, not
only throughout Judea, where this evil originated, but also
throughout the City [Rome], where all outrageous and
shameful things gather from every reign and are exalted."
This passage certainly contains a description of Christ, his
death, the spread of Christianity and its persecution. In
120 Suetonius testifies that only twenty years after the death
of Christ, in the reign of Emperor Claudius, the Jews in Rome
often quarreled about *Crestus,* a corruption of the Greek
word *Christos,* a translation of the Hebrew word *messiah.*
And finally Jesus or the Christians are mentioned in three
places in the writings of Josephus, the Jewish historian, and
though there is a dispute among scholars about the authenticity of a longish passage in his *Antiquities of the Jews* about
Jesus, most scholars agree about the validity of the other two.

In short, these four reference of writers of antiquity to our
Lord and the Christians seem to establish the fact of the
historicity of Christ even if no Christian sources existed.
Granted that such references are few, the reasons are readily
apparent. After all Galilee was a small, relatively poor, obscure, distant, troublesome province of Rome. There were
constant outbreaks there, so a new disturbance might well
be passed over as unimportant in the affairs of the Roman
Empire. Only when the Christians became numerically strong
enough to disturb the equilibrium of the residents of the
provinces and Rome itself would they come to the attention
of Rome-centered Roman authorities and authors, and this
is exactly what happened.

In addition to these non-Christian sources, there are many
Christian writings of the first centuries other than the New
Testament. These are the apocryphal books, such as gospels,
acts, epistles, originally held to be inspired and part of the
canon of the Scripture but later officially rejected by the
Church as not inspired, *pseudepigrapha* or ecclesiastical writings of various kinds, and deeds and short sayings attributed
to Christ found in the early Church writers called *agrapha*
or *logia.* Some of these were held in such high repute in the

early Christian era that some writers included them among
the Books of the New Testament. When the Church in 382
ruled on what belonged in the New Testament, these apocrypha were discarded. It is safe to assume that there were
many more stories of our Lord, his deeds and his sayings,
than are recorded in the New Testament. Many of the
apocrypha, though discredited as divinely inspired, are regarded by Biblical authorities as authentic as historical documents and invaluable sources of information about the times
and peoples they describe. Further we have the Evangelist
John's word that Jesus did many things not recorded by himself and his fellow Evangelists when at the conclusion of his
gospel he says: "There are, however, many other things that
Jesus did; but if every one of these should be written, not
even the world itself, I think, could hold the books that
would have to be written" (John 21:25).

And finally, of course, the Epistles are a rich source of
biographical information about Christ. Usually they confirm
some fact in the four gospels but sometimes one of the authors of the Epistles will include in one of his letters a saying
not contained in the gospels as for instance St. Paul's "It is a
more blessed thing to give than to receive" (Acts 20:35).

But in the final analysis the Four Gospels are the biography
of Jesus Christ, and the seeker of information about his life
should read them before any other biography. Of course, any
biographer worth his salt begins his work by acknowledging
the fact that here is his primary source. Having said this
though, it must be immediately added that a good biography
of our Lord can add immeasurably to one's knowledge of the
Christ. For, important though the Four Gospels are, they do
lack much of interest to the reader that the biographer can
supply.

In the first place, the Evangelists were writing for an audience fully knowledgeable about the laws, customs, habits and
conditions of Galilee of the time of Christ. They made no
attempt to explain things that were well known to their
readers. Christ himself did the same thing. He lived in an
agricultural society; consequently, his teachings are liberally
sprinkled with references to harvests, grain, beasts, birds, all
familiar to the countryman but quite unfamiliar to people liv-

ing in a mechanized and industrial society. He talks of wolves attacking sheep and the need and duties of the shepherd; he cites the parable of grain falling on rocky, barren, and fertile soil, he talks of the lilies in the fields. All these were familiar to his listeners, and his Evangelists, writing for the same audience, felt no need for explaining any of these things so familiar to the people of their background and era. But many of their references puzzle today's audience. A biographer is aware of this and explains such things to his readers.

The same thing applies to the customs of the day, the governmental system in Palestine, the position of the Jews in the Roman Empire. All these factors, so important for an understanding of the life of Christ, are mentioned matter of factly by the Evangelists just as we today would matter of factly refer to the relationship of states to the federal government of the United States, or of Commonwealth nations to Great Britain, or of the nations in the United Nations to each other and to the world organization. It is the task of the Christologist to make clear for the reader this complex of human relations and this background information, so necessary for a full understanding of Christ's human life.

Galilee was not an area in a vacuum. It was surrounded by neighboring nations which affected the people and lives of Galilee. Again an understanding of these neighboring states as well as of the peoples of the places Christ preached and lived is essential for a full comprehension of his life. What motivated these people, why were so many of them so receptive of Christ's teachings, why were others so fearful, why did the Romans become involved—all these things the Evangelists knew, as did their listeners; but for the modern reader much of it is incomprehensible and requires the assistance of one versed in these various points.

Most important too is the religion and history of the Jews. The story of the Chosen People is all of a pattern from the time of Adam and Eve to the present day, and if we do not know the religious background and history of the Jews we simply cannot have a full picture of Christ and his teaching. Our Lord said "Do not think that I have come to destroy the Law or the Prophets. I have come not to destroy, but to fulfill" (Matt. 5:17). He was simply pointing out that there is a continuity between Judaism and Christianity and without knowing of that heritage stretching from Abraham to the time of Christ we cannot grasp his mission. Pope Pius XII made the point so well when he said "We are all spiritual Semites."

There are constant references in Christ's sermons and actions to events and persons of the Old Testament. Unfortunately, today most Catholics do not have the knowledge of the Old Testament to appreciate fully these references. Obviously the way to correct this lack of knowledge is to study the Old Testament; but just as obviously, many have neither the time nor the inclination to do so. And so it behooves the good biographer of Christ to make these references and quotations understandable to his reader by filling in the gaps in his knowledge. In all fairness, too, it must be pointed out, as we did in discussing the Bible, that much of this material can be understood only in the light of years of intensive study. Thus, the reader expects the biographer of Christ to draw on his knowledge wherever needed to clear up points which would be incomprehensible except in the light of such study and knowledge.

In the same vein, it is essential for the biographer to be aware of the teaching of the Catholic Church. It is all very well for the unbeliever to produce a life of Christ which is accurate in all material and worldly details. But even one who does not believe in the divinity of Christ must admit that there was something in this life not explainable by the standards adduced to evaluate a man's contribution to mankind. At the very least, they must admit a spiritual-like appeal which transcends the appeal of an admittedly great human being. For the believer, of course, that appeal is divinity.

And it is precisely to transmit the promise of salvation and how it may be obtained that Christ founded his Church. The teachings of the Catholic Church are merely the extended application of the teachings of Christ. For centuries men have spent their lives studying and expounding these teachings. To understand the life of Christ these teachings must be understood and the appointed repository of that body of teaching is the Catholic Church. To know her teaching is to know what Christ taught—an essential element in knowing his life. It is clear then that the biographer who would tell of Christ's life must have this knowledge either from his own study or from those who have devoted their lives to the Church's teaching. And, though it is hindsight, knowledge of the Church's teaching as it has developed over the centuries often clarifies some teaching of the Lord which was prophetic in nature, not understood by his listeners, but clear to us in the light of subsequent developments.

All these points made above are specifically applicable to a biography and to a biographer of Christ. At the same time, though, the points that we make in the biography section of this *Guide* are all equally applicable to him as well. Knowledge of his subject and background, the ability to write understandably and preferably felicitously, and the capability to transmit the essence of his subject are all as necessary for the Christologist as they are for the biographer of a mere mortal.

If we may, we would strongly recommend to one interested in knowing the life of Christ that he read the Four Gospels immediately after he has read a biography of our Lord. The reader will be amazed at how a good life of Christ will fill in gaps, explain various sections, and supply background material which will make the four gospels more alive and more understandable. For broadening your knowledge of the most tremendous figure of all history, we unhesitatingly recommend a life of Christ. For a deeper knowledge of everything he taught and means read also the source material for all biographies of Christ—the writings of Matthew, Mark, Luke and John, the greatest of all Christologists.

It is an interesting fact that, although through the centuries countless lives of Christ have been written, each generation finds it necessary to write its own lives. In the list below you will find no life of Christ listed that was written more than fifty years ago. It is not that the compilers of this *Guide* did not wish to include any older biographies. It is just that the passage of time has inevitably caused previous lives to be read less and less as their appeal to new generations diminishes until they finally disappear and are supplanted by new biographies. This has been going on for cen-

turies and probably will for centuries to come. The sole
exception to this rule is what the Evangelists have written
about Christ. Ever fresh, ever new, the Gospels have an
irresistible appeal for all Christians in all ages in all places.
This comes as no surprise to all Catholics who consider them
inspired books of the Bible.

Finally, may we point out that there is a life of Christ for
every literary taste no matter how humble or how refined.
Read carefully the descriptions of those we have selected so
that you may begin with a suitable biography. Don't get dis-
couraged if you pick one that may not suit your tastes. Select
another, until you find what you want. Then read another
life. It is a truism that every good life of Christ gives the
reader new insights through the author's approach, a special
technique, a particular slant, a new discovery. Christ is a
source of infinite joy and happiness and knowledge; a good
biography of him is a path to a greater understanding of all
he offers.

ADAM, KARL. *Tho Christ of Faith*. Translated by Joyce
Crick. Pantheon, 1957. x, 364 p., index. $6.00. Mentor-
Omega, 1962. pa. 95¢.

Adam's work is a study of the Christology of the Church—
i.e., of what the Church teaches about Christ. Beginning
with the Gospels, the author traces the development of present Church teaching through the patristic period, the Middle Ages, the Renaissance, and modern times. He examines
the writings of individual fathers and doctors of the Church,
of the councils, and of papal pronouncements, giving background material from the history of each period examined.

ADAM, KARL. *Christ Our Brother*. Translated by Justin Mc-
Cana, o.s.b. Macmillan, 1931. vi, 210 p. $3.50. Collier, 1964.
pa. 95¢.

This is a collection of seven meditations on the life and
works of Christ, based upon the Gospel story. Various doctrinal and historical aspects of Christ's earthly life are studied
with applications made to the spiritual needs of modern
man. As a book of meditations, this work presupposes a
knowledge of elementary theological concepts, and so may

not be so useful to the layman as to the priest or religious.

ADAM, KARL. *The Son of God.* Translated by Philip Hereford. Image, 1960. 235 p. pa. 95¢.

The author's thesis is that if Christ is not God, then Christianity is merely a body of ethical beliefs; if, on the other hand, Christ is God, then Christianity is unquestionably the true religion. To prove his point Father Adam undertakes a thorough examination of Christ's claim to divinity, and an analysis of the belief that Christ is, in fact, God. This is a simple and straightforward discussion of a difficult and controversial subject.

BARBET, PIERRE (M.D.). *A Doctor at Calvary.* Translated by the Earl of Wicklow. Kenedy, 1958. 213 p., notes. $3.50. Image, 1963. pa. 85¢.

A surgeon's description of the passion of Christ, written with reverence but with scientific objectivity. From an examination of the Holy Shroud of Turin (the authenticity of which Dr. Barbet accepts from medical evidence) this book reconstructs Christ's agony and answers such questions as: What degree of physical torture did Christ suffer? What was the medical cause of his death? This is one of the most moving books ever written on the death of Christ; it is phrased in layman's language, in an excellent translation by the Earl of Wicklow.

BISHOP, JIM. *The Day Christ Died.* Harper, 1957. xvi, 336 p., bibliography, maps, index. $5.95. Perennial, 1965. pa. 75¢.

This is a re-creation, based on the New Testament story, of the first Good Friday. The author recounts, in a popular, journalistic style, the events from the taking of Christ in the Garden of Olives to the Crucifixion, filling in the material provided by the Evangelists with uncomplicated historical, social, and political background. The book is highly readable, instructive, and entertaining as well as inspiring.

CHESTERTON, G. K. *The Everlasting Man.* Image, 1955. 274 p. pa. 95¢.

An examination of the formula that Christ is only one of the many religious legends of history, and that his religion is only one of many similar religions. With the devastating wit characteristic of Chesterton at his best, the author points out that those theses are contradicted by a very striking fact—that this particular "religious legend" visited his world in person, as Creator, at an easily determined point in history.

DANIEL-ROPS, HENRI. *Jesus and His Times*. Translated by Ruby Millar. Dutton, 1956. 625 p., notes, appendices, bibliography, index. $6.50. Image, 1956 (2 vols.). pa. 95¢ ea.

In this study of the life of Jesus, the author has set out to re-create the atmosphere of the Holy Land in the time of Christ. Against that background, he explains Christ's teachings and the meaning of his words. Included are a section on the Dead Sea Scrolls, and a defense of the historical integrity of the Gospel narratives. This is an excellent life of Christ for the general reader.

FARRELL, WALTER (O.P.). *Only Son*. Sheed, 1953. v, 244 p. $3.50.

Father Farrell, an eminent theologian, studies the life of Christ in its Biblical accounts, explaining the meaning of various passages that are not clear and giving historical and theological background for the events of the life of Christ and for Christ's teachings. The book is well written and, although it does not take into account the most recent findings in Biblical research, it still has much of value for spiritual reading and meditation.

FOUARD, CONSTANT-HENRI. *The Life of Christ*. Guild, 1960. 415 p. pa. 95¢.

Father Fouard's *Life of Christ* was written in the first part of the nineteenth century, yet the story it tells and the way in which it is told is sufficiently timeless to make the book as popular today as it was at its first publication. The author covers the whole life of Christ, from the Nativity through the public life, the passion and crucifixion to the Resurrection. The book is not an historical study, but rather a spiritual biography; it is suitable, and recommended, for spiritual reading.

GORMAN, RALPH (C.P.). *The Last Hours of Jesus*. Sheed, 1960. vii, 277 p. $3.95.

Father Gorman presents, in popular language, the events and the significance of Jesus' passion and death. There is abundant historical background material, and the writing is clear and the narrative orderly. The book is suitable for spiritual reading and, in many instances, for meditation.

GRAHAM, AELRED (O.S.B.). *The Christ of Catholicism.* Image, 1957. 350 p., bibliography, indices. pa. 95¢.

A synthesis of scriptural testimony and the doctrine of the Church on the meaning of Christ. The author's approach is to explain, not to argue. Not a book of devotion or meditation, it will nonetheless be helpful to both because of its insight into Christ's life and teaching.

GUARDINI, ROMANO. *The Lord.* Translated by Elinor C. Briefs. Regnery, 1954. xi, 535 p. $6.50.

This work is a study of the mystery of Christ as savior, as man, and as God. The author places the events of Christ's earthly life in their proper historical context, and shows how Christ's teachings are related to the whole body of Church doctrine and practice. One particularly valuable aspect of the work is its incorporation of the wealth of modern Biblical criticism supplied by such scholars as Karl Barth.

OURSLER, FULTON. *The Greatest Story Ever Told.* Doubleday, 1949. 350 p. $3.50. Image, 1961. pa. 95¢.

Few books dealing with the life of Christ have attained such popularity as this one, and probably none other has been read by so many people. Basing himself on the events of the Gospels, the author weaves a colorful and fascinating story in the popular style for which the author was so well known.

RICCIOTTI, GIUSEPPE. *The Life of Christ.* Translated by Alba I. Zizzania. Bruce, 1947. xvi, 703 p., notes, illustrations, index. $7.50. (Abridged version, edited by Aloysius Croft. Bruce, 1952. xxxiii, 402 p., index. $3.50.)

Father Ricciotti's work is probably the best and most popular life of Christ to appear in the twentieth century. Although the book is intended for the general Catholic reader, the author's treatment is neither dogmatic nor controversial. While accepting wholly the traditional Catholic supernatural view of Christ's life, Ricciotti critically examines the findings of the rationalist interpretations and accepts such elements as clarify or supplement the Catholic position. Many readers will find the most interesting part of the book to be the author's vivid description of the Oriental background against which Christ spent his life. This work is unreservedly recommended.

SHEED, FRANK J. *To Know Christ Jesus.* Sheed, 1962. xx, 377 p., map. $5.00.

Basing himself upon the Gospels, Mr. Sheed writes a popular interpretative biography of Christ. He furnishes a wealth of detail to complement the New Testament narratives, emphasizing and revealing unusual facets of Christ's human personality and discussing interesting questions of Christ's public life. This is an unusual book, written in Mr. Sheed's polished and fast-moving style. It is recommended for spiritual reading as well as for just plain reading.

SHEEN, FULTON J., BISHOP. *The Life of Christ.* McGraw, 1958. xii, 599 p., index. $6.50. Popular, 1962. pa. 95¢.

This life of Christ by Bishop Sheen is one of the best known of Sheen's works. Along with a chronological narrative of the events of Christ's life on earth, beginning with the Annunciation and ending with the Ascension, Bishop Sheen presents a series of reflections and meditations on the significance of the various events for God's salvation plan. The book is not, nor is it intended to be, a scholarly presentation; it is rather a devotional book, in the better sense of the term, and it is excellent material for spiritual reading.

19. THE PAPACY

For a full understanding of the Catholic Church, one must know what the papacy is, how the office originated, how it has changed and grown through the centuries, and what is its unique role in the world today. It is safe to say that no center of authority has had such profound effects on Western history as the papacy. For centuries it was the mainspring of Western civilization and its evolution through the ages is a most intriguing study.

For Catholics, the first pope was St. Peter who was so appointed when Christ said to the apostle: "Thou art Peter, and upon this rock I will build my Church, and the gates of hell shall not prevail against it. And I will give thee the keys of the kingdom of heaven; and whatever thou shalt bind on earth shall be bound in heaven, and whatever thou shalt loose on earth shall be loosed in heaven" (Matt. 16:18–19). From that charge stems the whole authority of the papal office. And it is a dogma of the Church that when the pope speaks *ex cathedra*, i.e. when exercising his office as the shepherd and teacher of all Christians on a matter of faith and morals, he is infallible, i.e., safeguarded from any error by the Holy Spirit. Thus, infallibility is his by virtue of his office as the vicar of Christ on earth and as a consequence of his primacy. The primacy of the pope is his supreme power of jurisdiction to teach, rule and sanctify the universal Church and from this primacy flows his authority as head of the Roman Catholic Church.

Obviously, this is not the place to discuss the history and role of the papacy at any great length. Such information can be gleaned from the books listed below. But it may be worth considering briefly some of the reasons why the papacy is often a puzzle to some and so widely misunderstood by others.

High among such reasons is a simple physical fact. Many will accept that our Lord did designate Peter as the first among the apostles, charged with awesome responsibility; but

they become confused by the massiveness of the Church of
the twentieth century and the similarity between the first
Peter and the present pope is lost. Peter was one of a dozen
apostles, and Christians at that time were numbered in the
scores or at most in the hundreds. Today Pope Paul VI, as
bishop of Rome, is one of some 3000 bishops, and Christians
number hundreds of millions. The structure of the Church
today is complex and farflung, whereas in Peter's time it was
simple and concentrated in Galilee. What is not easily seen is
that, with the tremendous growth of the Church, a structure
was necessary; and as it grew larger that structure of necessity became more diffuse and more complex as the growing
Church organized and reorganized itself to meet the increasing and more difficult tasks facing it. Organization is necessary
for any growing organism. But the important point is that,
despite the massive and overwhelming organization we know
as the Church, basically, beneath the numbers and complexities, the role of the pope is the same today as when our Lord
appointed Peter. What the student of the papacy must realize
is that, though growth and expansion always cause a
change in structure, the significant fact is that the principle
remains unchanged.

As a point of comparison, consider the office of president
of the United States. Certainly the functions and duties of
the president of the United States in the third quarter of the
twentieth century in a highly industrialized and complex society are vastly expanded as compared to those exercised by
the first president in the last decade of the eighteenth century
in a simple agricultural economy. Any student of government
will accept this as a necessary factor in the growth and expansion of the country. Yet the basic principle of the presi-
dency as set forth in the Constitution adopted in 1789 remains the same today, two centuries later, as does also the
form of the American government. The first Congress had
65 Representatives and 26 Senators; today there are 435
Representatives and 100 Senators. Though the functions of
the Congress have changed in the past two centuries, the
principle of its role in the American republic remain the same.

So obvious are these facts that everyone accepts them as
a normal part of growth and development. If such drastic

changes occur in a government in two centuries, even greater changes must be expected in such an organization as the Catholic Church in twenty centuries as it expanded all over the world. The *form* has changed to meet changing conditions; but the basic *principles* set forth by Christ when he appointed Peter and organized his Church around the apostles remain the same.

Another cause for wonder and concern for many is that the Church has had "bad" popes. And the charge is true, as any good Catholic historian today will readily admit. What must be kept in mind is that, though Christ promised "I am with you all days, even unto the consummation of the world" (Matt. 28:20), the Church is ruled and staffed by men with all the imperfections of human beings. There have been dark periods in the history of the Church, when she was governed by men who were swayed by pride or greed or passion; there have been popes who gained their office by questionable means; popes have reigned who have used the papacy for their own gains and selfish purposes. But such popes have been comparatively few in number, and no other group of rulers have ever possessed the over-all dedication, ability, holiness, and interest of the organization they ruled as have the men who have occupied the chair of Peter. And Christ has always been true to his promise, for always he has rescued his Church when danger threatened to overwhelm it. Invariably, good men of great ability have come in times of crisis to renew and reform and reinvigorate the Church.

Indeed, this too is one of the hallmarks of the papacy. Time and again learned men have tolled the death knell of the papacy and always the papal office has been invested with renewed vigor and achieved even greater heights than before. As recently as 1870, the loss of the Papal States was considered by many to be the final blow that would end the papacy once and for all. There followed a succession of great popes who raised the papacy to a height that it had seldom reached before. Indeed, one would have to go far back in history to find a pope who so captured the world and raised the papacy to such prestige as did Pope John XXIII, less than a hundred years after the direfully predicted end of the papacy. As had happened so often before, a seemingly disastrous calamity, the loss of the Papal States, turned into a blessing as the papacy, relieved of the secular burden of its states, turned with renewed vigor to the spiritual welfare of the Church.

It must be evident, then, to any interested observer, that the papacy is a unique institution unlike anything devised by man. No other comparable office has endured for 2000 years; and not only has the Church endured but it has flourished so that today the Holy See is enjoying one of its peak periods of influence and prestige. To Catholics, the reason is to be found in something far deeper than capable men or saintly occupants of the papal throne, or skilled administrators. It is all these; but far more important is the fact that the papacy was divinely founded, "thou art Peter and upon this rock I will build my Church," and divinely protected "and the gates of hell shall not prevail against it."

BRUSHER, JOSEPH S. (s.J.). *Popes Through the Ages*, revised edition. Photographs collected and edited by Emanuel Borden. Van Nostrand, 1964. 530 p., illustrations, portraits, 9" × 12". $17.50.

Essentially, this is a picture gallery of the popes, from Saint Peter to Paul VI. There is a portrait of each pontiff, most of them taken from the work of contemporary artists, accompanied by a brief biographical sketch of the subject pope. Although the book provides basic historical facts on the life and times of each pope, and thus furnishes a general survey of Church history, primary interest lies in the variety and quality of the reproductions of medieval and Renaissance art.

BREZZI, PAOLO. *The Papacy: Its Origins and Historical Evolution*. Newman, 1958. xiii, 218 p., chronological tables, bibliography, index. $3.50.

This is a study of the papacy as an institution rather than as a succession of individual popes. The author discusses the foundation of the papacy by Christ, and traces the development of papal power and authority over the whole Church from Peter and the primitive Church, through the Middle Ages when papal power extended itself into every field, through the decline of the popes' spiritual and temporal prestige in the seventeenth, eighteenth, and early nineteenth centuries, up to the almost unparalleled centralization of executive powers in the papacy since the first Vatican Council of 1869–70. The author shows that, though no orthodox Catholic group has ever seriously questioned the primacy of the papacy within the Church, the nature of that primacy has often been in dispute. There are many interesting historical insights into the development of the process of selecting popes, the evolution of the papal court, etc.

CORBETT, JAMES A. *The Papacy: A Brief History.* Anvil, 1956. 191 p., bibliography, index. pa. $1.25.

Mr. Corbett tells, in a popular style, the general history of the papacy from its founding to the middle of the twentieth century. The second half of the book is devoted to a collection of important historical documents which have had a bearing on papal history. Though this is only a brief survey, it is historically sound and will provide an accurate over-all knowledge of the development of the institution of the papacy from its beginnings.

FARROW, JOHN. *Pageant of the Popes,* revised edition. Sheed, 1950. viii, 394 p., illustrations, bibliography, tables, indices. $5.00. All Saints, 1965. pa. 50¢.

This is a concise, fast-moving history of the popes from St. Peter to Pius XII. The narrative is presented in a continuous, strictly chronological form. It deals with each of the popes quite frankly, avoiding both sensationalism and whitewashing. The book was written for the general reader, presumes no historical background on the part of the reader, and provides a general introduction to the history of the papacy and, therefore, to the history of the Church.

HOLLIS, CHRISTOPHER, Editor. *The Papacy.* Macmillan, 1964. 304 p., illustrations, facsimiles, maps, portraits, 9″ × 12″. $25.00.

Mr. Hollis, an eminent historian and biographer, brings together twenty-six chapters, by as many European and American scholars, tracing the story of the Papacy from its foundation to the reign of Paul VI, in an authoritative and yet popularly written text. The book is enhanced by an abundance of excellent illustrations and reproductions, many of them in full color. *The Papacy* is an excellent work of historical popularization as well as a beautifully executed "art book."

JOHN, ERIC, Editor. *The Popes.* Biographies by J. M. W. Bean; historical synopses by Douglas Woodruff. Hawthorn, 1964. 496 p., illustrations, plates, portraits. $15.00.

This is a concise biographical history of the popes up to and including Paul VI. There is a brief biography of each pope, while the historical periods into which the papacy, as well as general history, is divided, are surveyed in connecting chapters. The illustrations and portraits of the popes are chosen mostly from contemporary works, and form a representative collection of Christian art from the Middle Ages to the present.

NEUVECELLE, JEAN. *The Vatican: Its Organization, Customs, and Way of Life.* Translated by George Libaire. Criterion, 1955. vi, 250 p., plates, index. $4.50.

Mr. Neuvecelle, a French journalist, delineates thoroughly the workings of the Holy See in its administration both of the Church and of Vatican City. There is a breakdown of the various congregations, offices, tribunals, etc., through which the pope rules the Church and the Vatican, an explanation of the duties of the major Vatican officials, and in general an intimate description of daily life in the Vatican. The book is sound both theologically and historically, is well written in a journalistic style, and will be of interest to all Catholics who have wondered about the way in which the pope governs through his officials.

PASTOR, LUDWIG VON. *The History of the Popes.* Translated by Frederick I. Antrobus, Ralph F. Kerr, and Ernest Graf. Herder, 1915–1938. 40 volumes.

Pastor's *History of the Popes* is one of the most monumental works of Catholic historical scholarship undertaken in modern times. It covers the five centuries from the close of the Middle Ages through the eighteenth century (1305 to 1799), discussing the reigns of sixty-one popes and antipopes, from Clement V to Pius VI, with an attention to detail and a scholarly exactitude that will make this the standard work on the papacy during that period for many years to come. The author had access, in his capacity of Austrian ambassador to the Holy See, to documents in the

Vatican archives which had not been accessible to scholars before him, and his thorough documentation makes this series an indispensable work of reference for historians of the period.

VAN LIERDE, PETER C. *The Holy See at Work*. Translated by James Tucek. Hawthorn, 1962. 254 p., notes, bibliography, glossary, index. $3.50.

Bishop van Lierde, an official of the Roman Curia, gives an account of the inner workings of the complicated administrative machinery of the Vatican. He discusses the basic principles which govern both the organization and the operation of the Curia and of other administrative and executive organs of the Holy See, from the papal office itself, the College of Cardinals, and the various congregations and tribunals and commissions of the Curia, to the local government of the churches at a diocesan level.

ENCYCLICALS

A special word must be said here about encyclicals, since they are an important instrument of the papacy and have often played a vital role in modern times. An encyclical is a letter addressed by the Supreme Pontiff to the bishops or to the faithful in their care, or even to all mankind (as was the case with Pope John's *Pacem in terris* or *Peace on Earth*, which was addressed to the bishops and faithful and also "to all men of good will") on a particular subject of special importance.

Encyclicals had their origin in the epistles of the New Testament. These epistles were letters written to various Christian communities instructing the Christians there, admonishing them when necessary. In general, they were a method by which the apostles, in their roles as bishops, explained Catholic belief, defined certain disputed doctrines and exercised the discipline inherent in their office. The encyclicals are the latter-day counterpart of these epistles.

The modern popes since Leo XIII have especially made use of encyclicals to instruct the faithful. A wide variety of topics has been covered by these letters and many of them have had profound effects not only on the Catholic community but on all society. The labor encyclicals of Popes Leo XIII, *Rerum novarum*, and Pius XI, *Quadragesimo anno*, became the charters of social justice all over the world; the Biblical encyclicals of Popes Leo XIII, *Providentissimus Deus*, and Pius XII, *Divino afflante spiritu*, unleashed the whole Catholic Bible revival which has had such a profound effect on every activity of the Church; Pope John XXIII's *Pacem in terris* evoked such an overwhelmingly enthusiastic response from leaders of all denominations and walks of life that it bids fair to become the Magna Carta of twentieth-century man in his quest for peace. It is safe to say that papal encyclicals are among the most important documents of our times.

Two further points should be made about encyclicals. First, the extent of their authority is uncertain. They are not infallible pronouncements, such as the formal proclamations of dogma promulgated by the pope speaking *ex cathedra* in his role as Supreme Pontiff; such declarations must be accepted as the basic, unquestioned teaching of the Church. But though encyclicals are not of this infallible character, they are extremely important pronouncements demanding the respect and attention of the faithful. Pope Pius XII forcefully defined their role in the Church in his encyclical *Humani generis* in these words: "Nor must it be thought that what is expounded in encyclical letters does not itself demand consent, on the pretext that in writing such letters the popes do not exercise the supreme power of their teaching authority. For these matters are taught with the ordinary teaching authority, of which it is true to say: 'He who heareth you, heareth Me' . . . if the supreme pontiffs in their official documents purposely pass judgement on a matter up to that time under dispute, it is obvious that the matter, according to the mind and will of the same pontiffs, cannot be any longer considered a question open to discussion among theologians." Such a statement emphasizes the extreme gravity the popes attach to encyclicals, and the faithful must treat them accordingly.

The second point we would make about encyclicals is that they are not easy reading. They often treat of difficult matters with profound learning and in formal and exact language. Concerned as they are with matters affecting the very life of the Church they could not be otherwise. When one deals with vital matters only the most careful and exhaustive treatment will suffice. And that is exactly how encyclicals are prepared. Consequently they are not for light reading but must be approached with the attitude of the student. They must be studied and meditated upon and applied to one's life. Encyclicals treat of matters vital to the Church, and knowing their contents is a responsibility for all Catholics. We have listed books in this section which will provide the text of the most important encyclicals and others which will provide commentaries on and insights into the encyclicals for the mature reader. This is not an easy task to read much of this material, but it can be of invaluable aid to the reader in learning the mind of the Church.

FREMANTLE, ANNE, Editor. *The Papal Encyclicals in Their Historic Context.* Introduction by Gustave Weigel, s.J. Mentor-Omega, 1956. 317 p., notes, bibliography, tables, index. pa. 50¢.

Here, in one volume, are assembled selections from the main encyclical letters of the popes, from St. Peter to Pius XII, on the teachings of the Church. The editor describes the historical era and circumstances surrounding the composition of each letter, and achieves a comprehensive historical view of the development of the doctrines of the Church. Among the issues of current interest treated are the relationship of spiritual and temporal authority, the position of the Church with respect to communism, and the Catholic attitudes toward social justice.

FULLAM, RAYMOND B. (s.J.). *The Popes on Youth.* McKay, 1957. xvii, 442 p., bibliography, index. $5.00.

This is a collection of texts from papal pronouncements on the formation and guidance of youth, issued during the reigns of Leo XIII, Pius X, Benedict XV, Pius XI, and Pius XII. The work is divided into four parts: the first contains excerpts concerning the authority and responsibility of the popes toward youth, the second presents principles for the formation of youth, the third lists directives on adult responsibilities toward youth, and the fourth studies adverse influences in the formation of youth.

HUGHES, PHILIP (MSGR.). *Catholic Faith in Practice.* Dimension, 1965. viii, 331 p., index. $5.95.

This collection of papal documents contains, in synopsis form, all of the important social encyclicals, letters, and addresses of the modern popes, from Leo XIII to Pius XII's early years as pope—the period 1878–1941. In some cases, the pope's words are given, while in others there is a synopsis of the encyclical, letter, or address. The documents are divided into nine sections, by subject, covering such questions of social importance as international relations, the extent and limitations of political authority, education, society, labor, etc. The most unusual feature of the book, and that one which most commends it to the reader, is the minutely detailed subject index which, for the period covered, will furnish a complete guide to papal pronouncements on subjects of social interest.

JOHN XXIII, POPE. *The Encyclicals and Other Messages of Pope John XXIII.* Commentaries by John F. Cronin, S.S., Francis X. Murphy, C.SS.R., and Ferrer Smith, O.P. The Pope Speaks, 1965. xi, 522 p., illustrations. $8.50.

This collection of the official writings and addresses of Pope John XXIII includes the complete texts of his eight encyclicals, and of eighteen of his most important letters and addresses, as well as excerpts from his addresses to the first session of Vatican II, his messages on various feast days of the liturgical year, and his formal allocutions. The messages are grouped in sections, each section corresponding to a topic of major importance to Pope John. There is a biographical introduction by Francis X. Murphy. The various commentaries give the historical context of each document, explain their significance, and interpret their meaning.

MARY CLAUDIA, SISTER (I.H.M.). *A Dictionary of Papal Pronouncements.* Kenedy, 1958. vi, 216 p., index. $6.50.

This useful work presents excerpts from papal encyclicals, letters, and addresses from the reign of Leo XIII to that of Pius XII, covering the period 1878 to 1957. The entries are arranged alphabetically by subject. This is a useful reference work for the home and for students.

LEO XIII, POPE. *The Church Speaks to the Modern World.*
Edited, with an introduction and notes, by Etienne Gilson.
Image, 1954. 348 p., notes, bibliography, index. pa. $1.25.

This is a collection of the writings of Pope Leo XIII on
social problems. The basic encyclicals of that pope are arranged in the order which he himself expressly indicated:
Aeterni Patris (On Christian Philosophy); *Libertas praestantissimum* (On Human Liberty); *Arcanum divinae sapientiae*
(On Christian Marriage); *Humanum genus* (On Freemasonry); *Diuturnum* (On Civil Government); *Immortale Dei*
(On the Christian Constitution of States); *Quod apostolici
muneris* (On Socialism); *Rerum novarum* (On the Rights
and Duties of Capital and Labor); *Sapientiae Christianae*
(On Christian Citizenship); *Inscrutabili* (On the Evils Affecting Modern Society); *In plurimis* (On Slavery); *Graves de
communi* (On Christian Democracy). The editor provides
historical perspective for each document in the introductory
sections, and explanatory notes and summaries of each encyclical.

LEO XIII, POPE. *Great Encyclical Letters.* Edited by John J.
Wynne. Benziger, 1903. 257 p. $5.00.

This is a collection of Pope Leo's encyclicals, written from
the time of his election to the papacy, in 1878, to his death
in 1903. The subjects treated are: The Christian Constitution
of States (*Immortale Dei,* 1885); Christian Marriage (*Arcanum divinae sapientiae,* 1880); Christian Citizenship
(*Quod apostolici muneris,* 1878); On the Duties of Labor
(*Rerum novarum,* 1891); The Holy Spirit (*Divinum illud
munus,* 1897); On Anglican Orders (*Apostolicae curae et
caritatis,* 1896); The Holy Eucharist (*Mirae caritatis,* 1902);
Christian Unity (*Satis cognitum,* 1896); and Christ the Redeemer (*Annum sacrum,* 1899).

LEO XIII, POPE, POPE PIUS XII, and POPE JOHN XXIII. *Seven
Great Encyclicals.* Paulist, 1965. 276 p., outlines. pa. $1.50.

This compilation contains the full texts of the following
encyclicals: *The Condition of Labor* by Leo XIII; *On Christian Marriage, On Atheistic Communism, On Christian Education,* and *On Reconstructing the Social Order* by Pius XII;
Peace on Earth and *Christianity and World Progress* by John
XXIII. There are discussion-club outlines for each encyclical.

Pius xi, Pope. *The Church and the Reconstruction of the Modern World.* Introduction, with notes and commentary, by Terence P. McLaughlin, c.s.p. Image, 1957. 433 p., notes, bibliography, index. pa. $1.25.

This collection of the social encyclicals of Pius XI contains the following documents: *Ubi arcano* (On the Peace of Christ in the Reign of Christ); *Quas primas* (On the Kingship of Christ); *Divini illius Magistri* (On the Christian Education of Youth); *Casti connubii* (On Christian Marriage); *Ad Catholici sacerdotii* (On the Priesthood); *Quadragesimo anno* (On the Reconstruction of the Social Order); *Caritate Christi* (On the Present Distress of the Human Race); *Non abbiamo bisogno* (On the Apostolate of the Laity); *Mit brennender Sorge* (On the Church in Germany); *Divini Redemptoris* (On Atheistic Communism); *Firmissimam constantiam* (On the Religious Situation in Mexico). The editor furnishes, for each encyclical, an introduction, a summary, and explanatory notes.

Pius xii, Pope. *The Pope Speaks.* Edited by Michael Chinigo with the cooperation of the Vatican Archives. Pantheon, 1957. 278 p., glossary, index. $4.50.

This is a collection of the most important pronouncements of Pope Pius XII on such matters as education, human relations, science, art, religion, society, the status of man, and politics. It contains the essence of his messages from 1937 to 1956, and answers many questions concerning the Christian duties of men and women in the family, in their professions, and in their capacity as citizens. In addition to its value as a guide to Pius XII's thought, the book is a handy reference work for the home and library.

Pius xii, Pope. *Selected Documents of His Holiness, Pope Pius XII.* National Catholic Welfare Conference, 1961. Various pagings. $7.50.

This is a collection of thirty-one documents of Pius XII, issued between 1939 and 1958, and including many of his encyclicals, addresses, allocutions, and letters. Among the subjects covered are: the function of state in the modern world, the Mystical Body, the dogma of the Assumption, married life, art, psychiatry and religion, Mary, the lay apostolate, and the liturgy. The encyclicals have individual study outlines and reading guides, and the entire volume has a detailed subject index. This is an invaluable reference work for all libraries.

WERTH, ALVIN (O.F.M. CAP.) and CLEMENT S. MIHANOVICH. *Papal Pronouncements on Marriage and the Family.* Bruce, 1955. xiii, 189 p., index. $3.50.

This is a compilation of papal documents on the subject of marriage and the family issued during the reigns of Leo XIII, Piux X, Benedict XV, Pius XI, and Pius XII—the period from 1878 to 1954. The material is arranged chronologically, and includes all of the most important papal pronouncements on marriage issued in modern times.

(Individual encyclicals of the modern popes are readily available. Most Catholic book stores carry these encyclicals in handy pamphlet form published by among others the N.C.W.C., 1312 Massachusetts Avenue, NE, Washington, D.C.; the Paulist Press, Glen Rock, New Jersey; America Press, 106 West 56th Street, New York, N.Y.)

20. PHILOSOPHY

Philosophy may be defined as the study of the highest or ultimate causes of things insofar as that knowledge may be attained through the use of natural reason. As such, it involves a consideration of the principles underlying all knowledge and leads the philosopher to a study of the most fundamental causes or principles of the universe and the role of the human person and his destiny in the universal plan. Since, over the centuries, man has compartmentalized his philosophical knowledge into particular systems with a specialized vocabulary and terminology, it is truly a science.

Of all man's studies, except for theology, philosophy represents the pinnacle of man's knowledge, for in philosophy are probed the very causes and reasons for existence. It dares to tread where the scientist and the pragmatist hesitate, for lack of empirical experience, to enter. For no other art or science of man gives scope to the imagination and rational aspect of man's being as does philosophy.

Man's rational mind is the human characteristic which puts him above all animals. That he can think is at once his greatest blessing and, alas too frequently, his greatest curse, and when man first began to exercise this God-given gift he was a true creature of God—a human being.

From the earliest days of mankind, wherever a civilization or culture developed, with it grew a philosophy. For as soon as man could think he began to question: What am I? Whence did I come? What is my destiny? What is earth? the moon? the sun? the stars? the universe? What is my role in all of this? And as his knowledge grew and was organized, he began to speculate on these basic problems of human existence and destiny, and philosophy was born.

We are so accustomed today to think of the modern age as the age of greatest knowledge that we are often prone to overlook the treasures of philosophical knowledge that have been developed through the ages. But it is only in the past two centuries that man has exploited so fully the physical sciences with the consequent effect on modern civilization of technological progress. So overcome were men by the wonders wrought on our lives by the scientific revolution of the past century that only now are we beginning to question a blind adherence to the directions scientific discoveries and advances have given us. Increasingly, men are coming to realize that a *philosophy* for the modern age is a requisite for living with the machines and drugs and space probes which are our inheritance from the science of the past century. The discoveries and advances and machines are not enough in themselves. We have allowed ourselves unthinkingly to be caught up in the forward movement of technological without pausing to develop a framework of thought to encompass the relation of these scientific developments to man, the rational animal. Speed, comfort, convenience, knowledge—all these are surely desirable for mankind. If, however, they become paramount, man will then truly be bereft of what has characterized every true forward movement in human history: a philosophy of being which brings these advances under his domination, rather than the opposite where his creations engulf him. For the first time in history, this fate could befall modern man. Nuclear devices, electronic gadgets, computers, automation, all have the potential to annihilate man as a rational, thinking person. He must contain and control his mind-children, and for this a philosophy of life which guarantees his domination of all creatures and of human creations is essential.

But such a philosophy does not spring full blown from any one era. Man must draw on the accumulated wisdom and knowledge of the ages. Scientific categorization of information is no more than a storehouse of knowledge. What is needed today is the application of wisdom to the use of the knowledge that we have accumulated, and that wisdom can be obtained from the great minds of the ages whose thinking and application of knowledge to human problems often has an immediacy that is startling. The accumulation of knowledge is a desirable and laudable undertaking, and a knowledge of the great systems of philosophy can be of inestimable worth for modern man. It is true that many of his problems are unique and a product of our times, but often their solution can be obtained by paths laid out by great minds of other ages. Too often, the problems are as old as mankind, for man can change his environment but human nature by and large has remained constant.

And so, it is fair to state that the study of the great philosophers and philosophical systems is a most useful and indeed an essential undertaking for any man who considers himself educated. But the question will be asked by the reader of this *Guide* whether the Christian should study any but Christian philosophy. (We have no intention, of course, of becoming involved, in these brief considerations, in the still heated controversy as to whether there is a true philosophy which is Christian. This we will leave to you the reader to explore in some of the volumes described in this section.) It seems to us that in today's world there can be but one answer to such a query. Not only should the Christian study the various philosophers but, if he is to bear witness to his Christianity today, he *must* study all philosophies. Especially must this be true of priests and religious and of all educated Catholics. How can one counter attacks on Christianity, as one example, if one does not know the beliefs of the attacker? How can one explain Christianity to the non-Christian if he does not even know his vocabulary to answer his queries and/or attacks in language understandable to the questioner?

Further, as Pope John so often emphasized, there is truth in all great thoughts. Granted, frequently, error can be and often is found in a particular philosophy. But where truth is found, how can the Catholic ignore it? The classic example of this point is St. Thomas and Aristotelianism. By building on the truths in Aristotle's philosophy Thomas produced a synthesis which bridged the gap between Christianity and paganism. He extracted the truths from a pagan philosophy, subjected them to the light of Christian revelation and teaching, and produced the *philosophia perennis* of the Christian world which has endured for centuries. In our own times, Teilhard de Chardin attempted the same synthesis between Christianity and the theory of evolution. His work is one of the greatest contributions to human thought in the twentieth century.

And so we have included studies of philosophies other than

Christian philosophies in this section. As will be evident, the main stress is on Christian philosophers and philosophies. But since a broader knowledge of philosophy is needed by today's Catholic, we suggest certain books which we feel will provide that knowledge. At the same time, always aware that there is an inherent danger to the novice in dipping into an alien philosophy, we have recommended works and editions by authors and editors who too are fully aware of this problem and provide the necessary safeguards. Obviously, no attempt is made by these men to water down the philosophies they present or discuss. But the treatment is based on the knowledge of the author or editor as a Catholic of the problems facing the Catholic when he or she probes other than Christian thought.

And to close this section we cannot refrain from quoting the words of a very wise man concerning philosophy and religion: "A little philosophy inclineth man's mind to atheism, but depth in philosophy bringeth men's minds about to religion." (Francis Bacon)

BOËTHIUS, ANICIUS MANLIUS SEVERINUS. *On the Consolation of Philosophy.* Translated by Richard Green. Bobbs, 1962. 199 p. $3.00. Liberal Arts, 1962. pa. $1.25.

One of the great classics of philosophy as well as of literature, this book was written early in the sixth century while its author awaited execution at the hands of Theodoric the Goth. It considers such subjects as the nature of Good, and shows that Good does not consist in power or wealth, but in the possession of God. The subject of free will is examined, and finally free will is reconciled with God's plan for man's salvation. Boëthius wrote before philosophy had developed an oppressive terminology, and his book requires no particular background in that discipline. It is required reading for the educated Christian.

CAPONIGRI, A. ROBERT, Editor. *Modern Catholic Thinkers.* Harper, 1960. xvi, 636 p. $10.00.

This anthology comprises thirty-seven selections under seven general headings: God, man, the Church, the political order, history, religion and culture, and witness. The contributors are, for the most part, well known Catholics of modern times; such as Maritain, Gilson, Dawson, etc. The editor provides an analytical commentary for each selection. The book is an interesting sampling of the various contributors' thought, as well as a representative cross-section of modern Catholic intellectual achievements.

COPLESTON, FREDERICK C. (S.J.). *Aquinas.* Penguin, 1955. 263 p., bibliography, index. pa. 85¢.

The author of the monumental *History of Philosophy,* Father Copleston examines in this work Aquinas' philosophical thought. His approach is non-technical, treating of the historical context of the Thomistic synthesis, the metaphysics of Aquinas, his concept of God, man as a creature and as a social being; a final chapter outlines the development of Aquinas' thought by subsequent "Thomist" schools from the end of the Middle Ages to the twentieth century.

COPLESTON, FREDERICK (S.J.). *A History of Philosophy.*

This is a series which eventually will comprise nine volumes covering the progress of philosophy from the earliest Greek thought to the contemporary systems. It is widely acknowledged as the best study of philosophers and their systems now available in English, and it will undoubtedly be the standard history of philosophy for many years to come. The author combines monumental scholarship with a clear, flexible, and interesting style; the rather abstruse nature of some of the contents, of course, necessitates attentive reading, but the value of this work more than compensates for the effort.

The following volumes are available at present:

Vol. I. *Greece & Rome.* Newman, 1946. 599 p., notes, bibliographies, appendices, index. $4.75. Image, 1962 (2 vols.). pa. 95¢ ea.

This first volume surveys the progress of Greek and Roman philosophical speculation from the pre-Socratics to the Neoplatonists, analyzing the systems of Thales, Anaximander, Pythagoras, Heraclitus, Parmenides, Zeno, and Socrates; there are particularly lucid analyses of the thought of Plato and Aristotle. The book concludes with a survey of post-Aristotelian philosophy: Stoics, Epicureans, Cynics, Sceptics, the Jewish-Hellenistic philosophers, the Neoplatonists.

Vol. II. *Mediaeval Philosophy.* Newman, 1950. 692 p., notes, bibliographies, appendices, index. $4.75. Image, 1962 (2 vols.). pa. 95¢ ea.

Here the author reviews the accomplishments of the schools of Western thought from the Patristic period and St. Augustine, through the Carolingian age, St. Bonaventure, and St. Thomas Aquinas, to Duns Scotus. The sections on Bonaventure and Aquinas are especially comprehensive and valuable.

Vol. III. *Late Mediaeval and Renaissance Philosophy.* Newman, 1953. 559 p., notes, bibliographies, appendices, index. $4.75. Image, 1963 (2 vols.). pa. 95¢ ea.

This volume considers the philosophy of the late Middle Ages and the early Renaissance and analyzes in detail two major influences of the period: first, the metaphysical basis of Thomism and the relation between philosophy and theology and, second, the emergence of the physical sciences as disciplines separate from philosophy. These themes are traced through a close study of such thinkers as William of Ockham, Marsilius of Padua, Nicholas of Cusa, the speculative mystics (Suso, Ruysbroeck, Tauler), the political philosophers (Machiavelli, Thomas More, Bodin, Grotius), Francis Bacon, and Suarez.

Vol. IV. *Modern Philosophy: Descartes to Leibniz.* Newman, 1957. 400 p., notes, bibliographies, appendix, index. $4.50. Image, 1963. pa. $1.35.

The fourth volume deals with the great rationalist systems of philosophy on the continent in the pre-Kantian period. The author traces the gradual emancipation of philosophy from theology through the systems of Descartes, Pascal, Malebranche, Spinoza, and Leibniz. The value of this volume is enhanced by a detailed introduction to the whole subject of modern philosophy, in which the spirit of modern thought is analyzed by tracing its continuity with late-medieval and early-Renaissance thought and by pointing out its new and revolutionary aspects.

Vol. V. *Modern Philosophy: The British Philosophers.* Newman, 1959. 472 p., notes, bibliographies, appendix, index. $4.75. Image, 1964 (2 vols.). pa. 95¢ ea.

The scope of this volume is the whole of British philosophy during the seventeenth and eighteenth centuries. Although most extensive treatment is accorded the giants of that period —Hobbes, Locke, Berkeley, Hume—other significant movements also are examined in detail: the Cambridge Platonists, the Ethicists, the Deists, and the "commonsense" successors of Hume.

Vol. VI. *Modern Philosophy: The French Enlightenment, The German Enlightenment.* Newman, 1960. 456 p., notes, bibliographies, index. $4.75. Image, 1964 (2 vols.). pa. 95¢ ea.

The sixth volume is concerned with the 18th century Continental philosophers. Beginning with the French Enlightenment, it surveys the work of Bayle, Fontenelle, Vauvenargues, Condillac, Helvetius, Montesquieu, the Encyclopedists, the early materialists, the philosophers of natural history, the Physiocrats, and finally—and in detail—Rousseau. The German Enlightenment is studied through the works of Lessing, Wolff, the various schools of education and psychology, and Deism. There follows a discussion of Bossuet, Vico, Voltaire, and Herder. The last half of this volume is devoted to an intensive examination of the thought of Kant and of his impact on nineteenth- and twentieth-century philosophy.

Vol. VII. *Fichte to Nietzsche.* Newman, 1963. 595 p., notes, bibliographies, appendices, index. $4.75. Image, 1965 (2 vols.). pa. 95¢ ea.

Here the author covers the entire range of opinion in German nineteenth-century philosophy from Fichte through Nietzsche, explaining in detail Schelling, Hegel, Schopenhauer, the transformation of idealism in the thought of Marx and Feuerbach, and the significance of Kierkegaard. A concluding chapter discusses the twentieth-century systems which developed principally through association with Husserl, Hartmann, and Heidegger.

COPLESTON, FREDERICK. *Medieval Philosophy.* Torchbooks, 1961. 194 p., bibliography, index. pa. $1.35.

As a survey of medieval philosophy, Father Copleston's work is hard to better. He treats of the great medieval syntheses comprehensively and clearly, tracing their origins and explaining their evolution within the context of the historical situations responsible for their appearance. The work is highly recommended.

CUENOT, CLAUDE. *Teilhard de Chardin.* Translated by Vincent Colimarc; edited by René Hague. Helicon, 1965. vi, 492 p., illustrations, bibliography. $9.75.

This is the most comprehensive and complete biography

of Teilhard de Chardin yet available in English. In addition to a substantial narrative of his subject's life, Cuenot offers also an interpretation of Teilhard's thought in synthesis form. Although the book presents a rather idealized Teilhard and treats very sketchily the reasons for and the reactions to the ecclesiastical ban on Teilhard's works, it may be recommended as an excellent general introduction to the life and thought of the great Jesuit philosopher and paleontologist.

FREMANTLE, ANNE. *The Age of Belief.* Mentor-Omega, 1955. 218 p., bibliography, index. pa. 75¢.

In the "age of belief," the period from the fifth to the early fifteenth centuries, philosophers discussed such problems as the nature of God, of Being, and of Man, with an intensity not known before or since. In this work, Mrs. Fremantle has taken selections from the basic writings of the most important thinkers of that period, such as Augustine, Aquinas, Bonaventure, Boëthius, Anselm, and Abelard, and, by means of a commentary interwoven with the texts, gives an interpretation of their philosophies. The book is an interesting introductory study of medieval philosophy, as well as a series of excellent sketches of individual philosophers.

GALLAGHER, KENNETH. *The Philosophy of Gabriel Marcel.* Foreword by Gabriel Marcel. Fordham, 1962. xvi, 179 p., notes, bibliography, index. $5.00.

Gabriel Marcel is an outstanding contemporary French philosopher and writer, a convert to Catholicism, and the most important spokesman for the school of modern philosophy called "Christian existentialism." Mr. Gallagher's book is a brief introduction to Marcel's philosophy, outlining his thought on several main points: the need for man's recognition of his utter dependence on God; the necessity for man's development of his total being; the distinction between "problem" and "mystery"; the ways of attaining union with God and with humanity; the role of creativity in human life. In the concluding chapters the author summarizes briefly some of Marcel's dramatic works and presents a final brief synthesis of the philosopher's system. There are passages in this work which are quite difficult, but most of it will be quite understandable to the educated layman. It will serve as a good introduction to this increasingly important Catholic thinker.

GARRIGOU-LAGRANGE, REGINALD (O.P.). *Reality: A Synthesis of Thomistic Thought.* Translated by Patrick Cummins, O.S.B. Herder, 1950. xiii, 419 p., bibliography, index. $6.00.

In this work, one of the great Thomistic philosopher-theologians of the twentieth century condenses the whole of traditional Thomistic thought into a readable synthesis. It is a book intended for the general reader rather than for the student or the specialist, and can serve as an excellent introduction to the thought, both philosophical and theological, of Aquinas.

GILSON, ETIENNE H. *The Christian Philosophy of St. Augustine.* Translated by L. E. M. Lynch. Random, 1960. xii, 398 p., bibliography, indices. $7.50.

M. Gilson presents a synthesis of Augustine's thought on the search for God through the intellect and through the will, and on the contemplation of God in his creatures. There is a comprehensive bibliography of Augustine's writings. Although this work is somewhat specialized in its subject, Gilson's exposition is not technical, and the book will appeal to the informed general reader as well as to the student.

GILSON, ETIENNE. *The Christian Philosophy of Thomas Aquinas.* Catalogue of Aquinas' works by I. T. Eschmann and L. K. Shook. Random, 1956. 502 p., notes, index. $7.95.

Professor Gilson presents in this work a synthesis of St. Thomas Aquinas' philosophical system in all its ramifications—natural theology, metaphysics, ethics, cosmology, etc.—establishing the main points of his thought in each branch and tieing them in with the content of other branches to form an intelligible whole. This is perhaps Gilson's most remarkable work, and it is undoubtedly the best synthetic presentation of the philosophy of St. Thomas that is available in English. There are sections that make for difficult reading, mainly because of the subtlety of the material; this work, however, is highly recommended to the serious reader.

GILSON, ETIENNE. *God and Philosophy.* Yale, 1941. xviii, 147 p., index. $2.00. Yale, 1959. pa. 95¢.

The subject of this study is the relationship between the human concept of God and the demonstration of God's existence. The author gives the historical background of the issue, beginning with the Greek philosophers and working through the medieval syntheses. There is a critique of the modern philosophers, by which the author demonstrates the reason for the eclipse of the philosophical approach to the existence of God since the Middle Ages. This is a book for the student of philosophy, and it requires a basic knowledge of the terminology of that discipline.

GILSON, ETIENNE. *The History of Christian Philosophy in the Middle Ages*. Random, 1955. 829 p. $7.50.

Gilson, a master philosopher and historian, examines the history of philosophy from the time of Augustine to that of Ockham in the fifteenth century. Although he treats the various thinkers individually, he is careful to present, by means of a synthetic development from chapter to chapter, a unified view of the age when a uniquely Christian view of the universe was crystallized. Unlike much of Gilson's work, the language, style and manner of the book make it suitable for the general reader as well as for the student.

GILSON, ETIENNE. *The Spirit of Medieval Philosophy*. Translated by A. H. C. Downes. ix, 490 p., notes, index. Scribner, 1936. $3.50.

This is a collection of Gilson's *Gifford Lectures*, delivered in 1931–32. The lectures or chapters together constitute a history of medieval philosophy and present the whole range of philosophic thought from the time of Augustine to that of the fourteenth century. The author's thesis is that Thomas Aquinas' philosophy was a harmonization of faith and reason, combining the thought of Augustine with that of Aristotle without distorting either. This work, one of Gilson's best, is rather difficult reading if the reader has no basic background in philosophy and history.

GILSON, ETIENNE. *The Unity of Philosophical Experience*. Scribner, 1937. xii, 331 p., bibliography, index. $4.50.

The underlying theme in this work is that all philosophical speculation is interconnected, regardless of the time in which such speculation takes place. To demonstrate this thesis, Gilson reviews the history of philosophy from the earliest times to the twentieth century and shows the dependence of later thought upon earlier philosophical concepts and systems, with particular emphasis upon the debt of medieval thought to Aristotle and upon that of modern thought to medieval philosophy. The book is not technical, nor does it presume a knowledge of philosophy, but it does require attentive reading.

Lepp, Ignatius. *Atheism in Our Time.* Translated by Bernard Murchland, c.s.c. Macmillan, 1963. 160 p. $5.00. Macmillan, 1964. pa. $1.45.

The author is a priest who is a former Marxist atheist. In the work, he discusses atheism as a unique phenomenon in that it attempts to break completely away from all faith and to establish a purely "natural" civilization. There is an analysis of the teachings of the leading exponents of atheism— Marx, Sartre, Malraux, etc.—and of the differences between the various forms of atheism. This unusual study is highly recommended to the discriminating reader.

Marcel, Gabriel. *The Philosophy of Existence.* Translated by Manya Harari. Citadel, 1961. 128 p. pa. $1.50.

This is an explanation of the meaning of existentialism, by the leader of the Christian existentialist school. The book has four parts, the first being on the nature and meaning of being, the second on the relationship between existence and freedom, the third on the various schools of existentialism, and the last being, in effect, a biography of the author. The work is a clear, concise introduction to the whole of existentialist thought. It requires no particular philosophical preparation, other than intellectual curiosity and a certain patience with a sometimes confusing translation.

Maritain, Jacques. *The Degrees of Knowledge.* Translated under the supervision of Gerald B. Phelan. Scribner, 1957. xix, 476 p., index. $7.50.

The Degrees of Knowledge is generally regarded as Maritain's finest and most important work. In it, he considers the three stages of abstraction by virtue of which, according to Thomistic principles, one attains to the three levels of knowledge: the knowledge of the senses, acquired through the empirical sciences; abstract or mathematical knowledge, arrived at through the intellect's ability to establish relations between external objects; and knowledge attained by mystical experience, which cannot originate in the intellect alone but which requires the aid of divine illumination. On the whole, the book deals with a rather abstruse point of scholastic thought and requires that the reader have a grasp of that system such as is usually found only among professional philosophers.

MARITAIN, JACQUES. *A Maritain Reader.* Edited, with an introduction, by Donald and Idella Gallagher. Image, 1966. 480 p. $1.45.

For more than half a century, Jacques Maritain has been occupied in evolving a truly contemporary Christian philosophy, and he is recognized as one of the strongest forces today in the current revival of religious thought in American intellectual circles. This work is a collection of representative selections from his writings, designed to cover those areas of philosophy in which Maritain has been most active: logic, ethics, the philosophy of science, epistemology, aesthetics, mysticism, political philosophy, and metaphysics. This comprehensive anthology covers the whole range of Maritain's thought in philosophy, and it is, for the general reader as well as for the student, an outstanding introductory study.

MARITAIN, JACQUES. *Moral Philosophy.* Translated by Matilde Mazzolari. Scribner, 1964. 468 p., notes, index. $7.95.

This is an historical and critical survey of the great moral and ethical systems of human behavior, from Socrates to the present time. Yet, it is not a history of moral philosophy so much as an appraisal of those systems which the author judges to have significance in human history. Thus, some of the great Catholic moralists—Augustine, Bernard, Aquinas—are not discussed, since Maritain regards them as theologians rather than as philosophers. It is less easy to understand the omission of such philosophers as Hume, Mill, and Bentham. This is one of the few Maritain books readily comprehensible to the general reader; unfortunately, it is perhaps the least satisfactory of them all.

MARITAIN, JACQUES. *On the Use of Philosophy.* Princeton, 1962. 71 p. $2.75.

In three short essays, the author explains the importance of the philosopher for the modern world and particularly for modern democracy, showing how philosophers should cooperate with one another both in the purely philosophical and in the religious fields. Thus, rather than a speculative work, this book deals with the practical applications of philosophical thought. It is a model of brilliant simplicity, and is highly recommended.

MARITAIN, JACQUES. *The Range of Reason*. Scribner, 1952. 227 p. $3.95. Scribner, 1961. pa. $1.25.

The collection contains Maritain's reflections on a variety of disconnected subjects, among which are: the value of human knowledge, the quality of artistic judgment, the immortality of the soul, pluralism in a democracy, the meaning of modern atheism, Christian humanism, and Machiavellianism in the contemporary world. Though there is no real unity of subject in the work, it is interesting as a cross-sampling of the great philosopher's thought on subjects ranging from political science to the knowledge of God.

NEILL, THOMAS P. *Makers of the Modern Mind*. Bruce, 1958. xiii, 420 p., index. pa. $2.25.

The author has selected and written studies on the ten men who, beginning with the Reformation, have had the greatest impact on the modern man's attitudes toward himself and the world. The ten are treated in the following order: Calvin, Rousseau, Freud, Bentham, Darwin, Newton, Locke, Kant, Luther, Marx, Descartes—a logical, rather than chronological, order. This is a well written, popularly slanted work.

PASCAL, BLAISE. *Pensées*. Translated by M. Jarrett-Kerr. Allenson, 1959. 135 p. $2.50. Penguin, 1965. pa. 95¢.

This classic work is a collection of random thoughts which were taken from Pascal's notes by his friends after his death. Essentially, the book constitutes an apologia for the Christian faith, addressed to a growing class of intellectual freethinkers among the French aristocracy in the seventeenth century. There is little doubt that Pascal was something of a fanatic, and not always an orthodox one. Because, however, of the lucidity and brilliance of his reflections on common moral as well as religious questions, the *Pensées* remain a source of guidance and information for those who wish to believe but are troubled by doubt, as well as a classic of modern literature.

PIEPER, JOSEF. *Guide to Thomas Aquinas*. Translated by Richard and Clara Winston. Mentor, 1962. ix, 181 p., bibliographical notes, index. pa. 60¢.

Professor Pieper sketches a portrait of Aquinas against a vivid historical background, both as a person and as a thinker of much influence and importance for the modern world. The treatment of Thomas' harmonization of religion and science is unusual and of special interest. This is an excellent survey.

PIEPER, JOSEF. *Leisure, the Basis of Culture*, revised edition. Translated by Alexander Dru; introduction by T. S. Eliot. Pantheon, 1964. 125 p., notes. $3.95. Mentor-Omega, 1964. pa. 60¢.

The thesis of this small but profound work is that true culture can flourish only on a foundation of leisure. In demonstrating that conclusion, Dr. Pieper demolishes our cherished puritanical-Calvinist belief that all labor is noble and that leisure is inherently sinful. Among the targets of the author's erudite wit are machine worship, the cult of youth, the cult of "the common man," and the idolization of technical know-how. This is a provocative little book, highly recommended to the general reader.

SULLIVAN, DANIEL J. *An Introduction to Philosophy*, revised edition. Bruce, 1963. xiii, 288 p., bibliography, index. $4.50.

This is a general introduction to the study of scholastic philosophy for the beginner. It provides historical and reference background as well as a basic synthesis of the traditional philosophical teachings of the Church, and it is so written as to satisfy the reader without confusing him.

TEILHARD DE CHARDIN, PIERRE (S.J.). *The Divine Milieu.* Harper, 1960. 144 p. $3.00.

The famous French Jesuit thinker investigates the question of how man, through his spiritual life, can participate in the destiny of the universe. His answer to the problem is that, through Christian asceticism, we may attain the "divinization of our activities"—or, at the risk of oversimplification, that we must put aside our own will, both exteriorly and interiorly, in conformity with God's will. This is a difficult book, but the informed reader will find, perhaps to his surprise, that it is quite intelligible.

TEILHARD DE CHARDIN, PIERRE (S.J.). *The Future of Man.* Translated by Norman Denny. Harper, 1964. 319 p. $5.00.

This is a collection of twenty-two of Teilhard's essays on the progress of man from his present state to a form of "super-Christianity" made possible by the advances of the experimental and social sciences. The book is, to a large extent, a commentary upon this author's *Phenomenon of Man,* and should preferably be read in conjunction with that work. The style of this work, however, is more suitable for a general audience.

TEILHARD DE CHARDIN, PIERRE (s.J.). *The Phenomenon of Man.* Translated by Bernard Wall; introduction by Julian Huxley. Harper, 1959. 318 p., index. $5.00. Torchbooks, 1961. pa. $1.75.

This famous work contains Teilhard's thought on the natural evolutionary processes of creation in general and of man in particular, and it is the groundwork for the remainder of his system. Although the book originally was regarded with some suspicion by conservatively inclined theologians, it has come to exert considerable influence on theological and philosophical thought among Catholics and non-Catholics alike. The general reader must be prepared for a continuous struggle with the author's terminology and with the subtlety of his ideas. Despite its large sales, the book remains easily comprehensible only to the specialist.

THOMAS AQUINAS, SAINT. *On the Truth of the Catholic Faith.* Translated by Charles J. O'Neil, Anton C. Pegis, James F. Anderson, and Vernon J. Bourke. Image, 1955 (5 vols.). Introductions, notes, indices. pa. 95¢ ea.

This is a translation of Aquinas' *Summa contra gentiles* (also called the *Summa philosophica*). In this work, Thomas attempts to explain, by reason alone, the truth of the Catholic faith. It is, then, basically a book of apologetics, and the source from which all later such works have been drawn. The work is divided into four books, or parts: the first, "God," treats of the existence and nature of God; the second, "Creation," deals with the notion of creation and with the interrelationship of creator and creatures; the third book, "Providence," examines the concept of God as the final good and end of all creatures, and studies the role of free will and of grace in that context; the fourth section examines the meaning of salvation and the ways of attaining it, such as the Church, the sacraments, etc., and is entitled "Salvation." Its depth and closeness of logic recommend it only to the serious reader.

THOMAS AQUINAS, SAINT. *The Pocket Aquinas.* Edited, with new passages translated, and a general introduction, by

Vernon Bourke. Washington Square, 1960. xxvi, 372 p., bibliography. pa. 60¢.

These selections from the writings of Aquinas are representative of both his philosophical and theological thought, and treat of such subjects as the manner and validity of human knowledge, the role of philosophy in Christian life, social and political theory, and the nature of theology. The book is an excellent guide to Aquinas' teachings on individual questions, but it is perhaps too fragmented to serve as a comprehensive introduction to his work.

VANN, GERALD (O.P.). *St. Thomas Aquinas.* Foreword by Charles A. Hart. Benziger, 1947. xxvii, 185 p., bibliography. $3.50.

This is a study in the practical aspects of Thomism, rather than, as the title might imply, a biography of St. Thomas. The author's purpose is to show how Aquinas' philosophical and theological thought is equipped to serve as a bridge between the oriental and the occidental minds. Whatever one's own views on the subject of Thomism, the book is well worth reading as an interesting and provocative study of the thought of Aquinas in relation to the modern world. It presupposes a general knowledge of scholasticism, but it should be intelligible to the careful general reader.

WARD, BARBARA. *Five Ideas That Change the World.* Norton, 1959. 188 p. $4.50. Norton, 1962. pa. $1.50.

Miss Ward, an eminent Catholic economist and social philosopher, offers a plan for the economic salvation of the under-developed nations. The basis of her thought is that a certain level of material well-being is essential to the spiritual and political well-being of man, and that the "have" nations have a spiritual, as well as a political obligation, to share their wealth with the "have-nots." Miss Ward is one of the few social scientists who is also an accomplished writer. Her thought is lucidly, and often entertainingly, expressed, and her work is always wholly intelligible to the lay reader.

COMMUNISM

The whole concept of Communism has been called the greatest threat to Christianity since Christ established his religion on earth. For the first time, the Church is faced with a world-wide attack by a powerful and ruthless force which has as one of its basic tenets the complete and total destruction of religion. It is not sufficient to fear such a force; if it is to be met and conquered, it must be understood. We believe the books below will explain the nature and philosophy of Communism in a manner which will reveal it fully and in all its manifestations.

BUDENZ, LOUIS. *The Technique of Communism.* Regnery, 1962. viii, 342 p. pa. $2.00.

The author, a former high-ranking member of the American Communist party and a convert to Catholicism, explains the aim and methods of Communism. Basing himself on official party books, documents, and directives, he provides an analysis and evaluation of Communist ideology and strategy in schools and in Communist groups. The book is non-technical in style and will provide a clear picture of Red activities in the United States when internal Communism was a force to be reckoned with.

CRONIN, JOHN FRANCIS (s.s.). *Communism: Threat to Freedom.* Paulist, 1962. 80 p., reading lists, study outline. pa. 50¢.

A general and popularly written exposition of Communist aims and methods, this book treats of theory and practice in the Cold War, subversion, economic warfare, Communism in the U.S., etc. It is an adequate introduction to the meaning and significance of contemporary Communism.

D'ARCY, MARTIN C. (s.j.). *Communism and Christianity.* Devin, 1957. xii, 242 p., bibliography. $4.00. Penguin, 1956. pa. 65¢.

The purpose of this book is to show the similarities and differences between Christianity and Communism. By an analysis of the two systems, the author demonstrates the fundamental incompatibility of their two philosophies of life. In addition to its value as a popularly written presentation of the philosophy of Communism, the book is worth reading for the insight it provides into the ideological bases of the East-West struggle.

DODD, BELLA VISONO. *School of Darkness*. Devin, 1963. 246 p., index. $2.75.

Bella Dodd was, for many years, a member of the National Committee of the Communist party in the United States. This book is her account of the activities of the Party while she was a member, of her eventual resignation of membership, and of her conversion to the Catholic Church. It is an interesting study of the Communist party at the height of its influence in the U.S. Although some readers will find the author's style rather bleak, the book is worth-while reading as the record of a period when Communism seemed to pose a serious internal threat to American security.

NEILL, THOMAS PATRICK and JAMES COLLINS. *Communism: Why and How It Works*. Introduction by R. J. Henle. Sheed, 1964. viii, 216 p. $4.50.

This concise history of Communism in Russia won the Freedom Foundation Award in 1964. It outlines the birth and growth of the Communist party in Czarist Russia, provides a graphic description of the seizure of power in 1917, and surveys the history of the party from those days through the Khrushchev era. The book is, in effect, an excellent history of twentieth-century Russia.

21. REFERENCE BOOKS

Although many reference works are excluded from the average home because of their size or price, it has seemed to us desirable to include a section on this most valuable category of books to indicate what is available in the Catholic field. Everyone is aware of such general standard reference books as dictionaries, but not so well known is the fact that there are several excellent Catholic dictionaries readily available and at a variety of reasonable prices; the *World Almanac* is widely known, but there is also a *Catholic Almanac* which has an amazing store of knowledge compressed into a single, easy-to-use volume. Many of these standard Catholic reference books are quite inexpensive and merit a place in every Catholic home.

A reference work is a fascinating storehouse of knowledge. In one sense, of course, any book one consults for information is a form of reference work; but we are using the term in its more limited sense, as a book which contains material designed to be found easily and quickly. It is thus a short-cut to information on persons, places and events. But in a larger sense, reference works provide a systematic presentation of man's knowledge on a particular subject and become a treasury of the knowledge man has accumulated through the ages and is uncovering today in every field of human endeavor. There have always been reference works, but no age has produced reference books on so many varied subjects, so accurately compiled, and so comprehensive in treatment as has the twentieth century. The ordinary citizen of today has at his finger-tips, in reference books, more knowledge than the giants of earlier ages ever dreamed of. The worth of reference books in a civilization so complex as our own cannot be overestimated. With such a wealth of information available at every turn it is incumbent on us to use it widely and wisely to our great advantage.

As is the case with all reference books, the user of Catholic reference tools should always, as a first step, know what the authors intend their work to be. Practically all reference books have a foreword or introduction explaining what the authors had in mind when they prepared the volume, how it should be used, and the particular aspects of it with which the reader should be familiar if he is to realize maximum value of the book. For example, the authors of *Dictionary of Catholic Biography* carefully explained in their foreword that no living figures were contained in its pages. And yet the publishers received numerous letters pointing out the names of prominent living individuals who were not included in its pages. The consulters of that *Dictionary* who wrote those letters obviously had not read the foreword. Similarly, in this *Guide* we have excluded books which are out of print and not readily available. Doing so means that some excellent titles have been omitted since we mean this *Guide* to be a working tool for the interested reader. In both cases anyone expecting more of the *Dictionary* or the *Guide* will be disappointed simply because they did not take the time to find the purpose of the volume.

Next, master the mechanics of using a reference work. This is particularly true in the more complex, multi-volumed works. Looking up a word in a dictionary (though even in this simple research knowing how to spell it is essential) is a comparatively simple task. But in the larger reference work, knowing how to find cross references, the meaning of certain abbreviations, under what heading certain material is to be found, how to use the index (it is incredible how many people do not know how to use an index to the fullest advantage)— these are some of the points that the user should learn about when consulting a reference work.

For those constantly using a reference book such as the *New Catholic Encyclopedia* or *Butler's Lives of the Saints*, study the work and learn how it is put together. Again, a short time spent in studying the make-up of a particular reference work will save hours of time and frustration for the student or scholar who will be using the work constantly. This is true of even the humblest book containing material which would classify it as a reference work.

One of the invaluable aids offered the seeker of knowledge by most reference works is the bibliography to be found at the end of any important article. The encyclopedia or handbook or whatever it is gives a concise summary of the subject or person but frequently the user will want further information. Here, conveniently at hand, is a list of books for more intensive study. Too often the reference-tool user ignores the worth of these lists. Compiled by experts in the field, they are the carefully evaluated selection of what is available for shedding further light on the subject. Much effort is expended in preparing these lists and the reference book user should take full advantage of them.

Interestingly enough, though reference works present articles on various matters which are meant to provide quick and concise information, even those seeking more complete information can find these articles most helpful. For instance, the period of the Thirty Years' War was a most complex one, with leaders changing sides, issues constantly changing, nations torn by conflicting loyalties, so that often the student is completely bewildered. Reading an article on this subject in an encyclopedia often will give the reader an over-all picture, an outline as it were, of this tragic period of history, which will make clear to him its mainstreams and directions. With this comprehensive concept in mind, he will find the more detailed studies delving into the more particularized aspects of his subject far more understandable as each fragment fits into the master plan he has learned from the shorter encyclopedia article. Frequently, using the reference-work article as the starting point in a research project, or even when one intends merely to make a personal study, is an excellent method of more easily and more intelligently approaching a subject.

Reference works are primarily, of course, as we have stressed, designed to make easily and compactly available information on a particular person or subject. If one does not wish to read a whole book on the Crusades, one turns to a reference work to get the information one wants. But may we suggest that reference works may well provide fascinating reading as well as quick access to needed information. The reader will be surprised at how interesting he will find it to browse through an almanac or an encyclopedia or a biographical dictionary. These books are an amazing source of knowledge and the modern reference work is usually well written, legibly printed, often well illustrated, and handsomely packaged. Next time you have looked up the particular topic you are checking, spend a few minutes browsing. You will be surprised at how interesting you will find it, and of course your store of information and knowledge is bound to be increased. Don't blame us, though, if the minutes melt into hours! They always do for the authors of this *Guide*, but we always enjoy such excursions. Why don't you try it?

ALTING VON GEUSAU, LEO, et al., Editors. *Concilium: Theology in the Age of Renewal.* Paulist, 1964–1969. (50 vols.). $4.50 ea. (by subscription, $159.00 per set).

Concilium is a series of books published over a five-year period intended to cover the theological and historical background of the changes within the Church put into effect by Vatican II. The series' editors are twenty-one of the modern Church's most respected thinkers, such as Yves Congar, Godfrey Diekmann, Hans Küng, Roland Murphy, Karl Rahner, and Edward Schillebeeckx. The fifty volumes, being published at the rate of ten volumes per year, cover ten main subjects: dogma, liturgy, pastoral theology, ecumenism, moral theology, the Church in the modern world, Church history, canon law, spirituality, and Scripture. The individual volumes, for the most part, are quite technical in approach and quite specialized in subject. They are suitable for use by theologians, but require in the non-professional reader a sound foundation in the various disciplines.

ATTWATER, DONALD. *Catholic Dictionary,* revised edition. Macmillan, 1961. xvi, 552 p. $5.95.

This is a dictionary of words, terms, names, and phrases in common use in theology, philosophy, canon law, the liturgy, ecclesiastical institutions and organizations. In addition, there are brief biographies of the best known saints. This is perhaps the most concise and comprehensive such work available, and it is an indispensable and easy-to-use reference book for any Catholic library or home.

ATTWATER, DONALD. *A Dictionary of Mary.* Kenedy, 1956. viii, 312 p. $6.50.

This was the first, and it still is the best, book in English which brings together all of the assorted bits of information and historical facts about the Virgin. The book is in dictionary format, listing and explaining, in alphabetical order, the facts of Mary's life, her privileges, the theology of Mary, her feasts, her shrines, etc. It is a valuable reference work for home and library.

ATTWATER, DONALD. *A Dictionary of Saints.* Kenedy, 1958. vii, 280 p. $4.50.

This is a one-volume revision of the standard authority on the lives and deeds of the saints, Butler's *Lives of the Saints.* The better known saints are included in this volume, in alphabetical order, and the details of their lives and miracles are given in easily readable language. This work is indispensable for libraries who do not have Butler's multi-volume work, and it is a valuable reference work for the home.

Book of Saints, 4th edition, revised and enlarged. Edited by the Benedictine Monks of St. Augustine's Abbey. Macmillan, 1947. xvii, 708 p., bibliography, appendix. $7.50.

This is a collection of lives of the saints, extracted from the official and unofficial martyrologies of the Church. The entries are arranged in alphabetical order and give brief biographical sketches of each saint as well as information concerning their patronage of occupations, countries, etc., and their feast days. There is a calendar of saints, or liturgical calendar, showing the feast days of the saints in chronological order. This is a concise and comprehensive work of reference, ideal for use in the home as well as in libraries.

BUTLER, ALBAN. *Lives of the Saints.* Edited, revised and supplemented by Herbert Thurston, S.J. and Donald Attwater. Foreword by Francis Cardinal Spellman. Kenedy, 1956. Vol. I: xxxii, 720 p.; Vol. II: xxii, 692 p.; Vol. III: xx, 705 p.; Vol. IV: xx, 707 p., bibliographies, indices. $39.50 (boxed).

Butler's classic work, written in the mid-eighteenth century, has long been regarded as the standard reference work on the saints of the Church. The editors have brought it up to date by including the names of saints canonized in modern times, revising Butler's material in the light of the discoveries of modern historical methods, and, where necessary, rephrasing the author's always elegant, but not always lucid, style into idiomatic modern English. This is the complete source of information on any saint, containing 2565 entries, and it is an indispensable reference book for Catholic libraries.

CODE, JOSEPH B., Editor. *Dictionary of the American Hierarchy.* J. F. Wagner, 1965. 452 p. $12.95.

This work is a biographical dictionary listing more than 850 leaders of the Catholic Church in America, about one-third of which are still alive. Under the appellation of "American Hierarchy" the editor includes not only heads of U.S. dioceses and their auxiliaries and coadjutors, but also missionary and other bishops with jurisdiction outside this country; he lists also non-American prelates who, for some reason or another, are identified with the American Church (e.g., Apostolic Delegates). The biographical sketches of the subjects are ample and painstakingly correct. This an authoritative and basic tool of reference, and should be in every public library as well as in that of every Catholic institution.

COULSON, JOHN. *The Saints: A Concise Biographical Dictionary.* Introduction by C. C. Martindale. Hawthorn, 1958. 496 p., bibliography. $12.95.

As the title indicates, this is an alphabetical listing of all of the better known saints to whom one might expect to find reference made either in the liturgy or in the history of the Church. There is a brief but comprehensive biography given of each saint, along with useful information concerning the particular saint's place in the liturgy.

DANIEL-ROPS, HENRI, Editor-in-Chief. *The Twentieth Century Encyclopedia of Catholicism.* Hawthorn, 1957– . (150 vols.) Price range: $2.95 to $3.50 ea.

The Twentieth Century Encyclopedia of Catholicism is not an encyclopedia in the traditional sense of being a collection of articles arranged alphabetically by subject; it is rather a series of volumes divided into sixteen categories, each volume of which is written by one author and treats of one particular subject. The categories and the number of volumes in each are as follows: I. Knowledge and Faith (15 volumes); II. The Basic Truths (13 volumes); III. The Nature of Man (8 volumes); IV. The Means of Redemption (11 volumes); V. The Life of Faith (12 volumes); VI. The Word of God (14 volumes); VII. The History of the Church (6 volumes); VIII. The Organization of the Church (9 volumes); IX. The Church and the Modern World (19 volumes); X. The Worship of the Church (8 volumes); XI. Catholicism and Literature (4 volumes); XII. Catholicism and the Arts (7 volumes); XIII. Catholicism and Science (8 volumes); XIV. Outside the Church (5 volumes); XV. Non-Christian Beliefs (7 volumes); XVI. General and Supplementary (4 volumes). As in all such works of composite authorship, there is a good deal of variance in quality of treatment and in approach among the individual volumes. (The reader is referred to appropriate subject classifications in the present book for a description of selected titles from the *Encyclopedia*.)

DELANEY, JOHN J. and JAMES E. TOBIN. *Dictionary of Catholic Biography*. Doubleday, 1961, xi, 1245 p., appendices. $18.50 (thumb-indexed, $19.95).

This work contains, in alphabetical order, concise but comprehensive biographies of some 13,000 important figures of Catholic history, exclusive of living persons. The material is intelligently arranged, clearly written with abundant cross-references, and includes suggestions for further reading on many subjects. This is an indispensable reference work for both Catholic and general libraries.

ENGLEBERT, OMER. *The Lives of the Saints*. Translated by Christopher and Anne Fremantle. McKay, 1951. 532 p., index, illustrations. $5.00.

This collection, by an eminent Catholic scholar and writer, narrates the lives of the saints in an easy-to-read and readable style. Included are all of the well known saints and many less known ones of particular interest, arranged chronologically according to feast days. The author, in selecting his material, has used modern historical methods of criticism, and his work is historically sound as well as inspirational and informative.

McCARTHY, THOMAS P., Editor. *A Guide to the Catholic Sisterhoods in the United States*, revised and enlarged edition. Foreword by Ameleto Cardinal Cicognani. Catholic University, 1964. 404 p., illustrations, appendices, index. $4.50. Catholic University, 1964. pa. $2.95.

This is an indispensable reference work for those who are interested in American convent life in any of its aspects. It contains information on the history, way of life, kind of work or works performed, and general admission qualifications of every order, society, and congregation of women in the

United States. This edition also contains a list of secular institutes, a list of communities that will accept older women, and an analytical index which shows the amount of time devoted in each community both to work and to prayer. Appendices provide, by geographic location, the addresses of all motherhouses, generalates, and provincial houses. There are photographs of the habits of all communities. In short, the reader will find just about any item of information in this book on the subject of women's religious orders.

McKENZIE, JOHN L. (s.j.). *Dictionary of the Bible.* Bruce, 1965. 976 p., tables, maps, illustrations. $17.95.

Father McKenzie has written almost two thousand separate articles, analyzing every book of both the Old and New Testaments. The reader will find practically every Biblical name identified, with essays on such major concepts as grace, faith, salvation, truth, etc., and with articles on the various civilizations of importance to Biblical study (Egyptian, Sumerian, Canaanite, Elamite, and Persian). Of particular value is the author's analysis of each book of the Bible according to content, literary character, date and time of composition, and themes. This is an excellent, easily understandable, reference work; it will be of great value for use in the home as well as in libraries.

NEVINS, ALBERT J. (M.M.), Editor. *The Maryknoll Catholic Dictionary.* Preface by Donald Attwater. Grosset, 1965. 710 p., tables, appendices. $9.95.

This simply written, up-to-date dictionary lists, in alphabetical order, information about the Church in all its aspects. The entries are in the form of explanations rather than of strict definitions, and unusual and foreign words are accompanied by phonetic pronunciation guides. The appendices include the names and addresses of Catholic organizations, and biographical sketches of the most prominent deceased Catholics of the U.S. and Canada. The book is a useful source of information for homes and libraries.

PASTOR, LUDWIG VON. *The History of the Popes.* Translated by Frederick I. Antrobus, Ralph F. Kerr, and Ernest Graf. Herder, 1915–1938. 40 volumes.

Pastor's *History of the Popes* is one of the most monumental works of Catholic historical scholarship undertaken in modern times. It covers the five centuries from the close of

the Middle Ages through the eighteenth century (1305 to
1799), discussing the reigns of sixty-one popes and antipopes, from Clement V to Pius VI, with an attention to detail and a scholarly exactitude that will make this the standard work on the papacy during that period for many years to
come. The author had access, in his capacity of Austrian
ambassador to the Holy See, to documents in the Vatican
archives which had not been accessible to scholars before
him, and his thorough documentation makes this series an
indispensable work of reference for historians of the period.

PEGIS, JESSIE CORRIGAN. *A Practical Catholic Dictionary.* All
Saints, 1961. ix, 260 p., appendices. pa. 50¢.
 This inexpensive work is an adequate dictionary of liturgical, theological, and spiritual terms in common use in the
Church, written in non-technical language. The appendices
include brief biographies of the best known saints, a chronological listing of the popes, and a list of the most important
papal documents. This is a suitable work of reference for
Catholic homes and for students.

RAHNER, KARL and HERBERT VORGRIMLER. *Theological Dictionary.* Edited by Cornelius Ernst, O.P.; translated by Richard Strachan. 493 p. $6.50.
 This work is not a "theological dictionary" in the proper
sense of the term. It is rather a concise theological encyclopedia, in that it comprises a group of approximately six
hundred short articles, alphabetically arranged, on various
concepts of dogmatic theology. The material provided gives
a succinct statement of the teachings of the Church with
respect to points of doctrine and their theological implications. Within those limits, it is an excellent work, by a master
of contemporary theological thought, and thoroughly up-to-
date.

ROMIG, WALTER and JOSEPH E. PLACEK, Editors. *The Guide
to Catholic Literature.* Catholic Library Association, 1939– .
(7 vols.). $9.00 ea.
 This work contains listings of all books of Catholic interest, both hard-cover and paperback, published in this
country from 1888 to the present. The following information
is given for each book: author, title, number of pages, date
of publication, publisher, and price at date of publication.
In addition, many of the listings contain a brief synopsis of

particular books, and some provide pertinent critical comments. Volume I covers 1888 to 1940; Volume II, 1940 to 1944; Volume III, 1944 to 1948; Volume IV, 1948 to 1951; Volume V, 1952 to 1955; Volume VI, 1956 to 1959; Volume VII, 1960 to 1965 (in preparation). The work will be of much value in the libraries of schools and religious institutions. (A paperbound "Annual" is available every year at a subscription rate of $6.00 per issue.)

THOMAS AQUINAS, SAINT. *Summa Theologiae.* McGraw, 1964– . Translated and edited with notes by the Dominican Fathers of the English-speaking provinces.

This monumental undertaking is a translation of the *Summa Theologiae* of St. Thomas into English. Each volume will deal with Aquinas' thought on one basic section of theology, giving both the Latin text of the original and an idiomatic English version, and each section is explained and commented upon by a system of introductions and notes. (The cost of the individual volumes runs from $5.50 to $7.50.)

VAN DEN BORN, ALFRED. *Encyclopedic Dictionary of the Bible.* Translated and adapted by Louis F. Hartman. McGraw, 1962. 2634 p., illustrations, plates, maps, bibliographies. $27.50.

This is one of the most complete and useful one-volume Biblical encyclopedias available in English. It identifies and discusses practically every word, concept, and name to be found in either the Old Testament or the New, in entries ranging in length from a few lines to several thousand words. The entries take into account non-Catholic, as well as Catholic, Biblical studies. Despite the relative absence of English-language works in the bibliographies, and an occasional lapse into jargon, this book is an excellent reference work for libraries and for the general reader.

22. RELIGIOUS ORDERS

One of the most unusual characteristics of the Catholic Church is the religious order, congregation, society, or community.* Broadly speaking, the religious order consists of a group of individuals united to pursue a religious way of life, bound by vows, and subject to a superior general.

So integral a part of the Church have these religious societies become that it would be difficult to conceive of the Catholic Church without them, and their importance to the Church can hardly be overestimated. It is significant that, all through history, the first step taken by a ruler or state intent on attacking the Church has been the dissolution of the religious orders. Whether it be a specific order, such as was the case in 1773 when Pope Clement XIV, under tremendous political pressure, suppressed the Jesuits, or all orders, as was the case during the anticlerical government in power in France in 1905, the enemies of the Church have always realized the importance of the religious order in the life of the Church and in human affairs and have made their destruction a primary objective.

Not only do religious orders play a vital role in the Church as an institution, but equally important to the welfare of the Church and society is the kind of men and women produced by the religious orders. From the earliest days, the religious life in community has produced a type of man and woman which has provided the Church with some of her greatest figures. Saints, popes, cardinals, philosophers, educators, diplomats, artists, authors, poets have come in an unending stream to people the Church with outstanding figures in every field of human activity. Dedicated completely as they are to God, their persons and their talents are ever at the dis-

* Each of these terms has a particular significance as defined in canon law, but in this discussion we will use the expression "order" as a generic term to cover all groups of men or women united in the religious life.

posal of the Church, and glorious chapters in the Church's history have been written by them in every century.

The religious life has had an appeal for Christians from the earliest days of Christianity. As early as the first century, the Christian virgins, dedicated to perfecting their lives through unity with God, were celebrated by the Church Fathers. Renowned for their continence and holiness, they were a source of inspiration to their fellow Christians, as were the early confessors who too practiced chastity and poverty as a means to achieve Christian perfection. But though these good men and women employed many of the virtuous habits so cultivated by religious today, there were notable differences particularly in their mode of living. These early religious did not withdraw from the society in which they lived but rather remained in it following their holy and ascetic practices in their own homes and in the midst of their fellow men. Further, they pursued their spiritual goals on an individual basis and were under no vow of obedience to a superior.

In the third century, a new dimension in religious life appeared in the practices of the Desert Fathers in the barren wastelands of the Egyptian deserts. Multitudes of men, disillusioned with the depravity of their world, fled to the deserts to follow their holy calling under the harsh conditions of desert life. At first, a life of solitude was the norm. In time, the holiness of certain eremites such as St. Antony and St. Paul of Thebes attracted followers who grouped themselves into monastic villages, which were the forerunners of monasteries. When St. Pachomius brought his followers under one roof, the cenobitic life began. In the fourth century, the beginnings of a monastic rule appeared in the regulations (in the form of questions and answers) which St. Basil drew up for his monastery in Pontus. Another development came from the genius of St. Augustine, who inaugurated the common life with his clergy and founded convents of nuns following the regulations he had laid down (especially in a letter to a community of nuns in 423) which later developed into the rule of St. Augustine. His influence on Western monastic life has been tremendous, surpassed only by St. Benedict, and his rule became the basis for the foundation of many religious orders, among them the Dominicans, Trinitarians, and Knights Hospitallers, as well as the clerks regular.

But the real founder of the monastic religious life as we know it today was St. Benedict. In the sixth century he promulgated a series of directives for his monks, known to this day as the *Rule of St. Benedict*. This Rule was the basis of all monastic life from the eighth to the twelfth century, and is observed today by thousands of religious in the Benedictine, Cistercian, Camaldolese, and many other orders which adopted and adapted his Rule as the basis of their religious life. It describes the government, daily life, and practices of a monastery, and provides the means by which men in a community should devote themselves to God's service by prayer and work. One of the most important innovations of his Rule is the vow of stability, in addition to those of poverty, chastity, and obedience, which bound the monk to the house in which he had been professed and ended the wandering about of monks so prevalent in Benedict's day.

Inevitably the next step was the grouping of different monasteries under one head. By the twelfth century, for example, the Cluny congregation had some two hundred monasteries under its authority. The significance of this development was that it brought into existence a feature common to religious orders today—the dispersal of an order over large geographical areas. No longer confined to an individual monastery, an order could spread all over Europe as it founded new monasteries far from the motherhouse.

In the twelfth century a tremendous new concept of religious life came into being through the genius of St. Francis of Assisi and St. Dominic. For centuries the monasteries were cultural oases scattered over Europe; with the passage of time, they became as well the center of wealth and often a source of scandal in the Church. All too frequently they lost contact completely with the common people who were living lives of incredible poverty and desperation. To many, the monasteries represented the epitome of opulence, luxurious living, and, for the poor, of oppression. The startling notion of the new mendicant orders put into dramatic practice by St. Francis and St. Dominic was that they would live in common a life of the utmost poverty, with no possessions or income, and would live their life of contemplation in the world—not bound to a monastery but wherever their wanderings might lead. Further, as the Franciscans and Dominicans grew, they put into effect a principle which introduced an entirely new element in the structure of the Church. Each mendicant would be responsible to his superior who in turn was responsible to his superior until the chain of command reached the superior general of the order. And general he was, for the hierarchy of these orders was almost military in nature and a military obedience was demanded. Most significant of all was that the orders were authorized by papal approval. At a stroke, the mendicant orders were freed from the authority of a local monastic superior or the bishop of a diocese or the metropolitan of a province. A whole new hierarchy was introduced into the structure of the Church.

By the sixteenth century new needs had arisen in the Church which called for new concepts for religious orders, and these needs were met by the founding of the various orders of clerks regular. The first of these was the Theotines in 1524, but the best known is the Society of Jesus founded by St. Ignatius of Loyola and his companions in 1540. These clerks regulars, like the orders preceding them, were groups of men who had taken religious vows, lived in community, and were governed by their rule. But, unlike their monastic and mendicant brothers, they were engaged in the active work of their ministry and were not bound to office in choir. The times called for a new freedom of action by religious which would permit them to engage in the work of salvation in an active and direct manner rather than from the cloister of the monastery.

Generally speaking, these three broad classifications, monastic, mendicant, clerks regular, encompass the various religious orders in the Church. An infinite variety of orders exists today—literally thousands of them. When and where a particular need arose, a religious order came into being. As time passed, many of the needs which brought an order into being disappeared, and the order was either dissolved, merged with another order, or found a new purpose for its existence. For instance, in the twelfth century a group of military orders came into existence. The Equestrian Order of

St. John of Jerusalem in 1118 (now the Knights of Malta), the Knights Templars in 1118, and the Teutonic Knights in 1190, were founded to defend the cause of the Church through armed might. As their need ceased, they were dissolved or, in some cases, became honorary orders. The Mercedarians were founded in 1225 to ransom captives taken by infidels, especially the Moors. They later engaged in hospital work as the ransoming of captives became unnecessary.

During these centuries, along with the men's religious orders, the women's orders too grew and flourished. Some were founded as companion orders to the men as was the case with the Franciscans and the Poor Clares founded by St. Clare. Others were founded for a particular purpose and were in no way related to any of the men's orders. Always though, whether the order was male or female, the purpose was constant—to do God's work on earth.

How well they have succeeded can be seen by the works in which the religious, male or female, are engaged today. Name any human need or activity and there will one find religious engaged. Care of the sick, the poor, the aged, the orphan; education; intellectual activity; missionary work; contemplation; and always, of course, concern for the spiritual well-being of their fellow humans.

Today the religious orders, like the entire Church, are engaged in a painful self-examination and renewal as they strive to make themselves and their goals relevant to the needs of the modern world and to adjust to the tempo of the times. The training of new members, a realignment of forces, the modification of methods, a reappraisal of goals, the application of new techniques to their chosen work, the renewal of their very essence—all these are the subject of intensive study for every religious order. Their generals and superiors realize clearly that this is a new and dangerous age that man has entered—the age of the atomic bomb and nuclear energy and exploration of outer space. All human society has been affected, and the old way of life is forever gone. Mankind is in a new age. And as has been true for centuries, the religious orders are meeting the new challenges head-on. They have always been the strong bulwark and support of the Church and today have taken to heart the charge of Pope

John for renewal and reform. Change is the order of the day, and the religious orders are in the forefront of the fray. They are today and they will be in centuries to come.

The books we have listed in this section reflect all of the above. They tell the history of the religious orders and their great leaders, how the concept of religious orders began, grew, and developed; and finally they bring the story up to date by describing what is going on among the religious communities today.

BRODRICK, JAMES (S.J.). *The Origin of the Jesuits*. Image, 1960. 233 p., notes, index. pa. 85¢.

This popularly written history of the beginnings of the Jesuits describes the era when such giants as Ignatius Loyola, Francis Xavier, and Diego Laynez worked to expand the tiny Society into the powerful organization that was one day to cover the globe and to affect the destinies of popes and kings.

CANU, JEAN. *Religious Orders of Men*. Translated by P. J. Hepburne-Scott. Hawthorn, 1960. 144 p., bibliography, index. $2.95.

This is an historical introduction to religious orders for men. The author divides his work into three chronological sections: fourth to twelfth centuries, thirteenth to fifteenth centuries, and sixteenth to twentieth centuries. In the first section he considers the institution of monasticism; in the second, that of the mendicant orders; and, in the last, modern religious orders, societies, and congregations. This is an excellent over-all treatment of the religious life in general and gives not only the history of each order but also explains how they are fulfilling their missions in the modern world. (Volume 85 of the *Twentieth Century Encyclopedia of Catholicism*.)

HANLEY, BONIFACE (O.F.M.) and SALVATOR FINK (O.F.M.). *The Franciscans: Love At Work*. St. Anthony's, 1962. 240 p., illustrations. $6.50. Image, 1966. pa. 95¢.

This is a pictorial essay describing the Franciscan Order. With 103 full-page photographs, the book tells the life of St. Francis, explains the application of the spirit of St. Francis in the twentieth century, and shows how that spirit is put to work today through mission work, teaching, preaching, and other activities in which the Franciscans are presently engaged.

HOMAN, HELEN W. *Knights of Christ.* Prentice, 1957. xxiv, 486 p., bibliography, index. $12.50.

This author, the writer of many popular biographies of saints, in the present work tells the stories of the major religious orders—the Benedictines, the Dominicans, the Franciscans, etc.—describing how and why they were founded, how they developed, and giving a brief but comprehensive and accurate history of each. There is also a concise and excellent biography of the founder of each order.

KANE, GEORGE LOUIS, Editor. *Why I Entered the Convent.* Introduction by Archbishop Richard J. Cushing. Newman, 1953. xvii, 214 p. $2.50. Newman, 1953. pa. $1.00.

In this book twenty-one nuns from various communities in the United States tell the stories of their vocations. Although the contributors are, for the most part, unknown beyond the walls of their respective convents, their stories make for interesting, and sometimes inspiring, reading.

KITTLER, GLENN D. *The Maryknoll Fathers.* World, 1961. 318 p., illustrations. $5.00. Guild, 1964. pa. 75¢.

The Catholic Foreign Missionary Society of America, popularly known as "the Maryknoll Fathers," was founded in 1911 by Fathers James A. Walsh and Thomas F. Price. In the fifty years between that date and the publication of this work, Maryknoll has sent, and is maintaining, missionaries in the Far East, Latin America, the Pacific islands, and Africa. In this book, Glenn Kittler tells the colorful story of that expansion from a small group of dedicated priests to a worldwide organization devoted to the establishment of Christianity in every corner of the world.

KITTLER, GLENN D. *The White Fathers.* Introduction by Laurian Cardinal Rugambwa. Image, 1961. 318 p. pa. 95¢.

The religious congregation known popularly as the "White Fathers" was established in 1868, as the Society of Missionaries of Africa, by Cardinal C. M. A. Lavigerie. The purpose of the Society is to work for the African missions, particularly among the Arabs. They are bound to live as much like the

natives as possible, and their dress closely resembles the flowing tunic and burnoose of the Arabs. Mr. Kittler tells in this
book the story of the founding of the Society, and of their
activities until the middle of the present century. The book
is as interesting as any story of adventure, and it is well and
colorfully written in a journalistic style.

LaFarge, John (s.j.). *A Report on the American Jesuits.*
Photographs by Margaret Bourke-White. Farrar, 1956.
236 p., illustrations. $4.95.

Father LaFarge, a well known Jesuit writer, describes the
history of the Jesuits, their growth in the United States, the
Jesuit approach to education, and their methods of dealing
with contemporary problems. The book furnishes a clear
picture of current activities of the Society in missionary work,
in the schools, and in various fields of learning and other
work. The book was written for those who know little about
the slightly mysterious Society of Jesus, and is an excellent
statement of the aims and spirit of that order.

McCarthy, Thomas P., Editor. *A Guide to the Catholic
Sisterhoods in the United States,* revised and enlarged edition. Foreword by Ameleto Cardinal Cicognani. Catholic
University, 1964. 404 p., illustrations, appendices, index.
$4.50. Catholic University, 1964. pa. $2.95.

This is an indispensable book for those who are interested
in American convent life in any of its aspects. It contains
information on the history, way of life, kind of work or works
performed, and general admission qualifications of every
order, society, and congregation of women in the United
States. This edition also contains a list of secular institutes, a
list of communities that will accept older women, and an
analytical index which shows the amount of time, in each
community, devoted both to work and to prayer. Appendices
provide, by geographic location, the addresses of all motherhouses, generalates, and provincial houses. There are photographs of the habits of all communities. In short, the reader
will find just about any item of information in this book on
the subject of women's religious orders.

Malard, Suzanne. *Religious Orders of Women.* Translated
by George J. Robinson. Hawthorn, 1964. 110 p. $3.50.

This volume explains the life of the modern nun in a simple
and comprehensive way. The author discusses religious life

for women in general, attempting to answer the question, "What is a nun?" There is a treatment of the importance and significance of the religious vows, and of the various kinds of religious orders for women: the contemplatives, the missionaries, those in the active apostolate, and the secular institutes. (Volume 86 of the *Twentieth Century Encyclopedia of Catholicism.*)

MARIA DEL REY, SISTER (C.M.). *No Two Alike.* Dodd, 1965. x, 240 p., illustrations. $5.00. Echo, 1966. pa. 85¢.

These biographical "profiles" of Maryknoll nuns are intended to do away with the quaint notion that all Sisters, like all West Pointers, look alike, talk alike, and act alike. In a fast-moving narrative, the author tells the story of Sister Patrice who worked among the lepers of Hawaii; of Mother Mary, who went on horseback into the jungles of Central America to found a hospital; of Sister Martin, a Negro social worker in Oregon; of Sister Magdalena and her life in China and Manchuria—and of a dozen others who resemble each other only in their dedication to God and in their love of humanity.

MARY FRANCIS, SISTER (C.P.). *A Right to be Merry.* x, 180 p. All Saints, 1962. pa. 50¢.

This little book will dispel forever the tale that life within convent walls is a drab, morose affair. Sister Mary Francis shows not only that nuns are happy beings, but also that they have a perfect "right to be merry"—a right based on the beauty and usefulness of the contemplative life. The content of the book, as well as its style, will appeal to nuns and to those curious about nuns.

MERTON, THOMAS. *The Waters of Siloe.* Harcourt, 1949. 399 p., notes, index. $5.00. Image, 1962. pa. $1.25.

An account of the history of the Trappists and an explanation of its ideals, aims, and way of life, including a complete account of the monk's daily life from his rising at two in the morning to sing Matins until his retirement after Compline at seven in the evening. The book is a logical sequel to this author's best-selling *Seven Storey Mountain,* and it is written in the same polished style as that book. It will answer just about any question on the purpose and way of life of the Trappist monks.

MEYERS, SISTER BERTRANDE (D.C.). *Sisters for the Twenty-First Century.* Introduction by Joseph Cardinal Ritter. Sheed, 1965. 364 p., index. $5.00.

The subject of this book is the process of growth, development, and adaptation by the women of religious orders to meet the demands of life in the modern world. The author treats of such controversial subjects as the relationship between conscience and the vow of obedience, the educational formation of teaching nuns, and the advisability of nuns undertaking an active apostolate in the world. The position throughout is one of moderate liberalism, and the book may be read with profit by anyone interested in the role of women religious in the Church.

23. THE SACRAMENTS

According to Catholic teaching, a sacrament is an outward sign of inward grace, instituted by Christ to signify sanctifying grace, by which grace is conveyed to the soul of the recipient. Though there are other methods of obtaining grace —prayer, repentance, and almsgiving for instance—the sacraments are by far the most efficacious and effective means of receiving grace. Since such is the case, the tremendous importance of the sacraments is obvious and all Catholics should understand what they are, how they were instituted, the forms under which they are conferred, and the graces they impart.

In the Constitution of the Sacred Liturgy, approved during the second session of Vatican Council II and promulgated by Pope Paul VI on December 4, 1963, the importance of the sacraments is reaffirmed. After stating that the purpose of the sacraments is "to sanctify men, to build up the body of Christ, and finally, to give worship to God," the Decree goes on to declare that they instruct the faithful and "by words and objects they also nourish, strengthen, and express" the faith which is why they are called sacraments of the faith. In addition to imparting grace "the very act of celebrating them most effectively disposes the faithful to receive this grace in a fruitful manner, to worship God duly, and to practice charity. It is therefore of the highest importance that the faithful . . . should frequent with great eagerness these sacraments which were instituted to nourish the Christian life." And to receive the maximum benefit to be achieved from frequenting the sacraments, it is most desirable that the faithful know something about them.

First and foremost is the fact that Christ instituted the sacraments as the ordinary channels of grace, and that there are seven sacraments: baptism, confirmation, Holy Eucharist, penance, anointing of the sick, holy orders and matrimony, each of which we shall consider below.

Essentially, three things are required of a sacrament:

the matter, the form, and the minister. The matter is something that can be seen, heard, tasted, touched, in short it is visible through the senses. It is capable of many different meanings but it receives its sacramental significance from the form. The form consists of the words used to give meaning and significance to the use to which the matter is being put. For example, in baptism the matter of the sacrament is the water. Now water may be used for many purposes, washing, cooling, drinking, etc. But in baptism the water is specifically used for washing away original sin—a purpose given to it by the form used in the sacrament. The form is the words pronounced by the person administering baptism: "I baptize thee in the name of the Father, and of the Son and of the Holy Spirit" which gives sacramental significance to the water—the matter. The minister is the person administering the sacrament, usually a priest but in an emergency anyone. To confer a sacrament validly, the minister must have the necessary power, the intention of doing what the Church does in the administration of the sacrament, and he must perform the necessary rite. Where there is doubt about the capability of a person to receive a sacrament, it may be administered conditionally; when the condition is verified, the sacrament is received validly by the recipient. Also once a person has reached the age of reason, he or she must intend to receive the sacraments as holy things, otherwise the sacrament is invalidly received.

The sacraments are divided into two groups, the sacraments of the dead: baptism and penance; and the sacraments of the living: confirmation, Holy Eucharist, anointing of the sick, holy orders, and matrimony.

The sacraments of the dead are so called because they give life through sanctifying grace, called "first grace," to those spiritually dead because of original sin or actual sin. The sacraments of the living are thus designated because their reception presupposes ordinarily that the recipient is in the state of grace. Normally they bestow "second grace" since they increase the sanctifying grace already present, though occasionally, since the sacraments always give grace, a sacrament of the dead may confer "second grace" (as in penance when the sinner receives absolution for venial sins only) and a sacrament of the living may confer "first grace" (as in the anointing of the sick when the recipient's sins are forgiven).

A brief consideration of the seven sacraments may be in order at this point.

Baptism confers the grace of spiritual regeneration. It cleanses the recipient of original sin, makes him one of the People of God, and an heir of heaven. It is necessary for salvation, can be received only once, and valid baptism is necessary for anyone to receive the other sacraments. Baptism by water is the usual method, but a person may attain salvation by "baptism of blood," wherein a person suffers martyrdom for the Catholic faith or some Christian virtue, or baptism of desire, i.e., perfect contrition with the implicit intention that the person wishes to do whatever God wills him to do for salvation. Christ himself emphasized the importance of baptism when he allowed John the Baptist to baptize him and in John 3:5 when he said "unless a man be born again of water and the Spirit, he cannot enter into the Kingdom of God."

Penance, the other sacrament of the dead, and also called confession, is the sacrament by which one is forgiven sins committed after baptism. The matter of the sacrament consists of the penitent's sorrow, for a supernatural motive (contrition), the confession of the sins, and the intention of the penitent to do the penance imposed by the confessor (satisfaction); the form consists of the words of absolution of the confessor who is the minister. Only a priest may administer the sacrament of penance, which was instituted by our Lord when he said "receive ye the Holy Ghost: whose sins you shall forgive they are forgiven them; and whose sins you shall retain, they are retained" (John 20:22–23). It may be received as often as the penitent may need to relieve him of mortal sin.

The remaining five sacraments, all sacraments of the living are:

Holy Eucharist is the sacrament in which the body and blood of Christ, under the appearances of bread and wine, are truly and substantially present and is the grace-producing food of the soul similar to the effect of food in our bodies. The matter of the sacrament is bread of wheat (unleavened in the Roman rite, leavened in the Eastern rite) and wine of grape. The form is the words of consecration spoken by the priest who is of course the minister. The institution of the sacrament by our Lord is described in Luke 22:15–20. The Eucharist may be received only by one in a state of grace who has observed the Eucharistic fast. Mass can be said and the Eucharist consecrated only by a priest, though under certain conditions a deacon or a layman may distribute holy communion. The sacrament may be received as often as the regulations of the Church permit; at the present time it is once a day for laymen, though a recent decree permits the reception of the Eucharist twice on Easter Sunday if one of the receptions was at midnight Mass.

Confirmation is the sacrament by which the individual receives the Holy Spirit, is strengthened in grace and becomes a soldier of Christ. It confers the grace of fortitude to practice and profess one's faith particularly under difficult conditions and is sometimes said to complete the work of baptism. The matter of the sacrament consists of the anointing with chrism in the sign of the cross on the forehead of the recipient and the imposition of the hands of the minister, usually a bishop though a priest may confirm under certain specified conditions. The form consists of the words spoken by the minister "I sign thee with the sign of the cross and confirm thee with the chrism of salvation in the name of the Father and of the Son and of the Holy Spirit." It may be received only once and was instituted by our Lord at Pentecost but was not conferred until after Pentecost since in it is given the fulness of the Holy Spirit which could not be until after Christ's resurrection and ascension ("it is expedient for you that I depart. For if I do not go, the Advocate will not come to you; but if I go, I will send him to you." John 16:7). It may be received only once.

Matrimony is the sacrament wherein a man and a woman agree to live together and to fulfill the duties of the married state—the procreation of children and their proper upbringing and education, and the loving mutual care of each for the other. The matter and form of the sacrament consist of the mutually offered and accepted matrimonial rights. The ministers of the sacrament are the man and woman (*not* the priest who officiates and acts as a witness) who minister the sacrament to each other but both must be baptized to receive the sacrament. Marriage was recognized as sacred in character in the Old Testament (Genesis: 24) but polygamous marriages were tolerated. Under Christ monogamy and the indissolubility of marriage were declared the divine law in the New Dispensation (Matt. 19:4-10; Mark 10:11-12; Luke 16:18; I Cor. 2–6). Our Lord's presence at Cana and the miracle he performed there are emphatic witness to His concern for this sacrament. Though validly contracted marriages are indissoluble, the sacrament may be received more than once as when a married person marries again after the death of his or her spouse.

The anointing of the sick (formerly extreme unction) is the sacrament administered to those seriously ill and in danger of death, and was promulgated in James 5:14-15. The sacrament confers grace to strengthen a sick person against imminent death, in some cases gives health of body if it is for the good of the soul and remission of venial sins and inculpably unconfessed mortal sins (though the person must have at least imperfect contrition). The matter of the sacrament is the anointing of the eyes, ears, nose, mouth, hands and feet of the afflicted person with specially blessed oil and the form is the words spoken by the minister who must be a priest. It may be received more than once if the life of the individual is again threatened after imminent danger has passed.

Holy Orders is the sacrament which gives the grace and spiritual power to an ordained minister which enables him to consecrate the Eucharist, forgive sins, and perform his priestly functions. The matter of the sacrament in the Western Church is the imposition of the hands by the prelate ordaining and his presenting to the ordinand the chalice containing wine and the paten containing a host; the form consists of the prayers of the ceremony. The minister of the sacrament is a bishop and it may be administered only once. It is the only sacrament which may be bestowed only on a man and its institution is described in Luke 22:19 when Christ commanded his disciples to "do this in remembrance of me." Also to be noted is Hebrews 5:1 "For every high priest taken from among men is appointed for men in the things pertaining to God, that he may offer gifts and sacrifices for sin."

The above, of course, is merely the briefest of descriptions of the sacraments and a consideration of what they are. But it is sufficient to indicate however slightly the immensity and complexity of these ordinary channels of grace which Christ instituted to confer sanctifying grace on those who place no obstacle to its reception. A whole literature has deservedly been written on every aspect of the sacraments, and we have selected for listing below those books which we feel will be of help to the general reader in acquiring a deeper understanding of the sacraments, so he may participate more fully in them and realize the fullest possible benefit from them.

DANIEL-ROPS, HENRI. *This Is the Mass,* revised edition. Translated, with notes, by Alastair Guinan. Photographs by Yousuf Karsh; foreword and introduction by Bishop Fulton J. Sheen. Hawthorn, 1965. 191 p., illustrations, notes. $5.95. Image, 1967. pa. 95¢.

This revised edition of a well known book incorporates all the latest changes made in the Mass as a result of the Church's liturgical renewal. After an introductory chapter explaining the nature of the Mass, each individual part of the Mass, from the opening prayers to the last blessing of the people, is explained by Daniel-Rops and illustrated by photographs of Bishop Sheen. It is a handsome book, as well as a useful one, and it is recommended to all Catholics.

DIDIER, JEAN-CHARLES. *Death and the Christian.* Translated by P. J. Hepburne-Scott. Hawthorn, 1961. 106 p., bibliography. $3.50.

In an introductory section, the author considers the Christian concept of the relationship of soul and body and the Christian attitude toward sickness and death. Then there is a detailed historical and liturgical consideration of the sacraments for the sick and dying and of the rites connected with them. This work, Volume 55 of the *Twentieth Century Encyclopedia of Catholicism,* is a very readable explanation of the sacramental means employed by the Church to bring relief to the souls, and sometimes to the bodies, of the sick and the dying.

GUARDINI, ROMANO. *Meditations Before Mass*. Translated by Elinor Castendyk Briefs. Newman, 1960. xiv, 202 p., notes. pa. $1.25.

Father Guardini, one of the most widely read spiritual writers of modern times, writes a series of meditations on the Mass. The book has two parts: Part I, entitled "Sacred Bearing," which is intended to put the reader in the proper frame of mind for deriving maximum benefit from the Mass; Part II, "Essence of the Mass," which explains in simple language the mystical and spiritual significance of what transpires at the altar.

HASTINGS, CECILY. *The Sacraments*. Sheed, 1961. 217 p., appendices. $3.50.

This popularly written work is divided into two parts. Part I discusses the nature of a sacrament, its relation to the nature of man, and the place of the Christian sacraments in salvation. Part II takes up each of the seven sacraments in detail, explaining the purpose of each and how each one is administered and by whom. There are two appendices, containing quotations from the Gospels and from the early Church Fathers on the sacraments. The book is an excellent over-all view of the sacraments.

HOWELL, CLIFFORD (S.J.). *Of Sacraments and Sacrifice*. Liturgical Press, 1952. 171 p., illustrations. $2.00.

One of the concepts traditionally associated with any interpretation of the meaning of the Mass in particular and of the sacraments in general is that of "sacrifice." In this work, Father Howell explains what is meant by that term, and develops that explanation into a study of the essentials of Mass and sacraments. His writing is clear and precise, and his approach is comprehensive enough to provide the reader with a valuable over-all view of the significance of the Eucharistic and sacramental rites.

LECUYER, JOSEPH. *What Is a Priest?* Translated by Lancelot D. Sheppard. Hawthorn, 1959. 125 p., bibliography. $3.50.

This work, volume 53 of the *Twentieth Century Encyclopedia of Catholicism,* is a popular explanation of the sacrament of Holy Orders. The author discusses the nature of the priesthood established by Our Lord at the Last Supper, and explains the relationship of the episcopate to the priestly power conferred by the sacrament as well as the participation in that power enjoyed by clerics in minor orders and by the laity. This is a well written and intelligible introduction to an understanding of what a priest is and what the priesthood signifies.

MERTON, THOMAS. *The Living Bread.* Introduction by Cardinal Agagianian. Farrar, 1956. 157 p. $3.50.

Thomas Merton has written a study of the Sacrament of the Eucharist in which he presents both a survey of the Church's teachings on that subject and a series of meditations on the significance for man of Christ's presence in the sacrament. The book was intended primarily for priests and religious, but it will be of value also to the layman with no formal training in theology.

NICOLAS, MARIE-JOSEPH (O.P.). *What Is the Eucharist?* Translated by R. F. Trevett. Hawthorn, 1960. 125 p., bibliography. $2.95.

This volume studies the meaning and the significance of the sacrament of the Holy Eucharist. The first section of the book discusses the institution of the sacrament by Christ and the Church's doctrine concerning the Eucharist. The second is a popular survey of the theology of the Eucharist. The third section clarifies the notion of the Eucharist as a sacrifice, and the fourth explains what is meant by "communion." The final chapters discuss the Eucharistic practice of the Church—what we mean by the "real presence," the importance of participation in the Mass, and the practice of frequent communion. This is not only an excellent introduction to the theoretical aspects of the Eucharist; it is also an extremely useful preparation for the worthy reception of communion.

O'CALLAGHAN, DENIS, Editor. *Sacraments, the Gestures of Christ.* Sheed, 1965. 194 p. $4.00.

This collection of chapters by several well known modern theologians emphasizes a particular, and particularly modern, aspect of the sacraments; i.e., that they are a personal encounter of the individual Christian with Christ, in which the individual, expressing his faith and love and receiving grace, engages in an active exchange with his Savior. This "per-

sonalist" concept of the sacraments is increasingly emphasized in the liturgical renewal, and Father O'Callaghan's
collection will be rewarding reading for the discriminating
Catholic.

PIAULT, BERNARD. *What Is a Sacrament?* Translated by A.
Manson. Hawthorn, 1963. 174 p., bibliography. $3.50.

The sacraments are the chief means by which the Church
accomplishes its saving mission in the world. The aim of
this book (Volume 49 of the *Twentieth Century Encyclopedia of Catholicism*) is to describe the human and the
spiritual function of the sacraments as the signs of God's
grace in the world and as the acts of Christ in the soul
through the rites of the Church. The author approaches his
subject from the standpoint of theology, of reason, and of
Scripture, discussing sacraments as signs, Christ's institution
of the sacraments, the way in which the seven sacraments
make men holy, and the action of Christ in the sacraments.
The book, even in its discussions of the theology of the
sacraments, in simply written and readily understandable,
and may be recommended as a layman's introduction to a
basic understanding of the meaning not only of the sacraments but also of the Church's significance.

RAHNER, KARL (S.J.). *The Church and the Sacraments.*
Translated by W. J. O'Hara. Herder & Herder, 1963. 116 p.
pa. $2.25.

Father Rahner, one of the most influential and widely read
of modern Catholic theologians, discusses in its general lines
the way in which the sacramental system of the Church
works, what its place is in the over-all plan of salvation, and
what is the significance of the sacraments, collectively, for
the spiritual life of the Catholic. The book is not always
easy reading, but the author's style in this work is nontechnical and any difficulty will be more than compensated
for by Father Rahner's comprehensive treatment of a difficult subject.

ROGUET, AIMON MARIE (O.P.). *Christ Acts Through the
Sacraments.* Translated by the Carisbrooke Dominicans.
Liturgical Press, 1954. 162 p. pa. $1.25.

Father Roguet, a well known French theologian and
liturgist, explains first the general concept of a sacrament,
and then discusses each one of the sacraments as a grace-

giving means by which Christ acts in the recipient of the sacrament. The book is written for the layman, and is well translated into thoroughly intelligible English.

SCHILLEBEECKX, EDWARD (O.P.). *Christ: The Sacrament of the Encounter with God.* Translated by Paul Barrett; English text revised by Mark Schoof and Laurence Bright. Sheed, 1963. 222 p., bibliographical notes. $4.50.

Father Schillebeeckx is widely respected as one of the most profound and original of the contemporary theologians. In this work, which has become something of a classic since its European publication in 1958, he studies the Catholic sacramental system. Particular stress is laid on the concept of the sacraments as actions of God in Christ, actions taking place in the Church as the Mystical Body of Christ, and on the grace which is the effect of those actions. This work requires an acquaintance with basic theological concepts and terminology, but it is highly recommended within those limits.

SHEERIN, JOHN B. (C.S.P.). *The Sacrament of Freedom.* Bruce, 1961. ix, 166 p. $3.50.

Father Sheerin discusses various difficulties which arise in the requirements for receiving the Sacrament of Penance. He treats such problems as what to do about venial sins, how to make a proper examination of conscience, what is meant by a "firm purpose of amendment," whether temptations must be confessed, how to deal with scruples, and how to make a general confession. The approach is eminently practical and frank, and the book will be especially valuable to the layman who wants to gain maximum benefit from his confessions.

SHEEN, FULTON J. *These Are the Sacraments.* Hawthorn, 1962. 191 p., illustrations. $4.95. Image, 1964. pa. 75¢.

A presentation and explanation of the seven Sacraments of the Church, with photographs by Yousuf Karsh. After analyzing the necessity for each Sacrament and indicating its origin, Bishop Sheen investigates each one, beginning with the rebirth of the Christian at Baptism and ending with a commentary on the nuptial blessing given to those who receive Matrimony. He explains the elements peculiar to each Sacrament, and points out what is necessary in each case for valid administration of the Sacrament.

SHEPPARD, LANCELOT. *The Mass in the West.* Hawthorn, 1962. 112 p., bibliography.

This is Volume 111 in the *Twentieth Century Encyclopedia of Catholicism.* The author discusses not so much the meaning of the Mass as its origins, history, and evolution into what is known today as the Mass of the Roman Rite. The book also explains the development of other Catholic rites—Ambrosian, Dominican, Carmelite, Slavonic, etc.—and notes briefly in what respects they differ from the Roman.

WILSON, ALFRED (C.P.). *Pardon and Peace.* Sheed, 1947. 257 p., appendices. $3.00. Image, 1965. pa. 95¢.

This is a lucid explanation of the psychological appropriateness of the sacrament of Penance, of the benefits to be derived from it, and of the best method of preparing for confession and of confessing. The central theme of the book is the importance of having the correct attitude toward confession. All readers, particularly those troubled by doubt and scruples, will benefit from this work.

24. SCIENCE AND THE CHURCH

It is generally agreed that modern science had its beginnings in the sixteenth century, and the publication of Copernicus' *De revolutionibus orbium coelestium* is often pinpointed as its birth year. During the four centuries since then, open warfare between the adherents of the Church and the protagonists of science has been the order of the day. Intermittently, an uneasy truce has prevailed, but this deceptive calm has always been punctuated by a fierce conflict which served to emphasize the irreconcilability of religion and science.

As early as the seventeenth century the battle lines were drawn in the Galileo controversy. Though it can readily be asserted that Galileo's chastisement was comparatively mild for the times, the fact still remains that an official body of the Church, the Inquisition, condemned the scientific findings of Galileo which supported the Copernican system of astronomy based on the revolution of the earth around the sun. That subsequent discoveries proved how correct Galileo was served in the eyes of many to put the Church in the camp of those impeding the progress of modern science.

As time passed, the lines hardened and the antagonism between churchmen and scientists tended to make the differences irreconcilable. To many churchmen, the scientists were attacking the very basis of religion. For example, to them, Galileo's theory that the earth revolved around the sun threatened the belief that man, as a creature of God, was the center of attention of an all powerful, universal Power. Earth as man's dwelling must be the center of the universe, and any attack on that belief was an attack on the Bible; for had not Joshua commanded "Stand still, O sun . . . And the sun stood still" (Jos. 10:12, 13)? Obviously, to anyone who accepted literally everything in the Bible, the sun must have revolved around the earth if Joshua were able to stay its movement.

Increasingly, to many scientists the Church became the citadel of superstition, outmoded beliefs, and a rigid dogma, refusing to face the facts that science was revealing as it probed into the many areas with which the natural sciences were concerning themselves. To many of these men the discoveries they were making were proof that religion had no basis in fact but was merely a carefully formulated structure to perpetuate tired, meaningless creeds. As increasingly, particularly after the Reformation and later the French Revolution, many scientists became atheists or agnostics, it seemed clear to many devout churchmen that these men were no less than creatures of the devil doing his work.

In the nineteenth century any tendencies on the part of some Catholics to attempt to bridge the gap between science and religion were blown sky high by Darwin's theory of evolution. Simply stated, Darwin's theory was that man was the highest form of animal life and had evolved in successive stages, over aeons of time, from lower animal forms. Again many churchmen took the widespread acceptance of Darwin's theory in scientific circles as a direct attack on the Church and an absolute contradiction of the Adam-and-Eve story in Genesis. Many scientifically minded individuals, on the other hand, simply accepted the theory of evolution as a fact and as a complete repudiation of the Biblical concept of the origins of man and a total demolition of the whole Christian religion.

But though science and religion seemed to be at each other's throats, there were men of good will on both sides who felt that a reconciliation of the two disciplines was not only possible but inevitable. For many decades, the folly of the Galileo controversy had been fully apparent to Catholics. Galileo had been right and those who had denounced him and his teaching had been completely wrong. The earth *did* revolve around the sun and in this fact was the Church's error. Further, it was becoming increasingly evident that this fact of science *could* be reconciled with the teaching of the Church. Indeed it was also becoming evident that many of the findings of science actually confirmed Church teachings which had been scoffed at by earlier scientists. Especially was this apparent in the field of archaeology where time and again actual excavations revealed the accuracy of Biblical statements which had been questioned in the past. More and more the findings of science, rather than threatening to de-

stroy religion were actually becoming a great buttress supporting many of the basic claims of religion. What so many
had overlooked in previous centuries was the fact that God is
the ultimate Truth. Any quest for truth could not destroy religion; it could only confirm it. Hence, any scientific investigation honestly and sincerely pursued can only produce truth—
and all truths are stepping stones to the ultimate Truth.

As men realized this, the supposed incompatibility of religion and science began to disintegrate. But the deep-rooted
fear of many churchmen that science was a threat to religion
burst forth in another area in the twentieth century. As
Freudian psychology began to gain disciples and adherents,
the whole field of psychology and psychiatry became suspect
to many in the Church. The whole massive investigation of
man's subconscious and the implications of these studies
seemed to them an impingement on the Christ-given powers
of the confessional and a direct attack on the Catholic concept
of the soul. The Freudians' belief that answers to all of men's
problems were to be found in the sexual drive seemed to be
an attack on the beliefs of Catholics in the efficacy of purity
as a concept and in the God-given power to exercise restraint.
As some of Freud's followers became more radical in advo-
cating the thrusting aside of traditional sexual mores, so many
churchmen became more rabid in their denunciation of this
new scientific discipline. One must also bear in mind that the
Church in this period was under attack from many sources
so that, to many, this radical new branch of science was one
more in a series of attacks to be repelled as fully and vigor-
ously as possible.

With the passage of time and the broadening of research,
it has become obvious that this new scientific discipline had
much to offer harassed mankind. Also, the excesses of the
earlier protagonists of psychology, and later of psychiatry, began to vanish as deeper and broader research added new
knowledge to the field. As these disciplines became respected
members of the scientific community, so too Church opposition slowly began to decline. No little credit for this changed
atmosphere must go to those Catholic psychologists and
psychiatrists who fought to make their co-religionists realize
the contributions of these sciences, while at the same time

they labored to convince their scientific brethren that nothing in their religion prevented their functioning as true scientists. Only in the past few years has this last war slowed down to occasional encounters. Even now there are flare-ups; but the war on this front is over as now even priests, nuns and religious are accredited psychologists, psychoanalysts, and psychiatrists.

The tragedy of all this is that, to many people, the Church has been one of the chief obstacles in the path of scientific progress. And the fact must be faced that the charge has all too frequently been true. But always there have been courageous men in the Church who have fought the good battle knowing that the quest for truth by man can never harm what the Church has always possessed—the Truth—but can only lead, though often by devious roads, to that Truth. That their number is increasing is obvious. Perhaps, the best example is the whole attitude of the Church toward Teilhard de Chardin and his theory of universal evolution. In less than a decade after his death in 1955, his theories had wide acceptance among many of his fellow Catholics. Though an admonition of the Holy Office pointed out several conflicts with Church teaching in his writings there was no condemnation or castigation. Today his theories are studied all over the Catholic world.

But though there has been great progress in cementing the relations between science and Catholicism, the past history of that relationship should be constantly borne in mind. There is no doubt that in the future science will explore areas of the body and mind of man, of the earth and of the universe, which at this moment are unknown. When these explorations seem to affect the validity of Catholic teaching, Catholics should remember what has so often happened in the past. And always the uppermost thought must be that the pursuit of the truth can never affect by one iota the ultimate Truth—that genuine, dedicated pursuit of the truth can only lead one to the ultimate Truth, which is God.

It is with these thoughts in mind that we have prepared the list of books below. They tell of the problems which have existed, discuss the different scientific disciplines and their relation to the Church, and in general give the interested reader new insights into the proper role of Catholic teaching as it relates to science.

BIOT, RENÉ. *What Is Life?* Translated by Eric Earnshaw Smith. Hawthorn, 1959. 93 p., bibliography. $2.95.

This slender volume is a highly competent, non-technical study of what it is that makes life. Dr. Biot discusses all the components of human life, beginning with the chemical or physiological and progressing through the sentiment of psychological to the spiritual, ending with a brief consideration of life at the supernatural level. (This work is Volume 32 of the *Twentieth Century Encyclopedia of Catholicism.*)

BRACELAND, FRANCIS J. (M.D.) and MICHAEL STOCK (O.P.). *Modern Psychiatry: A Handbook for Believers.* Doubleday, 1963. 346 p., glossary, index. $4.95. Image, 1966. pa. $1.25.

This is a survey of various aspects of modern psychiatry—its background, techniques, and its future, with particular emphasis on its relation to religious faith. Under the latter aspect, the authors demolish the popular belief that psychiatry poses a serious threat to religion, or vice versa. In addition to its value as a reconciliation of religion and psychiatry, the book is an excellent introduction for the layman to the meaning and methods of a much discussed, but widely misunderstood, science.

BRODRICK, JAMES (S.J.). *Galileo: The Man, His Work, His Misfortune.* Harper, 1965. 120 p., bibliography, index. $3.50.

Father Brodrick, a respected biographer and historian, reexamines one of the greatest men of science and one of the most famous scandals of the Church. Early in the 17th century, Galileo published a work asserting that the earth (and, by implication, man) was not the center of the universe. The Holy Office promptly condemned the theory and confined the theorizer to his quarters. Father Brodrick reviews the circumstances of the trial, the implications of Galileo's theories, describes the situation of the Church in history, and concludes that the Church's action had its cause in political expediency as well as in the fact that the reigning pope, Urban VIII, was not, on the whole, an intellectual giant.

CARREL, ALEXIS. *Man the Unknown.* Harper, 1939. 322 p. $4.95. Macfadden, 1961. pa. 60¢.

Man the Unknown, in addition to being a modern classic, is one of those odd books that seem to grow more pertinent as they grow older. Written in 1935 by a Nobel Prize winner, its purpose is to define man in terms of his mental and physical constitution. In addition to explaining how man's body and his mind function, however, the author goes a step further and forecasts the amazing things that the human mind will be capable of once its full potential is realized. Dr. Carrel, although he is a Catholic, does not always adhere to traditional Catholic beliefs; for example, his views on euthanasia are at variance with the accepted Catholic teaching on the subject. A careful reading of the book, however, combined with a certain wariness for unorthodox opinions, will open up to the reader a richly rewarding field of scientific speculation on man's future.

COLIN, REMY. *Evolution.* Translated by J. Tester. Hawthorn, 1959. 144 p., glossary, bibliography. $2.95.

Dr. Colin, a professor of medicine, explains briefly and in a non-technical manner what is meant by "evolution" with respect to human beings, what has been proved and what is still purely hypothesis, and what effect the theory of evolution has or may have on the traditional teachings of the Church. The book is recommended as a concise introduction to the subject for the layman. (*Evolution* is Volume 30 in Hawthorn's *Twentieth Century Encyclopedia of Catholicism.*)

CORTE, NICOLAS. *The Origins of Man.* Translated by Ernest E. Smith. Hawthorn, 1958. 144 p., bibliography. $2.95.

This, Volume 29 of the *Twentieth Century Encyclopedia of Catholicism*, is concerned with explaining the origins of the universe in general and of man in particular. The author (Corte is a pseudonym for Leon Cristiani, a respected philosopher and theologian) first surveys the answers given to the problem from the earliest times, in mythologies, philosophies, and scientific systems; he then develops and explains the Catholic position on the subject. The treatment is non-technical, and will appeal to students as well as to the mature reader.

CROMBIE, A. C. *Medieval and Early Modern Science,* second revised edition. Anchor, 1959. Vol. I: xxii, 289 p., illustrations, bibliography, index; Vol. II: xvii, 380 p., illustrations, bibliography, index. pa. 95¢ ea.

These two volumes comprise a valuable and popular survey of the history of science from the fifth to the seventeenth centuries. Volume I, covering the Middle Ages, discusses the great advances in industry, chemistry, agriculture and medicine, as well as such practical activities as spinning, weaving, and shipbuilding, and describes the discovery of harmony and counterpoint, the evolution of the Gothic vaulted arch, and the production of medieval stained glass. There are also delightful accounts of some of the less successful experiments of the medieval scientists, as in their attempts to predict the weather from the activity of fleas. Volume II covers the scientific revolution from the thirteenth to the seventeenth centuries, including the accomplishments of Galileo, Newton, Copernicus, Kepler, da Vinci, and Descartes. Both volumes are very well illustrated.

HAURET, CHARLES. *Beginnings: Genesis and Modern Science,* revised edition. Translated by John F. McDonnell, O.P. Priory, 1964. 240 p., illustrations, map. $4.95.

The problem of the origin of the world and of man has long been the battleground on which the "conflict" between religion and science was waged. The real difference, however, has never been whether science was right and religion wrong, or vice versa, but rather consisted in understanding how, in fact, there is no real conflict between the biblical and the scientific accounts of creation. This book studies that difficulty in the light of scientific discoveries and theological principles, and provides a synopsis of Catholic teachings on the subject. It is lucidly written, and will be an eye-opener to those who still feel that religion and science are irreconcilable enemies.

LECOMTE DU NOUY, PIERRE. *Human Destiny.* McKay, 1947. 289 p. $5.00. Mentor, 1960. pa. 50¢.

Lecomte du Nouy, a scientist and an associate of Alexis Carrel, attempts in this work to provide a scientific basis for Christian theology. He attacks materialism and atheism, and pleads with modern man, as the goal of creation and of evolution, to utilize his spiritual powers to avoid inevitable disaster. When the book first was published, it was acclaimed by some as a unique accomplishment, and by others as a fraud. Whatever the individual reader's reaction may be, the fact remains that the book contains much that is of value in understanding the rather unique situation of modern man.

LEONARDO DA VINCI. *The Notebooks of Leonardo da Vinci.* Translated and edited by Pamela Taylor. Mentor, 1960. 253 p., plates. pa. 75¢.

Leonardo's notes covered his investigations in almost every field of art and science. This collection consists of excerpts from those notes, and reveals Leonardo as one of the most universal geniuses of history. In addition to his insights into the nature of the fine arts, he foresaw and completed designs for many inventions that lay centuries in the future: the airplane, the submarine, tanks, poison gas, and he anticipated such milestones as the theory of gravitation, of the circulation of the blood, and the heliocentric theory. This collection makes fascinating, and sometimes amusing, reading.

NOGAR, RAYMOND J. (O.P.). *The Wisdom of Evolution.* Doubleday, 1963. 408 p., bibliographical notes, index. $5.75. Mentor-Omega, 1966. pa. 75¢.

This is an examination of the facts and of the limitations of the theory of evolution. The author explains and evaluates the proofs for the fact of evolution, shows which general conclusions may legitimately be drawn from available evidence and which may not, and then gives a synthesis of scientific evolution and a philosophy of life which is in harmony both with scientific fact and with Christian belief. The educated layman, the theologian and the philosopher, will find here all the facts he needs for an appraisal of the evidence for evolution.

STERN, KARL. *The Third Revolution.* Harcourt, 1954. 199 p., notes. $4.00. Image, 1961. pa. 75¢.

In this work a noted Catholic psychiatrist argues persuasively for a reconciliation of psychiatry and religion. The basic concepts of psychoanalysis are seen by the author to be not only compatible with the Christian concept of man but indeed to confirm that concept. The book is a well written and illuminating discussion aimed at the general reader.

ZILBOORG, GREGORY. *Psychoanalysis and Religion*. Edited with an introduction by Margaret Stone Zilboorg. Farrar, 1962. xi, 243 p., index, bibliographical notes. $4.95.

Gregory Zilboorg, a convert from Judaism to Catholicism, was a respected authority on Sigmund Freud. This book brings together some of his most important writings on the impact of Freudian psychology on traditional religious belief and on the achievement of a working synthesis between religion and psychoanalysis. Although the selections were not written primarily for a general audience, most of the author's terms are in sufficient general use to be familiar to the mature reader, and the book is highly recommended to that audience.

25. SPIRITUAL WRITING

Among the noble forms of literature, the writing of things spiritual ranks high. For the man of any religious bent, the quest for spiritual perfection, leading as it does to closer union with God, must be the primary goal of earthly existence. And even for the man of little or no interest in things religious, there still remains an indefinable appeal in spiritual writing. For whether he admits it or proclaims it or ignores it or denies it, there seems to be in every man an element of the spiritual always present. It is a part of human nature, and it is to be found in some form in every kind of man, from the aboriginal Australian bushman to the cultured sophisticates of the great capitals of the world.

Through the ages, certain men and women have been gifted with special spiritual insights. Through God's grace and their own unceasing efforts, they have been far more successful than most ordinary mortals in attaining high degrees of spiritual perfection. They have reached high stages on the ladder of perfection in a wide variety of ways. Some have chosen the way of the eremitic. Others have become priests and nuns and through their religious vocations have been able to approach their goal. Still others have attained sanctity through helping their fellow man. And some have been successful in their spiritual life while pursuing a secular career. The ways are as numerous as human nature is varied.

But one thing is certain, regardless of the method chosen by these people: they all have something of a spiritual nature to offer to their fellow man though, in their humility, they would be the first to deny any preeminence in holiness in their lives. But people have always recognized true sanctity and in varying degrees are interested in learning of the secrets and techniques employed by these holy men and women to further their devotion to their Creator. For fundamental to every human being is the realization that only the things of the spirit are important. Dynasties, cultures, cities, buildings—all material things eventually disappear. But as Christians we know that the soul is eternal and that the food of the eternal soul is God's love which we can only realize through our spiritual lives.

It is evident, then, that any means of improving our spiritual life are well worth exploring. And how better can such a happy state of affairs be realized than through learning from the holy ones of all ages? In the section on the lives of the saints we emphasized how much the saints have to offer us through the examples of their lives. But fortunately—through that miracle of communication we so lightly accept as an ordinary part of our times—the book—we have readily available the spiritual meditations and reflections of these holy men and women and their suggestions and advice for leading a life of holiness. There is a whole literature of such writings and much of it is, next to the Bible, the most inspired of all literature. For here are the very gems of spiritual wisdom from the lips of men and women best qualified to write on this lofty subject. And they come down to us from every age, from men and women in every position from pope and emperor to priest and beggar, from those in posts of importance to those with no material influence, from men of every race. In short a panorama of the whole human family is represented in the authors of books of a spiritual nature. All these blessed of God, however exalted or ascetic, had in common with all mankind the deep-rooted, burning desire to know God and to come closer to him.

Spiritual books can be of invaluable aid to any individual, but in considering a spiritual book suitable for one's own use a few ground rules should be set up. First, it should be pointed out, as we have mentioned above, that spiritual books have been written by all manner of men and women in every walk of life. It should be obvious then that not every spiritual work is suitable for every individual. You, as the reader, must select the work most appropriate for you, spiritually, intellectually, and emotionally. Obviously, works that appeal to the university professor may not have any attraction for the campus janitor. So, in considering a spiritual book, make certain it is suitable for your own temperament, background, position, and above all the stage of your spiritual life.

Though this statement is generally true, it is also a fact that there are certain spiritual writings which are of such a calibre that they appeal to the most diverse men. Such books are so illuminated by the holiness of the author that another dimension beside intellect can bring a clear understanding of the author's message. Though so frequently scoffed at by today's unbelievers, faith, too, can make clear such messages. So universal is the appeal of such a work that scholar and manual laborer alike can grasp the author's meaning, each in his own way but with perfect understanding. Such works are the great spiritual classics beloved by all which are avidly read in every century.

Even with works of such ageless appeal which transcend all barriers, a word of caution is in order. For every man's writing is circumscribed to some degree by his own culture and age. Though the basic message comes through clearly, it can be surrounded by the errors of the author's times. Even the Bible is susceptible to its human authorship. Though inspired by God and though God's message is inerrant, the actual words were written by men whose outlook and knowledge were conditioned by the state of knowledge of the civilization in which they lived. The important fact is that no such merely human considerations affect the validity of the central theme. That St. Thomas Aquinas' knowledge of natural history was faulty in terms of modern scientific knowledge has no bearing on the validity of his thought, since his remarks in the area of natural history are not the pivot on which his theology is based. Even today, an artist's belief that the earth is square could not affect his artistic ability to paint a portrait, as witness the great artistic classics of men in ages when such a belief was held by all.

But spiritual writing is not merely the wisdom of the past. Each age has been blessed by writers of spiritual works of high merit and our age is no exception. We are fortunate in having numerous men and women writing today who are able to express the great eternal spiritual truths in today's language and in the context of modern times and conditions. We are thus able in this field of writing to benefit, as in so many other areas of Catholic activity, from tradition—the great spiritual writing of the past—and the Church's constant renewal—the spiritual writing of our own times.

It is a curious fact that people today are as interested—if not more so—in spiritual writings as they have ever been. It is especially curious when one stops to consider that our whole contemporary culture is based on materialistic values. In a period when violence, selfishness, immorality, disregard of law and order, and concern for material luxuries seem the order of the day, there is a constant and widespread interest, seemingly increasing, in these spiritual books. Obviously, people as always are still interested in the salvation of their souls, and even those who might scoff at such a phrase have that deep-rooted belief in the supernatural that as we mentioned earlier is to be found even in the most skeptical of men. Thinking men know there is, and must be more, to this life than merely the satisfaction of physical wants and appetites. It is the recognition of that belief that leads men to God, and one way to that goal is the reading of spiritual books with the conscious desire to learn from the masters of the spiritual life who have so much to offer all of us.

AUGUSTINE OF HIPPO, SAINT. *Confessions.* Translated by Frank J. Sheed. Sheed, 1946. 429 p., notes, bibliography, index. $3.50. Image, 1960 (translated by John K. Ryan). pa. $1.35. Washington Square, n.d. (translated by Edward B. Pusey). pa. 45¢.

By common consent, the work known as the *Confessions* holds a special place among the world's great books. Although it is autobiographical in character, it is not a story of the author's life; yet, no other book has ever gone more deeply into an author's character and deed, expressed more incisive judgments about the inner man, or revealed its author more fully. The book is not only a penetrating psychological study of man in search of God, but a unique document for understanding the spiritual life and a treasurehouse of thought for the philosopher and the theologian. After a thousand five-hundred years, the book still attracts countless readers, from the professional theologian to the student of literature, from the expert in philosophy to the general reader. It is recommended to all readers of whatever category as an indispensable work for the educated Christian. (Of the three translations listed above, Frank Sheed's is a very readable modern rendition; that of Msgr. Ryan, in addition to being also quite modern and smooth, has excellent explanatory notes; Edward Pusey's edition is regarded as the classic translation and is itself a literary work of the first order; yet, occasionally, it is difficult to read with complete understanding.)

BASSET, BERNARD (s.j.). *The Noonday Devil: Spiritual Support in Middle Age.* Academy Guild, 1964. xi, 178 p. $3.95.

This is a book of spiritual guidance especially designed for those who experience the difficulties and crises peculiar to middle age. The contents include reflections on the importance of knowing oneself, one's obligations to one's neighbors, friendship, rational behavior, and prayer.

BASSET, BERNARD (s.j.). *We Neurotics.* Academy Guild, 1963. 135 p. $3.75.

Taking as his premise that everyone today is at least a little neurotic, Father Basset examines some of the episodes in the life of a typical (neurotic) layman in search of God. Under its funny-serious, sad-happy surface, the book is a solid and skillfully contrived guide to the spiritual life, filled with wisdom as well as with wit.

BOYLAN, EUGENE (o.c.s.o.). *Difficulties in Mental Prayer.* Newman, 1943. xv, 124 p. Newman, 1966. pa. 95¢.

This short work is one of the most widely read books of spirituality of our time, and represents an eminently successful attempt to isolate common obstacles encountered in mental prayer. It is not a theoretical work, but deals with problems and solutions, and it is highly recommended to everyone interested in mental prayer.

BOYLAN, EUGENE (c.s.o.). *This Tremendous Lover.* Newman, 1947. xviii, 345 p., bibliography. $3.00. Newman, 1966. pa. 95¢.

This is a work of general spirituality which has come to be regarded as a modern spiritual classic. Its intention is to examine man's relationship to God, and then to show how that relationship may be made more intimate and more perfect. Thus, the first part discusses the nature of man's relationship to God, the second explains the proper use of the ordinary means of perfection. A well written and authoritative work, *This Tremendous Lover* is recommended to all Christians at whatever stage of spiritual development.

CHAUTARD, JEAN-BAPTISTE (o.c.s.o.). *The Soul of the Apostolate*. Translated with an introduction by Thomas Merton. Image, 1961. 270 p., notes, appendix. pa. 85¢.

The author of this spiritual classic sets out the necessity for a solid spiritual foundation for those engaged in the active apostolate, and gives the broad lines of the problems and solutions which those workers are likely to encounter in cultivating a spiritual life while in the world. It is a book of great beauty, amazing aptness, and profound insight, and it is highly recommended to all readers.

EVELY, LOUIS. *That Man Is You*. Translated by Edmond Bonin. Newman, 1964. xv, 297 p. $4.50.

This re-telling of the Gospel message is aimed specifically at the modern Christian living in the world and sharing its problems and unrest. The author's material is presented in "thought phrases"—i.e., in short, simple sentences—as an aid to meditation, and all centers around one theme: salvation is a present-tense affair, to be attained on a day-by-day basis by taking advantage of the opportunities that present themselves at home, in the street, at work or at play. The book is recommended to all readers.

FRANCIS DE SALES, SAINT. *Introduction to the Devout Life*. Translated and edited, with introduction and notes, by John K. Ryan. Harper, 1950. 314 p., notes, index. $3.50. Image, 1955. pa. 95¢.

The purpose of this famous classic is to arouse in the reader a complete love of God and an absolute confidence in him. The author describes step by step the way to be followed, describes the practical obstacles which will occur and the way to overcome them, and throughout the book exhibits an amazing knowledge of human psychology. A very practical and lucid guide for everyone from the beginner to the mystic, in a competent translation by John K. Ryan.

FRANCIS DE SALES, SAINT. *On the Love of God*. Translated with an introduction by Msgr. John K. Ryan. Image, 1963.

Vol. I: 314 p. Vol. II: 354 p., notes, bibliography, index. 95¢ ea.

This is one of the most beautiful of the spiritual classics, and one which has remained extremely popular since its original publication in the seventeenth century. The work is divided into two parts: the fundamental principles of the author's concept of love, and the application of those principles to one's life. It is clear, practical, and, despite its age, eminently useful for the modern Christian.

FRANCIS OF ASSISI, SAINT. *The Little Flowers of St. Francis.* Introduction, notes, and biographical sketches by Raphael Brown. Image, 1962. 357 p., notes, map, appendix. pa. 95¢.

The Little Flowers of St. Francis was written not by St. Francis but by Brother Ugolino, who lived a century after the saint's death. It was written in order to capture and transmit the true Franciscan spirit in the lives and thoughts of the founder and his followers. This edition includes nineteen chapters which have never before appeared in English, and is enhanced by a valuable Introduction, and by extensive information on the historical background of the book, biographies of important persons appearing in the book, and complete critical apparatus.

GUARDINI, ROMANO. *The Life of Faith.* Translated by John Chapin. Newman, 1961. 131 p. Newman, 1963. pa. 75¢.

A collection of meditative essays by one of the finest spiritual writers of the twentieth century, the work considers, among other subjects, the origins and meaning of faith, the virtues of hope and love, the various ways of knowing God, and the role of faith in the Church. This is excellent material for spiritual reading.

GUARDINI, ROMANO. *Prayer in Practice.* Translated by Leopold von Loewenstein-Wertheim. Pantheon, 1957. 159 p. $3.95. Image, 1963. pa. 75¢.

A guide to the understanding of what prayer is and what forms prayer can take. The author touches on such matters as the perseverance in prayer during spiritual dryness and difficulty, a personal approach to prayer, mysticism, and prayers to the Virgin Mary and to the saints, and leads the reader step by step through every stage of the spiritual life within the context of prayer. The book is popularly written, practical, with concrete directions for personal improvement in prayer.

IGNATIUS LOYOLA, SAINT. *The Spiritual Exercises.* Translated by Louis J. Puhl, s.j. xv, 216 p. $2.25. Image, 1964 (translated by Anthony Motolla; introduction by Robert W. Gleason, s.j.). pa. 85¢.

Regarded as one of the masterpieces of ascetical theology, the *Exercises* are a guide to spiritual perfection that resulted from St. Ignatius' own experiences and meditations. The work is divided into four weeks of meditations and four key meditations—on the kingdom of God, the two standards (of Christ and of Satan), the three classes of man, and the three modes of humility. The whole is unified by the central theme of Christ.

JOHN XXIII, POPE. *Journal of a Soul.* Translated by Dorothy White. 453 p., illustrations, bibliography. $7.95.

This posthumous publication of Pope John's consists of his notes, in diary form, kept from his fourteenth year until the year before his death. Most of the material is in the form of simple spiritual reflections, but there are also a few letters, his spiritual testament to the Roncalli family, and his will. Since this is primarily a spiritual journal, there are few references to John's public life, but the book is useful in understanding the reasons and intentions of Pope John in undertaking to up-date the Church.

JOHN OF THE CROSS, SAINT. *The Ascent of Mount Carmel.* Translated, with introduction and notes, by E. Allison Peers. Image, 1958. 386 p., notes. pa. $1.45.

A guide to the spiritual life, written by the greatest of the mystic theologians. Addressed to informed Christians who want to grow in union with God, this work examines every category of spiritual experience—the spurious as well as the authentic—and explains how to achieve that union and how to avoid the pitfalls. The author, a man of the sixteenth century, shows an astonishing grasp of human psychology. Recommended for the serious reader.

JOHN OF THE CROSS, SAINT. *The Collected Works of St. John of the Cross.* Translated by Kieran Kavanaugh, o.c.d. and Otilio Rodriguez, o.c.d., with introductions by Kieran

Kavanaugh, o.c.d. Doubleday, 1964. 740 p., diagrams. $11.95.

This is a modern translation of the writings of Saint John, the greatest mystical theologian of the Church, containing all of his prose, poetry, and letters. There is, in addition to a general biographical and critical introduction on the saint and his works, an introduction to each one of the major works which the reader will find invaluable for an understanding of St. John's thought and of his methods. Among the most famous of the works in this volume are *Ascent of Mount Carmel, Dark Night of the Soul, Living Flame of Love,* and *Spiritual Canticle.* All of the poems of the great mystic are included in the original Spanish with parallel English translations.

JOHN OF THE CROSS, SAINT. *Complete Works of St. John of the Cross.* Translated, with introduction and notes, by E. Allison Peers. Newman, 1963. 463 p. $10.00.

This edition of the complete works of St. John contains his writings in the following order: *Ascent of Mt. Carmel, Dark Night of the Soul, Spiritual Canticle, Living Flame of Love, Cautions and Counsels, Spiritual Sentences and Maxims, Letters, Documents.* Mr. Peers is recognized as an eminent authority on the thought of the great Spanish mystic, and his introductions to the individual works and his notes are invaluable. On the other hand, his translation sometimes sacrifices clarity to scholarly interpretation and is not always easy to read with understanding. (For the individual works of St. John available in paperback editions, see other entries in this section.)

JOHN OF THE CROSS, SAINT. *The Dark Night of the Soul.* Translated with introduction and notes by E. Allison Peers. Image, 1959. 193 p., notes. pa. 85¢.

St. John's most famous work, *Dark Night* is an explanation of the spiritual phenomenon by which the soul is deprived of all sensible and intellectual consolation. St. John discusses the signs, the causes, and the purpose of the dark night. This is one of the great spiritual and literary classics of Catholicism, but it is rather difficult reading at times.

JOHN OF THE CROSS, SAINT. *Spiritual Canticle.* Translated and edited, with introduction and notes by E. Allison Peers. Image, 1961. 520 p., notes, appendix. pa. $1.45.

Using the simple metaphor of Spouse and Bride, St. John sketches a series of dialogues between God and the soul made rich with imagery drawn from nature. Together with the poet-saint's commentary on his verses, *Spiritual Canticle* forms one of the great artistic and mystical masterpieces of Catholic tradition. Although the author's organization of his work seems rather old-fashioned for twentieth-century tastes, Allison Peers' masterful and modern translation makes the book thoroughly understandable for the modern reader, while his introduction and explanatory notes fill in any gaps in the reader's knowledge of the historical circumstances of composition and of circumstances and images referred to in the text.

KNOX, RONALD A. (MSGR.). *A Retreat for Beginners.* Sheed, 1960. vi, 234 p. $3.50. Deus, 1964. pa. 95¢.

Monsignor Knox was famous in his lifetime for, among other qualities, his success as a retreat master. This volume presents twenty-two of the sermons he preached during retreats for young people. The material is given in logical order and the style is, as in all of Knox's works, entertaining as well as inspiring.

KNOX, RONALD A. (MSGR.). *A Retreat for Lay People.* Paulist Press, 1963. x, 258 p. pa. 95¢.

Monsignor Knox has collected into one volume some of the meditations which he had presented to various groups of retreatants. The author's delightfully unique style and originality of expression, as well as his spiritual perspicacity, make this book interesting reading and an excellent handbook for either a private retreat or for private use in a group retreat.

LEEN, EDWARD (C.S.SP.). *Progress Through Mental Prayer.* Sheed, 1935. x, 276 p. $3.50.

Father Leen's work is regarded as a classic of modern spirituality and as the standard treatment on the subject of mental prayer. He begins by distinguishing mental from other forms of prayer, then goes on to discuss the means of mental prayer, its form, its organization, its problems, its rewards, and its place in the spiritual life of the Catholic. This book is indispensable for the reader who is serious about making progress in the spiritual life.

LEWIS, C. S. *Screwtape Letters.* Macmillan, 1943. 160 p. $3.50. Macmillan, 1954. pa. 65¢.

This unusual book by a famous author comprises a series of fictional letters addressed to an apprentice demon by an older, more experienced devil. The opening letters introduce the characters of the correspondents and contain mostly words of encouragement to the young imp, but the tone soon changes to one of discouragement, and finally to bitter reproach when the apprentice flubs one job after another. The serious purpose of this little classic is to reveal the tricks and fallacies by which doubt and temptation may creep into the mind; Mr. Lewis accomplishes this end by portraying such doubts and temptations as strategems of the devils. (This volume also contains *Screwtape Prepares a Toast,* a sequel, in the same spirit, to *Letters.*)

LUBAC, HENRY DE (s.J.). *The Splendour of the Church.* Translated by Michael Mason. Paulist, 1958. xii, 289 p., bibliography. pa. $1.25.

In this work an eminent theologian presents a series of meditations on the founding of the Church by Christ, on its role in the divine plan of salvation, and on its practical function in the world. The work is, in fact, a beautifully written compendium of the theology of the Church, and is useful as a source of information as well as for meditation.

MERTON, THOMAS. *Life and Holiness.* Herder & Herder, 1963. 162 p. $3.50. Image, 1966. pa. 75¢.

This is an elementary examination of a few ideas basic to Christian spirituality. The book gives particular attention to grace, both sanctifying and actual, to the virtues of faith and charity, and to Pope John XXIII's teachings as expressed in *Mater et Magistra.*

MERTON, THOMAS. *No Man Is an Island.* Harcourt, 1955. xxiii, 264 p. $3.95. Dell, 1956. pa. 50¢.

This is a series of reflections on certain fundamental aspects of the spiritual life such as prayer, the virtues of faith, humility, and love, self-sacrifice, etc. The author's purpose is to treat of these elements as means by which man, guided by grace, frees himself from himself so as to love God and man with perfect charity.

MERTON, THOMAS. *Seeds of Contemplation*. Dell, 1953. 201 p. pa. 50¢.

This is a series of reflections or meditations on prayer and the spiritual life, by the author of *Seven Storey Mountain*. Merton expands especially on the value of the renunciation of self-will and on the spirit of solitude as indispensable concomitants to progress either in prayer or in the inner life. The work is excellent both for meditation and for spiritual reading.

MERTON, THOMAS. *The Seven Storey Mountain*. Harcourt, 1948. 429 p., index. $3.95.

This famous work is the autobiography of Thomas Merton, covering the period from his birth in 1915 to the end of World War II. Essentially, it narrates the spiritual odyssey of a modern American man with little religious background through the philosophical isms until he finally finds an intellectual and spiritual home in the Church.

MERTON, THOMAS. *The Sign of Jonas*. Harcourt, 1953. 352 p. $3.95. Image, 1956. pa. 95¢.

The day-by-day experiences and meditations of Thomas Merton, author of *The Seven Storey Mountain*. This book is a collection of personal notes, a sort of spiritual diary, written during the author's life at the Trappist seminary at Gethsemane, Kentucky. It will answer just about any question as to how and why men become Trappist monks, and what they do once they are Trappists.

MERTON, THOMAS. *A Thomas Merton Reader*. Edited by Thomas P. Donnell. Harcourt, 1962. xiv, 553 p. $5.75.

This anthology of the writings of Thomas Merton, the famous Trappist monk, includes selections from his best known books, such as *The Seven Storey Mountain*, *Seeds of Contemplation*, and *Ascent to Truth*, as well as a representative selection of his poetry.

NEWMAN, JOHN HENRY CARDINAL. *Apologia Pro Vita Sua*. Modern Library, n.d. 439 p. $1.95. Image, 1956. pa. $1.35.

The most famous of Newman's works, the *Apologia* is an explanation of his changes in religious opinion from his childhood until, after years of study, he entered the Catholic Church "in perfect peace and contentment." This undoubtedly is one of the great spiritual and literary classics of modern times, and it is recognized as one of the great autobiographies of the English language.

PAONE, ANTHONY J. (s.j.). *My Life with Christ.* Doubleday, 1962. 317 p. $4.50. Image, 1965. pa. 95¢.

Father Paone has written a book of meditations designed to guide readers toward mental, emotional, and moral growth. Each of the 183 meditations comprises a reading from the Gospels, a reflection on the incident described, an application of the reflection to daily life, and a colloquy intended to bring the reader into close personal union with Christ. Particularly suited to the contemporary layman.

QUOIST, MICHEL. *Prayers.* Translated by Agnes M. Forsyth and Anne-Marie de Commaille. Sheed, 1963. 179 p. $3.95.

This slender volume is more than a collection of prayers; it is rather an introduction to the life of prayer, showing how one can pray—that is, commune with God—at all times by what the author calls "reading the Gospel of daily life." Taking his material from that gospel, Father Quoist has composed meditations on such subjects as advertising, the subway, pornographic magazines, hospitals, and funerals. The author's simplicity of vision, spiritual wisdom, and forceful style will make this an unusually valuable book for all readers.

RAHNER, KARL (s.j.). *Spiritual Exercises.* Translated by Kenneth Baker, s.j. Herder & Herder, 1965. 285 p., glossary. $5.50.

This work of Rahner's is a commentary on the *Spiritual Exercises* of St. Ignatius Loyola. The author's purpose has been simply to explain the *Exercises,* with special attention to the needs of twentieth-century man, avoiding unnecessary excursions into irrelevant areas of theological speculation. The book is aimed at the layman without theological training, and it is a book of such insight and clarity as to warrant its eventual acceptance as a spiritual classic in its own right.

TANQUEREY, ADOLPHE (s.s.). *The Spiritual Life,* revised edition. Translated by Herman Branderis. Newman, 1945. lxiii, 771 p., bibliography, appendices, index. $6.00.

Tanquerey's *Spiritual Life* has become recognized, since its first publication in 1923, as the standard work on mystical and ascetical theology. It was written both for priests and for laymen, and combines a thorough treatment of all aspects of the spiritual life—from its beginnings through its highest levels—with clear language and logical presentation. It is an indispensable work for priests, directors, teachers, and for laymen who aspire to progress in the spiritual life.

TEILHARD DE CHARDIN, PIERRE (S.J.). *The Divine Milieu.* Harper, 1960. 144 p. $3.00.

The famous French Jesuit thinker investigates the question of how man, through his spiritual life, can participate in the destiny of the universe. His answer to the problem is that, through Christian asceticism, we may attain the "divinization" of our activities—or, at the risk of oversimplification, that we must put aside our own will, both exteriorly and interiorly, in conformity with God's will. This is a difficult book, but the informed reader will find, perhaps to his surprise, that it is quite intelligible.

TEILHARD DE CHARDIN, PIERRE (S.J.). *Hymn of the Universe.* Translated by Simone Bartholomew. Harper, 1965. 157 p., bibliographical notes. $3.00.

Hymn of the Universe might best be described as a mystical meditation consisting of three parts: Christ in the world of matter, the spiritual power of matter, and a collection of eighty-one short reflections gathered from all of Teilhard's works. It is a work of mystical theology rather than the ordered exposition of a philosophical thesis, and its value lies in its spiritual power. Like all of Teilhard's works, the book requires careful reading, but in this case it requires no technical background in the reader.

TEILHARD DE CHARDIN, PIERRE (S.J.). *The Making of a Mind.* Translated by Rene Hague. Harper, 1965. 316 p. $5.00.

This is a collection of letters written by Teilhard, between 1914 and 1919, to Marguerite Teilhard-Chambon, his cousin. The relationship to Teilhard, then a member of the French army, to his confidante allowed him to share with her his insights on suffering, death, prayer, hope, detachment, and above all on the necessity of reformulating Christianity in terms comprehensible and relevant to the modern world. This is an excellent introduction to the Jesuit philosopher's later works.

TERESA OF AVILA, SAINT. *The Autobiography of St. Teresa of Avila*. Translated with notes by E. Allison Peers. Newman, 1962. 397 p., notes. $4.50. Image, 1960. pa. $1.25.

The autobiography of St. Teresa of Avila was written at the command of her confessors, to give an accurate and detailed account of her spiritual progress. The first part of the book is an autobiography in the ordinary sense, describing the author's family, education, and the beginnings of her spiritual life. The last part describes the spiritual trials and triumphs of the saints and the effects of them in her soul.

TERESA OF AVILA, SAINT. *The Interior Castle*. Translated, with introduction and notes, by E. Allison Peers. Newman, 1948. 233 p., notes. $3.00. Image, 1961. pa. 75¢.

One of the most celebrated books on mystical theology, *Interior Castle* reflects the author's concept of the soul as "a castle made of a single diamond, in which there are many rooms, just as in Heaven there are many mansions." She describes the various rooms of this castle—the degrees of purgation and continual effort—through which the soul must pass in its search for perfection. This edition contains a valuable introduction and some explanatory notes by the translator.

TERESA OF AVILA, SAINT. *The Way of Perfection*. Translated by E. Allison Peers. Newman, 1947. 280 p., introduction, notes. $3.50. Image, 1964. 85¢.

A spiritual classic on the practice of prayer, this work is a practical guide to a deep and lasting love of communicating with God. St. Teresa first treats of the conditions of the soul that are ideal for prayer—detachment from material things, the spirit of love, etc.—and then considers the different ways of praying. The final part of the book contains her celebrated commentary on the Lord's Prayer. There are sections of the book that are rather difficult reading, but the effort is worth while.

THOMAS À KEMPIS. *The Imitation of Christ*. Translated by Ronald Knox and Michael Oakley. Sheed, 1960. 217 p. $2.50. Image, 1955. (Translated, edited with an introduction by Harold C. Gardiner). pa. 85¢.

Next to the Bible, *The Imitation of Christ* probably is the most widely read spiritual work in the history of Christianity. It was written early in the fifteenth century, with the intention of pointing the way by which everyone is able to follow

Christ's teachings and, by so doing, imitate his life. The author sets out, in a series of 114 short chapters, an eminently practical step-by-step method of attaining that end. In addition to the spiritual value of the book, it is regarded as one of the treasures of Christian letters. It is, in the words of Matthew Arnold, "the most exquisite document, after those of the New Testament, of all that the Christian spirit has ever inspired."

VAN ZELLER, HUBERT (O.S.B.). *A Book of Private Prayer.* Templegate, 1960. ix, 242 p. $3.25.

Father Van Zeller has compiled this book of "considerations" or meditations and occasional prayers to be used as a basis for, or in conjunction with, both mental and vocal prayer. There are 116 titles, including prayers for zeal, in adoration, in thanksgiving, and meditations on death, sin, fear, charity, and the Mass. This is an unusual work, combining spiritual vision with literary finesse.

VAN ZELLER, HUBERT (O.S.B.). *We Die Standing Up.* Image, 1961. 160 p. pa. 75¢. *We Live with Our Eyes Open.* Image, 1963. 182 p. pa. 75¢. *We Sing While There's Voice Left.* Image, 1964. 208 p. pa. 75¢. *We Work While the Light Lasts.* Image, 1962. 160 p. pa. 75¢.

The reason for grouping several works in one entry is that all four of the books listed above—form, for practical purposes, one continuous work broken up into volumes. The "We . . ." series as a whole has one purpose: to provide practical, pertinent meditation material for the man or woman living in the modern world. Thus, there are meditations on work, marriage, envy, security, children, conscience, perseverance, truth, integrity, teaching school, prayer—on just about any topic of interest to the layman who is seriously concerned with spiritual progress. Those who like their spiritual food liberally mixed with wit and common sense will find Father Van Zeller's work an answer to a prayer.

VANN, GERALD (O.P.). *The Divine Pity.* Image, 1961. 189 p. pa. 75¢.

This is a study in the social implications of the Beatitudes. Observing that modern man is lonely and isolated because of his total absorption in himself and in material goods, the author discusses the ways in which man can return to the abundant happiness of God's love: poverty of spirit, meekness as a means to strength, mourning and pity as ways to wisdom, etc. It is a very readable combination of wisdom and wit.

VANN, GERALD (O.P.). *The Heart of Man.* Image, 1960. 190 p. pa. 75¢.

This is a study of man in his functions of creator and lover. First the author analyzes the heart of man longing to become one with the universe about and beyond him, and shows how man can achieve this unity through love. Then he considers the ways in which man expresses that longing for unity—through art, the family, the world, and the Church. It is an unusual book, well written, and quite suitable for either meditation or spiritual reading.

WEAVER, BERTRAND (C.P.). *Joy.* Foreword by Msgr. John S. Kennedy. Sheed, 1964. 182 p. $3.95. Image, 1966. pa. 75¢.

Father Weaver points out that sadness is one of Satan's most powerful weapons, and yet, there are many people who, in circumstances where they might be expected to be sad, radiate joy. The answer to this paradox is to be found in the knowledge of their identity as children of God. This book explores the sources of this joy, drawing upon Scripture, the liturgy, the writings of popes and saints, and a wide range of Christian prose and poetry. The result is an excellent book for spiritual reading in which the spirit of Christian joy reveals itself.

26. THEOLOGY

The primary dictionary definition of theology is "knowledge of God and the supernatural" followed by the secondary definition of "The critical, historical, and psychological study of religion and religious ideas." Originating from the Greek *logos* meaning word and *theos* meaning god, perhaps the simplest way of defining theology is to combine the two definitions above and add to them the necessary Christian element. It is then "a science which treats of God and those things relating to God in the light of divine revelation." Some non-believers may scoff at the use of the term "science," but how better to define a formal body of knowledge, which has been the subject of intense study and investigation through the centuries and now constitutes the conclusions of these studies in a synthesis that has all the characteristics of a corpus of scientific knowledge.

Interestingly enough, the two dictionary definitions above describe the historical evolution of theology. For Catholics, much of the knowledge of God is based on the teachings of Christ. During his earthly stay, Christ wrote no textbooks on God or on the relation of man to God. But he did travel up and down Galilee preaching the word of God and teaching his listeners and apostles the basic concepts of the Catholic faith. These teachings are to be found in the writings of the apostles gathered together in the New Testament.

Though the wisdom gathered by the evangelists in the New Testament might be considered the first Catholic theology, it was not, nor was it meant to be, a systematic body of theological content. Rather it was a recording of Christ's life and teachings so that the purity of our Lord's words, actions, and miracles would be passed on undiluted to future generations after the first Christians had passed into eternity.

So too the early Christians were too occupied with living their faith to feel the necessity of gathering their beliefs into a systematic order. Indeed, the first centuries were a desperate struggle to keep the faith alive and allowed little or no time for the intellectual effort necessary to promulgate an ordered body of religious belief. But as time passed, Christianity spread into foreign lands and alien cultures. Questions were raised which called for considered replies. Gradually, as the Christian belief made deeper inroads, men began to appear who realized the need for preparing a systematic presentation of the faith which had been lived by the early Christians and passed from one generation to the next by example and by word of mouth. These were the early Church Fathers, and the theology they built up reached its epitome in the works of Augustine, whose thought became the cornerstone of Christian theology for almost a thousand years.

With the destruction of the Roman Empire, learning went into a gradual eclipse and was kept alive only in isolated spots by the monks in monasteries, which then became and remained for centuries almost the sole repositories of culture and learning. A resurgence took place late in the eighth century, with Charlemagne's encouragement of learning through Alcuin's palace schools. One of the developments which emerged in the centuries after Alcuin and which was to have tremendous importance for centuries to come was the reawakening of scholarly interest in the works of Aristotle. Schools began to appear in increasing numbers in the eleventh and twelfth centuries, and in the thirteenth century many of Aristotle's works were translated. The revolutionary concept that shook this period though was the conviction of many scholars that reason alone could provide knowledge of the nature of man and of reality, which meant that Scripture and scriptural commentary now had added to them the use of reason in structuring theology. St. Thomas Aquinas' *Summa* was the epitome of this movement, synthesizing faith and reason and was to become the cornerstone of all theology for centuries to come. Scholasticism was born.

As time passed scholasticism became more and more concerned with abstractions, lost touch with reality, and eventually reached the unhappy state of affairs in which the emphasis on exclusively rational and logical methods made theology a subject only for the specialist. By the time of the Reformation, theology was so concerned with its own miniscule studies it had completely alienated the overwhelming mass of the people and was the province of the specialized specialist if we may use such a term.

Low as its state was, it was to go even lower. For with the Reformation, theologians, both Catholic and Protestant, became completely engrossed in the task of refuting the other side. Theology became mainly polemical and defensive. Little thought was given to the creative thinking which is the life blood of theology. Though some attention obviously was given to certain aspects of theology (morals for example), the main concern of all involved was that of defending one's belief on the one hand and breaking the other side's wall by thundering denunciation buttressed by one-sided argumentation and biased presentations of relevant material.

So, pretty much, was the situation in the nineteenth century. Encouraged by Pope Leo XIII, attempts were made to revive the best of medieval scholasticism and to bring fresh insights to theology. Some progress was made and remarkable developments in Biblical scholarship spurred further efforts. With the accession of Pope John XXIII to the papacy and his revolutionary ideas for reform and renewal in the Church and for reunion with other Christian churches, a whole new vision of the role of theology opened up as every aspect of Church activity was subjected to searching scrutiny. Theology began to experience a whole new development as the areas in which it operates began to respond to the forces of renewal. As one of the most basic of all Church concerns, it was essential that theology be updated to meet the needs of the Church of the twentieth century.

As theologians eagerly meet the challenge and build a system of theology cognizant of modern forces and adapted to modern discoveries and needs, it is essential that the layman be aware of this dynamic development in the Church, and draw on it for his own purposes and to be qualified to explain his faith to his fellow man in terms the latter can accept and understand. The roots of the Church must reach to her members and theology must be the concern of all, not just of the few. For who would dare say that knowledge of God is not his concern? And that is exactly what theology is, as we have earlier defined it.

In view of what we have said above, it must be evident

that a whole new library of books is now appearing as theologians everywhere grapple with new concepts and define the Church's teaching in today's terms. Consequently, most of the books we are listing below are of recent date. But, as always, there is much to be learned from the past, and nothing said above is meant to jettison what is appropriate and has relevance for today from the rich heritage that we have. Thus, there will be books of other times included, for such books often add in a unique way to our knowledge and are undimmed by the passage of time. All in all, then, we feel the list is representative of the best of the Church's theology.

Before the reader begins considering the books described below, however, it might be worth giving a short breakdown of the various sections into which theology is divided. Any science proposing to treat of such a tremendous field as the knowledge of God must obviously be broken into units for the most profitable study.

Speaking for the general reader, theology may be studied under eight categories: dogmatic, moral, natural, supernatural, positive, mystical, ascetical, and pastoral.

Dogmatic theology is the branch of theology with which most people have at least a nodding acquaintance. It is the systematic presentation of the tenets of the faith based on the premise that the Church is the depository and guardian of revealed truth as expounded by Jesus Christ and taught by his apostles, their followers and descendants.

Moral theology too is a branch of theology which affects all of us since it treats of human acts in the light of the supernatural destiny which awaits all men. In developing the principles of moral theology both reason and the revelations of faith are employed to establish the rules which should govern human conduct.

Natural theology is the use of human reason to attain a knowledge of God. Some theologians contend that human reason cannot suffice to give us a knowledge of God, since God is so beyond human understanding that the only way man can ever attain this knowledge is through revelation— the knowledge of himself that God in his love for man has directly revealed to man through his son, the Scriptures, and in some cases personal insight. This concept is called supernatural theology. In general though, most theologians believe man through reason can approach God and comprehend of him though reason combined with revelation will bring us closer to the ultimate Truth.

Positive theology is a branch of supernatural theology devoted to discerning the truths of revelation and the dogmas of the faith from the *loci theologici*, the sources of theological knowledge. It is called positive inasmuch as it postulates these truths and dogmas but makes no attempts to refute the attacks by non-believers on the faith and its teachings.

Mystical theology, which in recent times has been increasingly attractive to many, treats of contemplation and things mystical based on the tradition of the Church and Sacred Scriptures. Akin to this branch of theology is ascetical theology, which considers the Christian virtues and the way to perfection and the methods to be used in attaining these goals.

And finally pastoral theology is that aspect of theology which treats of the care of souls and of course is chiefly the concern of priests. It combines the principles of dogmatic, moral and ascetic theology, and canon law, and applies these principles to every aspect of the daily work of the pastor and his assistants with the souls entrusted to them.

There are other more specialized areas of theology which are the province of the trained theologian, but for the general reader, for whom this *Guide* is intended, these branches of the science of theology described above will suffice. In the books we have chosen, there will inevitably be some overlapping of these various areas as most books on the subject, aside from textbooks which we do not include, treat of the science of theology as a whole. However, you will find here many approaches and styles, as each author develops his study in his own individual manner.

A word of caution is in order. Theology has not lightly been called "the queen of all sciences." It deals with the most exalted of man's drives—his quest for God. It discourses on things of great moment and leads to the heights of the spiritual life. On a subject of such magnitude and importance to us all, the reader must be prepared to devote the time he spends in the study of theology to serious effort. But the time so spent will be well worth any such effort. And while the word of caution is called for, it should not frighten away the interested reader. There are books described for every intellectual capacity. Read the descriptions carefully and then select the one most suitable for your personal needs. Even the most hardened skeptic must admit that "the queen of sciences" is a fascinating study. For Catholics, it should be high on the list of reading priorities.

ALTING VON GEUSAU, LEO, et al., Editors. *Concilium: Theology in the Age of Renewal*. Paulist, 1964–1969. (50 vols.). $4.50 ea. (by subscription, $159.00 per set).

Concilium is a series of books published over a five-year period intended to cover the theological and historical background of the changes within the Church put into effect by Vatican II. The series' editors are twenty-one of the modern Church's most respected thinkers, such as Yves Congar, Godfrey Diekmann, Hans Küng, Roland Murphy, Karl Rahner, and Edward Schillebeeckx. The fifty volumes, being published at the rate of ten volumes per year, cover ten main subjects: dogma, liturgy, pastoral theology, ecumenism, moral theology, the Church in the modern world, Church history, canon law, spirituality, and Scripture. The individual volumes, for the most part, are quite technical in approach and quite specialized in subject. They are suitable for use by theologians, as theological journals, but require in the nonprofessional reader a sound foundation in the various disciplines.

FARRELL, WALTER (O.P.). *A Companion to the Summa*. Sheed, 1938–1942. Vol. I: vii, 457 p., index; Vol. II: viii, 459 p., index; Vol. III: x, 530 p., index; Vol. IV: viii, 464 p., index. $4.50 ea.

This remarkable work is not a commentary on Thomas Aquinas' *Summa Theologica*, nor a translation of it; it is rather, in the author's words, "the *Summa* itself, reduced to popular language." Each of the four volumes corresponds to one part of the *Summa*. Volume I (*prima pars*) considers the existence and attributes of God, creation and creatures, and divine providence; Volume II (*prima secundae*) views man from a natural standpoint—as a moral, responsible being, pos-

sessing passions, emotions, and mental faculties; Volume III
(*secunda secundae*) describes the virtues, theological and
moral, and their corresponding vices; Volume IV (*tertia pars*)
is an exposition of the nature and means of redemption
and salvation—the Incarnation, Mary, the Sacraments, the
Church, etc. This work is for beginners and advanced students alike. Apart from the *Summa* itself, it is the best possible introduction to Catholic theology.

FARRELL, WALTER (O.P.) and MARTIN J. HEALEY. *My Way
of Life*. Confraternity of the Precious Blood, 1952. 630 p.
pa. $1.35.

My Way of Life is a condensation of St. Thomas Aquinas'
Summa Theologica. The authors have started at the beginning of that work, and digested and simplified the material
so that the entire work is contained in essence in this volume.
The book is highly recommended to all readers interested in
philosophy or theology; it requires no theological or philosophical preparation on the reader's part, but it does require
careful reading.

GARRIGOU-LAGRANGE, REGINALD (O.P.). *Reality: A Synthesis
of Thomistic Thought*. Translated by Patrick Cummins, O.S.B.
Herder, 1950. xiii, 419 p., bibliography, index. $6.00.

In this work, one of the great Thomistic philosopher-
theologians of the twentieth century condenses the whole of
traditional Thomistic thought into a readable synthesis. It is
a book intended for the general reader rather than for the
student or the specialist, and can serve as an excellent introduction to the thought, both philosophical and theological,
of Aquinas.

JOURNET, CHARLES. *The Meaning of Grace*. Translated by
A. V. Littledale. Kenedy, 1960. xii, 127 p. $3.50. Paulist,
1962. pa. 95¢.

This collection of essays examines the significance of grace
within the framework of the sacramental economy of the
Catholic Church. Father Journet treats of habitual and actual
grace, the relationship of grace to predestination, the role of
grace in salvation, the difference between grace in the Old
Testament and in the New, and the role of grace in the
Church. The book is clearly written and well organized; it
will be of value to the general reader with a taste for theology as well as to the student.

LEONARD, JOSEPH T. *Theology and Race Relations.* Foreword by Archbishop Patrick A. O'Boyle. Bruce, 1963. 316 p., bibliography. $5.00.

The author discusses the problem of race relations in America within the framework of Catholic theology, with emphasis on Negro-white relations. Among the specific questions discussed are: the Negro and organized labor, the obligations of property owners, Catholic Negroes and the parochial school system, and the morality of sit-in demonstrations and of freedom marches. The author presents a Christian sociological point of view, in a popularly written style. The book is recommended as a forthright expression of Catholic principles.

McAVOY, THOMAS J. *The American Heresy in Roman Catholicism: 1845–1900.* Notre Dame, 1963. 276 p., notes, bibliography, index. pa. $1.95.

In 1899, Pope Leo XIII condemned in his letter (called *Testem benevolentiae*) to Cardinal Gibbons the "errors of Americanism" or the "American heresy." That heresy amounted to this, that the Church should adapt itself to modern civilization, relax its rigorous rules, de-emphasize religious vows, show more sympathy for modern theories and methods, and generally allow for more individual expression of religious belief. Such "errors" would scarcely merit a second glance today, but, at the time, they represented scandalous innovations in theological thought. This work studies the origins of Americanism, its manifestations, European and American Catholic reactions both to the movement and to Pope Leo's action, and the eventual outcome of the controversy. The book presents a readable account of an important chapter in the history of the American Church.

MOUROUX, JEAN. *The Meaning of Man.* Translated by A. H. G. Downes. Image, 1961. 278 p., notes. pa. 95¢.

This is a Christian statement of the meaning of man. In opposition to those modern philosophies which challenge Christian reverence for the dignity of man as the image of God, the author explains the theology of man's relationship to God and how this relationship defines and directs man in both the temporal and spiritual aspects of his existence. Of special interest is the author's analysis of temporal and carnal values in relation to the human personality. It is not an easy book to read, but this is more than compensated for by the value of the author's views.

MURRAY, JOHN COURTNEY (S.J.). *The Problem of God, Yesterday and Today.* Yale, 1964. vii, 121 p. $4.95.

Father Murray, one of the best known spokesmen for the "progressive" school of philosophy and theology, in this work presents his thoughts on the concept of God as held by man at different stages in his historical development. For this purpose, the book is divided into three parts, treating respectively of God as seen in the Old Testament, in the full flowering of Christian thought, and finally in modern times. The last section gives special attention to the "death of God" movement in theology. The book is sufficiently non-technical to be intelligible to the reader with no formal training in theology.

PEGIS, ANTON C., Editor. *The Basic Writings of St. Thomas Aquinas.* Random, 1945. Vol. I: 1097 p., introduction, notes; Vol. II: 1179 p., notes. $15.00, boxed set.

Professor Pegis, an eminent authority on St. Thomas, has compiled a selection of the great philosopher's most significant writings. All of the selections—except one, from the *Summa contra gentiles*—are taken from what is regarded as Thomas' masterpiece, the *Summa Theologica*, even though, in many instances, the texts are either of both philosophical and theological interest or almost solely philosophical. The translation is that of the English Dominicans, painstakingly edited by Pegis for clarity of expression. There is an excellent introduction, situating Aquinas and the Thomistic system in their historical and intellectual context and pointing out the tremendous impact that Aquinas has had both on the Church and on the world, and notes explaining points of particular difficulty in the texts.

RAHNER, KARL and HERBERT VORGRIMLER. *Theological Dictionary.* Edited by Cornelius Ernst, O.P.; translated by Richard Strachan. 493 p. $6.50.

This work is not a "theological dictionary" in the proper sense of the term. It is rather a concise theological encyclopedia, in that it comprises a group of approximately six hundred short articles, alphabetically arranged, on various concepts of dogmatic theology. The material provided gives a succinct statement of the teachings of the Church with respect to points of doctrine and their theological implications.

Within those limits, it is an excellent work, by a master of contemporary theological thought, and thoroughly up-to-date.

SHEED, FRANK J. *Theology and Sanity*. Sheed, 1946. x, 407 p., index. $3.50.

This is the best general introduction to the theology of Christianity that is available today. The book is divided into three parts, discussing, respectively, God, creation as the work of God, and man as a part of God's work. In the first two sections, the author explains the fundamental truths of religion, such as the existence of God, God's attributes, the Trinity, God's providence, etc., while in the third part he shows the place of man in the divine plan of creation. This is not the ordinary book of apologetics, but a fresh approach to old truths. Mr. Sheed expresses himself with a precision of thought and a brilliance of style that makes the book a joy to read.

SHEED, FRANK J. *Theology for Beginners*. Sheed & Ward, 1957. x, 241 p. $3.00.

A prominent lay theologian sets out for laymen the basic principles of the knowledge of God. He covers such primary concepts as God's existence and nature, the origin and rule of the Church, and the general plan of salvation. The book is not only instructive and well written, but serves as an excellent introduction to the entire field of theology.

THOMAS AQUINAS, SAINT. *Summa Theologiae*. McGraw, 1964. Translated and edited with notes by the Dominican Fathers of the English-speaking provinces.

This monumental undertaking is a translation of the *Summa Theologiae* of St. Thomas into English. Each volume will deal with Aquinas' thought on one basic section of theology, giving both the Latin text of the original and an idiomatic English version, and each section is explained and commented upon by a system of introductions and notes. (The cost of the individual volumes runs from $5.50 to $7.50.)

WOLF, DONALD J. (S.J.) and JAMES V. SCHALL (S.J.), Editors. *Current Trends in Theology*. Doubleday, 1965. 285 p., notes, bibliography. $4.95. Image, 1966. pa. 85¢.

This book was designed to offer an understandable explanation of the advances being made, and of the new directions being taken, by Catholic theologians in the twentieth century. An introductory chapter traces the development of Catholic theology, by logical and historical stages, from the founding of the Church to the present. Subsequent chapters explain the progress being made in various fields of theological interest—methods of theological research, liturgy, Bible study, the role of the layman, Church-State relations, etc. Each of the thirteen chapters was written by an authority in the subject field. The book is highly recommended to the Catholic layman, as well as to the priest, as an excellent account of what is happening in his Church.

APPENDICES

    I. A Home Library for Catholic Books
   II. Catholic Book Clubs
  III. Catholic Magazines and Newspapers
  IV. Publishers of Books Listed

I. A HOME LIBRARY OF CATHOLIC BOOKS

Every Catholic home should have a basic library of Catholic books. The size of the library in any home, of course, is dependent on the reading tastes of those living there, the space available, and the cost of establishing a library. But it is a fact that with the millions of good, inexpensive paperbacks now available, cost is no longer the factor it once was in the purchase of books. Space is often a consideration but room can always be made for some books if there is the desire to do so. And finally, though reading tastes do vary, it is also a fact that 98% of Americans can read. There is simply no reason in the world why every Catholic family should not have a few basic Catholic books which would constitute their library of Catholic books.

In this section, the authors of this *Guide* have prepared a list of eleven areas of Catholic literature which provides the basis for a home library. The categories selected are basic in any approach to understanding the Church and her teaching through reading. We have deliberately kept the subject areas in this section to a bare minimum so the types of books we suggest are essential books which should be in every Catholic home. To begin a home library use this section as a guide for your basic selection referring to the proper section in the *Guide* to select the book in each area suitable to your own tastes and needs. To expand the scope of the library simply pick another area section in the body of the *Guide*, add it to the basic areas listed below and pick out a book suitable for your needs from the section you are adding. To broaden the selection, just add other books to those areas you have already established. By using this simple approach, a basic library can be established at once and can grow as one's interests become more closely involved with different aspects of Catholicism.

Cost is always an important factor in building a library so we have appended to this section a library of paperbooks based on the minimum areas outlined below which can be purchased for a total expenditure of about $15. Additions to this list may readily be made by consulting the body of the *Guide* for books to enlarge your basic library. At the same time, it should be stressed that a worthwhile library is an investment that should be approached with the same care and thought that one puts into any major household expenditure. How frequently one hears complaints about the costs of books from people who will spend more for movies or cigarettes in a year than they spend on books in ten years. A pack-a-day smoker spends about $150 a year on cigarettes and thinks nothing of it. When the year is over his $150 is literally gone in smoke. The same amount spent on good books can provide a lifetime of pleasure, information and inspiration. For any home, there can be no sounder investment than money spent for good books.

And so we recommend as basic for any home Catholic library at least one book in each of the following categories:

1. The Bible. It seems incredible that with all the emphasis on the need and desirability for Catholics to read the Bible, so few Catholics own a Bible. Here is *the* book of books, the basic book for the whole Christian world and yet so many Catholics neither own nor read it. If there is to be only one book in the Catholic home, obviously it should be a Bible.

2. A good life of Christ. Although all we know of Our Lord as told by his contemporaries is found in the New Testament, a good life of the Lord can provide background, insights, and information not available in the Bible. In view of the tremendous discoveries and findings of scholars of the past century, we know more about Jesus today than at any time in history. Next to the Bible, a life of Christ is the most needed book in a Catholic home.

3. A life of Mary. The Blessed Mother has always been an

integral part of Catholic life. Despite certain tendencies to play down her role in the Church, on the one hand, and the exaggerated claims made for her, on the other, the great masses of Catholics have always regarded her, as she is, as the mother of God and the mother of the Church. Knowing more about her and her true role in the Church should be obligatory for any Catholic.

4. A collection of lives of the saints. When Christ was on earth, he was the example par excellence for all men. We should all be doing our utmost to follow in his steps. Some men and women have been more successful in leading lives of holiness and sanctity and the Church has crowned their efforts by naming them saints. They are outstanding examples of what can be done in living lives that Christ wants us to and can serve as an inspiration for us all.

5. A history of the Catholic Church. During his stay on earth, Christ established the Church. For the 2000 years of her existence, the Church has always, with varying degrees of success, attempted to teach Christ's message. Every Catholic should know at least in broad outline how the Church has fulfilled the charge of her divine Founder.

6. A book on the teaching of the Church. Catholic teaching has always remained faithful to the teaching of Christ, but the methods and means of spreading his word have been modified where necessary to cope with varying conditions, events, and peoples. We should at all times have ready access to a book which explains the Church's teaching in terms of our own era and culture.

7. A Catholic reference work. Especially today is it essential for a Catholic to be informed on the meaning of words and expressions constantly used in the press, in books, and on radio and television. A Catholic dictionary or almanac provides this information quickly and precisely. In this connection, we cannot refrain from unreservedly recommending the *National Catholic Almanac*, published annually, which is a library of Catholic information all in itself.

8. Spiritual writing. A book of spiritual meditations or reflections can be a source of inspiration and consolation second to none. From the earliest days of Christianity to the present, such books have aided men and women in all walks of life.

Find the book or books which can help you spiritually and you will have a treasure which can help you all through life.

9. A collection of convert stories. The story of a man's quest for God is always among the most dramatic experiences in a man's life. Those who have gone through the spiritual awakening which led them to the Church have something of worth for all of us.

10. The social teachings of the Church. Our civilization today is the most complex and chaotic of any era in the history of man. Since the time of Pope Leo XIII, the Church has been increasingly aware of the complexities and injustices of today's world. A whole body of teaching has been propounded on the social problems of the modern world and their Christian solutions. The problems are world wide and affect us all. All Catholics should be aware of the Church's teaching in the area of human relations so that individually the Catholic can make common effort with his fellow man in providing a Christian solution to the world's troubles.

11. A selection of the great Christian writings of the ages. All through the centuries, great authors have written on every aspect of Christianity in biographies, novels, history, poetry, plays—in fact, in every literary form. They present in their writings rare insights into man's relation with God and his fellow man in the noble language and stirring terms of great literature. A selection of such writings or even a single volume of some great novel or poet should be a vital part of any Catholic home library.

A Basic Catholic Home Library in Paperback for $15

The Old Testament. Guild. $1.45
The New Testament. Image. 95¢
Jesus and His Times. by H. Daniel-Rops.
     2 volumes. Image. 95¢ each vol.
The Book of Mary. by H. Daniel-Rops. Image. 75¢
Saints for Our Times. by Theodore Maynard. Image. 95¢
A Popular History of the Catholic Church.
     by Philip Hughes. Macmillan. $1.95
A Handbook of the Catholic Faith.
     by Dr. N. C. M. Van Doornik,

Rev. S. Jelsma,
Rev. A. Van De Lisdonk.
Edited by Rev. John Greenwood. Image. $1.55
A *Catholic Dictionary*.
    by Donald Attwater. Macmillan. $2.45
The *Road to Damascus*.
    Edited by John A. O'Brien. Image. 85¢
The *Confessions of St. Augustine*.
    Translated by John A. Ryan. Image. $1.35
The *World's Great Catholic Literature*.
    Edited by George Shuster. Image. $1.45

II. CATHOLIC BOOK CLUBS

In 1927, a new and important element was introduced to the American book world with the launching of the first book club, the Book of the Month Club. The success of this new book distribution concept led in the years following to the founding of scores of book clubs offering selections for every conceivable literary taste.

Among the specialized areas of publishing which offered a potentially promising book club operation was the field of Catholic publishing. And so it was inevitable that Catholic book clubs would be founded. In 1928, just a year after the pioneer book club had begun operations, the Catholic Book Club was founded. In the years since then Catholic book clubs became flourishing institutions and there are now ten adult and two juvenile book clubs offering books for every Catholic reading taste. Since Catholic book clubs have been a most important factor in stimulating the reading of Catholic books—millions of their members have enjoyed books they have received through these clubs—the authors of this *Guide* felt it desirable to include this section describing the various Catholic clubs, the type of book they offer, and the general features of the book club operation.

At the same time we cannot refrain from stressing the merits of finding and patronizing a good Catholic book store. For while the book clubs serve a most worthwhile purpose, there are some drawbacks in depending entirely on the clubs for books. In the first place, they offer a monthly selection, usually of one book, which has been selected by the editor or editorial board of the club. But there are some 100–150 new Catholic titles published each month. The choice from clubs therefore is apt to be rather limited. It is only through regular visits to a good Catholic book store or library that the reader can come into contact with the full measure of Catholic books available today. Further many individuals prefer to make their own selection rather than have their book reading selected for them. Also contact with other readers, which can be so valuable, can be made through book stores and libraries but not at all through book clubs. And finally, the wealth of paperbacks at their attractive low prices is not available at all through book clubs, which to the present time have been unable to cope with this phenomenon of the contemporary book world.

On the other hand, there are definite advantages in book club membership. In the first place, generally speaking, the selections of the clubs are excellent. The men and women selecting the books for the clubs have had long experience with and are on familiar terms with the best of Catholic literature. Almost always the selections are current publications and invariably include the most popular and most discussed books of the day. The selections are offered at lower prices than elsewhere though there is usually some commitment on the part of the member to take a nominal number of books a year—usually four. All of the clubs offer real bargains as inducements for joining and some offer bonus books. But most important of all they offer folks with no ready access to Catholic book stores a simple method of getting the latest in Catholic reading. The importance of this latter point can be appreciated when one realizes there are at best 100–150 first rate outlets for Catholic books in the United States and many communities are miles away from any kind of Catholic outlet.

In general all Catholic book clubs follow the same procedure. Prospective members are approached by mail order campaigns or via newspaper advertising. The club offers a premium as an inducement to join and the individual agrees to take a certain number of books a year though some of the clubs require no commitment. There is a monthly selection, unless otherwise indicated, and after the member joins he is notified each month of the coming selection. At this time the member may decide to choose or refuse this particular selection. If he wants the selection, he need do nothing; the book and bill will be shipped to him and the process is repeated the following month. If he does not wish the selection, he must notify the club by a specified date and it is not shipped. Some few of the clubs have automatic shipment and these we will indicate below. The member is always free to drop out of the club after he has fulfilled his initial commitment; where there is no commitment he may drop out at any time. The commitment is usually for two to four books depending on the book offered the member for joining; occasionally it is higher if the book is very expensive.

For your guidance, we have listed below all the Catholic book clubs in the United States and have indicated the type of book they are offering. For further information about any aspect of any individual club, we suggest you write directly to the club in which you are interested.

Adult

The Catholic Book Club
106 West 56th Street, New York, N.Y. 10019
Conducted by the Jesuit Fathers who publish *America,* it offers books for the mature Catholic reader. Selections are of a high literary or intellectual character. The Club also sponsors the Campion Award annually to the author whose corpus of works over the years has made a distinguished contribution to Catholic letters.

The Catholic Digest Book Club
400 Community Drive, Manhasset, New York 11030
Selections are made by the editors of the *Catholic Digest* and are designed to provide interesting, entertaining, and morally and spiritually rewarding reading of a popular nature.

The Catholic Family Book Club
Garden City, New York
Published under the auspices of Doubleday & Co., Inc., this club offers entertaining, informative, and inspirational fiction and non-fiction with the stress on popular, readable books. An unusual feature is an omnibus volume offered each three months containing up to four complete books, some old and some new.

Catholic Know-Your-Bible Program
Garden City, New York
Sponsored by the Benedictines of Belmont Abbey, North Carolina, it offers original text and picture booklets by well known authors, devoted to key persons and themes of the Bible, which retell Bible stories interestingly and meaningfully for Catholic parents and children. These booklets are available only through the program.

The Catholic Literary Foundation
400 North Broadway, Milwaukee, Wisconsin
A division of the Bruce Publishing Company, its purpose is to offer wholesome, worthwhile reading on a planned basis to Catholics. A special feature of this club is its bonus system by which members receive a book free for purchasing a specified number of selections.

Franciscan Book Club
1634 West 51st Street, Chicago, Illinois 60609
A Franciscan enterprise, it makes available works of Franciscan interest to those interested in the Franciscan way of life. There are eight selections a year.

The Sisters Book League
180 North Wabash Avenue, Chicago, Illinois 60601
An activity of the Thomas More Association, it offers current books of particular interest to nuns. No commitment is required and the member is free to withdraw at any time.

Spiritual Book Associates
386 Park Avenue South, New York, N.Y. 10016
Now under the aegis of the Holy Cross Fathers at Notre

Dame, it offers only books of a spiritual nature to its members who agree to take seven newly published books spread over a one year period. The selections are shipped automatically.

The Theology Book Club
180 North Wabash Avenue, Chicago, Illinois 60601

Designed to meet the interest in the theological movement, it offers books in the field of theology useful for the intelligent reader in understanding the various aspects of contemporary theology. A Thomas More Association undertaking, and there is no commitment.

The Thomas More Book Club
180 North Wabash Avenue, Chicago, Illinois 60601

One of the earliest in the field the Thomas More Book Club offers works of high intellectual and literary content, frequently of a challenging and controversial nature. There is no commitment.

YOUNG ADULT

Catholic Digest Junior Book Shelf
400 Community Drive, Manhasset, N.Y. 11030

Its selections consist of biographies of contemporary and near-contemporary saints and heroes for youngsters in the 9–15 year age bracket. Selections, one a month, are shipped automatically, but members may drop out when they wish after their commitment has been met. Sponsored by the *Catholic Digest.*

Catholic Youth Book Club
Garden City, New York

Offers biographies of famous Catholic figures and fictional works based on great events in Catholic history for young adults in the 9–14 year age group. Books are shipped automatically once a month. Members may withdraw at any time after their initial commitment has been fulfilled. A division of Doubleday & Co., Inc.

III. CATHOLIC MAGAZINES AND NEWSPAPERS

Although this *Guide* is concerned primarily with books, a short listing of appropriate Catholic magazines was deemed advisable as a complement to your book reading activities. Though books provide the best means yet devised by man to transmit his thinking and knowledge in permanent, readily accessible form, magazines and newspapers do provide immediate information on current developments and trends which books because of the time required to publish cannot do. The great majority of magazines and newspapers are published daily, weekly and monthly and consequently can report on events and happenings much more rapidly than can books which usually take six months to a year to publish after the manuscript is completed. Events move at such a breakneck pace these days that the Catholic who would be informed and up to date must rely on newspapers and magazines to keep him abreast of the latest developments in his Church and in the world.

Also of value to the book reader is the fact that Catholic magazines and newspapers are the main source of his information about new books either through reviews, news stories, or publishers' advertising. This is particularly true of books of a religious nature which unfortunately are usually given short shrift indeed by general newspapers and magazines. Also religious books are much more apt to receive a more discerning treatment in Catholic papers than in general periodicals which often are unaware of the background, nuances and subtleties of many religious books.

Unfortunately, by and large, the great bulk of Catholic magazines and newspapers are not particularly good. A surprisingly high percentage of them are house organs—magazines run by a religious order solely to promote the purposes of that order. Certainly the motive is laudable but the result is all too often a badly edited, badly written, badly prepared magazine or newspaper. From the viewpoint of the literary purist, they could all be wiped out with no ill effects on literature; on the other hand their apologists point out they often are an invaluable adjunct to the laudable work and high purpose of their proprietors. Suffice to say they are house organs and should be regarded as just that.

The Catholic newspapers in the United States are almost all diocesan owned and controlled, and far too frequently are mere sounding boards and publicity sheets for their bishops. Often dull in make-up and content, they are no more than an extension of the type of magazine mentioned above as "house organ," the sole difference being that they are the house organ of the bishop.

On the other hand that such a state of affairs need not exist is attested by several first rate diocesan papers which are published in the United States. The advances made by some of the diocesan press in the past decade are most impressive. What is sorely needed is that more of the Catholic newspapers emulate the example of such outstanding diocesan papers as the Boston *Pilot*, the Cleveland *Universe Bulletin*, the Hartford *Transcript*, and the Davenport *Catholic Messenger*, to name just four of the excellent newspapers we have. Since diocesan papers are mainly available only in the dioceses in which they are published, the reader's choice in his selection of diocesan newspaper reading is limited to taking his own paper or leaving it which is an unfortunate state of affairs. Perhaps in the future nationally circulated Catholic newspapers will hopefully become available so the diocesan reader will have freedom of choice in his newspaper reading. One such paper which we describe below has appeared and the need for more newspapers distributed on a broader scale than merely diocesan distribution is readily apparent.

We make no attempt to provide any comprehensive list of Catholic periodicals here. Rather what we have done is select a baker's dozen of magazines which are outstanding and at the same time provide a good cross section for various intellectual needs. Further in view of the purpose of this *Guide* all of the periodicals in this listing provide book reviews which would be most helpful in keeping the reader current with the new books. In this sense, then, they provide excellent supplementary book commentaries to this *Guide* in addition to their main function of providing their readers with articles, opinions and differences of opinions on the current state of affairs, ecclesiastical and secular.

America. 106 West 56th Street, New York, N.Y. 10019

Edited by a group of Jesuit priests, *America* is a weekly journal of opinion which comments in a lively, far ranging manner on politics, education, economics, the arts, Church affairs, and foreign affairs, through comments and articles by the editors themselves or from authorities outside the magazine. A fine book section provides reviews of all important new books by authorities in the various areas covered by current books. Subscription: $8.00 a year.

Ave Maria. Notre Dame, Indiana

One of the oldest Catholic periodicals in the United States, it is also one of the broadest in appeal. It specializes in treating of complex problems in terms understandable to the average reader. Publishes articles on current topics, short stories, news briefs and several lively and popular columnists. Its book reviews are popular in approach, but coverage is limited to three or four an issue. Edited by the Holy Cross Fathers, it appears bi-weekly. Subscription: $7.00 a year.

Best Sellers. University of Scranton, Scranton, Pennsylvania

At first blush this may seem too specialized a publication for the general reader since it is published by the University of Scranton to provide evaluations of the new books for librarians. Actually it is the most comprehensive review medium in the Catholic field, reviews general as well as Catholic books in the context of Catholicism, and the reviews are down-to-earth and excellent for the general reader. Published semi-monthly. Subscription: $5.00 a year.

Catholic Digest. 2959 N. Hamline Avenue, St. Paul, Minnesota

Patterned after the enormously successful *Reader's Digest*, the *Catholic Digest* is one of the most popular Catholic magazines in the United States. Published every month, it offers digests of interesting articles from books and magazines and some original articles usually three or four pages in length but often longer. The material is selected from general as well as Catholic sources and gives a fine cross section of people and things of interest. Subscription: $4.00 a year.

Catholic World. 304 West 58th Street, New York, N.Y. 10019
The oldest Catholic periodical in the United States, it is
edited by the Paulist Fathers. It publishes serious articles on
Church and world affairs, literature, poetry, short stories, the
theater and movies. Its book section provides penetrating reviews on practically all the serious, important new books.
Published monthly. Subscription: $6.00 a year.

Commonweal. 232 Madison Avenue, New York, N.Y. 10016
For many years the storm center of Catholic publishing,
the developments of the past few years have justified many
of its at one time far out positions. Edited by laymen, it publishes weekly comments and articles on current events and
affairs, ecclesiastical and general. Strongly liberal, it is the
anathema of the conservatives. Intellectual throughout, it is
provocative, thought-provoking and often obtuse. Its book
section tends to learned reviews of little read and often
esoteric books. Published weekly. Subscription: $8.00 a year.

The Critic. 180 North Wabash Avenue, Chicago, Illinois
60601
This magazine is absolutely indispensable for anyone who
would keep up with literature, the arts, and Christian culture
in general. Sophisticated in tone, it features articles by leading authorities on books and authors, art, music and the theater, publishes short stories and poetry and is top-flight, in
every category. It has an excellent book review section with
informative reviews in depth on current books. It is published
6 times a year. Subscription: $5.00 a year.

Jubilee. 168 East 91st Street, New York, N.Y. 10028
A monthly magazine which combines picture stories, provocative articles and avant-garde layouts, its appeal is mainly
to the intellectual. It publishes heavily on the liturgy, ecumenism, poverty, sociological problems, race, and the Eastern churches. Subscription: $5.00 a year.

National Catholic Reporter. 300 East 36th Street, Kansas
City, Missouri
A weekly newspaper edited by laymen (the only Catholic
newspaper so conducted), it is nationally circulated and has
been the center of controversy since its first issue. Committed
to renewal, reform and progress, it is *the* spokesman for liberal causes in the Church. Outspoken and often highly criti-

cal in its approach, it has been praised ecstatically by its admirers and as vociferously attacked by its critics. Whether one agrees with its stands or not, one must admire the intellectual honesty and forthrightness of its staff, columnists and reporters. For a refreshing (or impudent according to its critics) and unfettered outlook on the whole range of Church activity, there is nothing quite like it. It reviews several books each issue usually on a topical and controversial issue. The reviews tend to be colored by the progressive views of the reviewer. Subscription: $6.00 a year.

The Sign. Monastery Place, Union City, N.J.

Designed for a wide audience, *Sign* is one of the best magazines of the picture-article type for a general audience. It aims at and usually achieves a nice balance between serious and light articles on subjects of current concern and has numerous columnists and special departments covering movies, sports, women's affairs. The book section provides short, pithy reviews and covers most new books of any importance. Published monthly by the Passionist Fathers. Subscription: $4.00 a year.

U.S. Catholic. 221 West Madison Street, Chicago, Illinois 60606

A monthly magazine of popular appeal, it offers articles on public affairs, photo stories, profiles of leading Catholic figures, covers the developments in various areas of the Church, such as the liturgy, education, marriage and family life, ecumenism, etc. An excellent periodical for the general reader with a good but not exceptional coverage of current books. Edited by the Claretian Fathers. Subscription: $4.00 a year.

The above are all of a general nature, offering the reader a broad coverage of many topics of interest to the general reader. We are adding to these magazines two periodicals of limited interest, but since their subject matter is of such vital concern in the Church today, we felt they should be included in this listing. They are:

The Bible Today. Collegeville, Minnesota

The Bible Today is devoted entirely to Biblical themes. In view of the tremendous effect of Biblical scholarship on every aspect of the Church, the general reader should at least be aware of it. Many of its articles are perfectly suitable for the general reader, but some are quite scholarly and limited in interest. Withal invaluable for anyone wishing to be knowledgeable with what is taking place in Biblical scholarship. Published by a group of Bible scholars 6 times a year. Subscription: $5.00 a year.

Worship. Collegeville, Minnesota
Devoted entirely to the liturgy, it is published by the Benedictine monks of St. John's Abbey. Not for the average or casual reader, it is *the* magazine to be informed on the liturgical movement. Published 10 times a year. Subscription: $4.00 a year.

IV. PUBLISHERS OF BOOKS LISTED

Abelard-Schuman, Ltd., 6 West 57th St., New York, N.Y. 10019
Academy Guild Press, 1317 Van Ness Ave., Fresno, California
Academy Library, an imprint of Harper & Row, Inc.
Alba House, 2187 Victory Blvd., Staten Island, N.Y. 10314
Alec R. Allenson, Inc., 635 East Ogden Ave., Naperville, Ill. 60540
All Saints, an imprint of Pocket Books, Inc.
America Press, 920 Broadway, New York, N.Y. 10010
American Heritage Publishing Co., 551 Fifth Ave., New York, N.Y. 10017
Anchor Books, an imprint of Doubleday & Co., Inc.
Angelus Books, an imprint of Guild Press, Inc.
Ann Arbor Books, an imprint of University of Michigan Press
Anvil Books, an imprint of D. Van Nostrand Co., Inc.
Appleton-Century, 60 East 42nd St., New York, N.Y. 10017
Ariel Books, an imprint of Farrar, Straus & Giroux
Atheneum Publishers, 162 East 38th St., New York, N.Y. 10016
Avon Books, 959 Eighth Ave., New York, N.Y. 10019

Ballantine Books, Inc., 101 Fifth Ave., New York, N.Y. 10003
Bantam Books, Inc., 271 Madison Ave., New York, N.Y. 10016
Barnes & Noble, Inc., 105 Fifth Ave., New York, N.Y. 10003
Basic Books, Inc., 404 Park Ave. So., New York, N.Y. 10016

Benziger Bros., Inc., 7 East 51st St., New York, N.Y. 10022
Bobbs-Merrill Co., Inc., 4300 West 62 St., Indianapolis, Indiana 46206
George Brazillier, Inc., 1 Park Ave., New York, N.Y. 10016
Bruce Publishing Co., Inc. 400 North Broadway, Milwaukee, Wisconsin 53201

Cambridge University Press, 32 East 57th St., New York, N.Y. 10022
Cardinal Editions, an imprint of Pocket Books
Catechetical Guild, 262 East 4th Street, St. Paul, Minnesota 55101
Cathedral Library, an imprint of Harper & Row, Inc.
Catholic University of America Press, 620 Michigan Ave. N.E., Washington, D.C. 20017
Chapel Books, an imprint of Harper & Row, Inc.
Citadel Press, 222 Park Ave. So., New York, N.Y. 10022
Cloister Books, an imprint of Harper & Row, Inc.
Collier Books, 60 Fifth Ave., New York, N.Y. 10011
Columbia University Press, 2960 Broadway, New York, N.Y. 10027
Compass Books, an imprint of The Viking Press
Confraternity of the Precious Blood, 5300 Fort Hamilton Parkway, Brooklyn, N.Y. 11219
Cornell University Press, 124 Roberts Place, Ithaca, N.Y. 14851
Coward-McCann, Inc., 200 Madison Ave., New York, N.Y. 10016
Crest Books, 67 West 44th St., New York, N.Y. 10036
Thomas Y. Crowell Co., 201 Park Ave. So., New York, N.Y. 10003
Crown Publishers, Inc., 419 Park Ave. So., New York, N.Y. 10016
Criterion Books, Inc., 6 West 57th St., New York, N.Y. 10019

Dell Publishing Co., Inc., 750 Third Ave., New York, N.Y. 10017
Devin-Adair Co., 23 East 26th St., New York, N.Y. 10010
Deus Books, an imprint of Paulist Press
Dial Press, Inc., 750 Third Ave., New York, N.Y. 10017
Dimension Books, Inc., Box 21, Wilkes-Barre, Pennsylvania 18703
Dodd, Mead & Co., Inc., 432 Park Ave. So., New York, N.Y. 10016

Dome Books, an imprint of Fides Pubs., Inc.
Doubleday & Co., Inc., 277 Park Ave., New York, N.Y.
10017
Dover Publications, Inc., 180 Varick St., New York, N.Y.
10014
Duell, Sloan & Pearce, Inc., 60 East 42nd St., New York, N.Y.
10017
Dufour Editions, Chester Springs, Pennsylvania 19425
E. P. Dutton & Co., Inc., 201 Park Ave. So., New York,
N.Y. 10003

Echo Books, an imprint of Doubleday & Co., Inc.
Everyman, an imprint of E. P. Dutton & Co., Inc.

Farrar, Straus & Giroux, Inc., 19 Union Square W., New York,
N.Y. 10003
Fawcett World Library, 67 West 44th St., New York, N.Y.
10036
Fides Publishers, Box 507, Notre Dame, Indiana 46556
Fleet Publishing Corp., 230 Park Ave., New York, N.Y. 10017
Follett Publishing Co., 1010 W. Washington Blvd., Chicago,
Illinois 60607
Fordham University Press, 441 East Fordham Road, Bronx,
New York 10458
Franciscan Herald Press, 1434 West 51st Street, Chicago,
Illinois 60609
Samuel French, Inc., 25 West 45th St., New York, N.Y.
10036
Funk & Wagnalls Co., 360 Lexington Ave., New York, N.Y.
10017

Galaxy Books, an imprint of Oxford University Press
Gateway Books, an imprint of Henry Regnery Co.
Grail Publications, St. Meinrad, Indiana
Grosset & Dunlap, Inc., 51 Madison Ave., New York, N.Y.
10010
Guild Press, Inc., North Road, Poughkeepsie, N.Y. 12601

Hanover House, an imprint of Doubleday & Co., Inc.
Harcourt, Brace & World, Inc., 757 Third Ave., New York,
N.Y. 10017
Harper & Row, Inc., 49 East 33rd St., New York, N.Y. 10016
Harvard University Press, 79 Garden St., Cambridge, Massa-
chusetts 02138

Harvest Books, an imprint of Harcourt, Brace & World, Inc.
Hawthorn Books, Inc., 70 Fifth Ave., New York, N.Y. 10011
Helicon Press, Inc., 1120 N. Calvert St., Baltimore, Maryland
21202
B. Herder Book Co., 314 North Jefferson St., St. Louis, Missouri 63103
Herder & Herder, Inc., 232 Madison Ave., New York, N.Y.
10016
Hill & Wang, Inc., 141 Fifth Ave., New York, N.Y. 10010
Holt, Rinehart & Winston, Inc., 383 Madison Ave., New York, N.Y. 10016
Horizon Books, an imprint of American Heritage Publishing Co., Inc.
Houghton Mifflin Co., 2 Park St., Boston, Massachusetts 02107

Image Books, an imprint of Doubleday & Co., Inc.

P. J. Kenedy & Son, 12 Barclay St., New York, N.Y. 10008
Keystone Books, an imprint of J. B. Lippincott Co.
Alfred A. Knopf, Inc., 501 Madison Ave., New York, N.Y.
10022

Liberal Arts Press, an imprint of Bobbs-Merrill Co., Inc.
J. B. Lippincott Co., East Washington Square, Philadelphia,
Pa. 19105
Little, Brown & Co., 34 Beacon St., Boston, Massachusetts
02106
Liturgical Press, Collegeville, Minnesota

McFadden-Bartell Corp., 205 East 42nd St., New York, N.Y.
10017
McGraw-Hill Book Co., Inc. 330 West 42nd St., New York,
N.Y. 10036
David McKay Co., Inc., 750 Third Ave., New York, N.Y.
10017
The Macmillan Company, 60 Fifth Ave., New York, N.Y.
10011
McMullen Books, an imprint of Farrar, Straus & Giroux
Marquette University Press, 1131 West Wisconsin Ave., Milwaukee, Wisconsin 53233
Mentor Books, an imprint of New American Library of World
Literature

Mentor-Omega Books, an imprint of New American Library of World Literature
Meredith Press, 1716 Locust St., Des Moines, Iowa 50303
Meridian Books, an imprint of the World Publishing Co.
Julian Messner, Inc., 8 West 40th St., New York, N.Y. 10018
Modern Library, 457 Madison Ave., New York, N.Y. 10022
Monarch Books, Inc., 529 Fifth Ave., New York, N.Y. 10017
Morehouse-Barlow, 14 East 41st St., New York, N.Y. 10017
William Morrow & Co., Inc., 425 Park Ave. So., New York, N.Y. 10016

Thos. Nelson & Sons, 18 East 41st St., New York, N.Y. 10017
New American Library of World Literature, 1301 Ave. of the Americas, New York, N.Y. 10019
Newman Press, Box 150, Westminster, Maryland 21157
Noonday Press, an imprint of Farrar, Straus & Giroux
W. W. Norton & Co., Inc., 55 Fifth Ave., New York, N.Y. 10003

Oxford University Press, 16-00 Pollitt Drive, Fairlawn, New Jersey 07410

Pantheon Books, Inc., 22 East 51st St., New York, N.Y. 10022
Paulist Press, Harristown Road, Glen Rock, New Jersey 07452
Penguin Books, Inc., 3300 Clipper Mill Road, Baltimore, Maryland 21211
Perennial Library, an imprint of Harper & Row, Inc.
Permabooks, an imprint of Pocket Books, Inc.
Philosophical Library, Inc., 15 East 40th St., New York, N.Y. 10016
Phoenix Books, an imprint of University of Chicago Press
Pocket Books, Inc., 630 Fifth Ave., New York, N.Y. 10020
Popular Library, Inc., 355 Lexington Ave., New York, N.Y. 10017
Frederick A. Praeger, Inc., 111 Fourth Ave., New York, N.Y. 10003
Premier Books, an imprint of Fawcett World Library
Prentice-Hall, Inc., Englewood Cliffs, New Jersey 07632
Princeton University Press, Princeton, New Jersey 08541
The Priory Press, 2005 South Ashland Ave., Chicago, Ill. 60608

G. P. Putnam's Sons, Inc., 200 Madison Ave., New York, N.Y. 10016

Random House, Inc., 457 Madison Ave., New York, N.Y. 10002
Henry Regnery Co., 64 East Jackson Blvd., Chicago 60604
Walter Romig, Publisher, 979 Lakepointe Road, Grosse Pointe, Michigan 48230

Saint Anthony Guild Press, 508 Marshall St., Paterson, New Jersey 07503
St. Martins Press, Inc., 175 Fifth Ave., New York, N.Y. 10010
Chas. Scribner's Sons, 597 Fifth Ave., New York, N.Y. 10017
Sheed & Ward, Inc., 64 University Place, New York, N.Y. 10003
Signet Books, an imprint of New American Library of World Literature
Simon & Schuster, Inc., 630 Fifth Ave., New York, N.Y. 10020
Peter Smith, Publisher, 6 Lexington Ave., Gloucester, Massachusetts 01932
Spectrum Books, an imprint of Prentice-Hall, Inc.
Spire Books, an imprint of Fides Pubs., Inc.

Taplinger Publishing Co., Inc., 119 West 57th St., New York, N.Y. 10019
Torchbooks, an imprint of Harper & Row, Inc.
Trident Press, Inc., 630 Fifth Avenue, New York, N.Y. 10020
Trumpet Books, an imprint of Fides Pubs., Inc.

Frederick Ungar Publishing Co., 131 East 23rd St., New York, N.Y. 10010
Universal Library, an imprint of Grosset & Dunlap, Inc.
University Books, Inc., 1615 Hillside Ave., New Hyde Park, New York 11041
University of Chicago Press, 5750 Ellis Ave., Chicago, Illinois 60637
University of Michigan Press, 615 East University Ave., Ann Arbor, Mich. 48106
University of Notre Dame Press, Notre Dame, Indiana 46556
D. Van Nostrand Co., Inc., 120 Alexander St., Princeton, N.J. 08540

The Viking Press, Inc., 625 Madison Ave., New York, N.Y. 10022

Vintage Books, an imprint of Random House

Vision Books, an imprint of Farrar, Straus & Giroux

Washington Square Press, Inc., 630 Fifth Ave., New York, N.Y. 10020

The World Publishing Company, 2231 West 110th St., Cleveland, Ohio 44102

Yale University Press, 149 York Street, New Haven, Connecticut 06511

INDEX

NOTES

NOTES

NOTES

NOTES

NOTES

NOTES

NOTES

NOTES